Women and Exercise

Routledge Research in Sport, Culture and Society

Women and Exercise

The Body, Health and Consumerism

Edited by
Eileen Kennedy and
Pirkko Markula

Routledge
Taylor & Francis Group

NEW YORK AND LONDON

First published 2011
by Routledge
711 Third Avenue, New York, NY 10017

Simultaneously published in the UK
by Routledge
2 Park Square, Milton Park, Abingdon, Oxon OX14 4RN

*Routledge is an imprint of the Taylor & Francis Group, an
informa business*

Typeset in Sabon by Swales & Willis Ltd, Exeter, Devon

Library of Congress Cataloging in Publication Data
Women and exercise : the body, health and consumerism / edited
by Eileen Kennedy and Pirkko Markula.
   p. cm.—(Routledge research in sport, culture, and society ; 5)
   Includes bibliographical references and index.
   1. Exercise for women. 2. Women in mass media.
   3. Women—Health and hygiene. I. Kennedy, Eileen.
   II. Markula, Pirkko, 1961–
   GV482.W66 2010
   613.7'045—dc22
   2010020097

ISBN13: 978–0–415–87120–4 (hbk)
ISBN13: 978–0–203–83930–0 (ebk)

Contents

Acknowledgments

We would like to warmly thank all the contributors whose commitment and passion for feminist research on exercise has made this book possible. In addition, Eileen Kennedy would like to thank the University of Alberta Faculty of Physical Education and Recreation's Visiting International Scholar Program for facilitating meetings between the editors during the final stages of preparation of the manuscript. She would also like to thank Phil Durrant for his support throughout this project. Pirkko Markula would like to thank the Faculty of Physical Education and Recreation, University of Alberta for providing academic support for editing this book and Jim Denison for his personal and professional support.

THE MEDIA AND THE IDEAL FIT BODY

Already in the 1980s, feminist researchers demonstrated that the fit body was reproduced within the ideological domain of media representation as a body "feminized" according to masculine, patriarchal representational logic. It was a body represented as thin, toned and sexually attractive for heterosexual relationships. From the perspective of these critical feminists, women's fitness, through representation of the ideal body, reproduced heteronormativity by "feminizing" women's physical activity (Kagan and Morse 1988; Lenskyj 1986; Theberge 1987, see also MacNeill 1998). This body is considered to contribute to women's oppression because of its sin-gularity: if only thin, toned and young women are considered attractive in a society where women come in a variety of different shapes, then most women are considered unattractive but nevertheless work continually to obtain the desired but unattainable body shape. At the same time, femi-nist researchers provided seminal Foucauldian readings of the oppressive nature of the media image of the ideal, thin, toned and youthful body (e.g., Bartky 1988; Bordo 1993; Spitzack 1990). Spitzack (1990) argued further that the cultural demand for attractiveness defined in these terms extends throughout women's lifespan and an appreciation of older women is increasingly connected to physical attractiveness and "aesthetics" of a healthy looking body. Concurrently, fitness has become an increasingly important tool for shaping the body into the narrowly defined, singular feminine ideal. Adopting a Foucauldian perspective, Lloyd observed an articulation between the textual production of aerobics and the feminine body in the U.K. to conclude that aerobics is promoted as producing "a svelte, toned and 'feminine' (or feminized) body" which is in "consonant with, and supportive of, the dominant feminine (white) aesthetic" (1996, 95). Duncan's (1994) analysis of the *Shape* magazine provided similar results from the U.S. More recently, Jette (2006) examined how promot-ing "feminine bodily norms" in Canada is combined with individual risk management to promote a neoliberal emphasis on personal responsibility for healthy pregnancy in the fitness magazine *Oxygen*.

Feminist fitness research has also explicated the power mechanisms underlying this widespread promotion of the oppressive feminine body ideal. The critical feminist researchers indicated that the feminine ideal was supported by the ideology of masculinity—it constructs femininity as the polar opposite and thus, inferior, to masculinity—in patriarchal society and implied that powerful groups (e.g., male media producers) purposefully provided such images to maintain women's oppression. Foucauldian feminists further point to the roles assigned to women in the reproduction of the oppressive ideal.

Duncan (1994) located her reading of "Success Stories" columns in the *Shape* magazine within Foucault's Panoptic power arrangement. These columns, she argued, are based on a personal initiative to lose weight:

successful women first confess their excess weight, usually through sudden revelation of how large they have grown, they then engage in a detailed exercise program that provides the desired better looking body (illustrated through vital before and after statistics) which also makes the women feel good. However, all this can be achieved only through publicly revealing bodily deficiencies and confessing shameful, out-of-control eating behavior. Through public confession, women control themselves as they continue to strive for the perfect body. Duncan concluded that these magazine columns work as a part of modern-day Panopticon where an invisible power continually controls individuals' behavior. In a later work, Eskes et al. (1998) extended their critique of *Shape* to incorporate Marcuse's (1964) analysis of advanced capitalism.

In the popular media texts, looking good (the ideal body) and feeling good (health) become closely intertwined. The thin and toned body is also celebrated as the healthy body. In this equation, the responsibility of the healthy looking body is assigned to individual women. In her analysis, Markula (2001) demonstrated how fitness magazines' advice on body image distortion (BID) creates a complex situation: these articles admit that their images of the unattainable ideal body cause BID which can lead to eating disorders. They further suggest, however, that the individual women's minds are out of order: they misperceive the media images and consequently, their minds have lost a sense of reality. The solution is that the women take responsibility to control their minds better and ignore the perfect images on the magazine pages. From a Foucauldian perspective, she analyzed how individual women are persuaded to look for individual solutions to an illness (BID) through medical discourse where health problems tend to be seen as individual choice: such problems are conceptualized a biological and physical manifestations of the individual body, not as social, political or environmental circumstances. Departing from the critical feminist perspective, however, it is neither the individual magazine editors (who continue to publish the images) nor the individual medical practitioners (who provide medical treatment for eating disorders) who are to blame per se. Both draw from the medical discourse without necessarily questioning its 'truth value' or being aware of its ill effects. Alongside the readers, they are "links in a set of power relations . . . that construct the media discourse on women's bodies. At the moment, they advance women's oppression by normalizing a certain body shape and encouraging certain attitudes toward health and the body" (Markula 2001, 174). Similar to Duncan (1994), Markula observed that avoiding or recovering from BID requires public confession of body dissatisfaction through which women learn to "adjust their behavior into the parameters of healthy femininity" (2001, 175). With the focus on individual behavior, women leave the societal construction of oppressive femininity unchallenged. Other Foucauldian feminists (Cole 1998; King 2003, 2006) also locate the representations of the fit body within the broader neoliberal rhetoric of personal responsibility for one's health through exercise. Dworkin and Wachs' (2009) recent work brings together the main themes of the fitness media research: construction of the ideal, feminine healthy looking body, and the individual's responsibility in attaining such a body.

Dworkin and Wachs (2009) located the ideal, fit, gendered body within the current consumer culture. They examined how popular fitness texts such as the *Self* magazine, *Men's Fitness*, *Men's Health*, *Shape Fit Pregnancy*, and *Ms Fitness* reproduced gender difference. While "men's objectified status still offers powerful forms of subjecthood, which were not included inside the frame of women's fitness magazines," women's magazines continued to focus on building the thin and toned feminine body by focusing on "lower body 'moves', toning, and light weights" (Dworkin and Wachs 2009, 162). They continued to promote white, heterosexual, middle-class notions of "'emphasized femininity' shaped in relation to hegemonic masculinity" (Dworkin and Wachs 2009, 162). The fitness magazines also reinforced neoliberal notions of individual responsibility for health: it is "through individualized solutions employed in the project of the self that one displays personal commitments of healthism" (Dworkin and Wachs 2009, 165). According to Dworkin and Wachs, fitness is sold by modifying feminist ideas of liberation and resistance into so-called commodity feminism:

> Over time, individual involvement becomes self-improvement and the neoliberal marketplace becomes an imperative part of the construction of the healthy self. At the same time, blame for the negative aspects of consumer culture or social injustices found within social structures is systematically displaced.
>
> (2009, 172–73)

Similar to Duncan (1994) and Markula (2001), they concluded that the magazines sold a body that looks and enacts gendered 'health' through sufficiently gendered signifiers (Dworkin and Wachs 2009, 174). Smith Maguire (2007) asserted further that such ideas about the exercising body provide seeds for an entire fitness lifestyle through which continued consumption of the fitness industry becomes possible.

In sum, feminist research, from various theoretical perspectives, indicates that media images of the fit body align closely with the singular ideal, thin, toned and youthful looking feminine body, which is tightly intertwined with health in this popular discourse. Women's health, this research uniformly confirms, is culturally expressed in aesthetic terms as a thin, healthy looking body. These researchers also agree that this image is unobtainable for the majority of women who, nevertheless, are persuaded to continually work toward it. Consequently, this dominant, singular image is deemed to be oppressing women.

Several authors in this book demonstrate how the formation of the fit body around aesthetics and health is constituted by discourses defining the field of fitness. As previous media research on fitness has shown, discourses circulate through different types of fitness texts such as popular fitness magazines, fitness videos, popular fitness books, exercise science text books, scholarly books and articles from where the discourses then percolate to the fitness practice through the expert advice from the fitness leaders and instructors. Eileen Kennedy and Evodokia Pappa in Chapter 1; Jaana Parviainen in Chapter 2; and Kerry McGannon, Christina Johnson and John Spence in Chapter 5, all analytically engage with discourses of exercise in a variety of media texts including magazines, newspapers and websites. While feminist research has been primarily concerned with how popular fitness texts circulate the discourse of the aesthetics of the ideal, healthy looking body, some scholars have analyzed how the discursive construction of health in such fitness media texts as exercise science text books shapes women's fitness.

Smith Maguire (2007) observed that exercise manuals, while providing more information about the specifics of doing exercise, tend to approach fitness as a motivational problem. From a Foucauldian perspective she demonstrated that these manuals are able to "individualize the question of physical fitness" (Smith Maguire 2007, 125) and present themselves as motivational experts. She further identified these manuals as governmental technologies that knit together "self-work" and "broader political, economic, and social agendas and goals" (Smith Maguire 2007, 126). To entice individuals to participate in the required self-work, these manuals highlight the associated health benefits of exercise: reduced risk of illness and increased confidence from improved appearance. The exercise practice itself is presented as a disciplinary activity that, if one is to persist with it, requires self-discipline, clear timetabling and continual body measurement. Through these techniques, the fitness manuals create a similar confessional environment to fitness magazines: the readers are to continually reflect upon their behavior, honestly confess any shortcomings and then engage in proper activity. Markula and Pringle (2006) continued this analysis by linking exercise practice with the discursive construction of health-related fitness.

From a Foucauldian perspective, a large part of fitness knowledge is based on medical, psychological and physiological research that unquestionably dominates the field of fitness (Markula 2001, Markula and Pringle 2006). In this literature, the most widely accepted justification for promoting fitness is its predicted health benefits as this research provides strong evidence to connect improved physical fitness to the prevention of coronary heart disease and related hypertension, diabetes, some types of cancer, osteoporosis, diabetes and anxiety. In general, then, scientific research postulates that the better one's physical fitness, the better one's predicted health. The theoretical position connected to this understanding of the fit body is characterized by the term 'health-related physical fitness' which includes four components: cardiovascular fitness, muscle strength and endurance, flexibility and body composition. An exercise prescription then comprises detailed instructions on how to improve each of these four components (for further details see Markula and Pringle 2006). It is important to observe that 'health' singularly denotes an absence of illness and such terms as 'health benefits,' 'health behavior' or 'healthy lifestyle' are presented as reducing the risk of illness. The World Health Organization's definition of health, nevertheless, is much broader encompassing physical, psychological and social well-being. From a Foucauldian perspective, when health is defined narrowly as an absence of illness, health-related fitness does not offer an alternative for the aesthetics of the healthy looking body, but rather further restricts women's exercise practices. These two discourses, the aesthetics of the healthy looking body and health as an absence of illness, also intertwine to promote thinness as 'healthy' and fatness/obesity as singularly unhealthy.

While feminist scholars have convincingly detected the dominant discursive formation of women's fitness knowledge in mediated texts, there has been limited research regarding the readers' meanings of these images. This is an area that obviously requires more attention from feminist researchers. In this book, McGannon and her co-authors go on to explore how women make sense of media discourses, and this is also a theme underlying the contributions by Louise Mansfield in Chapter 4; Emma Rich, John Evans and Laura De Pian in Chapter 7 and Jessica Chin in Chapter 11.

Some fitness researchers further argue that with the increased attention given to media images, limited attention has been paid to exercisers' lived experiences within the actual exercise setting. The magazines' glossy image world, they argue, has little to do with embodied ways of 'working out.' For example, while not from a feminist perspective, Crossley noted that "[r]elatively little empirical work has been done on and in gyms" to "focus upon more mundane, everyday forms of working out" (2006, 24). From a feminist perspective, Malin similarly observed that feminist critiques of the slender body have "ushered in the sometimes dangerous illusion that healthful exercise is unfeminist" (2010, 3). Consequently, many feminists 'hide' or 'segregate' their possible exercise lives from their critical work. Crossley (2004) further criticized 'grand theoretical' accounts that, often rooted in Foucauldian analysis, 'overgeneralize' as they gloss over the details of the actual workouts and rather than dealing with material collected from the gyms, base their conclusion on textual reading. These investigations, he added,

> portray the body as "docile" in relation to body maintenance . . .
> ignoring the active role of embodied agents in the practices and

eliding the difference between texts which prescribe ways of acting and the more messy and complex reality of those ways of acting.

(Crossley 2004, 41)

This critique leads to the second strand of feminist fitness research that focuses on women's lived experiences of fitness.

EXERCISERS' EXPERIENCES (WITH THE IDEAL BODY)

A body of literature that addresses Crossley's (2004, 2006) call for investigations of lived exercise experiences already exists. Many of these researchers openly engage in exercise practices as part of their inquiries using such methods as participant observation and ethnography. Similar to the media research on fitness, the accounts of women's exercise experiences draw from several theoretical perspectives. We begin this section by detailing interpretive accounts of women's embodied exercise experiences.

The interpretations of lived exercise experiences draw from several theoretical perspectives to understand gym experiences. They do not necessarily distinguish these experiences as gendered. In her ethnography, Sassatelli (1999) analyzed the micro-culture of an Italian gym. Employing Goffman's theoretical perspective, she argued that while the body culture within fitness gyms partly centers on building a perfect body, the gym also provides a place where a vast array of meanings and identities are negotiated. She provided a detailed description of the space and the 'expressive behavior' during exercise, to illustrate how each exerciser is exposed to the gaze of the others, yet uses irony as a strategy to gain distance from the toned, tight and slim body which exercise is deemed to produce. She concluded that although exercise practices are linked to the wider cultural body ideal, the definitions of the body are continuously and actively negotiated locally. The clients, however, are quite willing to assume a responsibility for creating a better-looking body.

As a part of larger social analysis of women's body practices, Gimlin (2002) observed aerobics classes in the U.S. Unlike the feminist research on the fitness media, she concluded that aerobics can serve as cultural resource for alternative constructions of female beauty. This was possible because,

Participation in aerobics allows women to construct accounts of their bodies that, first, release notions of selfhood from the physical and, second, provide a lens thorough which they can negotiate ideals of beauty. Aerobics provides women with alternative conceptions of beauty and the social context to support those ideals.

(Gimlin 2002, 51)

Aerobicizers attended classes to shape their bodies, but aerobics also offered a space where good mental characteristics such as willpower and determination compensated for the flawed body. Consequently, 'working out' made women feel better even without visible change. The flawed body is not an indication of a flawed 'self.' While women were able to emphasize the "personality implications of body work" (Gimlin 2002, 65), they also felt that building a toned body was a personally liberating, strong and active choice. The physical challenge for creating such a body was liberating because it was possible to obtain: everyone can build muscle with determination and thus, the toned body was achievable. The women were, thus, willing to assume personal responsibility for changing their bodies: it is up to each individual exerciser's willingness to engage in such body work.

The results of these investigations of lived exercise experiences seem parallel to the main findings of the fitness media research: obtaining an ideal body shape dominates exercise practices and participants gain self-confidence when they look good. In addition, individual exercisers seem to accept that it is their personal responsibility to engage in such body shaping. These studies, however, reveal that the lived world of exercise offers places to negotiate understandings of the body that, while indeed dominated by the main discourses of the fitness field, are also increasingly nuanced and varied. In this book, several authors elaborate on these descriptions of gym life using a similar theoretical perspective. In Chapter 12, Magdalena Petersson McIntyre exposes contradictions surrounding the recent phenomenon of striptease aerobics in Sweden. In Chapter 9, Elizabeth Pike examines older women's experiences of exercise through the lens of Goffman's theoretical perspective. Louise Mansfield, in Chapter 4, provides an ethnographic examination of exercisers' understandings of fatness employing Goffman's concept of stigma, but complements her reading with Elias's perspective on power relations. These authors all show the complexities involved in women's lived experience of the fit body.

From a phenomenological perspective, Crossley called for interpretive research which will "in different ways, explore the dual nature of the embodied agent, as both subject and object of change" (2004, 41). From his perspective, investigations of embodiment require an understanding of body techniques as "forms of shared practical reason, pre-representational and pre-reflective forms of collective understanding which complement and interact with 'collective representations'" (Crossley 2004, 38). He, therefore, turned to an analysis of reflexive embodiment: how exercisers act upon their embodied existence, actively "generating a bodily 'me'" (Crossley 2004, 38). His own research, while not explicitly investigating gendered experiences, focused on circuit training through which he analyzed how variety of forms of interacting with others in the class and engagement with the actual body techniques of this exercise form generated his own bodily 'him.' Lewis (2008) drew from Crossley's research to examine the meaning and motivation of yoga participation.

Through in-depth interviews and participant observation in a private yoga studio in the U.S., Lewis (2008) concluded that the participants found yoga often through a search for a lifestyle change to prevent or recover from illness or injury. Many had supportive family and friends who encouraged their healthy lifestyle and many also had a personal background in sport. In addition, yoga was understood to balance the work life stress and thus, providing a coping mechanism against the strains of everyday life. These participants understood yoga as very different from the 'gym' that individuals appear to frequent primarily to obtain a better body and compare their results with other gym goers. The yoga studio, instead, provides a protective, 'non-competitive' environment where the participants can obtain 'lean strength' without bulking up. Berman and de Souza (2005) confirmed that that the recreational exercisers in her study were primarily motivated to attend the 'gym' to lose weight and improve their appearance.

In this book, Synne Groven, Kari Solbrække and Gunn Engelsrud in Chapter 6 and Paula Lökman in Chapter 13 employ a phenomenological perspective to examine women's lived exercise experiences. Groven and her co-authors focus particularly on understanding large women's exercise experiences while Lökman traces how female beginners learn to practice Aikido.

From the interpretive perspective, researchers demonstrate that women can actively build a self through exercise—a self that, while influenced by the aesthetics of the feminine body, is not entirely suppressed by it. Critical feminist research expands on this theme to interrogate whether women's exercise is 'oppressive' or 'resistant.' Similar to the critical feminist research of the fitness media, these researchers see exercise as a feminizing activity that supports the oppressive ideology of masculinity which assigns women as polar opposite and thus, inferior to men. From this theoretical perspective, several studies demonstrate that women, indeed, generally exercise because they want to change their bodies toward the desired ideal (e.g., Dworkin 2003; Markula, 1995; Spielvogel 2002, 2003). Aerobics, particularly, has been deemed a disempowering technique of bodily discipline that mainly reinforces the oppressive physical ideal (e.g., Loland 2000; Maguire and Mansfield 1998; McDermott 2000; Prickett 1997). Prickett, for example, observed that "the desire to look better—clothed or unclothed—is a prime motivating factor behind the expanding aerobics phenomenon" (1997, 198). Hargreaves continued that "aerobics has been successfully packaged to persuade women, specifically, to participate in order to lose weight and improve their sex-appeal" (1994, 161). Fitness professionals tend to also promote the body beautiful through their instruction. Fitness instructors strongly shape the participants' exercise experiences because they design the exercise programs based on each client's goals. Research on personal trainers (PT) (Frew and McGilligvray 2005; Phillips and Drummond 2001; Smith Maguire 2007, 2001) concluded that these fitness professionals commonly accept the perfect body as an integral part of fitness culture and prescribe exercise to combat the clients' undesired fat and flab. They also expect consumers to want to work toward an idealized body shape when they come to train under their supervision. The PTs work hard to maintain their own bodies, which they believe is an indication of their dedication to fitness. PTs also grow easily impatient with consumers who expect results without continued hard work, dedication and proper diet. Frew and McGilligvray (2005) maintained that media images as well as staff attitudes and practices such as constant body measurement and progress checking foster the desire for a perfect body in fitness consumers. At the same time, women consumers also prefer to attend classes led by instructors with 'perfect' bodies (Evans et al. 2005). D'Abundo (2009) found that aerobics instructors in the U.S. also saw themselves as role models for the participants. While some instructors wanted to divorce thinness (the appearance) from health and promote 'being comfortable with one's appearance' as a better alternative, preoccupation with appearance tended to dominate the classes. Some of the instructors also expressed concern about being too fat themselves. From a critical perspective, with its persistent emphasis on appearance and body shaping, exercise is considered as oppressing women.

As a result, critical feminist researchers have turned to alternative forms of exercise to analyze resistant exercise practices that build a body differently from the feminine ideal. They have investigated such exercise forms as weight lifting and bodybuilding that are designed to increase women's musculature. As ideology of masculinity assigns visible musculature as a masculine body signifier, these exercise forms theoretically should provide resistant action to the production of the current feminine ideal. The findings, nevertheless, demonstrate that many women engage in these activities to improve their body shapes and carefully negotiate a feminine appearance with musculature (e.g., Bolin 1992, 2003; Boyle 2005; Dworkin 2001; Grogan et al. 2004; Heywood 1998; McGrath and Chananie-Hill 2009; Roussel Griffet and Duret 2003; St. Martin and Gavey 1996; Wesely 2001). Such ambivalence also tends to characterize later critical feminist scholarship of women's exercise. Despite the focus on appearance, this research concludes, women's exercise also develops physical health (Malin 2010) and strength (Dworkin 2003) as well as providing a social environment to be with other women (Malin 2010; Markula 2003a; Wray 2003) and allows participants to question the young, thin and toned media ideal (Craig and Liberty 2007; Haravon Collins 2002; Markula 1995, 2003a) or the dominance of westernized values of women's health and well-being (George and Rail 2006; Wray 2003). These reasons for exercise appear resistant to the domination of appearance concerns in these classes. For example, McDermott (2000) observed that aerobics provided Canadian women with empowering experiences, such as feeling better mentally and physically, in addition to working on a better-looking, thinner body. Such lived body experience also empowered women to feel more confident in their physical strength, endurance and competence. This provided alternative ways of understanding the feminine self. Craig and Liberty (2007) demonstrated that a chain of women-only gyms in the U.S., although 'feminized' places, also offered nonjudgmental, supportive space for noncompetitive sociability. Similarly, according to D'Abundo, aerobics instructors "seemed to be exhibiting agency" by creating a comfortable learning environment, providing encouragement, modifications, and practical applications for the movement patterns learned in their classes (2009, 314). Drawing from Bourdieu's notion of habitus, Waring (2008) further demonstrated that health club is a complex concept introduced for business professionals working in the city. Health clubs fuse work and leisure into a 'work-style' allowing professionals to entertain clients and improve their bodies into the appropriately 'healthy' business 'habitus' in their luxurious premier clubs. At the same time professionals enhance their physical capital within the work context which conflates the gender differences: women became strong and fit while men became aware of the need of being more 'presentable' and 'in shape.'

Parallel to interpretive researchers, critical feminists establish that women's exercise experiences are contradictory: while recognizing the oppressiveness of the narrowly defined body ideal, women nevertheless work relentlessly toward the same ideal. In addition, they theorize that resistance to the oppressive media image might be found by listening to the voices of exercising women. This scenario, however, results in an assumption of a binary between oppressive media images and resistant exercise experience: embodied fitness experiences are endorsed as more authentic representations of femininity than media representations. In this conceptualization, the focus on lived corporeality is seen as liberating the feminine body while the textual, critical readings of culture reveal the artificiality of the representational image—the logic of masculine thought that envelopes the feminine image body (Bray and Colebrook 1998). This viewpoint appears to endorse the existence of an authentic feminine self struggling to see the light through physical activity practices, but only succeeding in reproducing its own oppression. As a result, the studies of women's embodied experiences in fitness depict women's struggle within the dominant logic of femininity, but no change in the feminizing practices of fitness. For example, while the fitness industry practices have superficially changed, the orientation toward the same body ideal remains. Therefore, there is no evidence of 'resistance' that changes the oppressive 'feminized body' or the ideology of masculinity when the exercising women continue to act within the existing formation of fitness. Post-structuralist feminists argue that these theoretical approaches are limited by their tendency to rely on an assumption of authentic experience by a true and fixed self (e.g., Grosz 1997; Hekman 1990; Markula and Pringle 2006; Scott 1992).

From a post-structuralist perspective, an interpretive researcher focusing on experience assumes that it is possible to tap into a fitness field that allows women to turn themselves into autonomous subjects. In this 'non-ideological' field, subjects are presumably free from the control of ideological dominance and are empowered to take charge of their own bodies whereas the media is thoroughly permeated by oppressive ideological forces. In other words, women are able to find their 'true' selves in the gym. Even if critical feminist research acknowledges the ideological construction of the fit body, it assigns resistant agency through which women are able to act outside of ideological framing of exercise and find their 'true' embodied selves currently overpowered by various ideological constructions. Instead of searching for a 'true self,' Foucauldian scholars demonstrate how the power/discourse nexus subjectivates an exerciser into a limited feminine identity (e.g., Markula and Pringle 2006). Instead of the discovery of a 'true' self or authentic experience, identity construction itself needs to be challenged by adjusting the nexus. Therefore, there is no self, identity or embodied experience that takes place outside of discourse/power nexus. Because several authors use a Foucauldian perspective in this book, we will now briefly introduce Foucault's main concepts: discourse, power relations and the formation of the self.

Within Foucault's (1978) theoretical schema, knowledge formation (discourses) and power are inextricably linked. As established earlier in this chapter, two discourses—the popular discourse of aesthetics of the ideal, healthy looking body and the medical and exercise science discourse of exercise as illness prevention—dominate the fitness field (see also Chapters 5, 7, 8 and 10 in this book). Connected with particular, strategic use of power relations, these discourses have gained dominant positions in the fitness field. Foucault understood power operation through two main functions: bio-power and anatomo-political power.

Bio-politics refers to a function of power through "administering and controlling life in a particular multiplicity, provided the multiplicity is large (a population) and the space spread out or open" (Deleuze 1988, 61). Current governmental campaigns for active, healthy lifestyle, are aimed at increased longevity and illness prevention in a population. For example, obesity has been identified as one of the most serious threats to life within the westernized societies because fatness (and inactivity) is connected to many serious and costly illnesses. Such campaigns are often supported by bio-medical or exercise science research that have provided scientific evidence to link increased physical fitness and thinness with absence of illness. This governmental power/medical discourse nexus sustains certain forms of exercise that are deemed the best ways to prevent illness. Because the fitness industry provides exercise services, it benefits from these campaigns, but is also controlled by the scientific principles of health-related fitness that has become one of the dominant discourses of fitness suppressing other understandings of health and the fit body (Markula and Pringle 2006). In this book, Sharon Wray in Chapter 8, examines how White, Pakistani, British Muslim and African Caribbean women's exercise experiences are formed within the western bio-politics of health while Lisa McDermott, in Chapter 10, focuses on how physically active white women in Canada understand health within the nexus of bio-politics and health. While medical discourse and governmental bio-politics operate to support each other, power can also function through less formal structures by forming mobile strategies with other discourses.

Anatomo-politics (Deleuze 1988) refers to use of power that typically employs the technologies of discipline on a multiplicity of individuals. By analyzing this type of power, Foucault (1991) illustrated how power operates through techniques of discipline that normalize individuals into useful, docile bodies. Through these techniques, the activities of the human body are submitted to constant control. Such docility was achieved through isolation of space specific to activity, through selection of suitable, disciplinary activities, through organization of time and movement that then were combined into an effective system of control. In other words, the visible aspects of knowledge production are effectively harnessed for the function of power. In contemporary society, Foucault argued, such spaces as schools, hospitals, factories and the military work as effective locations for disciplinary techniques. Exercise can also be understood as a form of disciplinary technique through the ways it currently employs space, time and exercise practice to create certain type of bodies. The discursive construction of fitness and the practice of fitness, thus, create docile bodies. The discourses normalize a certain body type as ideal by linking it to the looks of beauty and health. The exercise practices then discipline the bodies (the exercisers) to follow these ideas of beauty and health. Foucault labeled this as the panoptic power arrangement. As established earlier in this chapter, subjected to such an arrangement the exercisers begin to actively survey any deviation of 'normalcy' themselves, confess their deficiencies and engage in practices to create better bodies without knowing exactly who asks them to do this or why it is necessary to conform to these models (e.g., Duncan 1994, Markula 1995). Fitness practices turn into discipline techniques that the exercisers follow in their never-ending quest for beauty and health.

Foucault acknowledged the effectiveness of the current bio-political and anatomo-political functions of power, but in his later work became increasingly interested in how individuals understand and transform themselves within the power/discourse nexus (see Foucault 1983a, 1983b, 1985, 1987, 1988a, 1988b). He began to move from the technologies of domination into the technologies of the self. Throughout his work, Foucault demonstrated how subjectivation has turned into subjection: how individuals, through disciplinary techniques, have turned into subjects under someone else's control. However, when knowledge formation is formalized through highly stratified ways of knowing—for example, the way we understand fitness is quite tightly codified through the discourse of health as absence of illness and the aesthetics of the ideal body—power operates in more flexible, localized and unstable manner. This means that it is not possible to locate power in certain spaces or certain individuals, groups, organizations or even the state (government), but rather all these, in addition to individual exercisers, instructors, club owners and program designers are part of power relations that affect fitness as a phenomenon. This does not mean that different individuals are not controlled by power relations in a different manner. In addition, governments have more means to affect exercise behaviors than individual fitness instructors. Power gains force, however, not necessarily only through formal structures, but through different channels by forming mobile strategies specific to each location. However, the flexible localization of power relations also means that each individual is a part of power relations and can also actively enact his/her force to create change. From a Foucauldian perspective, the individual exerciser is subjected to the current (neo-liberal) power/discourse nexus that, through exercise practices (formed based on the discourses) shape the individual's self. In his later work, nevertheless, Foucault (1983a, 1983b, 1985, 1987, 1988a, 1988b) was interested in exploring the slow formation of self experience; how individuals begin to understand themselves as subjects within power relations. It is important to emphasize that such a process still takes place within the nexus of discourse/power relations: an individual becomes a subject within power relations. The power relations and the existing discourses, far from being only oppressive, can also help the individual to 'heal' or recover from the subjection and become vitalized to engage in a relationship that is able to transform codes and dominance. For example, Markula (2004) examined how individual fitness instructors, through the technologies of the self, might be able to create change in the fitness industry.

Informed by Foucault's technologies of the self, Markula (2004), examined how mindful fitness instructors produced femininity through their practices (see also Markula and Pringle 2006). She discovered that while these instructors had an awareness of 'mindfulness,' they did not openly engage with mindful fitness to challenge the dominant discourse around the ideal feminine body. While they cared deeply about the quality of their instruction—they explained in detailed the proper execution of the movement and breathing techniques—their thoughts focused on the everyday teaching of their classes, not problematizing the larger discursive structures of identity construction and their manifestations in fitness practices. In this volume, Markula explores further possibilities for problematization of fitness practices but this time, assumes the role of an instructor herself. In her chapter, she employs the concept of fold developed from Foucault's work by Deleuze (1988) to explore possibilities to transgress the limited feminine identity constructed through the narrowly defined, normalized body ideal and the individualization of exercise/health practices. Deleuze's work has also inspired other post-structuralist researchers of women's fitness.

Deleuze's (1988, Deleuze and Guattari 1987) work bears close affinity to Foucault's work with a shared interest in the body. It is not surprising then that such work appears suitable to inform post-structuralist examinations of fitness. While Deleuze shared Foucault's conviction about an identity constructed within the intersections of knowledge formation and power, he also developed the ideas of active self-transformation that can actually change the current structure of domination further than Foucault. Markula (2006, 2009) has employed Deleuze's concept of the Body without Organs to examine how Pilates practices might be used to construct a femininity that is not dominated by the current discourses that define fitness. Drawing both from Foucault and Deleuze, Lea (2009) explores the possibilities Iyengar yoga practice offers for the type of care of the self that resists the codes and power. Gambs (2007), in her evocative, Deleuze-inspired autoethnography, shows how the exercising body might become a site of transformation through its affect (for other autobiographical and autoethnographic accounts of women's fitness see Malin 2010; Markula 2003b).

Beyond the Binaries

The scholarship collected together in this book presents a range of feminist perspectives on women and exercise in contemporary consumer culture. The contributions show how different theoretical approaches can illuminate the many aspects of women's complex relationship to embodiment, physical activity and health. Underlying all of the research is an awareness of the multiple layers of women's experience: the influence of gendered histories of the body and physical activity, the commercial orientation of the fitness industry, neo-liberal health policy agendas and the tyranny of idealized body images, alongside the pleasures of movement and the satisfaction of self-transformation. Some of the studies focus on the discursive construction of women's experience of exercise, others examine that experience itself. However, all of the authors are aware that media-saturated consumer culture forms the context of women's involvement in exercise and that it is impossible for women to escape its influence. This does not mean that women are incapable of resisting the messages that surround fitness, and many of the authors point to moments when this can occur. Nevertheless, the discursive construction of fitness and femininity inevitably shapes the fitness experience. The research collected in this volume is avowedly feminist and as such is committed to making a change in women's lives. By highlighting the difficulties created by the currently dominant discourses of fitness culture, the authors are moving toward the possibility of exercise practice free from the limitations of the present. To do this, it is as necessary to avoid a fetishization of an authentic exercising self as much as a focus on media discourse to the exclusion of experience. Our experience of exercise exists in relationship with its discursive construction in the mediated consumer society. This book, therefore, takes a tentative step away from binary separations of artificial media image and authentic experience; discourse and embodiment; oppression and resistance; critical feminist researcher and the participant in order to create better, transformative fitness practices for women.

THE STRUCTURE OF THE BOOK

This book, therefore, approaches women and exercise by drawing together research conducted from different perspectives. The book is divided into four parts that cut across different theoretical influences and investigations focused on texts and/or experiences. The first part, "The Business of Exercise: Selling and Consuming Fitness" considers the context of consumer culture in shaping women's exercise experience. This section explores the way exercising feminine subjectivities are formed within the discursive fitness field created by the media and the commercial fitness sector. The section investigates the way the fitness industry can both constrain and appear to provide alternatives to consumers as new products appear. New possibilities for engaging with and challenging the dominant definitions of fitness are explored.

In Chapter 1 "Love Your Body? The Discursive Construction of Exercise in Women's Lifestyle and Fitness Magazines," Eileen Kennedy and Evdokia Pappa consider the extent to which exercise is constructed as part of the pleasure of women's magazines. The authors examine a range of women's magazines across a spectrum of magazines pointing to the broad differences but also noting a similarity among all of the magazines. A disjuncture existed between the way exercise was presented on the cover and the way it was presented inside the magazine. Words and images on the covers constructed exercise as a simple and pleasurable means to achieving the desired future self. Yet, inside the magazine, women readers were no longer addressed in these terms, and the pleasure of exercise was consistently subsumed by the pleasure of consumption.

In Chapter 2, "Women Developing and Branding Fitness Products on the Global Market: The Method Putkisto Case," Jaana Parviainen explores the ways that women fitness entrepreneurs have been able to brand new fitness products, such as Method Putkisto (MP). Parviainen shows that the MP brand is constructed around a heroic version of the life story of its originator, Marja Putkisto. Marja Putkisto's femininity and individual body experience are interwoven into the brand, creating an interface that allows instructors and clients to identify with her, and thereby bond with MP products. As a result of this process, Parviainen argues that MP departs from the stereotypical youth and looks orientation of many global fitness products. Instead MP offers consumers encouragement to shape their bodies 'inside out.' Parviainen draws on feminist economics to show how MP highlights the way power is embedded in the fitness industry. While the MP brand and approach may empower its consumers, the business principles underlying the franchising of such fitness products create a hierarchy between the license owners and instructors, whose own agency is limited.

Pirkko Markula continues the critique of the fitness industry in Chapter 3, "'Folding': A Feminist Intervention in Mindful Fitness," but her approach proposes ways of making a difference to mindful fitness practices within a commercial environment. Markula draws on Gilles Deleuze's interpretation of Michel Foucault's work to introduce the concept of 'fold' as a way of creating positive change in the industry. Markula reports on an ethnographic project where she used her training as a Pilates instructor to encourage participants to problematize current codes of fitness, and transcend the narrow definitions of femininity and individualism of the industry. Markula reflects on her experience, arguing that this approach, while not always successful, is necessary to help exercise participants to feel the movement, to find their own rhythm and find their own bodies.

The second part of the book "Body Trouble: Fat Women and Exercise" investigates the cultural anxieties surrounding femininity, fatness and physical activity, and their effect on exercising women. The contradictions of promoting exercise as a means for re-shaping one's body, whilst simultaneously stigmatizing women perceived as 'failing' to embody the desired shape are highlighted. This section contributes to the debates surrounding obesity by exploring women's experience of engaging with these dominant discourses.

In Chapter 4 "Fit, Fat and Feminine? The Stigmatization of Fat Women in Fitness Gyms," Louise Mansfield presents a critique of the anti-fat ethic which she argues is pervasive within fitness gyms. Mansfield draws on the work of Goffman and Elias to conceptualize the stigmatization of the fat body within the fitness culture. Extensive participant observation and interviews with women attending or working in gyms have informed Mansfield's approach. Her findings reveal that anxieties about fat are mobilized within gym culture to exclude people who are perceived to be overweight and therefore unable to match up to socially constructed ideals of the body beautiful. Gym gossip works to stigmatize images of 'outsider' physicalities and generate embarrassment around the fat body. Mansfield concludes that fitness gyms reinforce dominant conceptions of female bodily perfection and marginalize fat women.

In Chapter 5: "I Am (Not) Big . . . It's the Pictures that Got Small: Examining Cultural and Personal Exercise Narratives and the Fear of Fat," Kerry R. McGannon, Christina R. Johnson and John C. Spence employ a feminist post-structuralist perspective to make connections between the media portrayal of health and fitness and women's experience of participation. McGannon and her co-authors analyzed a local newspaper fitness section to reveal narratives of fear and risk surrounding women's exercise. A case-study approach supplemented the media analysis, enabling the researchers to explore the ways that the exercise experience of one woman (Viv) was influenced by media constructions. Importantly, the authors show how Viv struggled to find her own, alternative understanding of exercise, in contrast to the dominant definitions.

Synne Groven, Kari Solbrække and Gunn Engelsrud adopt a phenomenological framework to explore "Large Women's Experiences of Exercise" in Chapter 6. The authors collected data from a medical setting in which an exercise program was offered to women defined as obese, using participant observation and interviews. The women experienced a challenging and uncomfortable program, which encouraged them to see themselves as out of control. An emphasis on visible results dominated the program, which closely conformed with mainstream fitness practice without being structured to the specific needs of the group. Despite the physical discomfort experienced by the women, 'pushing oneself' was seen as a culturally positive value. The authors argue that the effect of such programs is likely to increase bodily dissatisfaction and prevent larger women from exploring their own personal kinaesthetic experience.

In Chapter 7 "Obesity, Body Pedagogies and Young Women's Engagement with Exercise," Emma Rich, John Evans and Laura De Pian examine the impact of health discourses associated with obesity on young women's understanding of, and relationships with, exercise. Rich and her co-authors wish to problematize health promotion messages which suggest that young women are able to control their future lives and health as long as they engage in the regulative practices associated with health and obesity imperatives. Employing feminist post-structuralist theory to guide their approach to researching with students in a school setting, the authors examine how the prevailing discourses are understood by young women and how they inform their exercise practices. Findings showed that young women's engagement with exercise was influenced by the instrumental approach advocated within obesity discourse, rather than encouraging a joy of movement.

The third part of the book "In the Name of Health: Women's Exercise and Public Health" investigates the construction of exercise as a moral imperative within public health discourse. The section reflects on the historical emergence of these discourses and the way that the resulting exercise prescriptions have tended toward the homogenization of women's needs, without acknowledging their diversity in terms of age or ethnicity. Paradoxically, health discourses may be experienced by women, young and old, as constraining and as a disincentive to exercise. This section explores how far women can resist and reinterpret messages about exercise to suit their own needs.

In Chapter 8 "The Significance of Western Health Promotion Discourse for Older Women from Diverse Ethnic Backgrounds," Sharon Wray examines the differing perceptions of health promotion messages among ethnically diverse exercise class participants. Wray argues that western-centric health promotion discourses subjugate and marginalize alternative forms of knowledge, reinforcing individual responsibility for health while ignoring the structural and material causes of ill health. Wray draws on participant observation, focus groups and semi-structured interviews with participants and instructors at three exercise settings in the U.K.: an Asian women's center, a private gym and an African Caribbean community center. Her findings reveal differences in understandings of health needs among health and fitness instructors and Pakistani, British Muslim and African Caribbean participants. Wray's study effectively illuminates the ways that ethnic and cultural beliefs can form a resistance to western-centric perspectives on healthy lifestyle.

The specific needs of older women and exercise are brought sharply into focus by Elizabeth Pike in Chapter 9 "Growing Old (Dis)Gracefully? The Gender/Aging/Exercise Nexus." As life expectancy for women increases on a global scale, Pike shows that aging is inadequately understood in policy initiatives promoting physical activity among older people. Drawing on data from participant observation and interviews Pike explores the ways that age and gender intersect to construct the experience of exercise for British women over the age of 60. Informed by the work of Erving Goffman, Pike aims to avoid generalizing the experience of aging, focusing on the way older individuals understand their social worlds. The findings from her study indicate that exercise has multiple and contradictory meanings for older women. Exercise was associated with empowerment through its capacity to developing strength and mobility for independent living. However, the majority of women in the study felt oppressed by the pervasiveness of impossible body ideals privileging youth and traditional norms of femininity. Pike concludes by calling for closer attention to the experience of older women in health and exercise policy aimed at an aging population.

In Chapter 10 "'Doing Something That's Good for Me': Exploring Intersections of Physical Activity and Health," Lisa McDermott revisits data she collected in the late 1980s/early 1990s relating to a group of women's lived-body experiences of physical activity and exercise. Using a Foucaultian understanding of the self, government and bio-power,

McDermott considers the way that the seemingly private decisions of the women to engage in exercise were enmeshed in the health and neo-liberal discourses that were emerging at the time. By employing a retrospective analysis, McDermott is able to draw out the way that the women conceived of the relationship between exercise and health as working in the service of the self—in their own words "doing something that's good for me."

The final part of the book "Lived Body Experiences: Exercise, Embodiment and Performance" explores women's changing subjectivities in relation to physical activity and exercise. Shifting global cultural and economic patterns have resulted in new ways of managing the body, fitness and exercise for women. New exercise forms have been developed such as striptease aerobics which reflect the changing cultural expectations of fitness and femininity. Women's actual bodily experiences of 'doing' an activity such as running or learning an oriental physical art are explored phenomenologically to reveal the ways that women are involved in questioning gendered patterns of physical activity.

In Chapter 11 "The New 'Superwoman': Intersections of Fitness, Physical Culture and the Female Body in Romania," Jessica Chin uses a Foucauldian framework in her study of changing discourses of female physical activity in postcommunist Eastern Europe. Chin draws on ethnographic observation and interviews with sport and physical education students at a Romanian University. Two decades after the official fall of communism in 1989, Chin explores the complicated gendered terrain of postcommunist Romania. Chin argues that, accompanying the ideological shift from socialist equality to democratic freedoms, is a rhetoric of new opportunity, freedom and individual responsibility. This new rhetoric, however, only thinly veils the disciplining of female bodies by the fitness sector, constructing a 'postsocialist triple burden' for women of family, fitness and finances.

In Chapter 12 "Keep Your Clothes On! Fit and Sexy Through Striptease Aerobics" Magdalena Petersson McIntyre explores the phenomenon of striptease aerobics and pole dancing as fitness practices in Sweden. McIntyre views these new fitness practices through a framework of commodity feminism, whereby commodities tied to feminist imagery and a feminine appearance have come to represent feminism. Participant observation and interviews with three instructors provide the data for McIntyre's study. All three instructors negotiated the contradictions of empowerment and objectification of women that striptease aerobics simultaneously represents. McIntyre explores the ways instructors used strategies to understate sexual content of the activity, emphasize ironic representations of femininity and recharge the meanings of women's sexuality to create a space for women to exercise in ways that transgressed acceptable feminine behavior.

In Chapter 13 "Becoming Aware of Gendered Embodiment: Female Beginners Learning Aikido" Paula Lökman examines the potential of exercise to increase women's awareness of gendered embodiment. Lökman discusses how female beginners learning a Japanese self-defense sport, Aikido, experienced changes in gendered bodily dispositions and relations to movement. Employing a phenomenological framework, she shows how the women developed an understanding of 'the body' as the means through which one relates to and experiences their everyday world. Lökman argues that the women's new awareness of physicality was a positive experience that could not be separated from other aspects of the female Aikido learner's understanding of herself.

The final contribution to the book continues the phenomenological theme. Jacquelyn Allen-Collinson explores women's subjective, lived-body experiences of sport and exercise in Chapter 14 "Running Embodiment, Power and Vulnerability: Notes Toward a Feminist Phenomenology of Female Running." Allen-Collinson adopts autophenomenographic method to examine her own experiences of training for middle-/long-distance running in public spaces. The phenomenological analysis of her data allows her to explore the contradictory experience of inhabiting public space: the sense of danger from harassment, threat or attack as well as the feelings of empowerment, social agency, resistance, bodily power, strength and sensory pleasure. Allen-Collinson argues that feminist phenomenology offers a way of capturing the tensions of power and vulnerability in women's lived-body experiences of outdoor running.

Together, the contributors in this volume explore the interrelationship of discourse and experience in a shifting, globalized fitness culture. The limitations of dominant definitions of exercise and the ideal body are contrasted with how women actively create meanings of their exercise participation. As feminist researchers can also act as fitness instructors their attempts to negotiate the conflicting and partial understandings of health and fitness in their own exercise classes and their efforts to transcend the current discourses can form an aspect of feminist transformative agenda for social change. The chapters in this book effectively show the complex position that feminist researchers as well as the exercising women inevitably take up in contemporary fitness culture. The findings also foreshadow women's attempts to step away from the limitations of the current discursive construction of fitness to define their own engagement in exercise and physical activity.

REFERENCES

Bartky, S. 1988. Foucault, femininity, and the modernization of patriarchal power. In *Feminism and Foucault: Reflections on resistance*, ed. I. Diamond and L. Quinby, 61–86. Boston, MA: Northeastern University Press.

Berman, E. and M. J. de Souza. 2005. A qualitative examination of weight concerns, eating and exercise behaviors in recreational exercisers. *Women in Sport and Physical Activity Journal* 14: 24–38.

Bolin, A. 1992. Vandalized vanity: Feminist physiques betrayed and portrayed. In *Tattoo, torture, mutilation, and adornment: The denaturation of the body in culture and text*, ed. F. E. Mascia-Lees and P. Sharpe, 79–99. Albany NY: State University of New York Press.

—— 2003. Beauty or the beast: The subversive soma. In *Athletic intruders: Ethnographic research on women, culture, and exercise*, ed. A. Bolin and J. Granskog, 107–30. Albany, NY: State University of New York Press.

Bordo, S. 1993. *Unbearable weight: Feminism, western culture, and the body.* Berkeley, CA: University of California Press.

Boyle, L. 2005. Flexing the tensions of female muscularity: How female bodybuilders negotiate normative femininity in competitive bodybuilding. *Women's Studies Quarterly* 22(1/2): 134–49.

Bray, A. and C. Colebrook. 1998. The haunted flesh: Corporeal feminism and the politics of (dis)embodiment. *Signs: Journal of Women in Culture and Society* 24(1): 35–67.

Cole, C. L. 1998. Addition, exercise, and cyborgs: Technologies of deviant bodies. In *Sport in postmodern times*, ed. G. Rail, 261–76. Albany, NY: State University of New York Press.

Craig, M. L. and R. Liberty. 2007. "Cause that's what girls do": The making of a feminized gym. *Gender & Society* 21: 676–99.

Crossley, N. 2004. The circuit trainer's habitus: Reflexive body techniques and the sociality of the workout. *Body & Society* 10(1): 37–69.

—— 2006. In the gym: Motives, meaning and moral careers. *Body & Society* 12(3): 23–50.

D'Abundo, M. L. 2009. Issues of health, appearance and physical activity in aerobic classes for women. *Sport, Education and Society* 14(3): 301–19.

Deleuze, G. 1988. *Foucault.* London: Athlone.

Deleuze, G. and F. Guattari. 1987. *A thousand plateaus.* London and New York: Continuum.

Duncan, M. C. 1994. The politics of women's body images and practices: Foucault, and Panopticon and *Shape* magazine. *Journal of Sport & Social Issues* 18: 48–65.

Dworkin, S. L. 2001. "Holding back": Negotiating a glass ceiling on women's muscular strength. *Sociological Perspectives* 44(3): 333–50.

—— 2003. A woman's place is in the . . . cardiovascular room? Gender relations, the body, and the gym. In *Athletic intruders: Ethnographic research on women, culture, and exercise,* ed. A. Bolin and J. Granskog, 131–58. Albany, NY: State University of New York Press.

Dworkin, S. L. and F. L. Wachs. 2009. *Body panic: Gender, health, and the selling of fitness.* New York, NY: New York University Press.

Eskes, T. B., M. C. Duncan and E. M. Miller. 1998. The discourse of empowerment: Foucault, Marcuse, and women's fitness texts. *Journal of Sport and Social Issues* 22: 317–44.

Evans, R. R., E. M. Cotter and J. L. P. Roy. 2005. Preferred body type of fitness instructors among university students in exercise classes. *Perceptual and Motor Skills* 101: 257–66.

Foucault, M. 1978. *The history of sexuality, volume 1: An introduction*. London: Penguin Books.

—— 1983a. The subject and power. In *Michel Foucault: Beyond structuralism and hermeneutics*, ed. H. L. Dreyfus and P. Rabinow, 208–28. Chicago, IL: University of Chicago Press.

—— 1983b. On the genealogy of ethics: An overview of work in progress. In *Michel Foucault: Beyond structuralism and hermeneutics*, ed. H. L. Dreyfus and P. Rabinow, 229–52. Chicago, IL: University of Chicago Press.

—— 1985. *The history of sexuality volume 2: The use of pleasure*. London: Penguin Books.

—— 1988a. Technologies of the self. In *Technologies of the self: A seminar with Michel Foucault*, ed. L. H. Martin, H. Gutman and P. H. Hutton, 16–49. Amherst, MA: University of Massachusetts Press.

—— 1988b. An aesthetics of existence. In *Michel Foucault Politics, Philosophy, culture: Interviews and other writing 1977–1984*, ed. L. D. Kritzman, 47–56. London: Routledge.

—— 1991. *Discipline and punish: The birth of the prison*. London: Penguin Books.

Frew, M., and D. McGilligvray. 2005. Health clubs and body politics: Aesthetics and the quest for physical capital. *Leisure Studies* 24: 161–75.

Gambs, D. 2007. Myocellular transduction: When my cells trained my body-mind. In *The Affective Turn: Theorizing the Social*, ed. P. Ticineto Glouch and J. Halley, 106–18. Durham and London: Duke University Press.

George, T. and G. Rail. 2006. Barbie meets the Bindi: Constructions of health among second generation South Asian Canadian women. *Journal of Women's Health and Urban Life* 4(2): 45–67.

Gimlin, D. 2002. *Body work: Beauty and self-image in American culture*. Berkeley, CA: University of California Press.

Grogan, S., R. Evans, S. Wright and G. Hunter. 2004. Femininity and muscularity: Accounts of seven women body builders. *Journal of Gender Studies* 13(1): 49–61.

Grosz, E. 1997. Ontology and equivocation: Derrida's politics of sexual difference. In *Feminist interpretations of Jacques Derrida*, ed. N. J. Holland, 73–102. University Park, PA: Pennsylvania State University Press.

Haravon Collins, L. 2002. Working out contradictions: Feminism and aerobics. *Journal of Sport & Social Issues* 26: 85–109.

Hargreaves, J. 1994. *Sporting females: Critical issues in the history and sociology of women's sports*. London: Routledge.

Hekman, S. 1990. *Gender and knowledge: Elements of a postmodern feminism*. Boston, MA: Northeastern University Press.

Heywood, L. 1998. *Bodymakers: A cultural anatomy of women's bodybuilding*. New Brunswick, NJ: Rutgers University Press.

Jette, S. 2006. Fit for two? A critical discourse analysis of *Oxygen* Fitness Magazine. *Sociology of Sport Journal* 23: 331–51.

Kagan, E. and M. Morse. 1988. The body electronic: Aerobic exercise on video. *The Drama Review* 32: 164–80.

King, S. J. 2003. Doing good by running well. In *Foucault, cultural studies, governmentality*, ed. J. Z. Bratich, J. Packer and C. McCarthy, 285–301. New York: Simon & Schuster.

King, S. J. 2006. *Pink Ribbons, Inc.: Breast cancer and the politics of philan-thropy*. Minneapolis, MS: University of Minnesota Press.

Lea, J. 2009. Liberation or limitation? Understanding Iyengar yoga as a practice of the self. *Body & Society* 15(3): 71–92.

Lenskyj, H. 1986. *Out of bounds: Women, sport and sexuality*. Toronto: Women's Press.

Lewis, C. S. 2008. Life chances and wellness: Meaning and motion in the "yoga market". *Sport in Society* 11(5): 535–45.

Lloyd, M. 1996. Feminism, aerobics and the politics of the body. *Body & Society* 2(2): 79–98.

Loland, N. W. 2000. The art of concealment in a culture of display: Aerobicizing women's and men's experience and the use of their own bodies. *Sociology of Sport Journal* 17: 111–29.

MacNeill, M. 1998. Sex, lies, and videotape: The political and cultural economies of celebrity fitness videos. In *Sport and postmodern times*, ed. G. Rail, 163–84. Albany, NY: State University of New York Press.

Maguire, J. and L. Mansfield. 1998. "No-body is perfect": Women, aerobics, and the body beautiful. *Sociology of Sport Journal* 15: 109–37.

Malin, J. 2010. *My life at the gym: Feminist perspectives on community through the body*. Albany, NY: State University of New York Press.

Marcuse, H. 1964. *One dimensional man*. Boston: Beacon.

Markula, P. 1995. Firm but shapely, fit but sexy, strong but thin: The postmodern aerobicizing female bodies. *Sociology of Sport Journal* 12: 424–53.

—— 2001. Beyond the perfect body: Women's body image distortion in fitness magazine discourse. *Journal of Sport & Social Issues* 25: 158–79.

—— 2003a. Postmodern aerobics: Contradiction and resistance. In *Athletic intruders: Ethnographic research on women, culture, and exercise,* ed. A. Bolin and J. Granskog, 53–78. Albany, NY: State University of New York Press.

—— 2003b. Bodily dialogues: Writing the self. In *Moving writing: Crafting movement in sport research*, ed. J. Denison and P. Markula, 27–50. New York, NY: Peter Lang.

—— 2004. "Tuning into one's self": Foucault's technologies of the self and mind-ful fitness. *Sociology of Sport Journal* 21: 302–21.

—— 2006. Deleuze and the Body without Organs: Disreading the fit feminine identity. *Journal of Sport & Social Issues* 30: 29–44.

—— 2009. Affect[ing] Bodies: Performative Pedagogy of Pilates. *International Review of Qualitative Research* 3: 381–408.

Markula, P. and R. Pringle 2006. *Foucault, sport and exercise: Power, knowledge and transforming the self*. London: Routledge.

McDermott, L. 2000. A qualitative assessment of the significance of body percep-tion to women's physical activity experiences: Revisiting discussions of physi-calities. *Sociology of Sport Journal* 17: 331–63.

McGrath, S. A. and R. A. Chananie-Hill. 2009. "Big freaky-looking women": Normalizing gender transgression through bodybuilding. *Sociology of Sport Journal* 26: 235–54.

Phillips, J. N. and M. J. N. Drummond. 2001. An investigation into the body image perception, body satisfaction and exercise expectations of male fitness leaders: Implications for professional practice. *Leisure Studies* 20: 95–105.

Prickett, S. 1997. Aerobic dance and the city: Individual and social space. In *Dance in the city,* ed. H. Thomas, 198–217. New York: St. Martin.

Roussel, P., J. Griffet and P. Duret. 2003. The decline of female bodybuilding in France. *Sociology of Sport Journal* 20: 40–59.

Sassatelli, R. 1999. Interaction order and beyond: A field analysis of body culture within fitness gyms. *Body & Society* 5: 227–48.

Scott, J. 1992. Experience. In *Feminists theorize the political,* ed. Judith Butler and Joan Scott, 22–40. New York: Routledge.

Shilton, T. 2008. Creating and making the case: General advocacy for physical activity. *Journal of Physical Activity and Health* 5: 765–76.

Smith Maguire, J. 2001. Fit and flexible: The fitness industry, personal trainers and emotional service labor. *Sociology of Sport Journal* 18: 379–402.

—— 2007. *Fit for consumption: Sociology and the business of fitness.* London: Routledge.

Spielvogel, L. G. 2002. The discipline of space in a Japanese fitness club. *Sociology of Sport Journal* 19: 189–205.

—— 2003. *Working out in Japan: Shaping the female body in Tokyo fitness clubs.* Durham: Duke University Press.

Spitzack, C. 1990. *Confessing excess: Women and the politics of body reduction.* Albany, NY: State University of New York Press.

St. Martin, L. and N. Gavey. 1996. Women's bodybuilding: Feminist resistance and/or femininity's recuperation? *Body & Society* 2(4): 45–57.

Theberge, N. 1987. Sport and women's empowerment. *Women's Studies International Forum* 10: 387–93.

TNS Opinion and Social. 2010. Sport and Physical Activity (Special Euro-barometer Report). Brussels: TNS Opinion and Social. http://ec.europa.eu/public_opinion/archives/ebs/ebs_334_en.pdf

Waring, A. 2008. Health club use and "lifestyle": Exploring the boundaries between work and leisure. *Leisure Studies* 27(3): 295–309.

Waxman, A. 2004. WHO's global strategy on diet, physical activity and health: Response to a worldwide epidemic of non-communicable diseases. *Scandinavian Journal of Nutrition* 48(2): 58–60.

Wesely, J. 2001. Negotiating gender: Bodybuilding and the natural/unnatural continuum. *Sociology of Sport Journal* 18: 162–80.

Wray, S. 2003. Connecting ethnicity, gender and physicality: Muslim Pakistani women, physical activity and health. In *Gender and sport: A reader,* ed. S. Scraton, 127–40. London: Routledge.

Part I

The Business of Exercise

Selling and Consuming Fitness

1 Love Your Body?

The Discursive Construction of Exercise in Women's Lifestyle and Fitness Magazines

Eileen Kennedy and Evdokia Pappa

Exercise and fitness have come to form a vital segment of the media industry. Exercise has, for a long time, had its own specialist media, including magazines, DVDs and websites, but increasingly items related to exercise have begun to feature in mainstream media. It has long been acknowledged the media not only reflect but help construct women's social realities (Van Zoonen 1994). The media framing of exercise, therefore, can restrict or expand the imagined possibilities for exercise among women. Within the range of available media, women's magazines occupy a special place for articulations of fitness and embodiment. Abrahamson (2007) suggested that the unique features of magazines lend them an exceptional capacity to shape social life. According to this thesis, as a media form, magazines enjoy an unusually close connection with their audience. Magazine journalists often share a community of interest with their readers, and editorial content "is specifically designed by its editors and looked to by its readers as something that will lead to action" (Abrahamson 2007, 670). Magazines, therefore, may well not only offer women information about exercise but also provide the motivation and means to take part.

While scholars have been critical of the narrow way magazines frame exercise (Duncan 1994; Eskes et al. 1998; Markula 1995), analysis has so far tended to focus on fitness-oriented magazines. As exercise becomes a regular feature within a wider range of women's magazines, it might be anticipated that the framing of fitness may change. The diversity of women's magazines extends to titles focused on fashion, lifestyle, slimming, health, fitness and more. Each title vies with the others to attract the attention of the female consumer, and items related to exercise are increasingly featured in coverlines foreshadowing the magazine's "inside delights" (Winship 1987, 12). This wide range of competing titles aimed at different sectors of the female market suggests that women may have a greater choice than ever. This chapter provides a discourse analysis of the exercise content of titles drawn from across the spectrum of women's magazines to consider the range of options offered to readers.

FEMINIST RESEARCH ON WOMEN AND MAGAZINES

Feminist research has understood women's magazines as a key site for the construction of ideas about women, men and gender relations (Gill 2009). Much of this research has been critical of the magazines' restrictive image of femininity focused on fashion, beauty and 'how to get a man.' McRobbie (1999) pointed to the various 'stages' that scholarship on women's magazines has passed through. The first stage involved an angry repudiation of false and objectified images of women contained in the magazines. The second 'theory of ideology' stage drew on Althusser's (1971) work to characterize the consumer as a dupe of patriarchal power relations. This approach gradually gave way to a post-structuralist orientation that began to consider the role of the magazine in the discursive construction of women's realities. According to McRobbie, "post-structuralist feminism has argued that there is and can be no truth of womanhood just as there can be no single or true feminism" (1999, 193). The task of feminism is an ongoing investigation of the ways that magazines produce "great bundles of meaning" on a regular basis which compete to construct "the subjectivities of millions of female readers" (McRobbie 1999, 193). Readers might be unconsciously influenced by the messages of magazines, even if they consciously reject them. As a result, the second stage saw a growing interest in psychoanalysis, and the capacity of the magazine to produce desires and pleasures in the reader.

The third stage of feminist magazine research identified by McRobbie (1999) built on an interest in the relationship between the magazine and readers' pleasures to enable researchers to explore their love-hate relationship with women's magazines. Critics were able to admit there may be feminine pleasures to be found in the pages of the magazines. Winship's (1983; 1987) work has been most explicit in this regard. She observed that "above all, whatever practical information they might also offer, the editors of women's magazines have consistently been concerned to entertain their readers" (Winship 1983, 44). Winship (1983) argued that magazines were intended to provide a pleasurable read and escape and fantasy was an integral part of that pleasure. Winship (1987) has suggested that the defining characteristic of the cover image of women's magazines is the way that the female model holds the gaze of the reader: "with the model's gaze on 'you', the magazine invites you into its world" (Winship 1987, 12).

McCracken (1993) also took note of the pleasures offered by magazines. However, in her analysis, pleasure and insecurity were interlinked. McCracken (1993) argued that the magazine cover presents the reader with an idealized self, a version of identity that the reader would prefer to have. On the surface, magazine images of ideal beauty could be seen as positive projections of the reader's future self. Yet,

The attractive presentation frequently disguises the negativity close at hand: within this discursive structure, to be beautiful, one must fear being non-beautiful; to be in fashion, one must fear being out of fashion; to be self-confident, one must first feel insecure.

(McCracken 1993, 136)

The logic of magazines depends on this oppositional strategy to create the transitory pleasures of commodity consumption. Nevertheless, "one product or even several will never completely alleviate insecurities and the fear of being non-beautiful" (McCracken 1993, 136). The continued need to sell products means that readers' desires can never be completely fulfilled.

McCracken's approach acknowledged that the narrative structures of magazines could only attain "relative closure," and readers often negotiated contradictions by developing oppositional meanings (1993, 300). The shift from a focus on the text to the reader characterized McRobbie's (1999) fourth stage of magazine research. This stage aimed to rescue the women's magazine from its traditionally low cultural status by reconceptualizing readers as active consumers, rather than cultural dupes. Within this research, the magazine reader was considered as having the capacity to produce resistant readings rather than passively accept the meanings of the text.

However, Brook (2008) has argued that the emphasis on feminine pleasures and the ability of the reader to make their own meanings has resulted in a depoliticizing of the feminist critique of women's magazines. This perspective, she maintained, seemed to suggest that "exploitation is in the eye of the beholder" (Brook 2008, 141). Currie's (2001) study of young women's magazines found that, rather than resist the magazine's meanings, readers lent the magazine content a 'truth value' that overrode their own experience. Currie argued that the question and answer format of magazine advice pages encouraged young women to attribute authorship of the questions to a typical teenager, to whom they could compare themselves "and reject self-constructions in favour of those of the text" (Currie 2001, 277). While adult women may be a good deal savvier, Currie's study gives an indication of the power of textual constructions.

Gill (2009) observed that a more satisfactory response to the vexed question of ideology and reader agency would be to give up the search for one, stable meaning within the texts of magazines. For example, Winship (1987) argued that there was a plethora of contradictory and competing ideologies of femininity within the pages of women's magazines. Coleman's approach has been to emphasize the relationality of bodies and images, arguing that "women's bodies are often both subjects and objects of images and do not exist as an entity that is secure and bounded from images" (2008, 164). Women's relationship with magazines needs to be understood, therefore, as entailing a complex exchange of meanings, involving the reader in multiple investments in the shifting discourses of the magazine.

Magazines may produce both disciplinary and pleasurable subjectivities for the reader, which she must negotiate. This confusing array of meaning in women's magazines is captured by Smith (2008) who argued that 'chick lit' such as *Bridget Jones's Diary* (Fielding 1996) involves a critique of the problematic consumption practices endorsed by the magazines that their heroines read. Smith argued that authors such as Fielding "respond to the contradictory content of these magazines by depicting characters who struggle to follow the consumption guidelines offered by such publications" (2008, 13). Discourses of restrictive femininities may exist simultaneously with the promise of pleasurable possibilities within the magazines.

Research on magazines' construction of exercise, however, has tended not to focus on the possible pleasures made available to the female reader. Instead, this literature has adopted a post-structuralist approach, situating it broadly within the second stage of McRobbie's classification of feminist magazine research. Scholarship has drawn attention to the predominance of messages in women's magazines encouraging female bodyshaping in line with restrictive ideologies of femininity, for example, dieting, eating disorders, cosmetic surgery (Bordo 1993; Greer 1999; Wolf 1990). Magazines have been condemned within this research for "promulgating pernicious gender ideologies" (Gill 2009, 347). However, exercise and fitness have required a more complex theorization. Physical activity has the potential for women's self-transformation (Markula and Pringle 2006). Nevertheless, scholars such as Eskes et al. (1998) have denounced women's magazines for co-opting feminist exhortations to exercise to support their postfeminist empowerment ideology.

Research on exercise and physical activity has tended to concentrate on fitness-orientated titles, rather than mainstream women's magazines. Contradiction has been a theme within these studies. Following Bartky (1990), Duncan (1994) argued that women's magazines were involved in the duplicitous practice of encouraging women to alter their appearance in line with unrealistic feminine body ideals. While the overt function of this bodily discipline may be the pursuit of beauty, Duncan observed that "the covert function is female physical disempowerment" (1994, 49). It is no surprise, therefore, that the recurring theme of all women's magazines is "how to become healthier, fitter, thinner and more attractive" (Duncan 1994, 51). Duncan's analysis of two editions of *Shape* magazine drew on Foucault's (1977) discussion of the ways that the invisible but constant surveillance of panoptic prison architecture produced self-monitoring docile bodies (1994, 51). Duncan identified two "panoptic mechanisms" (1994, 51) used by *Shape* to encourage women to internalize unrealistic body ideals, becoming "objects for their own gaze" (1994, 50). The first of these mechanisms was seen in the magazine's focus on the "efficacy of initiative"—all you need is commitment—and the second was the subordination of health issues to beauty—"feeling good means looking good" (Duncan 1994, 51).

Eskes et al. (1998) highlighted the contradictions involved in magazines' employment of female empowerment ideology to promote exercise because physical health was reduced simply to beauty. Readers were told that, through fitness, they could become strong, healthy and attractive. However, while magazines may praise "perfect curves," "curvy is not intended to mean 'round'" but rather references the figures of the magazines' celebrity models, all "thin and muscular" (Eskes et al. 1998, 334). Scholars have also pointed to the contradictions involved in magazines' ostensible attempts to overcome this narrow and restrictive image of ideal femininity. Markula discussed the way that magazines can sometimes appear to present a diversity of body types, suggesting that "there is no single great 'look'" (1995, 447). However, the magazines continue to present versions of the same, thin, young and toned body, where the "only variable is their height" (Markula 1995, 447). While the magazines ostensibly encourage women to accept their bodies the way they are, they simultaneously present highly contradictory advice, suggesting women should disguise their bodies through judicious clothing choice.

Since the identification of the condition labeled 'body image distortion,' fitness magazines have even adopted a critical approach to representations of sculpted bodies that appear in their pages (Markula 2001). However, although the magazines may argue that images of impossibly slender bodies may help produce this condition in their readers, Markula (2001) observed that they prefer to disaggregate their responsibility by suggesting that readers should change their approach to the images, rather than change the images themselves. Markula (2001) argued that the magazines' continued use of unrealistic images and the associated feelings of imperfection that they create in the readers, tie the reader into a need to keep buying the magazine for "advice on thinning, toning, and how (while on a diet or exercising) to think positively about ourselves" (2001, 168). Eskes et al. suggested that "'talking out of both sides of your mouth' is the perfect phrase to describe fitness magazine texts preaching healthy living but highlighting impossible beauty ideals first" (1998, 342), citing a phrase from a reader's letter who wanted to express her anger at the magazine's ostensible condemnation, but continued use, of too-slender models.

Dworkin and Wachs (2009) argued that the combination of health messages and idealized body images within health and fitness magazines reproduce discourses of what they call healthism. Healthism situates the problem of health and disease at the level of the individual, and so operates to promote neo-liberal ideologies that "obscure the impact of government and structural contributions to health disparities" (Dworkin and Wachs 2009, 11). In this process, certain bodies are privileged and idealized and associated with greater moral worth. As a result, Dworkin and Wachs (2009) argued, the media are involved in reproducing an endless quest for bodily perfection.

Much of the research on exercise and fitness magazines points to the importance of consumer society as the context for the promotion of impossible ideals of bodily perfection that function to discipline and disempower the reader. However, there has been no corresponding exploration of the ways that exercise within women's magazines may be discursively constructed to produce pleasures for the reader. As Bordo observed, bodily control through diet and exercise can be understood as a response to consumer society's contradictory demands "to capitulate to desire and indulge in impulse" while also "repressing desires for immediate gratification" and cultivating the work ethic (1990, 96). Bordo (1990) argued that advertisements for diet and exercise programs try to mask these contradictions by using the imagery of instant gratification. Considered in this way, women's magazines are likely to present exercise as part of the pleasures of consumer society and the wide range of women's magazines available may construct exercise as differently pleasurable for their target readership.

However, existing studies of exercise and magazines have tended to concentrate on fitness titles and focus on close readings of one or two issues or articles within a single issue. The fitness boom shows no sign of abating, and in the U.K. context, exercise and physical activity are being regularly promoted in the mainstream media by both the government and the fitness industry through campaigns such as "Change4Life." It is, therefore, pertinent to consider the ways that exercise has begun to permeate the pages of mainstream women's magazines, and the different ways that fitness and fitness-oriented magazines construct physical activity. Within the pages of women's magazines, ranging from youth-oriented fashion and beauty titles, magazines aimed at older women, to special interest magazines focused on dieting, yoga or spa holidays, are there multiple fitness pleasures on offer to women? Health and fitness titles are differentiated on the basis of seriousness, fitness level or activity (for example, *Zest, Ultra Fit, Pilates Style*). Do these titles offer the potential of experiencing the fitness imperative in qualitatively different ways? This chapter presents an analysis of exercise in a range of women's magazines available in the U.K., posing the question, what are the similarities and differences in the ways exercise is discursively constructed in women's magazines? Is exercise part of the pleasure of women's magazines?

METHOD

In order to discover the limits of exercising subjectivities offered to women across the range of women's magazines, we conducted a discourse analysis of 34 women's magazines across a spectrum of fashion and lifestyle, diet, health and fitness. Titles comprised: *Brand New You, Cosmopolitan, Diet and Fitness, Easy Health, Easy Living, Elle, Essence, Essentials, Fitness, FitnessRx for Women, Glamour, Good Housekeeping, Harper's Bazaar, Health & Fitness, Healthy and Organic Living, InStyle, LighterLife, Luxury Spa Finder, Marie Claire, Natural Health, Pilates Style, Red, Shape, She, Slim At Home, Slimming World, Spa World, UltraFit, Vogue, Weightwatchers, Women's Fitness, Women's Health, Yoga and Health, Yoga Journal, Yoga Magazine* and *Zest*. Our approach to discourse analysis as a methodology derives from Foucault's (1972) understanding of discourse as practices, institutions and spaces through which regulatory power operates to enable what can be said, what (social, moral, political) positions can be adopted and what meanings can be ascribed to events, texts and objects. To analyze discourse is to pay attention to the repeated ways in which an issue is framed and to consider the effect of that framing on individuals' behavior, thoughts and opinions. Gaps or silences are equally important, since what is left out can have as powerful an effect as what is present.

Foucault (1972) considered discourse to be made up of groups of 'statements.' Statements can be thought of as those "utterances which have some institutional force and which are thus validated by some form of authority" (Mills 1997, 55) and which thereby claim to speak the truth. Within the magazines, we looked for discourses and statements within words and images, considering how they constructed truth claims about women and exercise. We were particularly interested in identifying repeated patterns of representation, or discursive formations (Foucault 1972) in the women's magazines. Our aim was to consider the way that the discursive framing of exercise within the different magazines addressed their readers. We wanted to identify the characteristics of the range of subject positions made available to the consumers of magazines. In order to do this we drew on scholarship on women's magazines by considering how combinations of visual and linguistic codes constructed an ideal self for women to identify with on the cover and inside the various magazines.

All of the magazines in our study were bought in the U.K. in June 2008, but the magazines' publication dates ranged from April to August. We identified all references to exercise, nutrition and bodyshaping in each magazine. We were particularly interested in the cover page as the first point of address to the ideal reader. We considered the title, cover image, coverlines and colors. Inside the magazine, we were interested in images accompanying the text, page layout the headings and subheadings. In total we examined 266 articles as well as each magazine cover. As a result, the number of magazines included in this study produced a very large data set. Following the approach taken by Gill whose method of discourse analysis fits with a "poststructuralist Foucaultian-influenced approach, which places emphasis upon power's material-discursive effects, rather than on a distinction between ideology and truth" (2009, 351) our discussion of the data we collected concentrates on a smaller sample in order to produce a more focused analysis. Our large data set enabled us to identify common patterns of representation both connecting and distinguishing the magazines. We discuss these differences and commonalities later using examples to illustrate our results.

THE SAME BUT DIFFERENT—EXERCISE ACROSS THE SPECTRUM OF WOMEN'S MAGAZINES

It was possible to identify broad differences within the discursive construction of exercise across the range of magazines. Magazine types could be differentiated by the images of bodies they contained in terms of size, age, fitness and activity. There were differences in detail and proposed intensity of exercise as well as the amount of space devoted to exercise. The magazines contained varying amounts of diet and nutritional advice, emphasis on appearance, weight loss, well-being, spirituality, fitness and performance. The range and type of expert advice and reader testimony included also differed, and the amount and character of advertising associated with exercise varied. On the basis of shared characteristics, it was possible to differentiate the magazines into four general types: 'fashion and lifestyle,' 'slimming,' 'health and spirituality' and 'fitness.'[1]

Taking *Elle* as an example, fashion and lifestyle magazines shared repeating features which included images of very slim, young bodies, with no discernible muscle toning or definition, depicted in passive poses linked to beauty and fashion. The emphasis on appearance throughout the magazines was reflected in their approach to exercise. For example, *Elle* contained one page devoted to yoga, but no practical guide, one page describing sporty fashion, and a page advising how to "style yourself slimmer," written by an expert "fashion director." The magazine contained a section called '*Elle*diet' which presented a reflection on readers' (assumed) interest in what other women eat, rather than nutritional advice or tips.

Slimming magazines such as *Weightwatchers* presented images of slightly older, fuller bodies, including women in their 30s, 40s and 50s. In *Weightwatchers*, models were posed in simulated exercise positions (for example, a model was dressed in a martial arts outfit with an arm outstretched as if punching the air). Eight pages were devoted to exercise and encouraged readers to start gentle activities such as walking or swimming, but also suggested less realistic goals such as learning water polo. Activities were accompanied by an estimation of typical calories burnt per hour. Expert advice drawn from personal experience was provided by named authors with designations such as "Head of Programme

Development for Weightwatchers." A total of 32 pages were given over to nutrition, mostly recipes. There were advertisements for a range of products including healthy or low-calorie food, beer, weightloss aids, spa holidays and Weightwatchers products featured in the articles.

Health and spirituality magazines contained images of similar body types, with a slightly extended age range. As an example of this type, *Natural Health* depicted models in natural settings with some adopting yoga positions. The emphasis was on well-being with articles such as "Hands On Healing" giving advice about positive mental and physical health strategies. The magazine contained 6 pages of advice and information related to nutrition, including a "Q and A" section and 2 pages of recipes and advertisements for healthy food products. Expertise was provided by named authors, but without information as to what qualifies them as experts.

Fitness magazines such as *Health & Fitness* contained images of mostly young, slim, defined and toned bodies in a range of active exercise poses, including fencing, running, weight training and stretching. Specific exercise routines were described, and 13 pages were collectively entitled an "exercise handbook." The emphasis on fitness was underscored by the inclusion of diagrams indicating which muscles were being activated by the exercise. The magazine contained 8 pages of diet and nutritional advice, including recipes, and expertise was provided by medically qualified, named individuals with the title 'Dr.' Advertisements were for fitness equipment, clothing for exercise and healthy food.

However, despite the different types of magazine, we also saw that there was an overarching pattern that united them all. There appeared to be a similar contrast between the way the magazine cover announced exercise-related contents and the way that exercise was covered inside the magazine. Pleasure was central to the construction of exercise in the magazine, but while the cover foreshadowed pleasure in exercise for the reader, this did not materialize inside. In the next section, we will explore the contradiction that existed between the promises made on the magazine cover and the related content inside the magazines.

GREAT EXPECTATIONS, DISAPPOINTING RESULTS

The ideal self constructed on the cover of many of the magazines contrasted sharply with the subject position offered by the article content inside. Many of the magazines portrayed exercise as easy to do with the promise of desired results without strain. For example, the cover of *Essence* (July 2008) suggested that readers should "Love Your Body" and promised an "Easy Summer Shape Up Guide." *Easy Living* (May 2008) demanded readers "Feel better!" and "Start Getting Results," suggesting that the magazine offered readers a way to "Achieve what you want at the hairdressers, in the shops and at the gym." A cover-line from *Glamour* (April 2008) promised that it was possible to achieve "Your Perfect Weight" with "5 tiny tweaks and you're there." However, inside the magazine, promises of achievable workouts were not met. *Easy Living*'s article on gyms was entitled "Are you being dim at the gym?" and presented seven rules of behavior to follow at the gym. The article warned readers that going to the gym was not enough, and that their workouts were unlikely to be effective unless they heeded the magazine's advice. The image accompanying the article showed a glamorous woman in full make-up, with an expression of delight, red high heels and long flowing hair, wearing a smart, silk summer dress, billowing behind her, on a stationary bicycle. The model wore a silver bangle on her arm that picked up the metal of the exercise machine. The image visually equated the experience of going to the gym with attending a summer garden party, linking exercise with ease, pleasure, good looks, health and high society. The model's attire and demeanor could not have been more unsuited to a workout.

The impossibility of this image was reflected in the logic of the article, since the advice given provided unrealistic guidelines that readers would be unlikely to be able to follow. For example, readers were advised against trusting erratic gym equipment such as calorie counters. The magazine advised that workouts would not be effective unless the exerciser can just "barely carry on a conversation and you stay in that state for about 45 minutes—then you are working hard enough to lose weight" (Le Poer Trench 2008, 133). Later, however, the article revealed that such exercise would still not be enough: "the fittest women might have a circuit-training programme they complete three times a week and then they choose a high-impact cardio class for their fourth and fifth workout to mix it up" (Le Poer Trench 2008, 134). The magazine also addressed readers' anticipated concerns about correct etiquette in the gym in a question and answer column accompanying the main article, where common gym situations (like meeting an acquaintance working out or being naked in the locker room) were presented as problems in need of solutions. Articles such as these build anxieties by asking readers to find fault with even the toughest of fitness regimes, as described earlier, and the everyday social encounters that surround exercise. Since the solutions offered are highly demanding, restrictive and inflexible, greater anxiety is likely to be generated by readers' inability to follow the advice. The magazines imply that it would be easier not to exercise at all.

A different approach but one with the same effect, was to persuade readers that it was normal for women not to exercise. *Glamour* (2008) asked readers "How normal are you about exercise?" suggesting that it was normal to exercise at home, to have a 'justified' reason not to work out (like hating school PE), to give excuses not to exercise, to be embarrassed to go to the gym, or to use the gym as a social network. An image of a slim model sitting on a beach in a bikini, casually holding a small pink dumbbell, accompanied the article, with the ironic caption "What? You mean I have to lift the thing as well?" This humorous item constructed a comforting, pleasurable discourse about 'normal' femininity, but in order to step into this normalized subject position, readers should give up any intention of engaging in exercise.

There was a similar disjuncture between the address of the cover of the health oriented magazine, *Zest* (May 2008) and its content. The cover presented a slim, blonde model on a beach, wearing shorts and a bra top, in semi-profile, looking over her shoulder and smiling. The coverline "The super simple 7-day diet" was positioned beside the model's flat stomach. This image of health and happiness was repeated inside the magazine, as the related article was accompanied by a close-up of a smiling model about to eat a slice of watermelon. However, in contrast to these images of pleasure and the promise of the relaxed and easy, super simple diet on the cover, the introductory words of the actual diet positioned the reader as "Desperate to lose weight?" While the cover image presented an ideal self to the reader, the diet implied the reader was out of control. The diet itself was not simple, containing the names of dishes without any preparation details. At the end of the article, the reader was encouraged to buy the book on which the diet was based, suggesting that the only solution is continued consumption of commodities.

The cover of *Health and Fitness* (April 2008) promised to make readers look and feel amazing. Coverlines such as "Stretch yourself slim" and "Exercise myths busted" promoted the possibility of knowledge and technique to help the reader construct herself in the image of the slim, smiling, blonde, relaxed and toned model. However, the articles inside the magazine contained conflicting advice about how to exercise safely. The article, "Fitness myths busted" (68) sought to alert readers to dangers in exercise of which they may not be aware. For example, in challenging the "Myth" of "I should always stretch before I do a workout," the article presented the "Fact" that stretching cold muscles before a workout can cause serious injury, despite stretching before exercise being advocated elsewhere in the magazine. In response to the "Myth" that "my workout shouldn't feel uncomfortable," the article presented the "Fact" that it was necessary to negotiate the fine line between discomfort and pain, and to challenge yourself "which feels tough." Nevertheless, "Stretch into shape" (111) advised readers not to "push your body to the threshold of serious discomfort and pain." The magazine presented a confusing message that could create anxieties in the reader attempting to interpret the magazine's advice correctly.

Pleasure and insecurity are both part of the packaging of exercise within women's magazines. As McCracken observed, images within magazines need to appear as "positive projections of the future self, for few would buy these publications were they overtly to present negative images"

(1993, 136). Exercise is presented as a simple and pleasurable means to a better future self through covers of the magazines. Yet, the magazines appear unable or unwilling to sustain this pleasurable approach to exercise. For McCracken, the magazine discourse exaggerates the importance of physical appearance to the neglect of other aspects of readers' lives. This emphasis is bound into the logic of consumer capitalism that supports the magazine industry. Magazine contents encourage readers "to dissect themselves conceptually into fragments that various products are promised to improve" (McCracken 1993, 138). Pleasure in exercise gives way inside the magazines to a more complex terrain where exercise advice becomes fraught with difficulty. McCracken argued that, while magazines may not be the initial cause of anxiety "they often encourage and exacerbate these feelings, and suggest that increased consumption is the remedy" (1993, 138). Accordingly, a repeated link to the consumption of commodities associated with exercise and fitness was a pattern across the magazines in our study. The next section explores the discursive construction of the relationship between exercise and consumption within the magazines.

ALL-CONSUMING FITNESS

An ideal self was assembled for the reader to identify with on the covers of the magazines, and exercise was presented as an easy means to step into that identity. However, inside the magazine, articles reminded the reader that this identity was out of reach. Instead, exercise was constructed as something 'normal' women did not do, and conflicting advice presented barriers to engaging in exercise. The articles no longer presented exercise as a simple step to an ideal self, but a minefield of anxiety and confusion. The ideal self of the magazine cover was disassembled inside, constructing an identity loop, whereby readers were promised a 'new you' only to find that the 'old you' was impossible to shake off. Across all the magazines, the reader was directed to the consumption of commodities associated with fitness, as the only progressive option. Exercise and consumption were inextricably intertwined.

For example, a *Good Housekeeping* (April 2008) coverline announced the possibility for readers to simply "Walk yourself slim with our achievable fitness campaign." The corresponding article inside the magazine was illustrated with images of readers who had signed up to join the magazine's walking program. The readers appeared to range in age from 20 to 50, and were not slim. The program presented a week-by-week guide to walking, with instructions of increasing complexity for walking in "time zones" and "ab walking" (115). Despite the low cost and straightforward nature of the activity (notwithstanding the refinements in the article), the reader was advised to consult the websites of two experts—a diet and movement specialist and a happiness coach—for further information. The expert websites were covered in sponsors' logos and associated products to buy. In addition, the magazine contained a promotion for a cholesterol-reducing yoghurt four pages further on from the walking program. The promotion took the form of a page-long article entitled "Positive steps," accompanied by an image of a woman (looking fitter and slimmer than the readers featured before) engaged in energetic walking. At points, the wording of this sponsored article was virtually indistinguishable from the previous article: the walking program advised "Aim for at least 30 minutes' continuous walking" (116), while the promotion suggested "Aim to do at least 30 minutes physical activity" (120). Exercise advice that purported to come from the magazine itself blended seamlessly into an advertising strategy for its sponsors. The fitter, slimmer image associated with the yoghurt promotion suggested also that the route to the ideal self was through the consumption of this product and not the walking program alone.

CONCLUSIONS

While exercise may have permeated the spectrum of magazines aimed at women, contradictions remain. There are differences in the ways that exercise is framed across the variety of magazine types, with varying amounts of space devoted to exercise and varying levels of detail in the articles. However, despite the differences, there was a pattern common to all the magazines. Exercise, diet and bodyshaping were built into the linguistic and visual codes of the magazine covers. Together they discursively constructed a better, fitter, firmer self made possible through exercise. The words and images on the covers constructed exercise as a simple and pleasurable means to achieving the desired future self. Yet, inside the magazine, women readers were no longer addressed in these terms. The articles dissuaded women from exercise, created problems around exercising, or presented complicated or conflicting advice that was difficult to follow. The discourse inside the magazines addressed women as struggling, flawed or imperfect and constructed obstacles to exercise. Articles constructed exercise as a complicated and anxiety-ridden activity. The simple exercise solutions promised on the cover evaporated inside the magazine, where the 'ordinary' state of femininity was revealed to be anxious and resistant to physical transformation. The mismatch between the cover and the inside features was a regularity across all of the magazines, as was an orientation toward the promotion of consumption. Commodity consumption was presented as the only progressive option available to women in all the magazines. Despite the range of magazines types and identifiable differences in approach to exercise, these commonalities severely limit the ways of engaging in exercise presented to women. The magazines are all involved in the manipulation of readers' anxieties about exercise. The promise of identification with the ideal self on the cover is disassembled inside where the reader is left anxious and confused.

The seemingly pleasurable constructions of exercise within the magazines give women readers an indication of the transformative potential of movement and physical activity. Yet, as McCracken observed, "the commodity base of . . . pleasure [is] so pervasive that it appears to be an essential characteristic of contemporary feminine desire" (1993, 299). The language of pleasure within the magazines does not seem to extend beyond consumption. Exercise, however, needs to be performed not consumed. The intertwining of commodity consumption and exercise undermines its potential for transformation, since it transforms it into something it can never be. Pleasures of consumption may provide the framework for exercise but cannot substitute for the activity itself. To extend the pleasure of exercise beyond the cover constructions, the discourse of women's magazines needs to imagine exercise outside of the logic of consumer culture and begin to frame exercise as pleasurable from image to practice.

NOTE

1 "Fashion and lifestyle" magazine patterns were common to *Essence, Glamour, Good Housekeeping, Elle, InStyle, Red, Cosmopolitan, Harper's Bazaar, She, Vogue, Marie Claire, Essentials* and *Easy Living.* "Slimming" magazine patterns were common to *Weightwatchers, LighterLife, Slim At Home, Diet and Fitness, Slimming World* and *Brand New You.* "Health and spirituality" patterns were found among *Zest, Yoga and Health, Health & Fitness, Natural Health, Easy Health, Pilates Style, Luxury Spa Finder, Healthy and Organic Living, Spa World, Yoga Magazine, Yoga Journal* and *Shape.* "Fitness" patterns were found in *UltraFit, Fitness, Women's Fitness, FitnessRx for Women* and *Women's Health.*

REFERENCES

Abrahamson, D. 2007. Magazine exceptionalism: The concept, the criteria, the challenge. *Journalism Studies* 8(4): 667–70.

Althusser, L. 1971. *Lenin and philosophy and other essays.* London: New Left Books.

Bartky, S. 1990. *Femininity and dominion: Studies in the phenomenology of oppression.* New York: Routledge.

Bordo, S. 1990. Reading the slender body. In *Body/Politics: Women and the discourses of science,* ed. M. Jacobus, E. Fox Keller and S. Shuttleworth, 83–112. London: Routledge.

—— 1993. *Unbearable Weight: Feminism, Western culture, and the body.* Berkeley: University of California Press.

Brook, H. 2008. Feed your face. *Continuum: Journal of Media & Cultural Studies* 22(1): 141–57.

Coleman, R. 2008. The becoming of bodies: Girls, media effects, and body image. *Feminist Media Studies* 8(2): 163–78.

Currie, D. 2001. Dear Abby: Advice pages as a site for the operation of power. *Feminist Theory* 2: 259–81.

Duncan, M. C. 1994. The politics of women's body image and practices: Foucault, the panopticon and *Shape* magazine. *Journal of Sport and Social Issues* 18: 48–65.

Dworkin, S. L. and F. L. Wachs. 2009. *Body panic: Gender, health and the selling of fitness.* New York: New York University Press.

Eskes, T. B., M. C. Duncan and E. M. Miller. 1998. The discourse of empowerment: Foucault, Marcuse, and women's fitness texts. *Journal of Sport and Social Issues* 22: 317–44.

Fielding, H. 1996. *Bridget Jones's diary.* London: Pan Macmillan.

Foucault, M. 1972. *The archaeology of knowledge.* London: Tavistock.

—— 1977. *Discipline and Punish: The birth of the prison.* London: Penguin.

Gill, R. 2009. Mediated intimacy and postfeminism: A discourse analytic examination of sex and relationships advice in a women's magazine. *Discourse and Communication* 3: 345–69.

Greer, G. 1999. *The whole woman.* London: Doubleday/Anchor.

Le Poer Trench, B. 2008. Are you being dim at the gym? *Easy Living*, May.

McCracken, E. 1993. *Decoding women's magazines from Mademoiselle to Ms.* Houndsmill: Macmillan.

McRobbie, A. 1999. More! New sexualities in girls' and women's magazines. In *Back to Reality? Social experience and cultural studies*, ed. A. McRobbie, 190–209. Manchester: Manchester University Press.

Markula, P. 1995. Firm but shapely, fit but sexy, strong but thin: The postmodern aerobicizing female bodies. *Sociology of Sport Journal* 12: 424–53.

—— 2001. Beyond the perfect body: Women's body image distortion in fitness magazine discourse. *Journal of Sport & Social Issues* 25(2): 158–79.

Markula. P. and R. Pringle. 2006. *Foucault, sport and exercise: Power, knowledge and transforming the self.* London: Routledge.

Mills, S. 1997. *Discourse.* London: Routledge.

Smith, C. J. 2008. *Cosmopolitan culture and consumerism in Chick Lit.* New York: Routledge.

Van Zoonen, L. 1994. *Feminist media studies.* London: Sage.

Winship, J. 1983. 'Options—for the way you want to live now', or a magazine for superwoman. *Theory, Culture and Society* 1(3): 44–65.

—— 1987. *Inside women's magazines.* London: Pandora.

Wolf, N. 1990. *The beauty myth.* London: Chatto and Windus.

2 Women Developing and Branding Fitness Products on the Global Market

The Method Putkisto Case

Jaana Parviainen

Fitness has become a dynamic global industry that produces new fitness forms in rapid succession. For instance in the U.K., fitness classes continue to represent an important and growing segment of the health and fitness market in spite of economic recession (Mintel 2009). In the past ten years, Yoga, Pilates and other mindful fitness classes have become increasingly popular with women. This *slow movement* of fitness activity can be seen as a part of a cultural trend that includes slow city (cittaslow), slow food and slow travel (Honoré 2004). A principal characteristic of the slow movement is that women look for physical exercise where they can enjoy the silence and tranquility of bodily movement. Focusing on movements in detail, they usually want to learn more about their bodies to develop tools for their well-being. One such fitness form is Method Putkisto (MP). The MP has not yet been internationally established, but it has gained popularity within the U.K. and Finland.

In this chapter, I will explore how the brand of the MP is constructed based on Marja Putkisto's heroic life story in which her body, femininity, expertise and slow movement take a central role. The MP is one of those body techniques through which women are advised to improve their self-image (Markula 2006). The MP can hardly be called a feminist approach, but it includes resistance to the traditional aerobic-oriented fitness culture. Body work in MP classes is work on the self and appearance. For example, Putkisto constantly emphasizes that the MP keeps the body looking youthful, but unlike mere body shaping, the method is 'working inside out' to improve the entire self. The body work of MP programs is based on relaxation, visualization, breathing, slow movement and using body weight. Before analyzing the success of MP program, I will detail my theoretical and methodological framework.

METHODOLOGY AND THEORETICAL FRAMEWORK

'Branding' has become a popular topic of studies in the marketing of sport equipment companies and professional athletes (Chavanat et al. 2009;

Yang and Shi 2009), but limited efforts have been undertaken to examine this phenomenon in the fitness setting. Given the increasing prevalence of marketing strategies for sport organizations, I want to explore the factors that constitute a fitness brand as a part of the well-being and lifestyle industry (Shove and Pantzar 2005). For example, beyond generating revenue, brands were introduced to enhance the emotional attachment between the consumer and the company (Gobe 2001). My purpose is to explore how the personality of Marja Putkisto creates an interface that allows instructors and clients to identify themselves with her and bond with MP products.[1] This is because a personality or a face is the most easily identifiable and perhaps also the most powerfully persuasive configuration of marketing sport and fitness products (Lury 2004, 90).

My study[2] of the brand building of the MP is based on a qualitative textual analysis methodology (see Fulton et al. 2005). Using items and interviews from the print media as textual material to interpret sport and fitness culture has become a popular methodological approach in sport studies. For example, sport sociologists have analyzed how magazines construct identities of female athletes (e.g., Kane and Parks 1992; Pirinen 1997; Vincent et al. 2007) or address women's body image distortion (Markula 2001). The textual material informing this chapter includes 50 interviews and items on Marja Putkisto and her method that appeared in the media (newspapers, magazines, websites) in Finland and the U.K. during the years 2000 to 2008. In addition to these print media texts and their associated websites,[3] the research material encompasses the texts of the official MP website and 10 books and fitness videos that Marja Putkisto has published to launch new programs and products.

My purpose is not only to describe how newspapers and magazines construct Marja Putkisto's identity but how Putkisto utilizes the print media, in particular women's magazines, to build the MP brand and market her products. In this analysis, my aim is not to evaluate or judge to what extent Putkisto's brand building has been intentional or unintentional, systematic or accidental. Instead, I outline the kind of narrative the media texts and autobiographical notes construct around Marja Putkisto. Fulton et al. suggests that the strategy of individualization of the print media is a marker of news discourse, particularly soft news and human interest stories which invite the audience to understand events, phenomena and institutions (2005, 237). It does not merely incorporate a 'character' into a story but also actively aims to associate events with individuals.

Because of the connection between media narratives and economic imperatives, most media narratives work persuasively in the same way as advertisements (Fulton et al. 2005, 5). In their analysis of autobiographical narratives, Ezzy (2000, 123) and Lightfoot (2004, 30) suggest that there are usually two main types of biographical accounts: heroic (agentic) and tragic (victim) narratives. Heroic narratives describe how active interventions in the world shape and control a person's circumstances. These actions are justified by an appeal to general values such as creativity and self-control (Ezzy 2000, 128). In tragic (victim) narratives, the protagonist is shaped by conditions beyond his or her control. Both types of story fundamentally build the individual agent's emotional relationships with potential clients and audiences.

In analyzing a narrative account of Marja Putkisto in media texts and her own writings, my aim is to understand the role of this narrative in the context of the fitness business. Based upon the theoretical framework of feminist economics (Baker and Kuiper 2003; Ferber and Nelson 1993) and feminist sociology of culture (Lury 2004), I will analyze the mechanism of brand as an interface between producers and clients. Feminist economics has critiqued many basic assumptions of mainstream economics to argue that financial markets are not simply neutral in terms of gender but enhance certain images and interpretations of men and women.

Criticism toward masculine economics emerged in the 1970s within radical feminism, when, for instance, Rubin (1975) criticized Marxism for what she claims is its incomplete analysis of sexism under capitalism. Feminist economics emerged with critiques of mainstream economics for the purpose of improving women's economic conditions (e.g., Bergmann 1986; Ferber and Nelson 1993). These feminists sought to expose the links between the social construction of gender and the social construction of economics. Moreover, many feminist economists have begun to be interested in the intersections of race, gender and class. Such feminist rethinking has resulted in the questioning of many core concepts, central assumptions and policy recommendations in economics (Strober 2003). Feminist economists have further claimed that mainstream economists have under-researched women's role and women's 'areas' in the global system of economics. They have attempted to look at power and who has access to it. They emphasize the relationship between micro and macro phenomena in economy (Evers 2003). This approach looks not only at an individual but also the system that constrains an individual's options. One strand in feminist analysis (Nelson 2009) demonstrates that the dualism between 'hard' rational and 'soft' affective features in economics is wildly overblown due to the crisis of global climate change, the development of a global service economy, and the significance of the images and brands in the post-industrial economy. I locate the MP system as a part of the current global service economy by focusing on the way its success has been created based on careful branding.

In Finland, while nearly three-fourths of the customers of fitness services in the private sector are female, most owners and managers of fitness companies are men. Very few studies analyze how the imbalance between female clients and male managers in the fitness industry constrains female clients' options to influence supply of fitness services and the content of classes. Since female fitness experts such as Moira Merrithew with Stott Pilates from Canada, Monica Linford with ChiBall from Australia and Marja Putkisto have begun to establish fitness businesses, this opens up an opportunity to examine the business models of these new enterprises through the lens of feminist economics. I will discuss to what extent the product development and brand building of the MP resists the established system of fitness industry and how the business system of the MP also constrains individual instructor's options to use their own expertise. Drawing on feminist economics, the purpose of the analysis is to understand the relation between micro and macro levels of fitness industry. While mainstream economics has neglected the role of embodiment in the economic success of the post-industrial society (Hewitson 2001), this treatment attempts to put the lived body back at the center of economic attention reflecting the body's role in building a fitness brand.

THE HEROIC STORY OF MARJA PUTKISTO

Marja Putkisto tells the same story using even the same words and phrases in most interviews. She says: "My hip was underdeveloped and needed correction" (Putkisto 2003, xi). "For the first eight months of my life my lower body was held in a static position with my legs forced into a constant 90-degree position" (Carpenter 2002; Putkisto 1997, 10; Perez 2004). "The initial problem had only been solved on a superficial level and I grew up 'off-centre'" (Putkisto 2003, xi).

As a girl, nevertheless, she had a strong desire to be physically active. She began ballet lessons but felt that some of the movements were impossible to master: "Every time I practiced pirouettes, I always seemed to find myself at a different end of the classroom compared with the rest of the group!" (Putkisto 2003, xi). She felt increasingly disappointed and frustrated: "According to one teacher I was considered an ungifted mover" (Putkisto 1997). Her doctor recommended giving up a career in physical activity or fitness. Instead of conceding, she continued studies in dance and physical education. During a voice workshop when she was 25 years old she was asked to breathe into her lower back. She tells about her feelings: "I couldn't feel anything. I was so upset that I started to investigate" (Carpenter 2002). At the turning point in discovering her problem she describes: "I was struck by the idea that my body is too short inside and hinders me to do certain movements" (Perez 2004). She continues: "I realized that the solution to overcoming the imbalance was simply to stretch my shortened muscles to a length that would allow my pelvis to fall in its neutral position which allowed my body to move freely" (Putkisto 2003, xii). This particular moment, she stresses, was the beginning of the MP deep-stretching program.

Putkisto declares that while the rest of the fitness world concentrated on celebrating aerobics "to feel the burn," she was working with long, intense, precise stretches and mastering her breathing technique. She seems to be convinced that her own method has transformed her body and it offers a suitable tool to change others' bodies as well. She repeats, tongue-in-cheek, the same sentence in interviews: "I don't think there's a single bone in the same place now" (Carpenter 2002; Keinänen 2002; Määttänen 2007). She believes that good posture affects overall well-being, improving breathing, circulation and digestion.

At the beginning of the 1990s in Finland, she noticed that "Nobody was interested in extension movement and deepening breathing . . . but the biggest problem was that I was young, blond and pretty woman" (Määttänen 2007). She continues: "They started to listen to me, when the big boys Jarmo Ahonen [physiotherapist of the Finnish Olympic team] and Jari-Pekka Keurulainen [a football coach] joined me. Everybody thought that they were the architects and I was a window trimmer" (Määttänen 2007, 68). After establishing her own company in 1992, she has sold over 200,000 copies of her books and videos in Finland and the U.K. In 1997, Marja Putkisto received an award from the Finnish government in recognition of the valuable contribution made by the MP toward improving people's health and well-being.

In this heroic life story I want to draw attention to the three features of the story which differentiate it from the typical fitness brand's celebration of beautiful, young, taut female bodies. The first feature is that the hero of the story is a woman who is not victimized but who, at first, misunderstood by her own people (Finns) goes on to become a highly esteemed person in her own community. She hints at gender discrimination by saying that nobody was listening to her due to her appearance. She also wants to say that she has succeeded because of her stamina and her questioning of the (male) authorities.

Another striking feature in her story is the body work and the body's active role as a leading subject in her story. Marja Putkisto's terminology of the body is physiologically-anatomically oriented giving the impression of physiological expertise. However, she uses words like 'breathing space' or 'stabilizing points' (Putkisto 2003) that refer to the notion of the lived body (Merleau-Ponty 1990). She 'listens' to her body and her body tells her how to proceed in healing herself and developing tools for well-being. She states in an interview:

> Combining this knowledge with my personal experience and training as a fitness and dance teacher, I developed this unique technique of deep stretching, strengthening and breathing to achieve optimum muscular balance, good posture, and superior levels of physical performance, appearance, health and well-being.
>
> (Salian 2008)

In addition to the two principal features—the female hero and the active body—there is also the third feature which emerges from the Putkisto narrative that I call *female bodily wisdom*. The heroic story shows how a woman can stand up to resist male experts' scientific knowledge based on her bodily knowledge and bodily wisdom. The story of Marja Putkisto represents a new type of ideal middle-class woman that is sensitive to her own body and lives 'naturally' according to its demands. For instance, she objects to cosmetic surgery. Putkisto's story suggests that she has a special knowledge of the body that she wants to share with other people (Parviainen 2002, 19).

Interestingly, the life stories that she tells in Finland and in England differ slightly from each other. In England, MP is a Finnish discipline and fitness method. Also Design Forum in Finland has started to market MP as a Finnish innovation. In the interviews with the Finnish media, the MP products do not include any 'Finnish' elements but are characterized as a combination of Yoga, Pilates and Alexander Technique. In fact, Marja Putkisto suggests that she developed the method in England where she finally met people who understood her views and ideas. She claims

> The "Putkisto" method was designed to stretch and free the body back to its neutral position, and release the stress. This way of thinking was approved with no reservation in the UK already some twenty years ago. Finns followed a decade later.
>
> (Putkisto 2006)

Journalists often remark in the articles how remarkable Putkisto looks. For example: "The first thing you notice about Marja Putkisto is her super-taut, heart-shaped jaw line—quite unfairly firm for a woman past 40" (Carpenter 2002). Her own body is presented as incontestable evidence of the functioning of the method. Highlighting the middle-aged female body when marketing fitness products, Putkisto's image has succeeded in broadening the beauty ideal of the young female body in the fitness industry. To further understand the role of this narrative in marketing MP products, I will next look at advertising strategies in the fitness industry and how the embodiment of Marja Putkisto creates an interface and interactivity that allows instructors and clients to reflect on their identity and bond them with MP products.

ADVERTISING

Till the 1990s, sport equipment and sportswear companies promoted their brands to consumers with an interest in a particular category of product, matching the profile of their customers in terms of age, gender and lifestyle (Nicholls et al. 1999). Shani et al. found that "advertisers made almost no attempt to appeal to the female market as a separate segment having different needs" (1992, 390), even if women spend almost as much as men on athletic footwear and sport equipments (Levin 1990). Shani et al. (1992) argue that sports marketing can potentially be effective for reaching the female population as well. In the 2000s, tennis became the first women's sport that produced truly mainstream celebrities, heralded as much for their style and sex appeal as for their athletic embodiment. According to marketing experts (*USA Today* 2003), female tennis players are perfect for product endorsements because their bodies represent an ideal combination of athletic, feminine, youthful, tall and slim. Marketing based on female tennis players, such as the Williams sisters, is supposed to appeal equally to female and male consumers.

The costs of new product/service development in the global market have risen to also prohibit the emergence of new brands. For example, while around 16,000 new products are launched in the U.S. every year, 95 percent of them are launched as extensions of existing brands (Murphy 1998, 5). Most successful brands, for example, Microsoft, Coca-Cola and Nokia provide the basis for long-standing dominance of certain markets and afford protection of long-term investment against risk. The high costs of advertising and marketing is one of the reasons why Method Putkisto Institute has developed new marketing strategies for their products.

As traditional advertising has begun to play less of a role in the fitness industry (Mintel 2009), fitness companies need new marketing strategies to attract new members and customers to fitness centers. Sport stores such as Niketowns are designed to encourage consumer activity in the space of the store: visitors are invited to try on shoes and clothing, test athletic equipment, watch videos, play computer games and listen to music and in some stores, there are indoor basketball spaces (Lury 2004, 40). Interaction frequently takes place across generations, as the store is full of parents who bring their children. The showroom thus becomes a laboratory for analyzing consumer reactions to different products. *Event-based marketing* may include sponsoring existing music, sporting and art events, as well as specially arranging events. Method Putkisto institute has hardly enough resources for free event-based marketing for its clients. Its strategy is to create extraordinary environments for exercise. For instance, it arranges workshops and fitness vacations in exotic surroundings such as the Scotland Highlands, Turkey and Eastern Finland. After the workshops, the clients are more attracted to attend weekly classes.

Method Putkisto Institute has invested a minimum sum of money in traditional advertisements. Instead of traditional advertising it has built the MP brand in Finland utilizing print media and TV journalism. The shift from advertising to journalism has happened in part because advertising is assumed to have lost most of its capacity to persuade consumers. Some theorists, for example, Lury argue that consumers are more or less passive subjects to be moved by advertising through various behavioral stages from product awareness to buying decision (2004, 38). In contrast, marketers have increasingly advocated the view that consumers are reflexive and resist the control of traditional marketing. Including features of *social marketing* such as word-of-mouth marketing (Weinreich 1999), *post-industrial marketing* has a different logic of value from that of the classic marketing approach. One form of social marketing is using news stories to market one's products. The aim of the new marketing through stories in the print media is to seek to fill the great gaps of meaning that exist in people's lives and to propose brands as ideas that people can live by (Grant 1999, 15). In the case of MP, this intimate marketing has taken place when mainly female journalists have acted as mediators between clients and Marja Putkisto.

The brand Method Putkisto is not yet widely known outside Finland. In the U.K., MP is marketed as the simple Finnish discipline. MP products are linked to a national (Finnish/exotic) fitness culture or seen in the context of Scandinavian 'white' minimalism. In Finland, however, MP is considered a growing international brand. MP products are sold by securing the trust of consumers, providing a guarantee of quality and emphasizing intimacy, peacefulness and individuality.

THE BRAND VALUE: CREATING INTERFACE THROUGH INTERACTIVITY

Many of the currently emerging brands are successful because they do not focus on a specific product. Instead they communicate clear values which can be extended across a plethora of different products and services (Hart 1998; Lury 2004, 32). Sport brands like 'Björn Borg' (a former tennis star) have become *lifestyle brands* that carry a range of products including jewelry, bags, cosmetics, spectacles, underwear, shoes, drinks, food, sheets, towels and bedding. The primary aim of this product line extension is to allow a greater number of customers to access the brand (Lury 2004, 62). Sport and fitness companies have benefited from this diffusion, since their success does not need to be limited to certain products/services or a sport event like a championship.

To create an attractive fitness brand, a company does not necessarily need innovative products/services but something or someone with a personality that gives vitality to the brand. The vitality of the fitness brand can be understood as an interface by which consumers have access to products (Lury 2004). Fitness brand is, thus, a combination of a community and the experiences generated by the commodity. These experiences are not created solely by the fitness programs but also, for example, by bodily feelings, music, apparel, shoes, books, DVDs, surroundings, co-movers and the emotional inspiration by the instructors. This means that the fitness brand innovation is no longer tied only to the fitness program per se. The power of the brand as an interface, then, sets new challenges for marketing commodities. Marketing becomes increasingly central to the internal communication of organization. Brands assume a dual role: they organize the exchange between producers and consumers and they organize the relations within the company itself (or between franchiser and franchisees). This latter role is sometimes described as *internal marketing* (Lury 2004, 33). This is important in particular fitness brands that are based on licenses and franchising principles. The franchiser is required to interpret and constitute themselves and their interests in relation to the goals of the company, and this may involve participating in the implementation of brand mission statement.

The MP brand is different from other fitness brands as it emphasizes the embodiment of the middle-aged woman, increased bodily awareness, slow movement and female bodily wisdom. In marketing, products must be defined both in terms of their similarity to or difference from other objects that might occupy the same social environment in relation to competitors or consumers (Lury 2004, 17). Brand designers are increasingly obliged to ascertain what emotional values they want consumers to attach to the product. For consumers, brands and brand values are a way for consumers to feel the product as part of their personalities (Lury 2004, 87). Certainly, clients do not need to meet Marja Putkisto in person to identify themselves with the MP products.

Even if the MP brand is tied to its creator's personality and embodiment Method Putkisto products would probably retain their value even if Marja Putkisto retires or gives up the company for some reason. The use of personality is not the signification of the individual as the origin of the product which the logo marks but rather an iconic signification of the brand (Pierce 1940). This means that the personality that sustains the brand need not necessarily be an embodied, real and alive individual, a fictional or deceased individual can also have the same effect. For instance, created in 1921 the fictional personality Betty Crocker whose handwritten signature marks a number of food products has had at least seven different portraits during the years of her imaginary existence. Not only does the name Betty Crocker mark a range of products, but it also authorizes recipes.

The interface of the MP brand is not located in a single place, at a single time. Rather, like the Internet, it is distributed across a number of surfaces (books, DVDs, backings); screens (magazines, television), sites (t-shirts, studios) or bodies (body shapes, gestures, facial expressions). The interface is the basis of two-way exchanges between producers and consumers that informs how consumers relate to producers and how producers relate to consumers. These exchanges, though they are two-way and dynamic, are not direct, symmetrical or reversible. The interface is a site of mediation or, more accurately, *interactivity*. The interface of the brand may be seen as both promoting and inhibiting exchange between producers and consumers, and informing this asymmetrical exchange through a range of performances of its own (Lury 2004, 50–51).

The interface of the Method Putkisto brand as a heroic story affects not just active practitioners but the general public. The brand communicates interactively but also selectively promotes and inhibits communication between MP products and consumers. While there are those clients who are convinced of the quality of MP products because they perhaps admire Marja Putkisto, there are as many people who avoid the products due to Marja Putkisto's personal image. Female and male clients can identify themselves emotionally with different parts of her heroic story (e.g., feeling strong embodied intuitions). When competing with other similar products, Method Putkisto Institute looks for clients that are loyal to MP programs and recommend them to their friends. This is called *brand loyalty* (Filo et al. 2008).

Interactivity has become a dominant model of how clients can be used to produce themselves as subjects instead of remaining the targets of traditional marketing. Interactivity is becoming a model for authority that does not take a disciplinary form. For example, fitness activity as the disciplinary technology was associated with the instructor's role who 'orders' clients around. Instead of the injunction, 'You must,' instructors nowadays use expressions that cheer and encourage clients. The principles, on which Method Putkisto is based, emphasize the need to 'give up pushing' and are associated with the injunction, 'you can': 'if you do it without pushing, you will reach.' In this interactive model, moving subjects are not disciplined; they are allowed to exercise to find themselves (Lury 2004, 131).

However, Slavoj Zizek (1997) suggests that interactivity should be more appropriately understood as 'interpassivity.' The user of interactive technologies such as computer games allows the machine to be active on the user's behalf. Fitness classes, in particular standardized and prechoreographed fitness programs like Les Mills (Felstead et al. 2007), are largely predictable, pre-selected, and highly circumscribed. When customers decide to follow a fitness program of the MP, in a way, they expect that the program will carry them 'automatically' to the promised outcome. As a consequence, interactivity and reflectivity become trivial and refer to a highly structured form instead of the mutual influence of the mover and the instructor / program.

From a managerial point of view, the structured fitness programs have a number of benefits. First, they routinize the labor process of MP instructing and therefore minimize its inherent unpredictability. The second benefit is that the popularity of a MP class no longer wholly relies on the instructors and the specificity of their class since the fitness service they deliver is the same (Felstead et al. 2007, 200). Third, it makes possible the global delivery system of MP fitness services.

FITNESS SERVICES ON THE GLOBAL MARKET

Until the early 1990s, the service sector was believed to be an unproductive and undesirable source of economic activities. Because fitness services had to be performed for the consumer, they were considered nontradable for a long time. Technological developments have allowed increasing tradability of fitness services. Recently the service sector has become a focal point of worldwide attention among both investors and policy makers (Aharoni 2000, 2; Hoy and Stanworth 2003). There is growing attention being paid to the best and most effective ways of organizing, managing and transferring fitness services globally.

The service companies necessitate a close interaction between the supplier and the consumer. The costs to the consumer include not only the price paid but also learning and other costs. Since services are intangible, non-storable and therefore cannot be transferred across national borders, they have to be produced at the time and place in which they are consumed. Most successful functional mechanisms for international expansion of service firms have been through *concepts, licenses* and *franchising agreements*. Franchising is a very efficient means to achieve international business expansion (Fladmoe-Lindquist 2000). A major contribution of franchising is the creation of linkages and network relationships. Franchise network culture sets common and shared beliefs, norms, and language that help to control franchisees' work.

In the fitness industry there are typically two types of franchising: fitness program (class) and fitness center franchise systems. The MP franchising principle is based on program franchising of fitness instructing concepts. Since the establishment of the Method Putkisto Institute in 1992 in Finland, more than 300 instructors have redeemed MP licenses after a 30-day training course in six months. The licensed MP instructors have opened several new MP studios in Finland. The official website of the Method Putkisto Institute states: "One of the most important tasks of the Method Putkisto Institute is to foster the trademark and the brand of Method Putkisto. The common sign brings for us a professional community and business advantage."

The Institute has developed three different fitness products: Method Putkisto (deep stretching method), Method Putkisto Pilates and Face School. The requirement of transformation of these basic products is actualized as tailoring classes and programs for new client groups. As Knorr Cetina argues, contemporary products/services are not defined by what they are but by what they will be (2000, 528). Her suggestion is that more and more objects exist not only as things-to-be-used but also things-to-be-transformed. Products/services continually undergo change: updates, versions and variations. They have a dual structure: they are simultaneously things-to-be-used and things-in-a-process-of-transformation. One of the MP services' new products is the 'stretch yourself slim in 30 days' program (Putkisto 2003). The program appeals to clients who want visible/measurable results and improvements in posture and body shape in a certain time period. This customizing aims at generating new fitness customers.

Even if the target of the Method Putkisto Institute is to grow the business into a large-scale corporation, it wants to retain an intimate touch between the instructor and the client. By way of MP instructors the Method Putkisto Institute has recruited mainly professionals such as dance teachers, physiotherapists or health care professionals for franchising the MP products. Since most MP instructors are already professionals—some instructors hold MAs—they could also work independently without this extra license. Working as MP instructors, instead of independent instructors, might bring them advantages in the fitness market. However, this requires effort from instructors to dedicate themselves not only to the MP principles but also to launching the MP in the fitness market (Instructor training 2009–10). From the instructors' point of view, brand loyalty is required to market MP products through their whole personality and the lived body (Nickson et al. 2001). As much as they are fitness instructors they are also fitness sellers.

The embodiment of MP instructors and their performance are an integral feature of the MP fitness marketing. While the MP license offers brand value and a script to instruct, the protection of MP products leaves little room for a professional instructor's own creativity, personal development and innovation of the method. The fear of 'going wrong' and, therefore, delivering 'heretic' MP classes can persist long after certification has been secured. In the long run, one of the consequences is that instructor skills are not really developed and as a result they learn little to stretch their abilities (Felstead et al. 2007). Fitness instructors' previously acquired multifaceted professional skills can degrade and wither through lack of use. An individual instructor's own understanding of the function of MP Pilates or deep stretching can conflict with that of the owner of the MP license.

Registering the Method Putkisto trademark in 1992 indicated fundamental economical and cultural changes in the fitness world. From the managerial point of view, the trademark was held for a twofold purpose: protection of the owner from unfair competition and protection of the consumer from confusion of the origin of the goods. However, the mushrooming of license-based fitness activity has created a new economical hierarchy in fitness activity: the license owners and the instructors who are conditional on the licenses. Previously, instructors used exercises and movements they had learned or seen in fitness classes freely. Their personal knowledge and expertise were considered guarantees of the quality of fitness programs. However, quality is no longer related to instructors' skills, formal education and their abilities of judgment but rather to fitness brands, fitness concepts or standardized choreographies. Fitness brands are being used as a guarantee of fitness quality.

CONCLUSION

My analysis of MP brand building from a perspective of feminist economics highlights two aspects in the new economic system of the fitness industry: female clients and female instructors. Feminist economics has drawn attention to where the power in a system lies and who has access to it. First, by offering a method for improving breathing, posture, body awareness and muscle relaxation slow movement techniques such as the MP method can empower women to improve their self-esteem and satisfaction with life (Impett et al. 2006). Beyond physical activity, the heroic story of the MP brand can be a powerful way for aging women to gain self-respect and embrace their femininity. While the stereotypical fit-body images of young women resonate with only a very small portion of the female population, the image given of Putkisto encourages women to concentrate on shaping their bodies inside out. One of the brand values of the MP is the way in which consumers feel the product as a part of their own bodies and become brand loyal toward MP products. This requires a close interactivity between instructors and clients, though this relation is not meant to be entirely symmetrical and reversible.

Second, considering the new status of the MP instructors, I suggest that the license-based fitness work has actually deadened rather than empowered professional instructors' scope for action in fitness industry. Losing the decision-making power of their own instruction, fitness instructors have become more dependent on license owners. Through the lens of feminist economics, the business model of the MP enterprise based on franchising principles has generated a new kind of hierarchy in the fitness culture between female instructors and female license owners. It appears that inequality between women in the fitness industry has increased rather than decreased since female fitness experts have begun to establish fitness companies.

In the last 15 years, pre-choreographed fitness programs, licenses, trademarks and brands have begun to take a more central role in guaranteeing the quality of fitness programs. This standardization of the fitness industry is hidden behind the instructor's 'natural' behavior to the extent that the average clients rarely recognize themselves being a part of 'global machinery.' The clients are to feel as if they chose individualized training programs, yet these programs are results of highly channeled, predetermined global fitness programs and instructor training.

NOTES

1 It is difficult to show a clear distinction between 'fitness goods' and 'fitness services' since classes or programs are hardly ever sold without some material goods and vice versa. By 'fitness products,' I mean fitness classes, programs and

services within all kinds of fitness accessories and equipments including guide books, DVDs and videos.

2 This research project is funded by the Emil Aaltonen Foundation and the Ministry of Education, Finland.

3 One of the examples of these media texts is an interview of Marja Putkisto, published on February 15, 2008, on the Aamulehti newspaper website: (http://www.aamulehti.fi/sunnuntai/teema/ihmiset_paajutut/6545595.shtml)

REFERENCES

Aharoni, Y., ed. 2000. *Globalization of services: Some implications for theory and practice.* London: Routledge.

Baker, D. K. and E. Kuiper. 2003. *Toward a feminist philosophy of economics.* London, New York: Routledge.

Bergmann, B. 1986. *The economic emergence of women.* New York: Basic Books.

Carpenter, S. 2002. How I stretched myself slim. *You,* 30 June 2002. http://srv12.louhi.net/~admin712/eng/articles/e_you0602.pdf

Chavanat, N., G. Martinent and A. Ferrand. 2009. Sponsor and sponsees interactions: effects on consumers' perceptions of brand image, brand attachment, and purchasing intention. *Journal of Sport Management* 23(5): 644–70.

Evers, B. 2003. Broadening the foundations of macro-economic models through a gender approach: New development. In *Macro-economics: Making gender matter,* ed. M. Gutiérrez, 3–21. London: Zed Books.

Ezzy, D. 2000. Fate and agency in job loss narratives. *Qualitative Sociology* 23: 121–34.

Felstead, A., A. Fuller, N. Jewson, K. Kakavelakis and L. Unwin. 2007. Grooving to the same tunes? Learning, training and productive systems in the aerobics studio. *Work, Employment and Society* 21(2): 189–208.

Ferber, M. A. and J. A. Nelson, eds. 1993. *Beyond economic man: Feminist theory and economics.* Chicago: The University of Chicago Press.

Filo, K, D. C. Funk and K. Alexandris. 2008. Exploring the role of brand trust on the relationship between brand associations and brand loyalty in sport and fitness. *International Journal of Sport Management and Marketing* 3(1–2): 39–57.

Fladmoe-Lindquist, K. 2000. International franchising: A network approach to FDI. In *Globalization of services: Some implications for theory and practice,* ed. Y. Aharoni, 197–213. London: Routledge.

Fulton, H., R. Huisman, J. Murphet and A. Dunn, eds. 2005. *Narrative and media.* Cambridge: Cambridge University Press.

Gobe, M. 2001. *Emotional branding.* New York: Allworth Press.

Grant, J. 1999. *The new marketing manifesto: The 12 rules for building successful brands in the 21st century.* London: Orion Business Books.

Hart, S. 1998. The future for brands. In *Brands: The new wealth creators,* eds. S. Hart and J. Murphy, 206–14. London: Macmillan Business.

Hewitson, G. 2001. The disavowal of the sexed body in neoclassical economics. In *Post-Modernism, economics & knowledge,* eds. J. Amariglio, S. E. Cullenberg and D. F. Ruccio, 221–45. London and New York: Routledge.

Honoré, C. 2004. *In praise of slow: How a worldwide movement is challenging the cult of speed*. New York: HarperCollins.

Hoy, F. and J. Stanworth, eds. 2003. *Franchising: An international perspective*. London: Routledge.

Impett, E. A., J. J. Daubenmier and A. L. Hirschman. 2006. Minding the body: Yoga, embodiment, and well-being. *Sexuality Research and Social Policy: Journal of NSRC* 3(4): 39–48.

Instructor training. 2009–10. http://www.methodputkisto.com.

Kane, M. J. and J. Parks. 1992. The social construction of gender difference and hierarchy in sport journalism: Few new twists on very old themes. *Women in Sport and Physical Activity Journal* 1: 49–83.

Keinänen, M. 2002. Marja Putkisto. Keho tutuksi metodien kautta. *Ilta-lehti* 15 May 2002. www.methodputkisto.com/fi/artikkelit/iltalehti15_5_02.pdf.

Knorr Cetina, K. 2000. Post-social theory. In *Hand-book of social theory*, eds. G. Ritzer and B. Smart, 520–37. London: Sage.

Levin, S. 1990. Hard bodies soft sell: How sporting goods companies are competing to win the hearts, minds and wallets of today's active women. *Women's Sports and Fitness*, November/December: 46–51.

Lightfoot, C. 2004. Fantastic self: A study of adolescents' fictional narratives, and aesthetic activity as identity work. In *Narrative analysis: Studying the development of individuals in society*, eds. C. Daiute and C. Lightfoot, 21–37. Thousand Oaks, California: Sage.

Lury, C. 2004. *Brands: The logos of the global economy*. London: Routledge.

Markula, Pirkko. 2001. Beyond the perfect body: Women's body image distortion in fitness magazine discourse. *Journal of Sport & Social Issues* 25(2): 158–79.

—— 2006. Deleuze and the body without organs. Disreading the fit feminine identity. *Journal of Sport & Social Issues* 30(1): 29–44.

Merleau-Ponty, M. 1990. *Phénoménologie de la perception*. [Originally published 1945]. Paris: Gallimard.

Method Putkisto http://www.methodputkisto.com/

Mintel. 2009. *Health and fitness clubs, UK, October 2009*. London: Mintel International Group Limited.

Murphy, J. 1998. What is branding? In *Brands: The new wealth creators*, eds. S. Hart and J. Murphy, 1–12. London: Macmillan Business.

Määttänen, M. 2007. Mrs Method eli totuus tuotteesta. *Sara* November 2007, 64–71.

Nelson, J. A. 2009. Between a rock and a soft place: Ecological and feminist economics in policy debates. *Ecological Economics* 69: 1–8.

Nicholls, J. A. F., S. Roslow and S. Dublish. 1999. Brand recall and brand preference at sponsored golf and tennis tournaments. *European Journal of Marketing* 33(3–4): 365–86.

Nickson, D., C. Warhurst, A. Witz and A-M. Cullen. 2001. The importance of being aesthetic: Work, employment and service organization. In *Customer service: Empowerment and entrapment*, eds. A. Sturdy, I. Grugulis and H. Willmott, 170–90. Houndmills: Palgrave.

Parviainen, J. 2002. Bodily knowledge: Epistemological reflections on dance. *Dance Research Journal* 34(1): 11–23.

Perez, T. 2004. Hitaan liikkeen kuningatar. *SpaNews*, March 2004 http://spanews. naantalispa.fi/sivu.php?jid = 60&lehti_id = 9 (accessed August 6, 2008).

Pierce, C. S. 1940. *The philosophy of Peirce: Selected writings*, ed. Justice Buchler. London: Routledge and Kegan Paul.

Pirinen, R. 1997. The construction of women's position in sport: A textual analysis of articles on female athletes in Finnish women's magazines. *Sociology of Sport Journal* 14: 290–301.

Putkisto, M. 1997. *Method Putkisto—Deep stretch your way to a firmer, leaner body*. London: Headline.

—— 2003. *The body lean & lifted*. London: A & C Black Publishers.

—— 2006. Body language talks. Embassy of Finland, London, Guest column, http://www.finemb.org.uk/Public/default.aspx?contentid = 98602&nodeid = 35867&contentlan = 2&culture = en-GB.

Rubin, Gayle. 1975. The traffic in women: Notes on the 'political economy' of sex. In *Toward an anthropology of women*, ed. R. Reiter, 157–210. New York and London: Monthly Review Press.

Salian, N. C. 2008. Stay in shape with Method Putkisto. http://archive.gulfnews. com/gnfocus/finland/more_stories/10052238.html.

Shani, D., D. M. Sandler and M. M. Long. 1992. Courting women using sports marketing: A content analysis of the US open. *International Journal of Advertising* 11(4): 377–92.

Shove, E. and M. Pantzar. 2005. Consumers, producers and practices: Understanding the invention and reinvention of Nordic walking. *Journal of Consumer Culture* 5: 43–64.

Strober, M. H. 2003. The application of mainstream economics constructs to education: A feminist analysis. In *Feminist economics today: Beyond economic man*, eds. M. A. Ferber and J. A. Nelson, 135–56. Chicago, London: The University of Chicago Press.

USA Today. 2003. Tennis players top sports marketers' wish list. 16 January.

Vincent, J., P. M. Pedersen, W. A. Whisenant and D. Massey. 2007. Analysing the print media coverage of professional tennis players: British newspaper narratives about female competitors in the Wimbledon Championships. *International Journal of Sport Management and Marketing* 2(3): 281–300.

Weinreich, N. K. 1999. *Hands-on social marketing: A step-by-step guide*. Thousand Oaks, California: Sage.

Yang, Y. and M. Shi. 2009. Estimating the value of brand alliances in professional team sports. *Marketing Science* 28(6): 1095–111.

Zizek, S. 1997. *The plague of fantasies*. London: Verso.

3 'Folding'

A Feminist Intervention in Mindful Fitness

Pirkko Markula

Feminist research often condemns the fitness industry as a site for women's oppression because it tends to reproduce the singular focus on the narrowly defined 'body beautiful.' Consequently, some of these researchers consider the fitness industry so thoroughly penetrated by negative commercialist ideologies that it is not worth further attention. At the same time, exercise and fitness are currently promoted as positive practices that contribute toward improved health. In westernized countries, the promotion of increased physical activity is a strong part of governmental health campaigns, but the responsibility of providing exercise services is usually left to the commercial fitness industry. This has further increased the commercial force of the fitness industry where promotion of health often blurs with aesthetics of the ideal body. As feminist researchers, we obviously need to continue to critique the discursive construction of the industry, but at the same time, there is no guarantee that such critique will actually change the way women's fitness is understood and practiced or even decrease the popularity of the industry. To provide a more active feminist intervention, I aim to analyze, through Gilles Deleuze's interpretation of Michel Foucault's work, how to create more positive practices within this industry. In my research, I focus particularly on how positive change might take place through so-called mindful fitness forms that have become an increasingly popular part of this industry.

As a Pilates instructor and a feminist researcher of women's exercise I have witnessed yoga and Pilates classes replacing aerobics and step classes in many health club timetables. In the commercial fitness world, *mindfulness* embeds such features as 'being present' during the activity, process orientation, slowness and embracing the activity itself (e.g., Monroe 1998). The most common mindful fitness forms are yoga, Pilates and Tai Chi although several hybrid forms as well as new adaptations such as Body Balance, Chi ball or Yogalates continually emerge in this environment. In addition, elements of 'mindfulness' are increasingly 'fused' into step, spinning or toning/strength classes, and personal training sessions. In this chapter, I will first locate mindful fitness and the commercial fitness industry in the current power/knowledge nexus. I will then problematize the formation of this knowledge and the exercising self within this nexus to conclude that alternative, more ethical fitness practices are needed. Constructing such alternatives is, nevertheless, a complicated task: despite substantial feminist critique of the fitness industry, there are very few feminist 'interventions' that investigate options for changing the current practices. Haravon Collins' (1995) study of yoga offers one brave attempt for creating fitness practices informed by feminist principles. In this chapter, I will present my struggle for a feminist exercise intervention in a Pilates class. To conclude I will analyze what positive force mindful fitness might have in contemporary society.

THE FORMATION OF THE CONTEMPORARY FITNESS INDUSTRY

Mindful fitness forms, some might argue, could transcend the discursive construction of such exercise practices as aerobics (Gimlin 2002; Markula 1995, 2003), circuit training (Craig and Liberty 2007), cardio-vascular training (Dworkin 2003) or even weight lifting and bodybuilding (e.g., Bolin 1992, 2003; Grogan et al. 2004; Heywood 1998; Roussel et al. 2003; St. Martin and Gavey 1996; Wesely 2001) that have been critiqued for reproducing heteronormativity through 'feminization' of the exerciser's body (see also Kagan and Morse 1988; Lloyd 1996; MacNeill 1998). Mindful fitness forms that propose to include the 'mind' into physical exercise can be argued to provide an alternative to the singular focus on building the 'body beautiful.' By embracing the activity itself, these forms provide multiple foci on the physical body, the mind and health. Do mindful fitness forms, regardless, have to negotiate the 'feminization' permeating the other fitness practices?

The Power/Discourse Nexus and Mindful Fitness

Mindful fitness forms differ from other commercial exercise practices through their search for mind-body integration. In these exercise classes, mind and body are to be united to create a holistic sense of self. This is possible through an engagement in physical exercise that is executed with a profound, inwardly directed awareness or focus (Monroe 1998). The awareness of the mind during exercise is to be achieved, for example, by focusing on proper breathing, bodily alignment, slow movement patterns and embracing the activity itself. Consequently, mindful fitness emphasizes process orientation: the participant is to be 'present' during the activity itself and concentrate, inwardly, into one's own movement patterns. Such refocus is particularly pertinent in a 'gym' environment where exercise is frequently understood as purely bodily enterprise—often so much so that the exercisers keenly escape the boredom of the monotonous physical exercise by engaging their minds by watching television, reading or listening to music. It is also common that the exercisers claim not to enjoy the exercise itself, but are happy with the results after the session, particularly with the improved looks of the body (Markula 2003). Therefore, they do not want to be 'present' in the actual exercise session. Against such unpleasant exercise experiences that entirely divide the mind from the body, mindful fitness aims to bring the 'mind' back into the gym to provide more meaningful and varied exercise practices. While building a holistic self appears to provide a positive exercise goal,[1] from a Foucauldian perspective, it is also constructed within the power/discourse nexus of fitness in contemporary society. Mindful fitness forms are, thus, a part of the same commercial fitness industry with other fitness practices. Therefore, they are also influenced by the dominant ways fitness is understood in this field. I will now analyze, through a Foucauldian lens, how mindful fitness practices are subjected to the powerful ways of knowing about the fit, feminine, healthy body.

Two main discourses or ways of knowing about fitness strongly shape the fitness field (see also the introduction and chapters 5, 7, 8 and 10 in this book). The discourse of aesthetics of the ideal, healthy looking body refers to the understanding of fitness as a means to achieve the ideal thin, toned and young body which is often also understood as the 'healthy body' (e.g., Duncan 1994; Dworkin and Wachs 2009; Eskes et al. 1998; Markula 1995). Medical discourse, in turn, promotes exercise as a means to ensure a disease-free body (e.g., Markula and Pringle 2006). For example, inactivity is often identified as a cause for obesity and consequently, a cause for numerous life-threatening illnesses. Both of these discourses place the responsibility for engaging in exercise and achieving a better looking, illness-free body on individual women (Cole 1998; Dworkin and Wachs 2009; Jette 2006; King 2003; Markula 2001). Connected with particular, strategic use of power relations, these discourses have gained dominant positions in the fitness field. I will now illustrate their impact on the ways mindful fitness is practiced.

Mindful Fitness and the Discourse of Health

Current governmental campaigns for active, healthy lifestyle, are aimed at increased longevity and illness prevention in a population. Foucault refers to this function of power as bio-politics (Deleuze 1988; Foucault 1978). Bio-medical or exercise science research functions as a reinforcement for bio-power as it connects scientific evidence of increased physical fitness and thinness with absence of illness. The fitness industry supports this discursive construction by providing exercise services that observe the scientific principles of health-related fitness. This governmental power/medical discourse nexus, thus, sustains certain forms of exercise as the correct ways to prevent illness (Markula and Pringle 2006).

As part of the fitness industry, mindful fitness forms operate within the same discursive formation. They can, thus, benefit from the medical discourse of illness prevention, but are also limited by it. For example, mindful fitness forms can be promoted as 'alternative medicine' that prevents or even cures 'diseases' ranging from cancer and back pain to psychosomatic conditions such as stress, anxiety, depression, fatigue, eating disorders, substance abuse problems, hypertension and chronic pain (Markula and Pringle 2006). While it is positive that exercise can function to prevent illness and promote longevity, this understanding of healthy exercise also controls the population because it tends to obscure the actual causes for ill-health. For example, relaxation in a mindful fitness class can offer stress relief. However, such relaxation often acts more like a pain killer that alleviates the symptoms, but does not necessarily cure the actual cause for stress that can stem from increased demands at work, tightened economical situation, or the general pressures of the lifestyle demanded from 'good,' successful, useful citizens. Several researchers observe that bio-politics also functions to place the responsibility of one's health entirely with individual women (see chapters 7, 8 and 10 in this book). This neo-liberalist rhetoric promotes individualism as the way of dealing with contemporary health problems. While medical discourse and governmental bio-politics operate to support each other, power can also function through less formal structures by forming mobile strategies with other discourses.

Mindful Fitness and the Aesthetics of the Healthy Looking Body

In addition to bio-politics, Foucault (1991) examined how power operates through techniques of discipline that normalize individuals into useful, docile bodies. Foucault named the use of power that typically employs the technologies of discipline on multiplicity of individuals, anatomo-politics (Deleuze 1988). Through the discourse of aesthetics of the body beautiful, exercise begins to function as an anatomo-political form of power: a form of disciplinary technique that legitimizes a particular, yet unachievable, body shape. This discourse normalizes the thin and toned body as the ideal fit, healthy-looking feminine body. Through normalization exercise practices turn into discipline techniques that the exercisers follow in their never-ending quest for beauty and health.

Because mindful fitness operates within the same diagram of anatomo-political power, it is not devoid of the disciplinary techniques that make docile bodies. Consequently, these fitness forms are easily colonized by the body beautiful discourse. When celebrity devotees market yoga as a means to a slimmer body and long, toned muscles, the idea is obviously to obtain a better looking body. When a yoga instructor assures clients that in yoga they gain muscles, but not bulky ones, she re-enforces the discourse of body beautiful. Or when Pilates is loudly advertised as a means for a 'slimmer tummy' or 'killer abs,' it is used for building the ideal looks. In addition to the body shape, mindful exercisers state that their minds are properly harnessed within the exercise session to further create docile, productive, stress-free citizens.

It is evident that mindful fitness is quite tightly codified through the discourses of health as absence of illness and the aesthetics of the ideal body. Such a codification of knowledge, allows power to operate in a flexible, localized and unstable manner. The current power/discourse nexus appears necessarily to produce docile exercise bodies. Even alternative forms, such as mindful fitness that might aim to emphasize other knowledges from the healthy looking body, tend to be harnessed and understood by the consumers through the current discursive framework (Markula 2004). After such a negative conclusion, one can only ask: Are women doomed forever into docility? Is it possible to change the discursive construction of fitness to operate with less dominance? Is it possible to provide exercise practices that do not build docile bodies? Is it possible to construct multiple fit feminine identities that transcend the aesthetics of the healthy body?

In his later work, Foucault began to shift from these technologies of domination into the technologies of the self: how individuals understand and transform themselves within the power/discourse nexus. I want to expand on this discussion to investigate further how to create less disciplinary exercise practices. To do this, I introduce the concept, 'fold,' developed from Foucault's work by Deleuze (1988) to explore possibilities of transgressing the limited feminine identity constructed through the narrowly defined, normalized body ideal and the individualization of exercise/health practices.

THE FOLD: HOW TO USE KNOWLEDGE WITHOUT BEING DEPENDENT ON IT

Throughout his work, Foucault demonstrated how subjectivation has turned into subjection: how individuals, through disciplinary techniques, have turned into subjects of someone else's control. For example, exercise acts as a disciplinary technique through which women try to shape themselves toward an ideal feminine body defined by someone else. Feminist research demonstrates that exercisers, with some hesitation, commonly accept the fit body as an ideal feminine body (e.g., Dworkin 2003; Gimlin 2002; Haravon Collins 2002; Loland 2000; Maguire and Mansfield 1998; Markula 1995, 2003; McDermott 2000; Prickett 1997; Sassatelli 1999; Spielvogel 2002). Like all exercise forms, mindful fitness forms are a part of same feminine identity construction.

Deleuze adds that "the modern individual has become tied to his [sic] own identity through self-knowledge obtained through all the techniques of moral and human sciences that go to make up a knowledge of the subject" (1988, 85). This refers particularly to the idea of a 'true self' that an individual is to endlessly search for with the help of numerous available therapies. Through this search an individual becomes tied to the confessional technique through which one is to first confess her constantly recurring or newly invented 'deficiencies' to an often invisible expert, engage in constant curative practice to reveal the true self never to be completely found. Dieting and exercise practices are often marketed in this manner when the consumers are first asked to face the fact that they are overweight, then advised to enroll in a specific, expert program that will help the individual to lose weight and finally, promised that they will discover the 'true,' healthy, successful person for whom everything is possible (Markula and Pringle 2006). With the emphasis on the (control of) mind, mindful fitness forms are sometimes linked with a therapeutic search for the true, calm, coherent self that is lost in the frenzied consumerism (Strauss 2005).[2] The notion of a true self increases the emphasis on individualism as the problems tend to be attributed to a woman who has lost sight of herself, not the social, cultural, economical or political forces that are at the root of many current troubles. In addition, the notion of a fixed true self results in a fixed identity defined by an invisible other. For example, exercise practices, among other contemporary practices targeting women, tend to fix the feminine identity with a certain narrowly defined body type that then comes to represent the 'true' femininity.

In his later work, nevertheless, Foucault was interested in exploring the slow formation of self experience: how we begin to understand ourselves as subjects within power relations (Markula and Pringle 2006). It is important to emphasize that such a process still takes place within the nexus of discourse/power relations: an individual becomes a subject within power relations. However, to re-establish a relation to ourselves, "[w]e need to resist two forms of subjection: individualization (through power relations) and being attracted to fixed identities. The struggle of subjectivity presents itself . . . as the right to difference, variation and metamorphosis" (Deleuze 1988, 87). According to Deleuze, the process of subjectivation requires bending power relations in a manner that allows an individual to be "recuperated by power-relations and relations of knowledge" because this allows "the relation to oneself" to be "continually reborn" (1988, 86). This means that the power relations and the existing discourses, far from being only oppressive, can also help the individual to 'heal' or recover from the subjection and become vitalized to engage in a relationship that is able to transform codes and dominance. Deleuze pictures this type of subjectivation or creation of the self occurring through what he calls 'foldings.'

By 'folding' an individual is able to fold forces to affect herself by herself (instead of being defined by someone else).[3] Foucault's fundamental idea, thus, was that subjectivity was to be derived from power and knowledge but without being dependent on them. To actively fold requires reflection, thinking and problematization for "[t]o think means to experiment and to problematize. Knowledge, power and the self are the triple root of a problematization of thought" (Deleuze 1988, 95). Consequently, we need to actively question: What can I know or see and articulate under certain conditions? I have already tried to articulate an answer for this question by mapping the field of fitness in this chapter. Further two questions, however, remain: What can I do, what power can I claim and what resistances may I encounter? What can I be, what folds can I surround myself with or how can I produce myself as a subject? In an attempt to 'fold,' I engaged in an ethnographic project where I aimed to use Pilates as a means to problematize the current codes of fitness.

METHOD

My ethnographic research design was developed around the two questions by Deleuze: What can I do as a researcher to problematize the fitness industry; How I can produce myself as a subject acting within this industry?

The Researcher's Self: How Can I Produce Myself as a Subject?

To problematize the individualization and the construction of a fixed feminine identity an individual is to fold forces to affect upon herself; to create a 'self-fold,' a dimension of subjectivity that is derived from power and knowledge without being dependent on them. While I could have investigated the exercisers' 'foldings,' it was quite evident from the previous literature that although they problematize the ideal body to a certain extent, they, with desire for the better, illness-free body, are quite dependent on the current power/knowledge knowledge nexus. My previous study of mindful fitness instructors (Markula 2004; Markula and Pringle 2006) also indicated that while the instructors were aware of the problems with the quest for the ideal body, they lacked the tools to actively shape their mindful practices with a different premise. In this project, I had to focus on my own practices for folding is a process that an individual actively engages herself with. However, this does not mean searching for one's 'true self.' On the contrary, "[t]he double is never a projection of the interior, on the contrary, it is an interiorization of the outside . . . It is not the emanation of an 'I'" (Deleuze 1988, 81).[4]

I had to reflect on my role as a researcher: how can a researcher create social change by folding the outside, become recuperated by power and knowledge without being dependent on them? I had to begin actively problematizing the fitness knowledges, the ways of instructing (mindful) fitness and the (mindful) fitness practices. Following Deleuze, I was to think what could I be as a researcher/mindful fitness instructor: how can I produce myself as a subject? As an academic I asked particularly: what can I know about mindful fitness in certain conditions that allows me to think differently, to problematize, to fold the outside into inside. What could I do with my knowledge of the fitness industry?

Research Setting and Research Methods: What Can I Do, What Power Can I Claim?

To begin my project I qualified as a Pilates instructor from a commercial instructor training program. I willfully chose a short 40-hour program as it was likely that this was the type of basic qualification most Pilates instructors who teach in commercial settings would acquire. I qualified officially by completing written assignments, a written test and a practical test. As a research project, I engaged in teaching a weekly Pilates class at a commercial recreation center operated in connection with the University where I worked at the time. The class met once a week, for 60 minutes at the time, throughout the year with a one-month summer break and a Christmas break. The class was open to the general public, but the majority of the participants worked at the University in various roles. The recreation center lacked a Pilates-specific space and thus, our class was scheduled in a martial arts dojo. The number of participants varied, depending on the time of year, from 10 to 30 people. While the majority were women, several men also attended the classes. I taught the class for 12 months.

During this time, I wrote detailed field notes based on my observations of the participants, but the notes also included reflections of my own teaching success, lesson planning (what worked, what did not work), and the numerous incidents that disrupted our daily class routines. In addition, I actively sought feedback from the participants through informal interviews before and after the class. I did not, however, conduct any formal interviews with the participants.

I want to emphasize that my purpose here is not to represent Pilates as an exemplary form of exercise practice—no exercise practice is inherently good or bad, but what matters is what is made out of it within the current power/discourse nexus—but to demonstrate how any exercise form can be problematized and then used in an attempt to change the current field of fitness. Therefore, other exercise forms, and not only mindful fitness forms, can also be used to fold, to problematize, identity construction and individualization. I chose Pilates purely as a personal preference, but also because it lacks the religious grounding of yoga and Tai Chi which would need to be analyzed as a discursive construction and disciplinary production of its own. This is not to argue that yoga or Tai Chi cannot be used to transform docility, but rather that there is an added discursive element that needs attention before a problematization of the westernized production of identity and individualism can take place.

FOLDING THE OUTSIDE WITH MOVEMENT INSTRUCTION

To think differently means problematizing mindful fitness as an activity: what are the aspects of it that discipline us to docile bodies, and bind us to individualism and confined identity? This would mean problematizing the aesthetics of the healthy body and the feminine identity it produces, the medical/health discourse and the individualism it embeds, and the actual practices of mindful fitness that produce the disciplined bodies. The most effective way of problematizing the feminine identity construction and individualism is probably to give talks and lectures that reveal the limitations of the articulable discourses maintaining them. I, of course, do this through my teaching, research writing and media campaigns where I have particularly challenged the construction of the ideal feminine body. In fitness classes, however, the body's practice is the main focus and the instructors spend most of their time providing instruction of how to execute the exercises correctly. It is definitely possible to give health instructions or provide an occasional comment to challenge the body ideal. It is equally possible not to talk about health in terms of illness prevention and not to ever bring up the 'body beautiful' during the class. I certainly made a concerted effort never to mention the looks of the body by refraining from, for example, promising my clients slimmer tummies, more toned legs, or 'bikini ready' bodies. However, when in a Pilates class the clients are there to move and thus, expect to be exercising. As a matter of fact, a common complaint in Pilates classes is that the instructor talks too much and the clients have too little chance to move. From Foucault's point of view, however, discourses manifest in practices and thus, to transform the discourses, one has to also transform bodily practices. Therefore, the most effective way to problematize identity construction and individualism in the context of an exercise class is to focus on the actual exercises and ask: How can I create exercise practices that transcend femininity and individualism instead of disciplining the exercisers into docile bodies? I will now explain how I attempted to fold the outside into the inside through movement practices that are recuperated, not controlled, by the current power/knowledge nexus.

For Foucault (1991), space and bodily practice were not innocent aspects of life, but similar to the discourses, these were an integral part of the process through which power relations diffuse through society. Therefore, it is important to carefully consider how these aspects of fitness knowledge intersect with current power relations and how they can be folded to create more ethical fitness practices. Foucault identified that disciplinary techniques of the body included such elements as time, space and control of the activity. As an instructor, I had more control over the activities done in class than the class space, the duration of the class or its position within the weekly timetable of the center. Therefore, my attempts at problematization were limited to the activities done in class.

Problematizing Identity Construction through Pilates Practice

Foucault (1991) demonstrates how repetitive, progressive exercise programs are designed to control the body and normalize it into the limited feminine identity. Pilates classes share many of the characteristics of disciplinary 'exercise': each class is segmented into warm up, exercise session and cool-down; correct execution of exercise is emphasized for maximum benefit; the exercises are organized to progressively become more intense and complex. The entire Pilates program could be described as 'series of series of exercise' where each exercise is carefully named with detailed instructions for execution and progression. Typically, while there might be several modifications of each exercise, no new exercises are added as a Pilates class should be constructed to include only exercises from the accepted Pilates vocabulary. From a Foucauldian perspective, such a program could ensure a continual and increased control of the body that leads only to docility. Why would anyone, then, choose such a highly codified, disciplinary exercise form to challenge the discourses that control the feminine body? Would one not be better off by creating an entirely new type of exercise class free of disciplinary segmentation and codified, progressive exercises? While this might be an option, from a Foucauldian perspective every practice is constructed through discourses and thus, nothing can be outside of power relations and certain control. Therefore, even a 'new' exercise class would be a form of codified practice, albeit through different discourses. In addition, codification is strong in the current fitness industry and Pilates, as a well-established practice, has a strong, existing client base which a 'new' class would not have. Therefore, my idea was to use the existing practice, with all its limitations, to problematize, to fold, the feminine identity construction.

Problematizing the Control of Activity

The key for my folding was to problematize the 'goal' of Pilates. Obviously, the goal of constructing the body beautiful needed to be replaced with another goal. Pilates already has a strong emphasis on improving alignment and core strength for better everyday movement ability and thus, my idea was to emphasize these through the actual exercises. According to Foucault (1991), segmenting time for effectiveness served as a disciplinary technique. My Pilates class continued to be loosely segmented into a warm-up during which we aimed to locate the body's 'natural' alignment, the deep abdominals and practice breathing. This was followed by the Pilates exercises and an ending which usually took a form of relaxation. These segments, nevertheless, departed from the health-related fitness premise that each of the components of physical fitness had to be fitted into the class to ensure improved physical fitness.

Foucault (1991) further asserted that an emphasis on correct execution of exercise to obtain maximally useful bodies creates docility. As most mindful exercise forms, Pilates exercises are performed in a detailed, precise manner to serve a specific purpose assigned to them. Usually these 'purposes' refer to either strengthening (e.g., the core, lower back) or obtaining more mobility (e.g., neck, lower back, pelvis) in certain body parts. This is the aspect of exercise that has also been harnessed to contribute to creation of the body beautiful when the 'benefits' of certain exercises have been re/misinterpreted for the purpose of body shaping. Therefore, it is important that the instructor is clear how each exercise, instead of guaranteeing a better looking body, might improve everyday movement ability or counteract the stresses of everyday life. Consequently, I continued to provide detailed instructions of how to keep the movement continuous, use the appropriate range of motion and engage the required body parts for the performance. To avoid disciplining the clients, they were to consider their own everyday needs (such as counteracting the strain of repetitive daily activities on their bodies). I also used music, but not to create an army of uniform exercisers (as might be the case in aerobics classes), but in the background. The exercisers were to work to the rhythm of their own breathing and thus, everyone started and ended their exercises at different times.

Problematizing the Organization of Genesis

In addition to control of each exercise, Foucault (1991) saw the disciplinary bodily techniques building into exercise systems. Successive segments with increasing complexity and intensity formed progressive systems to discipline individuals into docility. Clearly, Pilates could be considered as such a system of docility that locks individual women into an endless search for the healthy looking body (and mind). In my beginners' level class, I also incorporated modifications that were designed to progress into increasingly complex and intense work. The participants often requested that we 'work harder' as they did not 'feel anything.' This presented an interesting dilemma as the participants often did not know how to do the exercises in a manner that allowed them to 'feel' their bodies. Neither was it clear why they really needed to work harder. I interpreted this need stemming from the unquestioned force of discourses around the body beautiful: one needs to work hard, feel the 'burn,' to tone the body into the ideal shape. For me then, 'working hard' was a disciplinary technique that was difficult to counter. I often ended up providing more advanced modifications so that the clients could work harder although they did not possess the skills to do such modifications yet. It was also difficult to 'resist' the force of progression (to provide such difficult movements that every participant would be forced to 'feel' them) because it seemed like many of clients had lost the ability to 'feel' their bodies. I interpreted this to be partly due to the current disciplinary body training techniques that mechanically aid the exercisers through 'correct' movement pattern without the participants having to 'think' about it. For example, many resistance training machines are designed to strengthen isolated body parts (such as biceps brachii) through one dimensional, repetitive movement that leaves little room for deviation. In addition, the machine provides the resistance or intensity for the exercise instead of the exerciser 'feeling' it. In a Pilates class the exercises are based on the exerciser knowing/feeling themselves how to execute the movement and intensity is determined by adding more of one's own body weight. This provides possibilities for a less disciplined form of exercise where the individual can determine the intensity and complexity of exercise themselves instead of depending on the machine. However, it is not easy to fold the exercise practice this way as it requires thinking, feeling and concentration. Teaching the participants to 'feel' their bodies presented the most challenging task, particularly against the powerful notions of hard work and continuous progression. However, (re)learning this skill could then help each participant to problematize the need for progression or progress in a manner that is defined by them, not by the discourses surrounding the feminine aesthetics of the healthy body beautiful. In this sense, progression through increasingly complex and intense modifications of exercise is not, in itself, disciplinary, but there is a need to constantly problematize the goal and thus, the need for such progression.

Problematizing the Expert Knowledge

With the increase in the disciplinary techniques, Foucault (1978) demonstrated, there was a need for 'experts' who could provide definitive advice on how to do things correctly. A Pilates instructor can definitely be classified as such an expert who has obtained a special qualification to teach movement vocabulary commonly identified as Pilates. In Pilates classes, we are to teach only exercises developed and named by Joseph Pilates. While Pilates as an exercise form has grown into a large field with multiple 'systems' (such as the Stott Pilates, Body Control Pilates, Fletcher), qualified instructors are still the exclusive experts to teach this form. In a mat Pilates class like mine, the instructor controls the planning and organization of the class. This leadership is also expected by the clients who come to the class to follow a program planned for them by someone else. At first sight, one could imagine problematizing such an unquestioned position of control by overthrowing the entire idea of an instructor-led class in favor of a student-led class. While this is possible in a gym setting where everyone follows their individual programs (albeit planned for them by someone else, for example, a personal trainer), it is unlikely that the clients in the current cultural context would attend a student-centered class. Therefore, it was important for me to think how I could make my instructor-led class less disciplinary. Is an instructor-led class always necessarily disciplinary? What are the positives of being an expert?

It was clear that I knew a lot more about how the body works than the participants, was able to provide exercise alternatives and explain what muscles should be activated during each exercise. However, it was also important that I shared that knowledge with the participants instead of simply ordering them to do one exercise after another. I, therefore, aimed to explain why we were doing certain movements in addition to how to do them. I also believed that it was important to explain how the Pilates exercises might translate into moving in every day situations. For example, how might strengthening the deeper abdominals help in everyday situations? How does improving spinal twist aid in everyday life?

In addition to one's knowledge, in commercial fitness settings one's expertise is also determined by one's looks. Such a judgment, of course, draws from the feminine aesthetics of the ideal body. As an instructor, I tried to problematize this aspect of current construction of fitness expertise in favor of an ability of analyze movement performance. I always dressed in loose clothing instead of revealing, tight exercise wear. I also avoided demonstration, because I believed that the object was not for the participants to imitate my movements, but to learn to feel their own bodies that had different strengths and limitations from my body. This strategy did not always work well because in the contemporary world much of our perception is visual and we are often lost when that feed is taken away. Consequently, my clients were often confused with only verbal instruction, but at the very least they had to concentrate on their movement execution instead of mechanically following me.

My expertise on movement analysis stems from exercise sciences, the same discourses that construct the current understanding of health-related fitness. As I have demonstrated earlier, this discourse tends to produce docile bodies through individualism and the narrowly defined feminine identity. How could I, then, use the same discourse in my folding of individualism and feminine identity? It is important to remember that folding entails problematizing the discourses to be able to use them differently, to be recuperated, not dominated, by them. Therefore, this was my attempt to use my knowledge on movement analysis and anatomy—not unproblematically or unquestioningly for a better looking, illness-free body—to think of possible different understandings for exercise. This meant that while Pilates provided the overall structure to this effort, the actual class aimed to help participants think of their particular movement needs, their possibilities to move differently in everyday life, their limitations and strengths, and their preferences, movement sensations and enjoyment. However, providing comfortable movement experiences, I believed, meant also knowing about the body: how it works and how it moves. It was in this intersection that I felt movement 'expertise' was needed. Many clients, however, expressed continual 'movement needs' that appeared embedded in the medical discourse.

Problematizing Individualism through Pilates Practice

As an exercise form, Pilates is not constructed around the components of health-related fitness. For example, there is no cardio-vascular segment in the class. In this sense, it could be argued to be less embedded within the discursive construction of health as absence of disease than, for example, aerobics. Therefore, problematizing individualism of the health discourse, one would have thought, would be relatively easy: one could simply restrain from emphasizing Pilates as a form of illness prevention. This proved a bigger challenge than I expected as many of my clients were recommended Pilates by their physicians or their physiotherapists due to such conditions as back pain, MS, cancer or general muscle tension. How, then to think differently about 'health' in a Pilates class when many participants were there to seek a 'cure' to their existing, 'real' conditions? Because I was teaching a mindful fitness class, one solution could have been to emphasize an alternative 'eastern philosophy' rather than the 'western,' scientific, medical discourse. However, problematizing the 'health' discourse does not mean entirely denouncing it in favor of something else but rather asking: how can I derive from this knowledge without being dependent on it? Consequently, the solution is not to switch from 'bad westernized' discourses to 'good' eastern philosophy and then blindly follow this new discourse. On the other hand, if we create illness-free bodies through disciplined work in a mindful fitness class, we are defined by the medical discourse, not folding the outside to create diversity. To fold, one should problematize the prominent notion of health as illness prevention that pushes the responsibility for disease-free existence solely to the individual.

I could certainly not ignore the clients' existing conditions in the name of challenging the medical discourse. Instead, I did attempt to provide exercises modified for each client's particular condition and also provided modification of each exercise for clients to decide which level was the most suitable for them. 'Individualized' instruction is, nevertheless, impossible in a commercial fitness class where clients tend to come from all fitness levels with different exercise backgrounds.

Can such individualized programs and the focus on one's own body be considered as assigning the responsibility for illness prevention solely to the individual exerciser? Naturally, this can happen when the conditions for the individual body 'problems' are not problematized. However, it is also difficult to spend time in a commercial class talking about the work conditions or other life factors that might result in, for example, back pain. At the same, as the discourses manifest in the body, a detailed, 'thoughtful,' attention to its movements can also dismantle the previously 'numbed,' disciplined, 'voiceless' and docile body. It also seemed that touch played in important role in awakening some bodily feelings. For example, by touching I was able to direct a participant's attention to body parts that were tense or create a different movement path for limbs conditioned to take on extra strain. In contemporary society, some participants might perceive such touching as obtrusive. Forcing someone's limbs into unused positions can also be dangerous. However, even with these prerequisites, touching seems to often help clients sense the movement patterns and many of them commented positively of such individual attention. Again, there was not enough time to provide that to everyone, all the time. Nevertheless, I felt much better prepared to problematize the aesthetics of the body beautiful than the powerful discourse of health as an absence of illness. This was particularly difficult when faced with participants with debilitating conditions. I also felt that my Pilates training did not address such special conditions—and it was definitely made clear during the course that it prepared us only to work with so-called 'normal' clients, not with clients who had 'special' needs—and I was surprised by the amount of participants referred to Pilates classes by medical professionals. My fold of discourse of health needs to be deeper as continual work is required to negotiate this discourse in the commercial fitness setting.

CONCLUSION

Following Foucault and Deleuze, I engaged in 'folding' knowledge to transform myself as a fitness instructor informed, but, hopefully, not defined by this knowledge. My aim was to problematize the discourse of aesthetics of the healthy body—that locks women into a limited, predetermined identity—and individualism stemming from the medical discourse that defined health narrowly as an absence of illness. I focused particularly on how the actual movement practices can be changed as a result of such folding. Following Deleuze, I attempted a double unhooking or "differentiation" that occurs when the exercises that enable one to govern oneself "become detached both from power as a relation between forces and from knowledge as a stratified form, 'code of virtue'" (1988, 83). The responses to my attempts to fold were not always positive. I encountered plenty of resistance by the participants who, informed by previous fitness knowledges, had preconceived notions of Pilates or exercise in general. Not all my movement experimentation was successful and I certainly needed more tools to challenge the individualization of the medical discourse. It is clear, thus, that 'folding' requires one to continually problematize building a self, a body and a practice.

Because discourses manifest in the actual practices, it is important to change the practices that align with the dominant discourses. This means that we have to actively problematize the movement patterns in 'traditional' forms of mindful exercise such as Pilates also. We need to think of each exercise—what does it do?—by using knowledge of science but not becoming dependent on it. We need to think about the meaning of the movement, not copy pre-established patterns. We need to teach participants to feel the movement, to find their own rhythm, to find their own bodies.

Folding through movement education requires a problematization of the self, discourse and power dimensions. This also necessitates problematizing the actual movement practices and the meaning of 'authentic' exercise forms. To fold, to transform individualization and limited identities through (mindful) fitness, to create a self recuperated within power/discourse nexus means asking: What is this practice for? What is its discursive construction within the westernized commercial settings? What can instructors transform by problematizing their practice? How can an individual practitioner/instructor fold forces to affect upon herself—to create a 'self-fold,' a dimension of subjectivity that is derived from power and knowledge without being dependent on them?

NOTES

1 Despite the attempts for integration, mindfulness has not necessarily created a seamlessly integrated exerciser. When probing the origins of the most popular mindful fitness forms, instead of body-mind integration, a tendency for domination of the mind appears to replace the emphasis on the physical body. For example, yoga and Tai Chi stem from religious traditions that advocate control of the mind. Tai Chi originally draws from Taoism that advocates control of the mind that is achieved when the body is controlled. Yoga that originally refers to the union of the individual self with the Universal Self (Strauss 2005) is a practice that was eventually designed to enable an evolution of the soul freed from the body. Pilates, while an exercise form officially created in the U.S., was originally titled 'Contrology' to denote its creator Joseph Pilates' idea of an exercise system that combined science and art to develop coordinated body-mind-spirit through natural movements but under strict control of the will (e.g., Gallagher and Kryzanowska 1999). Thus, the mind-body integration is not a simple matter: practicing mindful fitness forms, in one way or another, appears to denote that the body is controlled by the mind—a strong mind (self) is achieved when the body is controlled.

2 For Foucault (1988a; 1988b), the entire notion of true self is embedded in western humanism and diverts the individual from actively creating an ethical self in favor of looking for something that can never be found.

3 Foucault saw the ancient Greeks engaging in this type of folding through the exercises of self-governance which became "detached both from power as a relation between forces and from knowledge as a stratified form, 'code of virtue'" (Deleuze 1988, 83). They bent the outside forces through a series of practical exercises which then became a version of doubling through differentiation and reflection: "Far from ignoring interiority, individuality or subjectivity, they invented the subject, but only as a derivate or the product of

76   *Pirkko Markula*

a 'subjectivation.'" They discovered the "'aesthetic of existence'—the doubling or relation with oneself" (Deleuze 1988, 84).

4 Deleuze (1988 72) explains that Foucault distinguished between exteriority and outside. Exteriority refers to the outside world whereas outside "is farther away than any external world." Outside is a type of force without a form that exists is relation to other forces. Similarly, inside differs from interiority (the self). The inside is a type of force created by folding the outside, not a creation of a new 'self.'

REFERENCES

Bolin, A. 1992. Vandalized vanity: Feminist physiques betrayed and portrayed. In *Tattoo, torture, mutilation, and adornment: The denaturation of the body in culture and text*, ed. F. E. Mascia-Lees and P. Sharpe, 79–99. Albany NY: State University of New York Press.

—— 2003. Beauty or the beast: The subversive soma. In *Athletic intruders: Ethnographic research on women, culture, and exercise*, ed. A. Bolin and J. Granskoog, 107–30. Albany, NY: State University of New York Press.

Cole, C. L. 1998. Addition, exercise, and cyborgs: Technologies of deviant bodies. In *Sport in postmodern times,* ed. G. Rail, 261–76. Albany, NY: State University of New York Press.

Craig, M. L. and R. Liberty. 2007. 'Cause that's what girls do': The making of a feminized gym. *Gender & Society* 21: 676–99.

Deleuze, G. 1988. *Foucault.* London: Athlone Press.

Duncan, M. C. 1994. The politics of women's body image and practices: Foucault, the panopticon and *Shape* magazine. *Journal of Sport and Social Issues* 18: 48–65.

Dworkin, S. 2003. A woman's place is in the . . . cardiovascular room? Gender relations, the body, and the gym. In *Athletic intruders: Ethnographic research on women, culture, and exercise,* ed. A. Bolin and J. Granskoog, 131–58. Albany, NY: State University of New York Press.

Dworkin, S. and F. L. Wachs. 2009. Body panic: Gender, health and the selling of fitness. New York: New York University Press.

Eskes, T. B., M. C. Duncan and E. M. Miller. 1998. The discourse of empowerment: Foucault, Marcuse, and women's fitness texts. *Journal of Sport and Social Issues* 22: 317–44.

Foucault, M. 1978. *History of sexuality. Volume 1: An introduction.* London: Penguin Books.

—— 1988a. An aesthetics of existence. In *Michel Foucault politics, philosophy, culture: Interviews and other writing 1977–1984,* ed. L. D. Kritzman, 47–56. London: Routledge.

—— 1988b. Technologies of the self. In *Technologies of the Self: A seminar with Michel Foucault,* ed. L. H. Martin, H. Gutman and P. H. Hutton, 16–40. Amherst, MA: University of Massachusetts Press.

—— 1991. *Discipline and punish: The birth of the prison.* London: Penguin Books.

Gallagher, S. P. and R. Kryzanowska. 1999. *The Pilates method of body conditioning.* Philadelphia, PA: BainBridgeBooks.

Gimlin, D. 2002. *Body work: Beauty and self-image in American culture.* Berkeley, CA: University of California Press.

Grogan, S., R. Evans, S. Wright and G. Hunter. 2004. Femininity and muscularity: Accounts of seven women body builders. *Journal of Gender Studies* 13(1): 49–61.

Haravon Collins, L. 1995. Exercises in empowerment: Toward a feminist aerobic pedagogy. *Women in Sport and Physical Activity Journal* 2: 23–44.

—— 2002. Working out contradictions: Feminism and aerobics. *Journal of Sport & Social Issues* 26: 85–109.

Heywood, L. 1998. *Bodymakers: A cultural anatomy of women's body building.* New Brunswick, NJ: Rutgers University Press.

Jette, S. 2006. Fit for two? A critical discourse analysis of *Oxygen* Fitness Magazine. *Sociology of Sport Journal* 23: 331–51.

Kagan, E. and M. Morse. 1988. The body electronic: Aerobic exercise on video. *The Drama Review* 32: 164–80.

King, S. J. 2003. Doing good by running well. In *Foucault, cultural studies, governmentality*, ed. J. Z. Bratich, J. Packer and C. McCarthy, 285–301. New York: Simon & Schuster.

Lloyd, M. 1996. Feminism, aerobics and the politics of the body. *Body & Society* 2: 79–98.

Loland, N. W. 2000. The art of concealment in a culture of display: Aerobicizing women's and men's experience and the use of their own bodies. *Sociology of Sport Journal* 17: 111–29.

McDermott, L. 2000. A qualitative assessment of the significance of body perception to women's physical activity experiences: Revisiting discussions of physicalities. *Sociology of Sport Journal* 17: 331–63

MacNeill, M. 1998. Sex, lies, and videotape: The political and cultural economies of celebrity fitness videos. In *Sport and postmodern times*, ed. G. Rail, 163–84. Albany, NY: State University of New York Press.

Maguire, J. and L. Mansfield. 1998. 'No-body is perfect': Women, aerobics, and the body beautiful. *Sociology of Sport Journal* 15: 109–37.

Markula, P. 1995. Firm but shapely, fit but sexy, strong but thin: The postmodern aerobicizing female bodies. *Sociology of Sport Journal* 12: 424–53.

—— 2001. Beyond the perfect body: Women's body image distortion in fitness magazine discourse. *Journal of Sport & Social Issues* 25: 158–79.

—— 2003. Postmodern aerobics: Contradiction and resistance. In *Athletic intruders: Ethnographic research on women, culture, and exercise*, ed. A. Bolin and J. Granskoog, 53–78. Albany, NY: State University of New York Press.

—— 2004. 'Tuning into one's self': Foucault's technologies of the self and mindful fitness. *Sociology of Sport Journal* 21: 302–21.

Markula. P. and R. Pringle. 2006. *Foucault, sport and exercise: Power, knowledge and transforming the self.* London: Routledge.

Monroe, M. 1998. Mind-body fitness goes mainstream. *IDEA Health and Fitness Source*, June–July: 34–44.

Prickett, S. 1997. Aerobic dance and the city: Individual and social space. In *Dance in the city*, ed. H. Thomas, 198–217. New York: St. Martin.

Roussel, P., J. Griffet and P. Duret. 2003. The decline of female bodybuilding in France. *Sociology of Sport Journal* 20: 40–59.

Sassatelli, R. 1999. Interaction order and beyond: A field analysis of body culture within fitness gyms. *Body & Society*, 5: 227–48.

Spielvogel, L. G. 2002. The discipline of space in a Japanese fitness club. *Sociology of Sport Journal* 19: 189–205.

St. Martin, L. and N. Gavey. 1996. Women's bodybuilding: Feminist resistance and/or femininity's recuperation? *Body & Society* 2: 45–57.

Strauss, S. 2005. *Positioning yoga: Balancing acts across cultures*. New York: Berg.

Wesely, J. 2001. Negotiating gender: Bodybuilding and the natural/unnatural continuum. *Sociology of Sport Journal* 18: 162–80.

Part II

Body Trouble

Fat Women and Exercise

4 Fit, Fat and Feminine?

The Stigmatization of Fat Women in Fitness Gyms

Louise Mansfield

FITNESS GYMS AND THE ANTI-FAT ETHIC

An anti-fat ethic is pervasive in fitness cultures, and perhaps most clearly evidenced in the fitness gym that provides a cultural space in which people manage the twin corporeal purposes of (internal) health and (external) appearance. Contemporary self-consciousness about the body, and the significance of corporeality in the production, reproduction and perception of the self is connected to long-term transformations in the economic, technological and political configurations in society that have contributed to the emergence of consumer culture (Burkitt 1999; Cole 1993, 2002; Shilling 1993; Turner 1996). The emphasis on sport, fitness and leisure in late capitalism is marked by commercialization of the body linked to the shift from industrial capitalism toward a "postindustrial culture" founded on a global economy, service industries, advertising and consumerism (Turner 1996, 3). A focus on the body beautiful, denial of the aging/diseased body, and the value of physical fitness and health, then, reflects the increasing consumerist concern with the body.

For Featherstone (1991) the commercialization of exercise, diet and cosmetic fitness practices illustrates the emphasis on bodily appearance and corporeal preservation in late capitalism. Such "self-preservationist" conceptions of corporeality are linked to the idea that the body represents a sphere of hedonistic practices, desire and pleasure (Featherstone 1991, 170). Within consumer culture, the reward for 'body-work,' such as diet, exercise and cosmetic regimes is an improved 'look,' a more marketable self, the increased potential for self-expression and the experience of pleasure. Specifically, body imagery in consumer culture is associated with the themes of beauty, youth, energy, enjoyment, freedom, luxury and romance. There is a moral value placed on the achievement of such themes and the promise of these pleasures requires a sharpened, more reflexive awareness of one's own and others' appearance (Featherstone 1991; Lupton 1996, 1997; Shilling 1993; Turner 1996). The tendency, then, in contemporary Western life, is for people to perceive that their bodies should be worked-on, and worked-out as a means of representing and expressing the individual self.

Fitness gyms are characterized by the promotion and prescription of exercise regimes for improved fitness and health measured and monitored by body weight, shape, size and posture, and the ability to perform specified physical tasks, be that through muscular strength and endurance or cardiovascular efficiency. In the dominant fitness discourse, the fat body tends to be afforded stigmatized status, positioned as the deviant or abnormal 'other' against which the socially esteemed fit and healthy body defines itself; and fatness is identified as a 'problem' for the full realization of a host of individual and social goals, from productivity and competitiveness to happiness and fulfillment (Smith Maguire et al. 2009). That said, fitness gyms vary in type and attract a range of people from different socio-cultural backgrounds. Fitness also invests bodies with power and opens up the possibility for practices of the self and challenges to the dominant discourse about fat some of which may have the potential to disrupt or at least complicate the stigmatization of fat bodies.

This chapter discusses the production and reproduction of a cultural distaste for fat in fitness gyms. It recognizes the relevance of the concept of stigma (Goffman 1973) and explores in more detail the socio-dynamics of stigmatization (Elias and Scotson 1994) for understanding how the appearance and display of fat in fitness cultures is denigrated and devalued, serving to classify fat women as the stigmatized 'other' in the gym environment and wider social life.

WOMEN WORKING OUT: ETHNOGRAPHY AND THE FITNESS EXPERIENCE

My research interest in fitness cultures and fat bodies has arisen out of a long-term practical and academic involvement in sport and leisure (Mansfield 2005, 2007, 2008). Broadly speaking such research represents an examination of the status, motivations, meanings and significance of women in cultures of fitness, and the impact of their involvement in fitness activities on the construction of their sense of femininity, and it is founded on an ethical commitment to producing knowledge upon which practical solutions to the problematic of gender, femininity and fitness can be based. It is, then, feminist work. At the same time the research has been guided by the principles of figurational/process sociology (Elias 1978; Mennell 1992; Van Krieken 1998) so that the overarching rationale is concerned with understanding the development and structural characteristics of cultures of fitness and the consequences of those characteristics on the self-conceptions and relative power of women in fitness activities.

The discussion in this chapter draws on participant observation and interview material collected in the context of public and private fitness centers in England, U.K., over the past decade that has centered on questions about fitness, female participation and femininities. Along with an extensive collection of participant observation field notes collected in a variety of fitness settings almost on a weekly basis, I have also conducted approximately 60 formal, in-depth, semi-structured or unstructured interviews with women about their fitness experiences. Some of these are one-off conversations, some are based upon a life-history approach and engage women in 4 to 5 interviews about different fitness themes, and my most recent discussions have included focus groups as a method for examining women's ideas about fitness cultures (Maguire and Mansfield 1998; Mansfield 2002, 2005, 2007, 2008, 2009a; Mansfield and Maguire 1999). Mainly, although not exclusively, the women I have exercised with and spoken to have been white, aged between 20–40 years, orientated toward middle-class lifestyles and heterosexual. However, I have conducted a research project with 10 Indian women aged between 50–80 years (Mansfield 2008, 2009b) and my more recent focus group work has begun to include the views of lesbian women (Mansfield 2009a).

My interpretation of fit bodies and fatness is not simply a description of events and occurrences but a translation of a particular reality in fitness cultures in which I, as the researcher, am involved. In Wheaton's terms this is critical sub-cultural ethnography and is best described as "the researcher's written representation of that culture" (2002, 248). I was always mindful of the impact my involvement might have on interpreting and understanding fitness and fatness. Throughout the research the challenge has been to balance my involved position with the subject matter with an appropriate degree of distance from the fitness activities themselves and from my personal politics about fit bodies and fat bodies. A feminist sense of critical self-reflection has been important in this regard to managing my-self in the research setting, in balancing the tasks of sociologist as participant and inquirer and in bringing an appropriate balance of passion and reason to the analysis (Mansfield 2007, 2008).

Observations were recorded as field notes; the "symbol of the ethnographer" (Sands 2002, 75). The evidence was collected in a fairly unstructured manner. I did not set out and follow a detailed plan, nor did I fix the themes of analysis from the outset. I wrote detailed notes in a notebook immediately after teaching or participating in exercise classes or after working-out in the gym, pool or park so that I could remember as accurately as possible things that were said and done when I typed up the full accounts. Sometimes I had more time to keep field notes and they were more immediate in terms of the time lag between participating and observing and writing, and sometimes there were more opportunities than others to directly type them into a laptop computer. At other times my notes were brief and I needed to recall from memory what I had seen and heard. I collected brochures, adverts, articles from newspapers and magazines and conducted searches of relevant Internet sites that provided information about how contemporary fitness cultures produce and reproduce socio-cultural ideas about femininity.

While field notes and interview material have been invaluable to my analysis in this chapter, they still remain partial in terms of building a picture of the relationship between fitness cultures and fat bodies. I did not set out to study fat exercisers. Fat was a key issue in all my discussions with women about fitness and the body beautiful although it was never on my agenda of discussion topics. That is to say these women's perceptions of their body—its shape, size and texture—were orientated toward ideas about fat. I never measured how fat these women were, nor did I judge them in terms of whether or not they were fat. Nevertheless, all those I spoke with defined themselves in relation to fat; losing fat, gaining fat, being and becoming fat, and fearing fat. It has been through a more recent re-engagement with my observation notes and interview material that I have come to see the centrality of anti-fat models of corporeality in the production of fit bodies and cultures of fitness. As I have become more attuned to the critical debate surrounding the so-called global obesity crisis and have become immersed in the work of fat activists and academics engaging in critiques of anti-fat ethics through such groups as Fat Studies in the U.K. (Tomrley and Kaloski-Naylor 2009) I have come to understand further the cultural distaste for fat that is central to the production of fit bodies and a recurring narrative in the conversations that I have had with women throughout my research.

FAT FEMALE BODIES IN THE FITNESS GYM: FITNESS, 'OTHER' WOMEN AND STIGMA

The fitness ideal varies from fashion and film ideals as Markula (1995) points out, by virtue of the desire for tight/toned muscles. Fit female bodies are a type of stylized corporeality and are defined and characterized by lean physiques and the omnipresence of fat stigma. For example, one of the respondents in my own research (Beth) clearly identified the character of idealized female fitness. "The ideal shape?" she questioned. "Very tall and very lean but not big. . . . Muscular but smaller and thinner. . . . a bit of definition but. . . . leaner . . . low fat or . . . no fat" and Charlie explicitly stated: "fat bothers me." Therefore, while thinness may not be the only requirement for such female bodies, fat is the problem. Few authors have focused specifically on issues connected to fat bodies and fitness cultures although, as previously noted, there is a wealth of literature that contributes to an understanding of the complexities of body image in sport and fitness. There is a developing body of scholarly work focusing on fat, overweight and obesity which addresses the politics of fat as well as providing a critical account of the construction and mediation of the so-called global obesity epidemic (see, for example, Gard and Wright 1995; Monaghan 2008; Rich et al. 2009; Solovay and Rothblum 2009; Tomrley and Kaloski-Naylor 2009). The discussion that follows hopes to make a contribution to such literature by examining the processes by which fat is stigmatized in fitness gyms.

Goffman's (1973) work on stigma is initially useful in understanding that fat people are effectively marginalized from the exercise endeavor and from social life more broadly. For Goffman (1973) there is a stigma associated with the disfigured, the blind, the paralyzed or those with absent limbs (bodily stigma), those with mental impairment and people considered to have impaired personal characters (mental and moral stigma), and those of racial or religious minority groups (tribal stigma). Different types of stigma influence and can be influenced by human relationships in many different contexts. All human beings are identified and represented by their bodies regardless of physical and mental impairment. While Goffman did not discuss fat bodies in his *Notes on the Management of Spoiled Identity*, he shed some light on the ways that being fat in contemporary western societies leads to judgments of inadequacy, undesirability and stigma. Like the disfigured, the blind, the epileptic, the amputee and the ex-mental health patient in Goffman's (1973) study, those who are fat tend to be perceived as socially abnormal, inferior human beings. Being fat constitutes both a bodily and moral defect that is connected to oversimplified and inaccurate stereotypical notions of fat people as lazy, unhealthy or unhygienic.

Of particular importance to Goffman's (1973) examination of stigma and the self was the ways in which bodies are central to personal interaction. For Goffman, it is commonly the visible and physical signs of abnormality that serve as a basis for the production and reproduction of the stigmatized self. Interchanges between people with so-called bodily defects and those considering themselves as normal result in what Goffman refers to as "interaction-uneasiness" (1973, 30). The stigmatized fat person may be defensive or withdrawn, the 'normal' person may react with embarrassment, guarded references to the defective characteristic may be made, common words such as fat, big, large and overweight may become taboo in face-to-face exchanges, and the 'normal' individual may react by overzealous acceptance or rejection of the stigmatized individual. As will be discussed in the final section of this chapter fat bodies in fitness gyms are most often connected with feelings of shame and embarrassment. Whispered conversations, raised eyebrows and shakes of the head characterize reactions to fatness and, indeed the word fat has become somewhat of a taboo in the sense that people are unsure whether to use it as a description since it is wholly associated with a pejorative characterization. As Fiona explained; "I suppose it's not nice to call someone fat really . . . fat . . . listen it really means lazy and something not very nice . . . I talk about the 'larger' lady . . . it's more polite in front of them."

Gyms are a place where fears and anxieties about fat are mobilized. Being or becoming fat or looking at others who were deemed to be fat tended to elicit feelings of alienation from the body, and discomfort and isolation from slim/normal people. The gym was commonly thought of as an intimidating place for those who were not well versed in the fitness regimes and those who did not look good/fit. Fitness gyms are sites where bodies are on display and such visibility presents an opportunity for fat bodies to be labeled as different and inferior. To some extent, negative emotional experiences connected to fitness cultures are associated with demeaning and patronizing attitudes of key personnel in the fitness industries as well as the negative attitudes of fitness gym members who hold stereotypical views of fat and, without always meaning to, reinforce the stigma attached to fat bodies.

Goffman (1973), then, provides some insights into the production and reproduction of stigmatized identities that are relevant to understanding experiences of fat women in fitness cultures. However, the focus of his work is on face-to-face interaction and his analysis tends to be restricted to the realm of individual, personal experience. His study of stigma focuses on situations where the 'normal' and 'abnormal' meet. However, stigma is not solely constructed through face-to-face relationships and in the case of fat cannot be fully explained by the simplistic and dualistic differentiation between slim/normal people and fat/abnormal people. All human beings have some experience of corporeal shape and size and the complexities of physicality cannot be understood in simple dichotomous terms. There are multiple and nuanced meanings of fat that cannot adequately be accounted for in Goffman's face-to-face situational explanation. Moreover, the production and reproduction of superior images of lean physiques in fitness cultures, and concomitantly the emergence of a cultural distaste for fat, is connected to the long-term development of global fitness cultures characterized by a network of interdependencies between personnel in the sport, health, fitness, medical and physical education industries. Following Oliver's critique of Goffman, it becomes clear that a Goffmanian account of stigma is "reducible to the individual" and lacks a coherent "structural account of stigma" (1990, 66–67). Stigma, in Goffman's terms, does not allow for the idea that people with impairments or so-called 'abnormalites' can challenge and reject their stigmas, or that stigma can be lessened or eradicated.

Contra Goffman, stigma, prejudice and marginality are not simply rooted in the personality structures of individual people. Broader aspects of cultural, social, political and economic structures of power influence the lives of stigmatized people such as those who are considered to be fat, overweight or obese. Processes of stigmatization, like systems and practices of representation happen in the context of specific power relations between and within human groups. Some people have a greater degree of power in constructing corporeal meaning than others. Examining relations of power is central to understanding stigma, marginality, fatness and femininities. In another account of stigmatization, Norbert Elias was particularly concerned with the relationships between more and less powerful groups. For Elias, stigmatization is a process that concerns the ability of human beings to label outsiders as inferior while constructing more favorable images of established groups. An introduction to the fundamental principles of his account of power and its relationship to the socio-dynamics of stigmatization will help to further the discussion in this chapter.

CORPOREAL POWER, ESTABLISHED-OUTSIDER RELATIONS AND STIGMATIZATION

Throughout his work, Elias was concerned with the centrality of power in human relationships. As he put it power is "a structural characteristic of human relationships—of *all* human relationships" (Elias 1978, 71). His ideas center on understanding the relative power balances or power ratios between people. He emphasized the processual character of human relationships explaining how those relationships change when distributions of power change (Elias 1998).

Elias argues that in order to understand human behavior and emotion it is necessary to consider how and to what extent people are bonded to others and how those bonds shift and change over time and in specific social contexts. In other words, consideration must be made of the needs through which people become interdependent. Such needs include those associated with physical, emotional, intellectual and material well-being (Elias 1998). Relationships, and therefore balances of power, develop between people because they have varying degrees of value to each other; a "functional interdependence" between each other (Elias 1998, 116). Some balances of power develop in situations where people value others highly. It is also possible that balances of power develop out of relationships whereby people place little or no value between themselves and another human being. For example, exclusionary actions connected to marginalization and stigmatization emerge because the stigmatized 'other' is not valued or is de-valued. Following Elias's line of argument, it may be said that the degree to which people depend on others is characterized by reciprocal relationships that involve varying degrees of inequality.

Uneven balances of power (power ratios) between people impact on their behaviors and emotions. Some people are able to withhold what others want and operate a power of constraint. Some people are able to exert influence from a position of relative inferiority and are able to shift the balance of power in their favor operating an enabling power or a power of resistance or agency. Such constraining-enabling balances of power are reflected in tensions and conflicts characteristic of social life. Power, then, is relational in character and is best understood in terms of who has more and who has less power in specific social conditions. Moreover, power balances are at least "bi-polar" and more usually "multi-polar" (Elias

1998, 116). One of the consequences of Elias's conceptualization of power was his theory of established-outsider relations (Elias and Scotson 1994). Here he sought to explain power tensions between dominant and non-dominant groups and his ideas are significant in understanding the unequal relations of corporeal power invested in different female physiques in fitness cultures.

Drawing on Elias's ideas, the stigmatization of fat in fitness gyms involves the monopolization of corporeal power, networks of gossip about bodies within communities of exercisers and the making of group charisma and group disgrace connected to perceptions and emotional understandings of the female body beautiful. The discussion that follows examines these aspects of the socio-dynamics of stigmatization that primarily serve to reinforce the negative images attached to fatness and fat women in the fitness gym.

FATNESS, FITNESS AND FEMININITY: MONOPOLIZING THE FEMALE BODY BEAUTIFUL

In relationships between established and outsider groups, effective stigmatization is principally founded on the ability of one group to monopolize some kind of power resource (Elias and Scotson 1994). In fitness gyms power is invested in the appearance of the body beautiful, ideals of bodily perfection and in the attainment of optimum physical measures of health and fitness. People who are overweight, fat or obese are stigmatized and relatively excluded from fitness gyms because they are perceived by the 'fit,' and often by themselves, as being unable to match up to socially constructed ideals of appearance and performance. Arguably, such ideals are rooted in the dominance of traditional views of white, heterosexual and middle-class femininity and masculinity, and are associated with established notions of physical capability in fitness cultures (leanness, muscular tone, endurance and skill). As Hargreaves explains in terms of sport, sporting culture glorifies the "commodified, glamorised, ultra-feminine image of flawlessness" (2000, 186–87). Such corporeal ideals dominate fitness cultures and reinforce desires connected to bodily perfection and fat-less bodies, thus, maintaining the internalized anxieties and exclusionary behaviors that surround fat. What is principally at issue in understanding the predominance of particular images of femininity in fitness gyms and the stigmatization of fat is the relative capacities of those involved in fitness cultures to 'control' ideals of the female body.

Bodies represent a symbolic resource in the production and reproduction of femininities. The exercise behaviors, physical appearance and corporeal capabilities of fitness gym users as well as key personnel involved in the fitness industries, and the way fit and fat bodies are mediated and consumed are connected to the ability to secure a preferred definition of the fit female body. I have argued in this chapter like others have done that there is no singular definition of the female body beautiful. However, in cultures of fitness lean/slender women through their appearance, performance and knowledge exert more influence over the production and reproduction of female body ideals than fat women. In other words, particular power ratios between and within groups of slim and fat women serve to construct and reconstruct female body ideals that provide the foundation for the marginalization and stigmatization of fat women.

Take the relatively large power ratio between fitness instructors (specialists) and new clients (non-specialists) as an example that illustrates how those 'who know' (instructors) about the body hold a relatively high capacity to 'control' idealized notions of female beauty and performance. Observing such relationships and listening to their dialogues revealed that there is a particular power relationship between the specialist and non-specialist that develops by virtue of the "functional interdependence" between them (Elias 1998, 116). The instructors' primary role is to teach people the correct use of equipment, the purpose for which particular exercises are intended, and the appropriate frequency, duration and intensity of activity for achieving particular performance and appearance objectives. Instructors also act as monitors in the gym checking that people are exercising in the right way to achieve a 'good' or 'fit' body. Fitness instructors are constantly vigilant of exercise behaviors and correct mistakes in bodily performance. While clients tended to be more dependent on instructors for acquiring body knowledge and structuring their exercise behaviors it should be recognized that instructors do not have an unlimited "capacity to compel" female clients to use exercise as a means of acquiring an idealized physique (Elias 1998, 122). Instructor/client relationships are reciprocal, yet unequal, ones. The superiority of an instructor over a client is never total, and does not remain constant.

In terms of the female clients at the gym, not all were equally dependent on instructors. However, new female exercisers who did not meet established appearance criteria were deemed to have not yet learned the correct exercise techniques and were perceived as being the least knowledgeable group of clients. They appeared to be relatively dependent on fitness experts for their body and exercise knowledge. This is not to say that such clients always sought the advice of fitness instructors for some were quite reticent in showing their lack of expertise but fitness instructors were certainly adept at approaching clients who appeared confused when using exercise equipment or who were adopting incorrect techniques. In the fitness gym, there is a hierarchy of those who know how to achieve female body ideals. Along with instructors, established participants, both female and male, held the tacit knowledge needed to achieve established markers of successful performance and appearance. In other words, at the top of the hierarchy of body knowledge were those who looked good and demonstrated their superior knowledge and ability in executing particular exercise techniques. Specialist body knowledge signified instructor status.

In the specialist-non-specialist relationship the rules of the workout were logged in personal exercise programs and embodied in the exercise regime. In these relationships clients work out according to dominant biological and social markers of female fitness. Instructors were consistent in advocating cardiovascular type exercise such as walking, jogging, rowing, cycling and stepping for 20 minutes, three times per week, as a way to improve the efficiency of the heart and lungs and achieve weight (fat) loss. And all exercise programs included muscle sculpting regimes intended to improve strength, posture and aesthetic appearance. Such advice reflects accepted guidelines and professional conduct in exercise testing and prescription advocated by experts in the field of exercise programming. It also reinforces messages and images about the desirability and superiority of lean and toned female bodies mediated in various ways through the wider fitness and health industries. Fitness instructors, then, have a relatively high degree of control over the overall network of processes that shape the gendered rules of gym culture. It appears that instructors and established participants spread particular messages about what counts as the female body beautiful. Moreover, instructors teach techniques for achieving preferred body ideals. So, they keep in motion a set of corporeal rules that permeate the actions and emotions of those who work out.

Fat women are not totally excluded from the fitness gym environment. Some instructors and clients wish to advocate a more positive view of fat and a more inclusive approach to fat exercisers. One instructor Fiona, for example, knew of "larger women" who wanted to work out. She wanted to encourage them to participate at the fitness gym. But she explained that "larger ladies" were intimidated by the culture of slimness saying: "look . . . I speak to these women and they really want to come at times when they don't have to be embarrassed being fat . . . I can understand that . . . I'm embarrassed when I am heavy." She continued by explaining the intimidation that can be felt by those who do not fit the ideals of the female body beautiful and said "It's a scary thing . . . to have your body visible . . . especially when it doesn't really look good." Fiona's comments illustrate the complexities of inclusive/exclusive strategies about fat exercisers and highlights the relatively low potential for fat women to exert an influence over what counts as acceptable female beauty. At the same time Fiona offered support to those who were overweight she noted that she would advise them to work out at "less busy times . . . times when the fit and gorgeous people are not in." And in her mind fat women welcomed her approach as one that countered their own anxieties and embarrassment at coming to the gym. But Fiona's comments reflect the cultural distaste for fat in the fitness gym and her strategy of inclusion quite literally pushes fat women 'behind the scenes' of the fitness gym.

There appears to be a great deal of uncertainty regarding the acceptance of fat bodies in the fitness gym. The desire for inclusion in the exercise activities is opposed by feelings of intimidation and anxiety about displaying fat bodies. Harnessing Elias's (1998) ideas once again, this example illustrates that one of the consequences of corporeal power is the disadvantage that results from strong disagreements, confusion and tension in values of 'outsider' groups. In his words:

> If groups formed by weaker players do not have strong inner tensions, that is a power factor to their advantage. Conversely, if groups formed of weaker players do have strong inner tensions, that is a power factor to the advantage of their opponent.
>
> (Elias 1998, 124)

As will be discussed further on in the chapter, anxiety, shame and embarrassment surrounded the imagery and appearance of female bodies that are fat and such feelings serve to limit the potential opportunities for collective resistance against the anti-fat ethic.

THE GOOD, THE BAD AND THE UGLY: GYM GOSSIP AND THE STIGMATIZATION OF FAT BODIES

Several researchers have explored the significance of women's talk to female kin and friendship networks in leisure experiences (Coates 1996; Green et al. 1990; Green 1998; Hey 1997). As Green (1998) argues, women's talk as 'friendship' represents a key site of leisure and a mechanism through which feminine subjectivities are produced and reproduced. Women's and girls' talk includes discourses that simultaneously reflect traditional ideals of femininity and embrace "contradictory or counter discourses of difference" (Green 1998, 183). While, in common parlance, the word gossip has come to refer to derogatory talk about other people's misfortunes closer investigations of gossip reveal it to have both negative and positive functions (Elias and Scotson 1994; McDonald et al. 2007)

Drawing on Elias's ideas about the socio-dynamics of stigmatization it can be argued that gossip tends to stigmatize outsider/other images of feminine beauty and physicality such as those associated with fat bodies. Gossip surrounds various corporeal issues but fat women, in particular, are gossip-worthy because they are widely considered to transgress the norms of fitness and health. Becoming fat however temporarily and whether through excess eating and drinking, illness, injury or pregnancy is also a source of gossip. Fat women can be discredited by defamatory comments about their bodily appearance and performance or what Elias and Scotson (1994) refer to as 'blame gossip.' At the same time 'praise gossip,' in the form of glorification about the body beautiful and regard for

corporeality. In other words dominant images of fit female bodies are founded upon the most extreme beliefs about acceptable appearance and performance that only a few fitness participants achieve (minority of the best). Concomitantly, there is a tendency in gym gossip for images of fat bodies to be modeled on the emotional generalizations about negative aesthetic and performative qualities (minority of the worst).

There is evidence that the selective gossip of the gym culture contributes to a somewhat distorted self-image in the women participants. Many of the criticisms they make of their own, and others', bodies grossly exaggerate their bodily deficiencies particularly in relation to fat. Blame and praise gossip is characterized by internalized emotional modes of thinking about being and becoming fat; a fear of fat. There is a tendency for women to be shamed by their own exercise behavior when it does not meet acceptable levels of workout frequency, intensity or mastery of technique and when their appearance is not within acceptable limits of attractiveness. Charlie illustrated such emotion at work when she talked about her feelings on days when she did not work out. She noted that: "I feel awful on days I don't do it (work out). I run so I won't get fat and so I can eat I suppose. I have to do it or I feel guilty." Another exerciser, Anna, also expressed the intensity of emotion surrounding the problem of fat in her response to a question regarding the importance of exercise saying; "Absolutely very, very, very [important]. I have to go [to the gym] everyday. I feel crap when I am undisciplined and put on weight. That's (fat) absolutely gutting, disgusting."

FEELING 'THE BURN': THE EMBODIMENT OF GROUP CHARISMA AND GROUP DISGRACE

Networks of gossip and the development of narrow definitions of fit female bodies based on images of the minority of the best and worst bodies are related to another mechanism in the process of stigmatization; the development of 'group charisma' and 'group disgrace' (Elias and Scotson 1994). Fit women in fitness gyms embrace a 'group charisma' by virtue of their appearance and ability which are based upon the highly valued traits of independence, physical discipline, mental toughness and (hetero) sex appeal. The language, discourse and values of fitness that are reflected in the media as well as in the organization and practice of fitness cultures tend to favor slimness, hard bodies and ability over fat, soft bodies and inability. Fat women in fitness gyms are endowed with a 'group disgrace' on the basis of their so-called 'flabby' or 'wobbly' bodies and their assumed physical inability.

The production and reproduction of group charisma and group disgrace is connected to feelings of shame and embarrassment that for Elias (2000) are central to human social life (Elias 2000). Goffman (1967, 1973) also makes reference to shame and embarrassment and in his language shame, embarrassment and humiliation are important to the way human beings manage themselves in the face of others. Most important is embarrassment evident in everyday feelings of uneasiness and Goffman provides some rich descriptions of embarrassing situations. However, the opportunity to explore in detail the character of, and relationship between, shame and embarrassment does not appear to be taken in Goffman's (1967, 1973) analysis. In Scheff's view Goffman's account of embarrassment and shame are "fleeting" and only analyzed "in passing" (2004, 238). For Elias (2000) shame, embarrassment and indeed disgust or repugnance characterize a driving affective-mechanism of social control. The main thrust of his analysis of such emotions is that over time, in European societies at least, shame and embarrassment have become increasingly internalized, operating to intensify levels and degrees of self-control in the face of such feelings.

Following Elias's ideas, shame is "a fear of social degradation or, more generally, of other people's gestures of superiority" (Elias 2000, 414–15). Habitual expressions of such shame-fear surrounding being and becoming fat were evident in Helen's experiences of the fitness gym when she said:

> I'm not as slim as I can be . . . or want to be . . . I've got loads of fat to lose. I look at some women. . . . who look great. . . . and I wish I looked like that. I really try to look like them and keep up with them . . . and do what they do . . . then I might be able to be more confident . . . I'm too embarrassed to wear tight clothes or even go to the front of the class . . . you've got to know the routine and look good . . . imagine if you weren't . . . I've never seen anyone (fat) do it.

Sarah, echoed Helen's sentiments and illustrated the internalization and habituation of feelings of shame-fear and corporeal disgust that represent a type of group disgrace when she exclaimed to a friend: "There are one or two women who come down here who look absolutely fabulous. They can make you feel bad . . . you know [horrible, disgusting, fat] . . . I don't know how they do it!" These comments reflect Elias's ideas about shame in that such feelings do not simply represent a conflict between individual women and the prevailing cultural attitudes toward fit and unfit bodies but illustrate that these women's exercise behaviors and their bodies are conflicting with a part of themselves that is aware of and believes in the dominant fitness aesthetic.

Inseparable from shame are feelings of embarrassment. "Embarrassment is displeasure or anxiety which arises when another person threatens to breach, or breaches, society's prohibitions represented by one's own super-ego" (Elias 2000, 418). I have already demonstrated the type of embarrassment that surrounds fat women exercisers as alluded to by some fitness instructors. One female exerciser (Rachel) also expressed a sense of embarrassment about the performances of fat and unfit women saying "I can't see the point of them coming. . . . They don't or can't put the effort in . . . and they sort of stand at the back and don't do much . . . . what's the point . . . it makes me feel a bit embarrassed for them." One further example is provided by another instructor, Anna who noted "this (fitness gym) is not the place if you are fat . . . I feel sorry for them . . . a bit embarrassed . . . it is intimidating." Shame and embarrassment about not achieving idealized female physiques serve to produce collective feelings of disgrace around unfit and fat bodies and mobilize women's exercise and dietary behaviors in their efforts to achieve the body beautiful.

The production of a sense of group disgrace goes hand in hand with the development of a sense of gratification and pride in sharing an appropriate mastery of fitness regimes and a slender and muscularly toned appearance symbolic of feminine body ideals which can be thought of as group charisma. Charlie, for example, explained "I am good at it (working out) and I can do it and I feel really good about that . . . and obviously I do it for the body thing . . . I do it because I am more confident if I am smaller or thinner." The positive feelings evidenced in Charlie's comments reveal the social value of the body beautiful. Improved self-esteem comes with the achievement of a slim, tight physique. Such gains reflect the emotional compensation that some women experience for their efforts in bodily self-restraint and discipline. Feeling good about exercise, as well as looking good when exercising, generates a group charisma. Pride, satisfaction and gratification characterize the collective charisma in the fitness gym. Charisma is also evident in the vocal displays of success that established women express in some exercise settings. In the exercise to music classes, for example, established women who dominate the front of the class sing the words, they whoop, cheer, shout and clap enthusiastically as they perform creating at atmosphere of excitement. Feelings of pleasure are associated with the physical experience of working ones muscles often to the point of fatigue. A psychological 'high' is associated with intense work outs that can produce an immediate or delayed physical 'burning' or 'tingling' sensation in the muscles that many exercisers find pleasurable. Feeling the 'burn' and experiencing excitement, pleasure and fun in the exercise setting is the foundation for the charismatic aspect of the fitness experience. Still, group charisma like group disgrace is produced in relation to the formation of gossip, the internalization of anxieties about being or becoming fat and unfit, and self-control toward bodily discipline of which fitness regimes are a part.

Networks of gossip about female bodies and fatness, the centrality of emotional attachment to the aesthetics and functionality of the body, and the associated development of group charisma and group disgrace extend beyond the immediate environment of the gym. These women are interwoven with the longer gossip chains of the 'exercise body beautiful complex' (Maguire and Mansfield 1998; Mansfield and Maguire 1999;

Mansfield 2002, 2005). The media, for example, are a source of stories and pictures about the exercise and dietary habits of rich, famous, more usually white, western women (Carlisle-Duncan 1994). For the women in this study, stories about female models, singers and actresses who had lost weight (fat), gained fat, and/or sculpted their bodies to improve their (hetero) sexiness provide a source of shared interest in the body. Such personal interest stories are gossip-worthy and are featured in fitness industry magazines reinforcing dominant ideals of (heterosexual) female beauty as well as integrating established women into a fitness culture defined by feelings of repugnance about fat. Eva confirmed the influence of the media as a source of gossip, a provider of knowledge about achieving an acceptable 'look' and its effectiveness in reinforcing both pride and shame about the female body when she said:

> I started buying those slimming magazines. One every month. And I really liked reading those success stories, looking at these pictures of these women who were really fat and had lost 4 stone or something and I loved that and that inspired me and taught me about food values and diets and aerobic exercise and so I got into the body image thing.

Media representations of fat women also tend to pathologize fat and reinforce acceptable images of weight (fat) loss associated with overcoming tragedy, and striving for normality rather than presenting the more self-defined images of those who have fat or are defined as overweight or obese.

Fatness is founded on undesirable characteristics such as passivity, weakness, dependence and unattractive bodies. Fatness and fitness tend to be artificially divided and are considered mutually exclusive corporeal states in fitness cultures. The established ideology of slimness is conflated with ability, perfection and normality in the fitness gym and the production of such body ideals effectively stigmatizes, marginalizes and excludes fat women by assigning collective feelings of shame, embarrassment and disgrace to fatness.

CONCLUSION

It was not my intention in this chapter to compare and contrast Goffman's (1973) ideas about stigma with Elias's theory of the socio-dynamics of stigmatization for understanding the marginal status of fat and fat women in fitness gyms. Goffman's work is significant and there is scope to explore the interplay between bodily stigma, mental and moral stigma and tribal stigma, and face-to-face experiences of embarrassment and humiliation in making sense of the ways that fat bodies are stigmatized in fitness cultures and wider social life. However, in Elias's account of the socio-dynamics of stigmatization there is potential for examining the relationship between the personal emotional experiences of fatness and the broader socio-cultural structures of power that influence the lives of those who are stigmatized for being or becoming fat. The mechanisms of stigmatization in the fitness gym; the monopolization of corporeal power, gossip and taboo and emotional constructions of group charisma and disgrace support and reinforce divisions between fat and slim female bodies and mobilize processes that tend to marginalize/stigmatize fat women. One of the central tenets of the socio-dynamics of stigmatization is the relative character of power in established-outsider relations and while there has been no space to develop the idea, Elias's work can be used to shed light on processes of resistance, challenge and change to dominant anti-fat discourses in the fitness field and other social contexts.

It is not the case that fat is totally abhorred by fitness participants or that fat women are completely excluded from fitness gyms. Some fat women are proud to be big and promote a more positive view of fat bodies and physical activity (Cooper 2009). I have participated in circuit training and spinning (cycling) classes where some of the fittest women are fat. And there are some fitness professionals engaging in pioneering work to promote plus size fitness. On her website, for example, Emma Britton, a U.K.-based plus size health and fitness expert promotes fitness regardless of body shape, size and weight. I would make a call for further research that examines the ways that women defined as fat, overweight or obese experience their physicality. In fitness gyms there appears to be a considerable degree of anxiety, shame and embarrassment about fat female bodies that limits 'fat' as an oppositional image to the preferred ideals of slim, tight physiques. The potential for fat to symbolize a more positive body image is weak. Fitness gyms, especially the commercially orientated ones, are dominated by a cultural distaste for fat that reinforces established conceptions of female bodily perfection and is a site for the stigmatization and marginalization of fat women.

REFERENCES

Burkitt, I. 1999. *Bodies of thought: Embodiment, identity and modernity.* London: Sage.

Carlisle-Duncan, M. 1994. The politics of women's body images and practices: Foucault, the Panopticon and Shape magazine. *Journal of Sport and Social Issues* 18(1): 48–65.

Coates, J. 1996. *Women talk.* Blackwell: Oxford.

Cole, C. 1993. Resisting the canon: Feminist cultural studies, sport and technologies of the body. *Journal of Sport and Social Issues* 17(2): 77–97.

——— 2002. Body studies in the sociology of sport. In J. Coakley and E. Dunning, eds. *Handbook of Sport Studies* 439–61. London: Sage.

Cooper, C. 2009. Fat girl on a bike: Introducing Health at Every Size. Paper Presented at the LSA Annual Conference. July 7–9. Canterbury. UK.

Elias, N. 1978. *What is sociology?* London: Hutchinson.

—— 1998. *On civilization, power and knowledge.* London and Chicago: University of Chicago Press:

—— 2000. *The civilising process: Sociogenetic and psychogenetic investigations.* Oxford: Blackwell.

Elias, N. and J. Scotson. 1994. *The established and the outsiders.* London: Sage.

Featherstone, M. 1991. The body in consumer culture. In M. Featherstone, M. Hepworth and B. Turner, eds. *The body: Social process and cultural theory,* 170–97. London: Sage.

Gard, M. and Wright, J. 1995. *The obesity epidemic: Science, morality and ideology.* London: Routledge.

Goffman, E. 1967. *Interaction ritual.* New York: Anchor.

—— 1973. *Stigma: Notes on the management of spoiled identity.* Harmondsworth: Penguin.

Green, E. 1998. 'Women doing friendship': An analysis of women's leisure as a site of identity construction, empowerment and resistance. *Leisure Studies* 17: 171–85.

Green, E., S. Hebron and D. Woodward. 1990. *Women's leisure, what leisure?* London: Macmillan.

Hargreaves, J. 2000. *Heroines of sport: The politics of difference and identity.* London: Routledge.

Hey, V. 1997. *The company she keeps: An ethnography of girls' friendships.* Buckingham: Open University Press

Lupton, D. 1996. *Food, the body and the self.* London: Sage.

—— 1997. *The imperative of health: Public health and the regulated body.* London: Sage

McDonald, K., M. Putallaz, C. Grimes, J. Kupersmidt and J. Coie. 2007. Girl talk: Gossip, friendship and sociometric status. *Merrill-Palmer Quarterly* 53(3): 381–411.

Maguire, J. and L. Mansfield. 1998. 'No-body's perfect'. Women, aerobics and the body beautiful. *Sociology of Sport Journal* 15: 109–37.

Mansfield, L. 2002. Feminist thought and figurational (process) sociology. In J. Maguire and K. Young, eds. *Theory, sport and society,* 317–35. London. JAI Elsevier Science.

—— 2005. Gender power and identities in the fitness gym: Towards a sociology of the 'exercise body beautiful complex'. PhD Dissertation. Loughborough University.

—— 2007. Involved-detachment: A balance of passion and reason in feminisms and gender-related research in sport, tourism and sports tourism. *Journal of Sport and Tourism* 12(2): 115–42.

—— 2008. Reconsidering feminisms and the work of Norbert Elias for understanding gender, sport and sport-related activities. *European Physical Education Review* 14(1): 93–121.

—— 2009a. 'Sexercise': Heterosexuality and femininity in Jane Fonda's fitness books 1980–90. Paper presented at the British Sociological Association one-day conference Sexy Spaces: Leisure and Geography Intersectionalities. May 22, in Brighton, UK.

—— 2009b. Fit bodies and intersectionality: The experiences of older Indian women. Paper presented at the LSA Annual Conference July 7th–9th, in Canterbury, UK.

Mansfield, L. and J. Maguire. 1999. Active women, power relations and gendered identities: Embodied experiences of aerobics. In Sasha Roseneil and Julie Seymour, eds. *Practising identities: Power and resistance*, 81–107. London: Macmillan.

Markula, P. 1995. *Firm but shapely, fit but sexy, strong but thin: The postmodern* aerobicizing female bodies. *Sociology of Sport Journal* 12: 424–533.

Mennell, S. 1992. *Norbert Elias. An introduction.* Oxford: Blackwell.

Monaghan, L. 2008. *Men and the war on obesity: A sociological study.* London: Routledge.

Oliver, M. 1990. *The politics of disablement.* London: Macmillan.

Rich, E., L. Monaghan and L. Aphramor, eds. 2009. *Expanding the obesity debate*, London: Palgrave.

Sands, R. 2002. *Sport ethnography.* Leeds: Human Kinetics Publishers.

Scheff, T. 2004. Elias, Freud and Goffman: Shame as the master emotion. In S. Loyal and S. Quilley, eds. *The Sociology of Norbert Elias*, 229–45. Cambridge: Polity.

Shilling, C. 1993. *The body and social theory.* London: Sage.

Smith Maguire, J., L. Mansfield and H. Curtis. 2009. Fat Bodies in Sport and Leisure: Discourses of Resistance and Change? Paper presented at the LSA Annual Conference July 7–July 9, in Canterbury, UK.

Solovay, S. and E. Rothblum. eds. 2009. *The fat studies reader*, New York: New York University Press.

Tomrley, C. and A. Kaloski-Naylor, eds. 2009. *Fat studies in the UK.* York, Raw Nerve Books.

Turner, B. 1996. *The body and society.* 2nd ed. London: Sage.

Van Krieken, R. 1998. *Norbert Elias.* London: Routledge.

Wheaton, B. 2002. Babes on the beach, women in the surf: Researching gender, power and difference in the windsurfing culture. In *Power games: A critical sociology of sport*, eds. J. Sugden and A. Tomlinson, 240–66. London: Routledge.

5 I Am (Not) Big . . . It's the Pictures that Got Small

Examining Cultural and Personal Exercise Narratives and the Fear of Fat

Kerry R. McGannon, Christina R. Johnson and John C. Spence

Media representations of health and fitness are often framed within obesity epidemic, fear of fatness and moral panic discourses (Boero 2007; Bonfiglioli et al. 2007; Saguy and Almeling 2008; Saguy and Riley, 2005). However, a growing body of critical literature (e.g., Bovey 2000; Brabazon 2006; Campos et al. 2006; Evans-Braziel and LeBesco 2001; LeBesco 2004; Throsby 2007; Tischner and Malson 2008) challenges morality-based fears around fatness and overweight at cultural and individual levels. Such literature argues for the revaluing and politicization of fat bodies: one can be "fit and fat" and/or not all women's fitness needs to focus on thinness. Moreover, this scholarship is important because it deconstructs taken-for-granted assumptions associated with fitness and fatness so that healthy and empowering forms of physical activity for women can be located.

How can we further deconstruct and understand fitness and morality narratives surrounding women's bodies to make healthful representations of physical activity more likely and more frequently connected to positive self-related views? The purpose of this chapter is to use feminist post-structuralism (Gavey 1997; Henriques et al. 1998; Hollway 1989; Weedon 1997) to explore the impact of media representations of fit bodies on women's exercise participation. To first provide a context for women's exercise experiences, we outline how the media constructs women's fitness. We then discuss our post-structuralist theoretical position before presenting the case study method to examine one woman's experiences with a pursuit to become fit. We then explore the links between subject positions constructed by media discourses and personal/individual identities in relation to exercise through our findings. We conclude by discussing the implications of what we learned about how subject positions can be constructed against fitness and health-related media discourses.

CONSTRUCTING WOMEN'S EXERCISE THROUGH THE MEDIA

Previous literature on media representations of fit feminine bodies typically find three interrelated themes: the ideal, fit feminine body is characterized narrowly as thin, toned and young; the ideal fit body is intertwined with the notion of health, and the responsibility for obtaining such a body is left to the individual women. We will now discuss each of these themes separately to provide context for individual's exercise experiences. To illustrate our discussion, we provide examples from women's exercise and weightloss narratives within a special interest section (i.e., ACCENT) in a Midwestern U.S. newspaper (i.e., *Cedar Rapids Gazette*, Iowa) (McGannon et al. 2008).

ACCENT: THE IDEAL FIT, FEMININE BODY

Several feminist researchers have demonstrated that a 'perfect body' is closely connected to fitness and ideal femininity. Such body shape emphasizes thinness and tightly toned muscles (Bordo 1993; Choi 2000; Duncan 1994; Krane et al. 2004; Lloyd 1996; Markula 1995, 2003). In addition, gendered exercises (e.g., aerobics, lifting light weights) are often promoted as the means to achieve the ideal. For example, the ACCENT section in a local newspaper revealed a particular vision of feminine exercise with such tag lines as 'Benefits of belly dancing,' 'Dance-based fitness classes are back' and 'Tomorrow: Ballet-inspired styles are graceful, feminine and tutu cute.'

Through these texts, women's fitness is closely aligned with dance which is established as a feminine style of exercise. In addition, images accompanying exercise articles (re)produced similar understandings as they drew upon appearance, weight loss and heteronormative discourses. For example, an article title "Give your arms, shoulders a lift: Ladies work out an upper body routine" pictured a young, white, blonde woman wearing a tight leotard. She demonstrated 'proper form' holding light weights and is shown from the side, revealing her flat stomach and large breasts. Here fitness was equated with weight loss, appearance, youth and 'feminine' forms of exercise (e.g., lifting light weights). Women are also positioned as helpless and unsure of how to exercise properly within these discourses, thus reinforcing particular notions of 'woman's exercise.'

In addition, the body ideal emphasizes a young, white, middle-upper class and heterosexual femininity. Women's exercise is often sold at the promise of 'landing a man' or being in a successful relationship with a man if results are achieved (i.e., doing it right, achieving appearance goals) (Hollway 1983; Weedon 1997). For example, in the ACCENT column an article titled "Raise the bar with Smith Machine" was accompanied by a picture of a white, blonde and youthful woman, wearing a form-fitting leotard, squatting, buttocks lifted on the Smith Machine. The article explained:

> You want to get strong, lean and lithe? Set your sights on Smith—the Smith Machine. Yes, it's that ominous looking large machine sporting a fixed bar across its middle. Don't let it scare you . . . Smith may just be the safe, secure and stable partner you've always wanted to be set up with.
>
> (ACCENT February 21, 2005, 3E)

Within these articles, women are depicted as small, weak and polite, whose femininity is naturalized by a particular expression of heterosexuality. Women were also naturalized as weaker partners whose subject position is that of an emotional, irrational and ignorant woman (e.g., "*don't let your impulsive heart overwhelm* the common sense of your cool, logical head"; "*Yes, it's that ominous looking large machine* sporting a fixed bar across its middle. *Don't let it scare you*"). Such positioning accomplishes particular social objectives (Hollway 1989, 1983) to reinforce gendered relations, to reinforce that women's bodies are flawed when falling outside of 'femininity,' and to sell particular products/forms of exercise to women to achieve femininity.

As demonstrated through previous literature, such constructions of fitness, exercise and femaleness make specific kinds of selves and ways of being—sites of subjectivity or subject positions (e.g., 'feminine women' are small and graceful and need help with their exercise) —while subordinating others (e.g., 'feminine women' can be large, strong and muscular and knowledgeable about their exercise). The 'improper bodies' in fitness media tend to be positioned as imperfect and depart from ideal femininity by being too fat, too muscular, too thin, too old, and/or not white and heterosexual (Day and Keys 2008; Evans-Braziel and LeBesco 2001; Krane et al. 2004; Markula 1995; Tischner and Malson 2008).

ACCENT: RISKY BEHAVIOR/RISKY BUSINESS

Several researchers demonstrate that news stories tend to generate fear surrounding fatness and/or lack of weight loss by positioning exercise and women's bodies within risk of life-threatening disease (Boero 2007; Murray 2008; Saguy and Riley 2005). This fear of illness further legitimates constructions of 'women's exercise' as a weight management tool, as it is not solely about appearance and vanity, but about being healthy and disease-free. Saguy and Riley (2005) called this a risky behavior framing, whereby news stories on obesity positioned inactivity as immoral and something to be feared. Therefore, fat, overweight and/or sedentary bodies are read as evidence of willfully 'catching' preventable illness and thus, being 'fat' is constructed as a moral failure. Such articles around obesity continue to position women as weak, flawed, at risk and in need of fixing. They assume an ethical duty by drawing attention to preventing further cases, even if this might worsen stigma associated with 'fat' bodies. Framing obesity and inactivity as risky behavior also implies the need for *individual* education and action, with women, positioned as ignorant, irrational and in need of expert help. Additionally, lifestyle behaviors such as exercise are portrayed as under one's control or should be controlled with 'help.' Therefore, women can (and should) personally control their body weight and appearance via adoption of such behaviors (Bonfiglioli et al. 2007).

In the following ACCENT story "Fine-tuning: Fitness routine makeovers for 2005—Tips from a pro" depicts that by not exercising women risk a life-threatening disease:

> Goal: she would like to lose another 17 pounds, which would put her at a healthy weight for her height. She hopes that in reaching her goal weight, she can lower her blood pressure and cholesterol levels enough to go off medications. "When I was younger, it was all about how I looked and today it's about health . . ."

Another story excerpt entitled "Pre-diabetes should not be disregarded" uses scientific research and medical authority to legitimate risk-claims of overweight and fatness and attributes these into a failure of an individual to follow proper diet, adequate exercise and exercise self-control:

> What's the big deal? Ignore "pre-diabetes" and you will probably go on to develop full-blown type 2 diabetes for which there is no cure. Solid research has identified five behavior changes that can prevent or delay the onset of diabetes: If you are overweight, lose at least 5 percent of our current weight. That's just five pounds for every hundred pounds you weigh . . .

Both article excerpts position exercise primarily as a form of weight control and the means by which women can literally exercise individualized control over their health. Using a feminist post-structuralist lens allows us to extend understandings of how such representations of exercise and women's bodies may have implications for self-related views and subjectivity.

THEORETICAL CONTEXT: FEMINIST POST-STRUCTURALISM

In this chapter, we draw upon feminist post-structuralism as informed by cultural theorist Chris Weedon (1997). Weedon suggested post-structuralism provides a useful foundation for feminist practice, describing feminist post-structuralism as "a mode of knowledge production which uses post-structuralist theories of language, subjectivity, social processes and institutions to understand existing power relations and to identify areas and strategies for change" (1997, 40–41). Central to our analyses and discussion of the personal story/case are the following ideas: 1) self and subjectivity are constituted in language and discourse (i.e., the self is a discursive accomplishment); 2) language and discourse are therefore of interest in understanding what people hold to be true about themselves and others and 3) exploring the self as a discursive accomplishment requires a consideration of how power (i.e., social processes) allows for the acceptance and validation of some forms of self-related knowledge over others.

Weedon's ideas are grounded in Foucault's (1978) concept of discourse whereby language is always located in discourse. Discourse can be understood as providing the meanings—in the case of our research examples particular meanings about "thin," "fat," "overweight" and "women's exercise"—that constitute people's everyday practices (e.g., what people think, feel and say about themselves in relation to exercise, the type of exercise one does and/or the types of exercise one avoids). Thus, discourses not only "systematically form the objects of which they speak" (Foucault 1978, 49) but they have material/concrete implications for bodies and embodiment (Markula et al. 2008).

To understand the role and impact of discourse in women's everyday lives, Weedon places primacy on understanding how discourses offer competing and (potentially) contradictory ways of giving meaning to the world and how we view ourselves. Some scholars name these *subject positions* of options that individuals take up (Davies and Harré 1990; Hollway 1989; Weedon 1997; Willig 2000). These positions are conditions of possibility for constituting subjectivity (selves, identities, understandings of the world) and vary in terms of the power they afford people (Weedon 1997). Philosophers/discourse theorists Davies and Harré's explanation of a subject position parallels Weedon's ideas:

> A subject position incorporates both a conceptual repertoire and a location for persons within the structure of rights for those that use that repertoire. Once having taken up a particular position as one's own, a person inevitably sees the world from the vantage point of that position and in terms of the particular images, metaphors, storylines and concepts which are made relevant within the particular discursive practice in which they are positioned. At least a possibility of notional choice is inevitably involved because there are many and contradictory discursive practices that each person could engage in.
> (Davies and Harré 1990, 46)

In exercise contexts women, regardless of their size and shape, acquire a sense of self and subjectivity and interpret the world from a particular perspective by participating in discursive practices that allocate meanings to particular categories (e.g., thin/fat, fit female body/unfit female body, exerciser/non-exerciser). The self is then positioned in relation to the storylines articulated around those categories and people have particular psychological and emotional experiences associated with that world view (Davies and Harré 1990).

Earlier we noted that a "fat is bad; thin is good" doctrine permeates fitness and exercise discourse. Such discourses are further reinforced as factual via the use of rhetorical strategies (e.g., statistics, quoting of experts, metaphors) within scientific, medical and morality discourses. By constructing "fat," "thin" and "fit" within such discourses, the primary subject position (i.e., storyline, image and identity) in relation to those categories available for women is that of a flawed, undisciplined woman whose body is unhealthy and in need of fixing (McGannon and Busanich 2010; McGannon and Spence 2010). At the same time, the meaning of "exercise" emerges within scientific discourse primarily as a disciplining and weightloss tool for bodies—whether fat or thin—that women can and *should* use to take control of, and fix, their flawed selves. Women positioned within such discourses may experience shame, loathing, fear and guilt in relation to their bodies—regardless of their size and regardless of whether or not they are exercising (McGannon and Spence 2010).

Research suggests that women's participation in fitness and exercise is extremely complex with women resisting the current body ideal in varying degrees (Brabazon 2006; Haravon Collins 2002; Krane et al. 2004; Markula 2003; Markula and Pringle 2006; McGannon and Spence 2010). How and why this is the case may relate to women literally *exercising* agency via the tactical usage of discourses to negotiate a new and different subject position. For example, in their study of women self-identifying as "large," Tischner and Malson showed that women *actively* rejected imposed subject positions of "lazy gluttons who sit there all day" (2008, 265). Additionally, women were able to renegotiate the meaning of surveillance in relation to their bodies, playing an active role in the politics of visibility. Resistance to dominant discourses was accomplished by women positioning their larger bodies as members of a community that is nourished, accepted and an advocate for other large women within health and wellness discourses. Viewed in this way, while the site of subjectivity one occupies in a discourse carries with it conventions as to how one will think, feel and behave, individuals are not passive and have some choice when positioning themselves in discourses (Weedon 1997).

Women can (and do) negotiate new subject positions by refusing the current dominant ones and taking up alternative physical activities (e.g., recreational physical activity or sport). Feminist post-structuralist scholars such as Weedon (1997) therefore advocate that the power/discourse nexus can be confronted and resisted by taking up a new or different subject position within discourse. Research on larger athletic women's experiences of their bodies as healthy, fit, powerful, strong, empowered and capable—as opposed to flawed, unfeminine or weak (Chase 2008; Krane et al. 2004; Scott-Dixon 2008)—further underscores the notion of positioning within discourse as a source of understanding how women might resist, change or transform disempowering discourses.

Using Weedon's (1997) feminist post-structuralism, therefore, allows us to understand how women may experience exercise against the backdrop of dominant discourses that morally position the self and exercise primarily within weight loss, appearance and risk of illness discourses. We identified several research questions. First, do women internalize fear and guilt of dominant discourses, and if so, what are the effects for women's subjectivity and lives? If women can and do resist dominant discourses, how do they do so and what are the effects for their subjectivity and lives? In order to answer these questions, we go on to explore how an individual woman constructs a subject position through exercise. In the following section we introduce our method: a critical feminist case-study (Reinharz 1992; Stake 2005) that explores the lived exercise experience of one woman, 52-year-old 'Vivian' or 'Viv,' through personal narratives.[1]

METHOD

Vivian's narratives were drawn from nine interviews that occurred weekly during a 10-week exercise intervention conducted by author Christina Johnson (Johnson 2005). Viv's narratives were drawn from a case-study project that was constructed in keeping with the feminist goal to end sexist oppression (hooks 1984). Vivian and Christina were co-participants in a service outreach project for a seminar course in Christina's doctoral coursework. Vivian was recruited from a convenience sample as a representative of a population of interest (peri- and post-menopausal women). The broader goals of the service project were to understand and promote physical activity in the community. Vivian's case took on the characteristics of an intrinsic case study (Stake 2005). As is typical for intrinsic casework, Vivian's case was previously identified for Christina. In this instance, Vivian and Christina were paired by a faculty supervisor. A description of Vivian's experience was not directed toward theory building or describing abstract phenomena. Instead, Vivian's case was taken on because "[the researcher] wants better understanding of this particular case" (Stake 2005, 445).

The case-study approach is fitting within a feminist post-structuralist analytic framework for a number of reasons. Weedon proposed feminist post-structuralism as a theory "which can address forms of social organization and the social meanings and values which guarantee or contest them (the forms of social organization)" (1997, 12). Weedon's feminist post-structuralism also forms the grounds for a theory of individual con-sciousness by providing analytic insights into the interconnectedness of language, discourse and subjectivity. To the extent that an individual takes on a system of meanings and values, she is said to have adopted a particular subjectivity or subject position. Case-study work allows for "close attention to the influence of [the case's] social, political, and other context" (Stake 2005, 444). This focus on the case as embedded within broader contexts is congruent with the post-structuralist goal to examine the ways social and discursive forces work on the construction of per-sonal narratives.

Although a case-study approach to gathering narratives does not exclu-sively promote a feminist post-structuralist analytic strategy, narratives drawn from case-studies can be used in that way. Vivian's narratives stemmed from an in-depth examination of her attitudes, beliefs, and val-ues with regard to physical activity. Her accounts went beyond physical activity, as she indicated the interconnectedness of exercise with other areas of her life. By examining Vivian's narratives from a feminist post-structuralist perspective, it is possible to examine what Weedon terms, "subjectivity in process" (1997, 86) in which certain types of subjectivity are adopted, reiterated and enacted while others are resisted.

It is at this point in the chapter that a shift in voice is necessary. Many feminist theoretical positions advocate recognizing the diversity of voices and experiences among women (Mohanty 1988; Trinh 1989). A move-ment within qualitative research toward reflexive and reflective writing arose in parallel to the recommendations of feminist scholars to recognize multiple voices and multiple experiences, (Fine 1992; Fine et al. 2000; Lincoln 1997). Correspondingly, I (Christina) find my own voice intri-cately interwoven in our (Viv's and my own) narrative. To the extent that feminist post-structuralist work seeks to examine the ways in which individuals enact and articulate subject positions (Weedon 1997), my (Christina's) own position as author becomes very important. Following my growing feminist ideals (Tierney and Lincoln 1997; Wolf 1992) we had agreed that Viv would play an active role in our project and voice her own experiences.

Each of our sessions lasted approximately one hour. We focused largely on Viv's progress maintaining an exercise program. Viv and I often talked about other topics such as work, stress, religion, musical activities and her personal relationships. Viv did not view physical activity in isolation from the rest of her life. Her views on exercise were embedded in her day-to-day practices, even if actual physical movement was not part of her day-to-day life. Because Viv's talk about physical activity was deeply interwoven with talk about other topics, I transcribed Viv's narratives verbatim and examined them as a whole.

Although Vivian never discussed reading ACCENT (a section from the local paper) directly, she was a self-proclaimed 'news junkie' and an active consumer of news information via newspapers, television, and Internet sources. Because of this, my choice to focus on ACCENT as a cultural site of analysis in conjunction with Viv's personal narratives is appropriate. By juxtaposing some of the narratives that emerge from ACCENT, particularly the ideal fit, feminine body and risk narratives, with Viv's own narratives, I explore the ways in which Viv took on certain subject positions and resisted others (Weedon 1997).

Vivian: The Ideal, Fit, Feminine Body

Viv seemed to be glaringly aware of the idealized fit, feminine form and often referred to my shape in that way. Frequently, her comments of, 'Look at you, strong-skinny, marathoning, martial-arts girl' left me feeling both flattered and vaguely uncomfortable. Viv's adoption of a vision of her ideal self reflected exercise narratives evident in ACCENT and many other cultural contexts including Hollywood movies, television and print media (Evans-Braziel and LeBesco 2001). During our early sessions, Viv and I talked about movies frequently. Viv compared our "walking adventures" to the latest James Bond picture that she and her partner had seen:

> It's so sexy. Its like a teenage boy's wet dream, the way Bond is tough, and sporty, and always right, and always . . . always gets the girl. We could be like Bond girls . . . out here adventuring through the streets.

Viv overlooked that neither of us outwardly appeared like the more recent Bond girls. While Viv's talk centered on what counts as sexy; she offered a thoroughly entrenched notion that where she was at the time was not sexy, and perhaps not even adequate.

Viv frequently stated, "I want my body back" and referred to herself as a "worn out, but tough old broad." During a later session, Vivian declared, again, "I want my body back" and flashed a picture of herself at age 18, thin, smiling, and standing on a mountain top with her hair blowing in the wind. She continued, "This is my goal . . . look at me, I was beautiful, powerful, I could do anything, I could climb mountains . . ." and then broke into a chorus of "Climb Every Mountain." When she finished, out of breath, she gasped, "Life was so perfect then. Look at me now." I read Viv's futilely narrow vision of perfect self—18 years old, before the decades had exacted a toll on her body—against her physical form at age 52. Viv had begun to indicate a clear distinction between her vision of a perfect self which looked very much like popular media portrayals of ideal femininity and her actual, transgressive self. She had developed a subject position as being the owner of a flawed body. Much like Davies and Harré suggest, she "inevitably [saw] the world from the vantage point of that position" (1990, 46), the position of a woman with a flawed body.

Viv further took on the position that her body was inadequate. In her repeated comments about my physique, she acknowledged my body as more perfect—at age 24, I had never experienced major injury, illness, or weight gain. And Viv, although quite agile, reiterated her self image as weak and at risk for injury with the following comments:

> When we walk outside in the winter, it's nice, you know? The temperature is right for me . . . in the summer it's too hot, you're gonna die of heat stroke if you go out in that humidity crap . . . But the ice in the winter. I'm gonna fall and break a hip if we keep this up. I'm 52 years old. Ladies my age break! But, we're [walking] together, I'll grab your arm. That's why I don't do this alone. I'd fall and die in a snow bank.

However, Viv's characterization of herself as a transgressive body deepened as our story wove on. She struggled to find a comfortable place for exercise. In subtle ways, she used her struggle to resist dominant exercise regimes. A simple solution for Viv to resolve her exercise conundrum would have been to invest in mainstream approaches. She could have purchased a gym membership, visited one of the area's free indoor tracks, or joined the legions of mall-walkers in the area's two major shopping centers. Yet, in response to my question about finding a place indoors to exercise, she expressed conflict as follows:

> I've got a friend, mother of three, full-time job, full-time husband, family . . . she's got it all. She goes down to the track at the rec center and walks for an hour every day. Her kids in a jogger out in front, and one trailing behind. And I say, why can't I have that? [Int: Why can't you?] (Laughing) Because I can't! I just can't. [Int: Are there other . . .] I can't go with those old ladies at the mall. I'm not an old lady. I can't be part of 'mommy-time' at the track. (voice takes an edge) I just can't. And the gym . . . that's nothing but a meat market. Nobody wants an old broad on the treadmill. [Int: So . . .] So I'll just trudge along. Venture out when the weather's nice. Feel guilty when it isn't.

At first, Vivian's resistance to mainstream exercise and her dedication to "wanting her body back" appeared irrational to me; she wanted desperately to gain fitness and lose fat, but rejected available fitness contexts as not suiting her needs. Her emotions spanned guilt, anger, fatigue and a sense of futility that deepened the more she discussed exercise. By looking more deeply, however, Viv's resistance to mainstream exercise practices indicates to me that her discontent with her physical self was outweighed by her discontent with the cultural, social and physical resources available to her. Her repeated comments of "I can't . . . I just can't . . ." when discussing contexts in which other women exercise can be read as a form of resistance to the cultural norms that romanticize one's relationship with exercise and exercise equipment and enforce those norms by reminding women, repeatedly, of the ways in which their bodies transgress from a narrow image of perfection.

Viv may not have been able or prepared to articulate resistance to the dominant portrayals of women's fitness. Media sources like ACCENT almost exclusively provide the message that women's perfect bodies *must* exercise to fulfill their moral duty of achieving slenderness, gracefulness and occupying as little space as possible (Bordo 1993; Choi 2000; Duncan 1994; Krane et al. 2004; Lloyd 1996; Markula 1995, 2003). Further, when women exercise, sources like ACCENT provide evidence that women are weak, silly and at risk of injury. In Viv's case, these ubiquitous discourses about women's fitness left her with little choice about how to view her physical activity in relation to her self.

Moments of resistance, like Vivian's in which exercise is refused, cannot be accounted for in the news media. Because of this, women who refuse dominant exercise practices like walking on indoor tracks, joining fitness clubs or even walking the interiors of shopping malls, are silenced. Further silenced are women who choose to exercise for reasons other than attaining and maintaining the physical markers of ideal femininity. At worst, the subject positions of women who do not choose traditional fitness practices are denied by the media. At best, women—both those who do not exercise and those who do—are portrayed as faulty, flawed and in need of fixing. Following the analytic suggestions of Weedon (1997) and Hollway (1983) Viv's narratives demonstrated an internalization of the discourse that ideal selves were women who ascribed to traditional exercise practices and thereby developed toned, slender bodies. Further, Viv's adoption of a subject position as flawed and transgressive comes through in her repetition of "I want my body back." Finally, the incongruence between her internalized vision of perfect and her positioning as transgressive led her to considerable distress.

FEAR, GUILT, INADEQUACY

By repeating "I want my body back" I saw Viv's investment in the moralizing body ideal discourses that accompany news coverage of physical activity. She did not, or perhaps could not, articulate that women's exercise was constructed in the media and consumed by women in very troubling ways. Instead, Viv seized the power to resist exercise itself. Such resistance was not consistent; at times she seemed very much to want to exercise, while at times she refused. During our meetings, Viv walked along, with acquiescence. However, she expressed resistance by saying, "I wouldn't be doing this (walking) if it weren't for you and these little forced marches." Her resistance was not clear—when she did not exercise, she described feeling "wonderfully lazy" and suggested "isn't it grand to spend Saturday morning drinking coffee and reading the paper [instead of walking]." In separate instances, she described feeling "guilt, guilt about everything" and said, "I'm the most happy when I'm moving, feel better about myself, can do my day without guilt for that one day. But that's only if I can get out the door and get moving that day."

In ACCENT, products and expert advice are rhetorical strategies that reinforce women as flawed and in need of help. The same products and services are offered as a means to fix or control slothful and flawed bodies to be desirable to the opposite sex. These solutions in ACCENT target a class of women who have both leisure time and money by recommending gym memberships, products and services with the aim of achieving an idealized self. Viv's reality did not look so simple.

Guilt and Conflict

Vivian sought solutions. Since she feared the ice on the sidewalks, and found the indoor track was not a realistic option, Vivian purchased a set of winter spikes she could wear over her shoes for traction. She did not wear them. I read this as another form of resistance. Although the newspaper/ACCENT narratives suggested that by purchasing a product, exercise problems could be solved, Vivian had not yet found resolution. Despite the promise of resolution in the daily news, Viv's lack of resolution solidified into a sense of futility and frustration mixed with unreasonable goals. In our penultimate session, Viv stated,

> What is IT all about? What's the deal? What is it? I just can't figure what it all means.
> What *it* means. Why we exercise, why we work. Why *it's* all so futile. Maybe that's *it,* futility. Futility. That's all there is. No fairytale castle, no happy ending.

Yet in an email follow-up from her last session, she wrote,

> These are the things I know from our time together . . . and the fact that I feel better . . . maybe even a little hopeful . . . that I REALLY WILL get rid of 60 lbs before too much longer. (Oh yes, during our time together my cholesterols got in the right order and the blood pressure came down to 110/70. . . . just in time for the new guidelines!)

And near the end of 10 weeks, Viv said:

> I guess when we first started [walking], I was borrowing your energy. You asked me last time about doing things for outside reasons. I

guess I do. I walk because you're here to make me. I couldn't do it on my own, so, I borrowed your body. Don't worry, I'll give it back. I just keep thinking, like "(singing) Someday my prince will come" only its "Someday my clothes will fit!" It's the Disney version of exercise, right? Everything will turn out OK in the end. For now, I'm borrowing your body, but I'll get my own body back. I want my body back.

By this time, Vivian had conceded to exercise but she had not yet begun to critique the ways in which exercise was framed. But she had ceased to resist the practice of exercise. It did not feel like a victory to me. Although she was willing to walk, Vivian's concession seemed as if she had been "strong-armed" (ACCENT February 21, 2005, 3E) into the activity and I had been the agent in charge of assuring her compliance. My own guilt, first for my inability to help her toward her goals and second for my contribution to her mounting sense of frustration and futility, was deeper than ever.

Toward the end our time together and without suggestion from me, Viv had begun logging her progress. In doing so, Viv engaged in the self-monitoring practices/process encouraged by the dominant discourses about exercise. Such monitoring was a source of great guilt for her but it also marked her growing acceptance of dominant exercise practices. Although she talked about not keeping the log because she found herself angst-ridden over it, she insisted that it was the "right thing" to do:

Guilt . . . its everywhere, isn't it? I don't walk, the calendar is blank and I think to myself, "Oh my god, what have I done?" It's like that scene in *The Hours* where she steps into the river and drowns herself. Its like my mind just closes in on me, and I can't function. So, I'm breaking the rules. My new motto is this: an inch is as good as a mile. For my meager little 10 minutes of walking, this week I put a big fat W on the calendar. And I refuse to feel guilty about it. So that's better, right? To walk a little and not feel guilty? Do I get to not feel guilty?

Vivian's guilt indicates the power of discourse. Women who have failed at sustaining an exercise program, experience real emotional consequences such as guilt. This leads to an internalization of the self as inadequate and flawed (Weedon, 1997).

Vivian: Risky Business/Risky Behavior

On numerous occasions, Vivian expressed fear of exercise, reiterating a popular media discourse that exercise is inherently a risky behavior. Repeatedly, Viv expressed fear of icy sidewalks. She spoke from the limited subject position of a weak woman—a subject position I had yet to experience—and so, I gave argument. When she repeated her sense of being at risk when exercising, I pushed for solutions. I was stymied when another element of risk and fear surfaced.

While we walked in the park one sunny Saturday morning, Viv constructed a fear of finding a dead body—"a woman raped and murdered"—in the trees, and potentially becoming the next victim. Vivian's fears, whether rational or irrational, reinforced her investment in a discourse of risk. She had come to see her body as flawed and herself as a victim—of broken bones on icy sidewalks, of heat exhaustion or of a random act of violence. By coupling the risky business of exercise with the risk of sedentary behavior, Viv emphasized a fear of becoming a victim of cardiovascular disease. She constructed an explicit fear of lethal fat:

> . . . what gets me out the door [to walk]? It's the big guy . . . you know the one, Mr. Grim Reaper . . . with the cape and sickle. I could stroke out at any minute, I'm heart disease waiting to happen. I work in the hospital, I've seen it happen, I know what fat can do and it's scary. So, fear. Fear motivates me.

Viv's fears indicate her investment in the complicated, contradictory discourses found in ACCENT and similar media sources that exercise is risky but sedentary behavior is equally risky. Viv adopted a position accepting that she was at risk by exercising *and* by being sedentary.

Viv's fears could be seen as a form of resistance to exercise and all of the potential subject positions that accompanied exercise (Weedon 1997). She expressed and was hindered by a fear of icy sidewalks and corpses in the park. Because of this, fear provided a reason to avoid exercise. The fear and the paralysis that flowed from it were grounds for an array of secondary emotional consequences including guilt and frustration. In the end, Vivian's fears were reinforced when she succumbed to injury. Having suffered chronic shoulder pain from a torn rotator cuff, she elected to have surgery to repair the tear. Although her walking nearly ceased after the surgery, her reflections did not:

> . . . Just futility. Think of the bullshit they start feeding you when you're a kid. Just keep going, and it'll all be OK. But here I am, 52 years old, gonna die of a heart attack with my arm in a sling. I kept going, and it's not OK.

Viv's tirade on the "bullshit they start feeding you when you're a kid" could be understood as a rejection of mainstream discourses on women's bodies and exercise and the available subject positions for women to make meaning of exercise experiences.

Vivian's disillusionment transcended her exercise experiences. She expressed a sense of powerlessness about her hobbies and her job. She and I even reflected on our sense of powerlessness about our national political situation—which at the time, we agreed, seemed to be using a rhetoric of fear and the threat of a repeated terrorist attack to paralyze the voting populace. Yet her sense of futility, frustration and fear about exercise and weight loss were most evident in our conversations. Viv met her mantras of "I want my body back" with reassurances of "An inch is as good as a mile," "so I can do my day without guilt" and 10 minutes of walking is better than no minutes." Yet, she did not see the progress promised to her in the fitness pages of the local paper.

FROM EXERCISE TO MOVEMENT

Viv joked, "What gets me to exercise? The M&M's (candies) in my desk drawer. They helped me get through the day, but now they're threatening to kill me if I don't go for a walk." Even in jest, Vivian reproduced a narrative in which food is lethal, and eating certain kinds of food is bad, and therefore the responsibility of women to police and control. And, although exercise might be risky, fat is fatal. Viv showed sparks of resistance to dominant fitness discourses first by refusing exercise. Later, she began to critique how exercise was framed by insisting that she would not allow herself to feel guilty, even if she only walked for 10 minutes. She marked her calendar in exactly the same way as if she had walked for 30 minutes. It was much later that spring when Viv and I finally settled on a new means of resistance. Viv decided to reject exercise and the discourses associated with it, and instead to move. In a follow-up to our sessions, she composed an email as follows:

> Thank you for instigating the movement that brought me my little Guilt-Away diddie: AN INCH IS AS GOOD AS A MILE. Thank you for the experience of talking about movement (notice I didn't say exercise) while moving. How holistic. And what a luxury . . . one-to-one mutual pontification . . . how could the citizens of [the town] have guessed as we, I, huffed and puffed our way through their sleepy little neighborhoods and parks that movement is fun . . .

Viv made a number of discursive moves in this passage. First, she reinforced her claim on the mantra, "An inch is as good as a mile." I take this to mean that Viv rejected the idea that her exercise efforts were failed if she did not achieve 30 minutes of daily physical activity. Second, she abandons the term "exercise," and instead claims the term "movement." The word "exercise," for Viv, connoted structured, planned and measured physical activity. For her, exercise and the subject position of exerciser was fear-laden and destructive. Movement did not carry the same connotations. Finally, Vivian indicated her belief that the people around her, the "citizens of [the town]" might find it novel to see movement as enjoyable.

That Vivian would find it novel to think "movement is fun" speaks to the power of the dominant exercises discourses that promote exercise as a means to achieving a slender end. For Viv, "movement" was not fraught with subtexts of risk, romance or transgression. Further, the novelty that Viv expressed about movement and fun indicates the strength and entrenchment of fear discourses: one, we should fear fatness since fatness is risky and lethal via diabetes or heart disease, and two, that we should fear exercise practices—since we are almost certainly exercising improperly and will hurt ourselves with our shoddy attempts. In the end, Viv forced me to recognize that "movement" was safer and more desirable for her than "exercise." In her resistance, she reframed the act of walking away from a risky, romantic exercise designed to help the exerciser recoup a lost or nonexistent perfect self. Instead, Viv restructured exercise as movement. Movement, for Viv, and more recently for me, was at least fun, perhaps less dangerous, and felt notably more whole.

CONCLUSIONS

The current chapter discussed news stories and a personal story/case study (i.e., Viv) within the context of Weedon's feminist post-structuralism to explore how news media discursively construct exercise and fat phobia and the implications for women's subjectivity and exercise participation. Our presentation of these original research examples highlights the complexity of this process, particularly with respect to how dominant health and fitness discourses may enter into, and impact, real women's everyday lives and exercise practices.

The media example revealed that ACCENT news stories reinforced broader cultural narratives that construct exercise and women's bodies in a narrow manner (e.g., as gendered, as linked to weight loss and appearance, as a tool to achieve an ideal feminine body), creating a limited subject position for women as irrational, ignorant, weak, flawed and at risk with respect to exercise. The ACCENT narratives also suggest that women's flawed and at risk selves can be fixed by purchasing a product, joining a gym, or consulting an expert (e.g., doctor, personal trainer, exercise leader). The news stories achieve this result by tacitly assuming that women want to exercise—and if they don't, they should feel guilty and even ashamed.

Viv's story reveals that the process of reiterating, consuming or resisting the aforementioned discourses and subject positions by women is not straightforward. When taking up the subject position of a flawed and at risk woman within dominant health and fitness discourses Viv experienced fear, failure and futility in relation to her body and exercise. However, Viv's exercise—or lack thereof—emerged as a conscious form of resistance. Viv (re)constructed the notion of 'women's exercise' as 'movement' by repositioning her physical activity within discourses of fun and freedom outside of notions of fear or futility.

Overall, Viv's narratives revealed the difficulties of challenging dominant discourses that construct and frame exercise in particular ways because such discourses are ubiquitous and often taken to be the truth (Markula and Pringle 2006; McGannon and Spence 2010). Moreover, such discourses are politically charged by the ideologies of consumerism and economic interests (e.g., the diet and fitness industry). Social and institutional practices (e.g., the way health and fitness are marketed and promoted) and the broader health and fitness discourses have to change for women to experience new and different views of their physical selves and experience the benefits of physical activity more often (McGannon and Spence 2010).

Apart from larger institutional changes, Viv's and Christina's individual resistance practices highlight the power of individual action in the process of resisting dominant discourses and reconfiguring the discourse/power nexus. Such resistance points to women becoming politically aware and literally *actively* resistant, questioning the limits of 'natural' identities and practices in exercise formed through the games of truth that may disempower women (see Markula 2004). Thus women can challenge/resist dominant discourses by *consciously* embracing their shape as fit and feminine regardless of weight/size, building a muscular body apart from appearance aspirations, changing the meaning of the term 'exercise' to movement, and enjoying the freedom and fun that comes from movement apart from appearance, reconfiguring dominant discourses of femininity (Haravon Collins 2002; Markula 1995, 2003, 2004; Markula and Pringle 2006).

Finally, as a means of challenging and changing dominant discourses and associated practices at cultural and individual levels, this chapter points to the value of research employing feminist post-structuralism. Using feminist post-structuralism as a theoretical tool allowed us to focus on the specific and nuanced role of language and discourse in constructing exercise and female subjectivities, allowing for feminist consciousness to be raised at individual, social and cultural levels. While our research only modestly contributes toward this endeavor, future research can continue to contribute toward resistance of dominant discourses and use feminist post-structuralism to study media texts (e.g., television, magazines, film, websites) to learn more about how women's bodies are (re)presented, and the implications for psychological and behavioral experiences for recreational (non)exercisers. These types of analyses can further contribute toward the broader goal of media literacy and raising feminist consciousness by deconstructing what is taken for granted in the realm of women's physical activity and fitness, and how this impacts health. Opening such a window and dialogue is something that both researchers and practitioners can benefit from in order to promote physical activity—at cultural and individual levels—in ways that lead to more healthful outcomes for women.

NOTES

1 Our media example is part of a larger eclectic discourse analysis (see Gough 2006), which found that the information in ACCENT on health, exercise and food is typically skewed toward women. The larger analysis included 33 stories about women's physical activity collected daily for three consecutive weeks over two time periods (i.e., December 20 to January 9, 2005 and February 14 to March 6, 2005). A portion of this research was supported through a grant from the Canadian Institutes of Health Research (CIHR) awarded to Dr Spence.

REFERENCES

Boero, N. 2007. All the news that's fat to print: The American 'obesity epidemic' and the media. *Qualitative Sociology* 30(41): 41–60.

Bonfiglioli, C., B. J. Smith, L. A. King, S. F. Chapman and S. J. Holding. 2007. Choice and voice: Obesity debates in television news. *Medical Journal of Australia* 15: 442–45.

Bordo, S. 1993. *Unbearable weight: Feminism, western culture and the body.* Berkeley, CA: University of California Press.

Bovey, S. 2000. *Sizeable reflections: Big women living full lives.* London: The Women's Press.

Brabazon, T. 2006. Fitness is a feminist issue. *Australian Feminist Studies* 21: 65–83.

Campos, P., A. Saguy, P. Ernsberger, E. Oliver and G. Gaesser. 2006. The epidemiology of overweight and obesity: Public health crisis or moral panic? *International Journal of Epidemiology* 35: 55–60.

Chase, L. F. 2008. Running big: Clydesdale runners and technologies of the body. *Sociology of Sport Journal* 25: 130–47.

Choi, P. 2000. *Femininity and the physically active woman.* London: Routledge.

Davies, B. and R. Harré. 1990. Positioning: The discursive production of selves. *Journal for the Theory of Social Behavior* 20: 43–63.

Day, K. and T. Keys. 2008. Starving in cyberspace: The construction of identity on 'pro-eating-disorder' websites. In *Critical bodies: Representations, identities and practices of weight and body management,* ed. S. Riley, M. Burns, H. Frith, S. Wiggins and P. Markula, 81–100. NY: Palgrave MacMillan publishers.

Duncan, M. C. 1994. The politics of women's body images and practices: Foucault, the panopticon, and Shape magazine. *Journal of Sport and Social Issue* 18: 48–65.

Evans-Braziel, J. and K. LeBesco. 2001. *Bodies out of bounds: Fatness and transgression.* Berkeley, CA: University of California Press.

Fine, M. 1992. *Disruptive voices*. Ann Arbor: University of Michigan Press.

Fine, M., L. Weis, S. Weseen and L. M. Wong. 2000. For whom? Qualitative research, representations and social responsibilities. In *Handbook of qualitative research* eds. N. K. Denzin and Y. S. Lincoln, 2nd ed., 107–32. Thousand Oaks, CA: Sage.

Foucault, M. 1978. *The history of sexuality, volume 1: An introduction*. London: Penguin Books.

Gavey, N. 1997. Feminist post-structuralism and discourse analysis. In *Toward a new psychology of gender: A reader*, eds. M. M. Gergen and S. N. Davis, 49–64. New York: Routledge.

Gough, B. 2006. Try to be healthy but don't forgo your masculinity: Deconstructing men's health discourse in the media. *Social Science and Medicine* 63: 2476–88.

Haravon Collins, L. 2002. Working out the contradictions: Feminism and aerobics. *Journal of Sport and Social Issues* 26: 85–109.

Henriques, J., W. Hollway, C. Urwin, C. Venn and C. Walkerdine. 1998. *Changing the subject*. London: Methuen.

Hollway, W. 1983. Heterosexual sex: Power and desire for the other. In *Sex and Love: New thoughts on old contradictions,* ed. S. Cartledge and J. Ryan, 124–40. London: Women's Press.

—— 1989. *Subjectivity and method in psychology: Constructing gender, meaning and science*. London: Sage.

hooks, b. 1984. *Feminist theory from margin to center*. Boston: South End Press.

Johnson, C.R. 2005. The body snatcher: Fear, guilt, and exercise intervention. Paper presented at the annual meeting of the Association for the Advancement of Applied Sport Psychology, Vancouver, BC, Canada, October, 2005.

Krane, V., P. Choi, S. M. Baird, C. M. Aimar and K. J. Kauer. 2004. Living the paradox: Female athletes negotiate femininity and muscularity. *Sex Roles* 50: 315–29.

Lebesco, K. 2004. *Revolting bodies? The struggle to redefine fat identity*. Amherst: University of Massachusetts Press.

Lincoln, Y.S. 1997. Self, subject, audience, text: Living at the edge, writing in the margins. In *Representation and the text*, eds. W.G. Tierney and Y.S. Lincoln, 37–55. Albany: State University of New York Press.

Lloyd, M. 1996. Feminism, aerobics and the politics of the body. *Body and Society* 2: 79–98.

McGannon, K. R. and J. C. Spence. 2010. Speaking of the self and exercise participation: What discursive psychology can tell us about an old problem. *Qualitative Research in Sport and Exercise* 2: 17–28.

McGannon, K. R., C. R. Johnson and J. C. Spence 2008. Constructing failure in I-O-Weigh: Accenting women's physical activity in Midwestern news discourse. Paper presented at the International Society for Behavioral Nutrition and Physical Activity conference, Banff, AB, Canada.

Markula, P. 1995. Firm but shapely, fit but sexy, strong but thin: The postmodern aerobicizing female bodies. *Sociology of Sport Journal* 12: 424–53.

—— 2003. Postmodern aerobics: Contradiction and resistance. In *Athletic intruders: Ethnographic research on women, culture and exercise*, ed. A. Bolin and J. Granskog, 53–78. Albany, NY: State University of New York Press.

—— 2004. 'Tuning into one's self': Foucault's technologies of the self and mindful fitness. *Sociology of Sport Journal* 21: 302–21.

Markula, P. and R. Pringle. 2006. *Foucault, sport and exercise: Power, knowledge and transforming the self*. Madison Avenue, NY: Routledge.

Markula, P., M. Burns and S. Riley. 2008. Introducing critical bodies: Representations, identities and practices of weight and body management. In *Critical bodies: Representations, identities and practices of weight and body management*, ed. S. Riley, M. Burns, H. Frith, S. Wiggins and P. Markula, 1–22. NY: Palgrave Macmillan publishers.

Mohanty, C. 1988. Under Western eyes: Feminist scholarship and colonial discourses. *Feminist Review* 30: 60–88.

Murray, S. 2008. Pathologizing 'fatness': Medical authority and popular culture. *Sociology of Sport Journal* 25: 7–21.

Reinharz, S. 1992. *Feminist methods in social research*. New York: Oxford University Press.

Saguy, A. C. and R. Almeling. 2008. Fat in the fire? Science, the news media, and the 'obesity epidemic'. *Sociological Forum* 33(1): 53–83.

Saguy, A. C. and K. Riley. 2005. Weighing both sides: Morality, mortality and framing contests over obesity. *Journal of Health Politics, Policy, and Law* 30(5): 869–921.

Scott-Dixon, K. 2008. Big girls don't cry: Fitness, fatness, and the production of feminist knowledge. *Sociology of Sport Journal*, 25: 22–47.

Stake, R. E. 2005. Qualitative case studies. In *Handbook of Qualitative Research*, eds. N. K. Denzin and Y. S. Lincoln, 3rd ed., 443–66. Thousand Oaks, CA: Sage.

Throsby, K. 2007. 'How could you let yourself get like that?': Stories of the origins of obesity in accounts of weight loss surgery. *Social Science and Medicine* 65: 1561–71.

Tierney, W. G. and Y. S. Lincoln. 1997. *Representation and the text: Reframing the narrative voice*. Albany: State University of New York Press.

Tischner, I. and H. Malson. 2008. Exploring the politics of women's in/visible 'large' bodies. *Feminism and Psychology* 18: 260–67.

Trinh, T. M-ha. 1989. *Woman, native, other: Writing post-coloniality and feminism*. Bloomington: University of Indiana Press.

Weedon, C. 1997. *Feminist practice and post-structuralist theory* (2nd ed.). Malden, MA: Blackwell Publishing.

Willig, C. 2000. A discourse-dynamic approach to the study of subjectivity in health psychology. *Theory and Psychology* 10: 547–70.

Wolf, M. 1992. *A thrice told tale: Feminism, postmodernism and ethnographic responsibility*. Stanford, CA: Stanford University Press.

6 Large Women's Experiences of Exercise

Karen Synne Groven, Kari Nyheim Solbrække and Gunn Engelsrud

In recent years, obesity has been presented as a major epidemic of the western world. In Norway, obesity is also considered a growing problem and health authorities and medical professionals continuously remind people to exercise to avoid weight gain. Women (in particular) seem to be accused of becoming obese as a result of poor self-control or lack of adequate knowledge about exercise and diet. At the same time, several researchers have pointed to the ways exercise has become a part of consumerism: exercise is primarily performed to achieve physical change, the 'healthy-looking body' (Berry 2008; Dworkin and Wachs 2009; Sassatelli 1999, 2007). In Norway, where fitness in the 1990s was characterized by a strong focus on health and functionality, there has also been a shift toward the looks-orientation of other westernized countries (Steen-Johnsen 2004, 76). Feminist researchers (Engelsrud 2009; Haravon Collins 2002; Lloyd 1996; Maguire and Mansfield 1998; Markula 1995) have criticized fitness activities aimed at women accusing them of promoting sexual commodification rather than empowering women to be 'healthy.' This chapter takes a critical approach to the growing public interest in obesity, pointing to the negative, 'unhealthy' aspects of the current fitness and exercise movement. Large women are often caught between contradictory meanings of the 'healthy-looking' body. In this chapter, we will show how large women deal with obesity in a Norwegian exercise context.

Australian feminist Samantha Murray (2005) argues that the predominant association of negative traits with large women reflects a negative culture of "collective knowingness" about fatness: "As members of western society, we presume we know the histories of all fat bodies, particularly those of fat women. We believe we know their desires (which must be out of control) and their will (which must be weak)" (Murray 2005, 154). In this study, we use the term "large" instead of "obese" or "fat." We consider the term "obese" a medical term which refers to the medical understanding of fatness as a disease. "Fat" implies, as we interpret it, an objectification of women as it refers to appearance. Consequently, we prefer the term "large" as less stigmatizing and objectifying. Moreover, our participants mainly talked about themselves as "large" during the interviews. In this chapter, we will first provide a brief introduction to our phenomenological framework before explaining further details about the interviews and observation of an exercise program organized by the Norwegian public health service for individuals defined as obese. We will then discuss how these large women experienced their exercising bodies in this context.

PHENOMENOLOGICAL FRAMEWORK

Our approach to research is especially influenced by the phenomenological concept of "the lived body" which transcends perspectives of the body as a physical object (Merleau-Ponty 2002). According to Merleau-Ponty (2004), the lived body reaches out in the world and the lived body is an active, perceiving and experiencing body. The lived body is a subject and an object, visible and viewing; touched and touching—always both at the same time, yet the two sides of the body cannot be reduced to one another. The lived body not only perceives, but also *produces* a spatio-temporal field around itself. This spatiotemporal field around the subject sensitizes the subject to how much movement is possible in a specific situation. As Maurice Merleau-Ponty so clearly states ". . . it is never an objective body that moves, but a phenomenological body" (2002, 121). From a phenomenological perspective the body is first and foremost a body-subject and a lived body and not an object to be controlled (Svenaeus 2000). Taking a phenomenological approach enables us to sensitize the *relation* between women and exercise as an experienced phenomenon. Consequently, our questions are: How do women who are defined as obese experience exercise? What are their interests and 'investments' in exercising?

METHODS

The data collection was carried out in a medical context that offered group exercising practice for obese persons in an average Norwegian city. The material was derived from participant observation during the exercise practice as well as interviews with five female participants. The training space was typical and similar to the commercial fitness context. The space was equipped with different recourses for exercising: training machines, weights, training cycles and apparatus designed for exercising different muscle groups. The walls were covered with representations of the skeleton and anatomical outlines of muscle groups. In line with the images and training machines focusing on different body parts, the training program was closely related to this organization of the space. The program was organized as circle training, one exercise per station, accompanied by pop music. Every exercise was performed for 1 minute with 60 percent to 70 percent of maximal intensity, then there was a short break, and the same exercise was repeated for one more minute. A total of 12 exercises were performed throughout the one-hour exercise program.

The group met twice a week and an experienced physiotherapist was in charge of the training. Initially, every participant had been given an adjusted personalized program by the physiotherapist, which depended on their physical shape and general health status. The treatment also included group discussion for one hour per month. Topics such as muscle physiology, dietary advice and how each one would go about changing their own lifestyle were emphasized in the instruction as well as in the discussion group. One important aspect of this treatment program was to measure the Body Mass Index (BMI). BMI ranging over 35 is defined as obese.[1] The participants' body weight and BMI were measured by the physiotherapist on a regular basis, usually every second week. A weight loss of half to one kilo each month was considered to be satisfactory in terms of progress. All the participants were strongly advised to stay in the program for a complete year. According to the physiotherapist, this one-year "membership" would ensure that each participant would not "give up easily".

Participants

The five women who were included in our study represented a diverse sample in terms of age, weight histories, marital status, education and area of work. One of the women had a university degree, two of the women had a college degree, and two had no formal education after high school. They were aged 35 to 63, years and when we met them they had been overweight for more than ten years. One of the women had been what she called "big" since childhood. One had started to gain weight in her teens, whereas one had become what she labeled as "overweight" after a struma operation in her early twenties. The labels 'large,' 'overweight,' 'fat' or 'obese' have different cultural values, and as we already stated our informants mostly used "large" when they spoke about themselves in the interviews. They had in common that living as large and heavy has been more or less their continuous situation. Moreover, all five women portrayed themselves as people that had tried numerous diets and exercise programs in different contexts before attending the treatment program in a medical context.

Segregated to a separate training space, the large women already experienced that their bodies were problematic and wrong as judged by others. Doctors had recommended that they participate in this program which they had agreed to follow up for at least one year. In addition, they allowed the physiotherapist to call them if they were prevented from coming.

Research Considerations

One of the authors (KSG) participated in the circle training and conducted the interviews. She still recalls the informal and social atmosphere that predominated when she joined the group on her first observation day. With pop music in the background, she observed how the participants were making social small talk before the class started. Some of the participants had placed themselves near the bicycles ready to start warm-up activities, whereas others were eagerly talking to the physiotherapist. They all seemed to know each other quite well. By contrast, the researcher felt quite uncomfortable standing by herself with pen and notebook. In addition, she noticed how several of the participants stared at her, and this made her worry about their reactions when she went about observing and writing notes 'about them.' Her mind was filled with questions: "How would they react?" "Would they feel stared at?" "Would they feel provoked?" These considerations made her change her research approach from the very first day. Rather than obtaining a distant position by observing the participants during training, she decided to join them, doing the exercises as if she were a member of the group. This strategy made her less visible and more comfortable as a researcher. Moving together changes the focus from visual perception to bodily engagement where the senses, sweating and heart beats contributes to 'forgetting' oneself. In this situation she felt more included in the group through moving. She even joined in the small talk during the intervals, enabling her to gain firsthand experience of the exercisers' reaction to the training. One remarkable experience was the difficulty and intensity of the program. KSG felt exhausted at the end of the first class, and felt that she did not experience any 'advantage' of having a smaller body, in doing the program.

Qualitative Interviews

Bearing her firsthand experiences with the group in mind, KSG conducted in-depth interviews with five of the female participants at a place of the women's own choosing (three chose their own homes, two chose a local café). The women were interviewed when they had participated in the program for nearly ten months. Our intention was to interview the women once again after they had finished the program; meaning after 12 months since this was a one-year course. However, the physiotherapist in charge of the group became seriously ill. The treatment therefore stopped after 10 months and a new group treatment did not start until 4 months later when the physiotherapist had found a substitute.

Semi-structured interviews were conducted in order to capture the uniqueness of each participant's experiences while at the same time enabling a focus on the topics in question (Kvale and Brinkman 2009).

This meant that KSG worked with a predetermined topic guide covering the main areas of enquiry whilst allowing room for departure to pursue novel topics introduced by the interviewee. Their expressions and answers were followed up by further questions in order to clarify the content and illuminate the uniqueness of each woman's experiences. Similarly, KSG would encourage the women to "give an example" when they talked about experiences that needed clarification or expansion of a topic. As the interviews were done face-to-face, both topics and order could be adjusted for each encounter based upon the researcher's perception as to what seemed most appropriate. This approach brought up several novel topics. For example, the women were eager to talk about their negative experiences with training and physical activity prior to joining the treatment program.

The interviews were tape-recorded with the women's permission and transcribed verbatim enabling quotations to be highlighted in the presentation of the results. Each interview lasted between 1.5 to 2 hours, resulting in a total of 140 pages of transcribed texts.

To maintain confidentiality, pseudonyms are used throughout this chapter. The study was approved by the Research Ethics Committee of Medicine in Norway.

Analysis of the Material

Our analysis can be described as following Kvale and Brinkman's (2009) idea of research as "bricolage." In this eclectic form of generating meaning, the researcher adapts mixed approaches moving freely between different "analytic techniques and concepts" (Kvale and Brinkman 2009, 233). Our analysis consisted of several phases. Although the phases overlap and interplay, we will describe this process as a stepwise procedure for the sake of clarity.

First, the transcriptions were read through a couple of times to get a general impression of the women's experiences with training and physical activity. In this stage, KSG and GE focused on the topics that first caught their attention, marking them as notes in the margin. The second stage can be described as what Kvale and Brinkman term a "meaning condensation" (2009, 205–207). Meaning condensation entails abridgement of the meanings expressed by the interviewees into shorter formulations. Long statements are compressed into briefer statements in which the main sense of what is said is rephrased in a few words (units of meanings). Then, the central theme that dominates the meaning unit is restated as simply as possible, thematizing the statement from the informant's viewpoint as understood by the researcher. Our next step was to find related patterns between the central themes. Following the phenomenological approach, certain themes were considered to have a common origin, were related, or both.

Our final step of analysis consisted of "meaning interpretation" (Kvale and Brinkman 2009, 207–208). Meaning interpretation goes beyond a restructuring of the manifest meanings of the text to a deeper or more critical interpretation of the text. According to Kvale, "the researcher has a perspective on what is investigated and interprets the interviews from this perspective (1996, 201). This kind of interpretation goes beyond what the informants have said directly so as to reveal the opinions and relations that are not evident. At this stage of analysis, it was quite useful to have Nyheim Solbrække as a critical reader. As a sociologist with a feminist approach, she focused particularly on Judith Butler's understanding of gender as a social practice. This made us pay particular attention to the ways the women talked about the training as exemplifying taking action in relation to their weight. Moreover, their repetitive argument that "diets don't work" could now be interpreted as a decisive move toward a qualitatively different kind of intervention that was proportionate to the problems that they faced. From this perspective, they could be seen as positioning themselves as subjects—or credible women—actively involved in the work of weight management rather than its vilified objects. At the same time, their decision to join a treatment program could be seen in terms of submission, since the women were accepting their doctors' advice to get professional help with their weight problems. Moreover, they had agreed to join the program for at least one year. In this sense, they revealed a sense of being out of control of their weightloss project, expressing their need to hand over control to a health professional rather than seeing it as a matter of individual responsibility. The position the women obtained in the interviews illuminated some ambiguous and contradictory positions. They were regarded by themselves and others as both subjects and objects of the "war on obesity." Based on the interviews, we organized the analysis around three main phrases: "Is it inside me or not?" "I want to see results" and "We are not here for fun."

IS IT INSIDE ME OR NOT?

Certain experience of discomfort and dissatisfaction seem to characterize women's negotiations with the choices during exercise sessions. Even in cases where they had quit after a short-time membership, they spoke vividly about the gaze of other members as an uncomfortable and painful memory. Negative experiences, nevertheless, in a Norwegian context, encompasses 'normal' cultural meanings. 'No pain, no gain' and 'not giving up exercising,' despite emotional strain and anxiety is consonant with dominate cultural ideas. (Dworkin and Wachs 2009). One woman said: "Sometimes I felt sick before going to the fitness training. I couldn't stand the idea of being stared at." In the beginning, she tried to suppress her negative experiences: "I decided not to care. But it did not work. I felt sick and miserable and decided to quit." Another common expression was: "I really felt like a failure. I have pain in my knees, in my back, in my groin." Even though our material stems from exercising in a medical context the experiences are ambiguous and intertwined with strong sensations and emotional memories. Discomfort and comfort were changeable and led to fluctuating emotions in our informants' talk about the training. They indicated that their bodies hurt as a result of the training. Training was unpleasant, wearisome and tedious at times, but still they continued to do it. This finding may be linked to a perception that losing weight demands both willpower and discipline, and that tolerating discomfort is seen as a sign of control over one's own body. From a phenomenological perspective the body is first and foremost a body-subject and a lived body and not an object to be controlled. However a large female body, may, if we borrow an expression from the Swedish philosopher Frederik Svenaeus (2000) be experienced as 'unhomelike' in the world and its limitations and size attain a thematic, explicit focus that may be reinforced by the bio-medical knowledge upon which the treatment program is based.

Exercising and dieting without success affected the participants in the study and contributed to the production of shame and self blame. One woman explained: "It was really depressing. It is so depressing when you realize that this is not something I will be able to go through with. I wouldn't make it this time either." She explained that she started worrying about her mental strength and figured that she must be "mentally weak" because she could not lose weight without regaining it soon after. Significantly, these understandings are also evident in the interviews with the other women. Dominant expressions concern the way the discourses about 'eating less, exercising more' are presented by the health authorities and the medical professionals. One woman said: "They think it is just about eating less and then you will become thinner. But here is something inside your head that blocks." In a similar vein, other women blame their "heads":

> It is inside me, I think it is placed between my ears, inside my head, like a mental block, because I know what to do. I know what's wrong, but still I am not able to lose weight. There must be something wrong with me . . . with my head.

To use expressions like "mental block" and "something wrong with my head," locating constant worries and feelings of shame and failure "inside me," can be understood as the dualistic and hegemonic language that both phenomenology and feminist theory have criticized.

The idea of representing women as "mentally blocked" can be traced back to the early nineteenth century (Johannisson 1996). Medical technology and power have contributed to legitimizing specific models of illness applied to women. By portraying women as more gendered and bodily than men—making use of biological arguments claiming that they had a more fragile nervous system—medicine legitimized a view of woman as the second (weaker) sex. When our informants used the expression "mental block" about themselves, this expression clearly does not only stem from "inside" the women, but refers to specific labels that have defined women within the history of medicine. That this feeling is closely linked to cultural norms of masculinity and femininity was not part of the women's interpretation of their experience—for them, "it is just me" that has a weaker mental state. Body shape becomes a sign of each woman's 'inner' personality—be it either 'mental weakness' or 'strong motivation.' Being slender and well-trained is associated with self-discipline and control, whereas being fat has negative connotations: laziness and lack of self-discipline.

I WANT TO SEE RESULTS

The women's interest in results took up considerable time during the interviews. Results were measurable effects in the visible body shape and synonymous with losing weight. All but one of our informants lost weight while they participated in the training program. According to the physiotherapist a 'normal' loss of weight is from 5 to 15 kilos. The defined weight loss was described as "a result" that has motivated them to continue with the program. The values of losing weight and thereby obtaining results were emphasized in various expressions like: "I wanted to see results, and that's what I got here. And that is what kept me going here."

Although the women placed great emphasis on the importance of seeing results from the training program in measurable weight loss, they were also anxious about developing bulging muscles. As a cultural idea our informants expressed gaining muscles as unwanted and unpleasant: "But I don't want muscles. And anyway, you're supposed to have long muscles." This informant expressed a definite perception of how the body is supposed to look. It must be both slender and firm – with little body fat and long, slender musculature. The feminist sociologist Pirkko Markula (1995) identifies the dominant ideas of postmodern aerobicizing female bodies that aim at being "Firm but Shapely, Fit but Strong, Strong but Thin." By using this striking title to her article, Markula addresses how narrow ideas of the female body appear to be central and unavoidable components of exercising in a fitness context. Because an obese female body can be seen as a failure or even as an offence against cultural ideas of the body, health and gender, these ideas have a considerable impact on obese women. Several aspects of the results indicate that this includes avoiding the development of prominent musculature. The guidelines of the program are also based on the assumption that this is the sort of change that is to be affected. One woman described the goals of the program as: "How to get small muscles and large muscles and no muscles. How the body reacts to different things. So then I wondered if I should use 30 kilos and do 50 repetitions or 50 kilos and 20 repetitions." As a result, they stuck strictly to the program and did not increase the weights appreciably.

Moreover, measurable weight loss alone was not considered to be a satisfactory result by the women. The women also desired a feeling of freedom, engagement and the feeling of "a kick." When they had developed a taste for measurable results they became occupied with the idea of losing even more. One of the women expressed that she would not be satisfied until she had taken off 30 kilos, because:

> If I really want to reach my ideal weight and get into . . . how should I put it . . . liberating form so that nothing is weighing me down, then I do have to lose 30 kilos. So I have a long way to go really. But it's in here (points to her heart). I really, really want to lose weight so that I can feel free.

Simone de Beauvoir (2000) has argued that freedom is a central phenomenon that women must fight for, and to achieve freedom (even if it is always limited) from today's cultural western ideal by gaining a critical distance from the limiting body ideals perpetuated in the worlds of media and medicine. Our material indicated that the exercises that large women are performing are not adapted to who they are and what they feel *during* moving. Even if they are training in a separated space, their practice follows mainstream 'normal' ideas about exercise and little attention is given to their personal experiences and abilities. Since achieving results is important, making great efforts tends to be a key aspect of the exercise and a prerequisite for attaining the various physiological effects. Efforts were confirmed by encouraging the women to continue "giving their all." By "giving their all" the potential for good health was communicated as obtainable. The instruction played on the present potential for improvement, the will to stretch oneself and "go for it." It seemed that attempts to ignore discomfort created fatigue, irritation and alienation. However, to experience and display oneself as functioning well, and being presentable, gives social advantages and credibility as a modern successful woman. Health becomes synonymous with the individual self-presentation that can be exhibited through the body, whether this is an individual physiological goal or a firm body.

However, as Sassatelli clearly states, achieving this "result" depends on spending one's spare time in making oneself physically desirable (2007, 169). Interestingly, in Norway these kinds of norms are not quite new ones. On the contrary these ideas have a long and manifest significance in sport and outdoor life in Norway, as core activities and often as a collective phenomenon. However, in Norway (Steen-Johnsen 2004) traditional activities have decreased and activities like aerobic and fitness training have become increasingly important due to the symbolic power of commercial fitness practices. In this context, we find it especially interesting that the women talk a lot about how they should exercise to lose weight and at the same time get a more slender, well-trained body. In addition, because achieving training results is central, pushing the body is regarded as a necessity. When physical discomfort or pain is felt, it is interpreted first and foremost as a sign that the body is still too heavy or in bad 'shape.'

WE ARE NOT HERE FOR FUN

In contrast to tradition of Norwegian sport and outdoor life which is regarded as pleasurable in itself, it was unusual to hear women's exercise discussed in terms of enjoyment and pleasure. Pleasure was regarded as a reward *after* exercising. During exercise lessons it was common to hear the instructor motivate them to endure the lesson with sentences like: "You will soon be finished." The tendency to take a position where pain and negative experiences resulting from the exercises must be tolerated seemed to be a normal attitude. However, the heavy bodies of our informants meant that their skeletons were subject to great strain during exercise. Their willingness to forego pleasure in order to follow the difficult program appeared to be having some negative consequences. One participant said: "I find that I hurt a lot in the afternoon and evening, but I think the reason is that I'm still very overweight and it puts a strain on my knees." Despite the knee pain, she thought the training was beneficial:

> The fact that you actually exercise your whole body, you go through all the muscles in the body. I think that is very important, not least because of all that about burning up fat. And you have to make a bit of effort to get it going, as it were.

One aspect of the physical discomfort is tolerance. Some of the women had experience with alternative forms of exercise. One had completed a course in Mensendieck gymnastics,[2] and had very positive experience of this kind of exercise, which she found very suitable for her. She mentioned that the slow exercises, in particular, are comfortable. She took these courses for almost three years.

> I didn't lose weight, though. But it was nice finding the muscles. Feeling how they worked. And it was a very gentle pace and very pleasant, really. It suited me then, in a way . . . It was nice. So I did that for several years.

The only problem with the gymnastics she liked was that one did not lose any weight. Comparing this program with that of the overweight groups where training with weights is uncomfortable for the body, the participant said: "It was awful in the beginning. I could hardly manage anything. I had to push myself. That was heavy-going. It was a strain." She found pushing her body both alienating and disagreeable. She talked about how the training put her in a sort of position outside herself, in contrast to the more comfortable exercises which suited her. She gave her reasons for deciding to persevere as follows: "The others keep going, so I must also keep going. That helped to motivate me . . . And if I don't carry on I'll be really round." This example shows that pushing oneself is understood as necessary for losing weight. However, the discomfort of pushing oneself is moderated by being part of a group, which made it easier to continue the training. By witnessing the efforts of the others exercising in the same room, seeing that the others "can stand" physical discomfort and persevere, she wanted to do the same. This seems like another kind of social construction of how to be a 'good' woman, along with the others perpetuated by the media and the medical world.

From the descriptions of the participants, "pushing oneself" was interpreted as a culturally positive value. Our informants stated that they take advantage of each other's desires to "be fit":

> I have the impression that everybody who goes to our course is very serious and really give it all they've got. They really want to be fit, is my impression. They're not coming here for fun, in other words. They aren't.

To exercise in a challenging and strenuous way helped form a positive perception in the group that one is serious about losing weight and "getting results." With regard to their own efforts, the women performed exercise in a "resolute" way and were "never slack." One participant says:

> Sometimes I think I can't face [attending the program] . . . And there are mornings when I really don't feel like it. But then you get dressed and go and it passes . . . No, I have never been absent unless I've been sick. Then . . . and then I know that [I have to] . . . get dressed and stop messing around . . . I have to get tired, because if I don't get tired, then there's no point my being here. And when I go home I have a very good feeling—that I've done it today too . . .

This excerpt from the interview indicates that even though this participant dreaded the exercise program, she was determined to work hard in order to get results in return for her efforts. The cultural idea of exercise engages in an agreement to lose weight. The women seemed conscious of this requirement. One of the main messages in this treatment program was, as shown previously, the importance of "focusing" and "keeping up the pace" of the training so as not to gain weight again. In the earlier excerpt, the good feeling after exercise might refer to the feeling of a good conscience as a result of doing one's duty once again. Another woman talked in a similar way: "If I don't exercise I get so fat. . . . But the feeling after [exercise] is very good. Then I feel better in a way. I guess I can say that I feel more cheerful." She talked about the training as something she *ought* to do—a sort of duty which is not fun at the time, but which yields positive results afterwards: both physical (her body is not "as fat") and psychological (she feels better mentally).

By becoming aware of how the others see them as overweight women, the women adopted an external perspective on themselves, which made them feel uncomfortable and ashamed of themselves. Moreover, it enhanced their view of themselves as fat and unattractive. According to Merleau-Ponty, the feeling of shame is closely connected to sensing the gaze of others:

> Shame and immodesty, then, take their place in a dialectic of the self and the other which is that of master and slave: in so far as I have a body, I may be reduced to the status of an object beneath the gaze of another person, and no longer count as a person for him.
>
> (2002, 193)

The objectifying gaze of others is a tacit premise that works directly on the bodies' kinaesthetic and emotional self-awareness. To normalize these bodily states the continuous work to change one's appearance moderates the tension between self and cultural ideas.

UNATTAINABLE RESULTS

As a response to being controlled by the weight, the "inner picture" of an acceptable body does not harmonize with what our informants saw when they look in the mirror. They often questioned how their large bodies relate to their personality. Culturally inappropriate bodies are at stake in negotiations about "who am I." If they achieved results from the exercises, their attitudes toward their own body improved: "I notice that my body is beginning to feel a little more like my own again. That I'm finding my way back to the person inside here."

Being large can contribute to a perception of the body as an appendage to the personality. The body is perceived mainly as problem. Expressions such as "I do not like my body" maintain dualistic conceptions of the body as 'separate' from the person. The married women among our informants reported that their husbands became critical of their weight gain. Hurtful comments about their body as "outer objects" were commonplace. Insecurity and loss of attractiveness, however, did not stop the women from still hoping to *get back the old body,* the one they had before the children arrived. Their concern with changing the shape of their bodies was perceived as an important value. Questions that might be posed in line with such experiences are: Who is changing? What does it mean to like or not like one's body? Obviously, no outer relationship between "me and my body" exists and as Merleau-Ponty (2002) might have said: I belong to my body and the body belongs to me. Not like other things belongs to me, and not as a thing I can manipulate as an object outside me. Moreover, living with a large body, certainly made our informants critical of their bodies, the body became a "thing" that they did not like. Since the body belongs to the person and the person to the body there is, however, no way of escaping this 'reality.' The visibility of the large body might function as a confirmation or manifestation of the undesirable side of living with a body that 'nobody' appreciates.

Drawing on de Beauvoir's (2000) description of "the narcissist," we might say that the women who participated in this study were striving to become someone else, unsuccessfully. All the plans to change gained an important place in their lifeworld. They continuously lived with that idea that they one day would reach stable weight. Our data indicated that the large women developed a somewhat self-observing relationship with their bodies. From Merleau-Ponty's perspective, the lived body is always subject and object, visible and viewing, touched and touching, yet the two sides of the body cannot be reduced to one another. Therefore, phenomena are always determined through their relationship with one another. De Beauvoir (2000) might argue that the women may seem to be at risk of alienation when they focus solely on body change instead of experiencing the exercise. The responsibility for changing one's body shape diverts attention from the discomfort and pain when they exercise. Remaining in a professionally controlled training program may lead to a feeling that they cannot continue the training on their own. In other words, their feelings of not being good enough are reinforced and their perception of themselves as 'the other' further internalized.

Managing the pace of the exercise program was a struggle for many interviewees. While struggling with intensive exercise to change their bodies into the 'healthy' ideal, they did not have an opportunity to dwell on the excessiveness of such behavior. As Haravon Collins so clearly puts it, being objectified is bad enough, but being ordered around is blatantly oppressive, particularly when the instructors assume that all of the participants are there for the same purpose: slimming down and shaping up (2002, 94).

Although some experiences of strain and effort may be part of 'normal' exercise, being under constant pressure can be counterproductive for obtaining good health. For example, while bio-medical sources state that exercise produces favorable effects on health when measured by a number of physiological variables, other research shows that excessive exercise can result in ill health (Kenttä 2001). In addition, exercising relentlessly reduces the chances of exploring movement from one's own perception of the situation. The actual moving and the flow of movement seem to be undermined and not promoted. Instead, feelings of loneliness and vulnerability were viewed as 'something wrong' rather than valuable experiences that might create awareness of space and one's own bodily history. In spite of the fact that the exercising caused pain and discomfort, the interviewed women kept up with the program.

Our material shows that the potential to enjoy exercise could help women to resist the western individualization processes. But this possibility is deferred in favor of a continuous pressure or obligation to obtain a thinner body shape. The interviewed women felt pressure when they were constantly told to push even further, make greater efforts, keep at it, and give what they could. These values may shed light on why the feelings of loneliness and vulnerability arose during exercise and why these feelings increased with a lack of opportunity to discuss the difficult experiences with others. Instead, the women were expected to deal with these feelings on their own. Although the feelings were suppressed, during exercise, the women's movements became visible and 'naked': heavy sweating and breathing were exposed and expressed. On the one hand these bodily reactions helped to affiliate the obese women to 'normal' women who exercise. On the other hand, it is exactly these expressions that contribute to stigma against body size. Sweating and being out of breath are often connected with fatness and this intensified the sense of the judging gaze of others by the large women, particularly, as the large women are culturally accused of becoming obese as a result of poor self-control or lack of adequate knowledge about exercise and diet.

We emphasize that women defined as obese did not want to lose weight solely for the sake of health, but were also struggling to become 'normal' women. The *result* of exercise is given priority, not the expressive and kinaesthetically subjective body. However, if large women are seen to make a visible effort to become smaller, this can provide them with credibility as 'normal' women. However, exercise with a focus on effort may contribute to an objectification of the body. As de Beauvoir argued (2000) when the body's subjective experience is considered secondary, the body, due to a lack of freedom and human transcendence, becomes objectified. The women in our study certainly described their training as something they ought to do: a duty which is unpleasant, but which yields positive 'physical' and 'psychological' results afterwards. It was obvious that they emphasized the effects of training. The measurable effect also receives most focus in the medical context where the training results are regarded as the only valid knowledge.

While our analyses strongly indicated that participating in exercise increased large women's credibility as 'normal' women, it was rarely possible or realistic that they would attain the ideal slim, hard, fit and energetic body. Therefore, success measured through the reduction of body size is problematic. On the one hand, obese women are portrayed as lazy, unethical and acceptable by others in the world of media and medicine. Women are, thus, expected to be responsible for their choices and actions. On the other hand, women who are defined as obese exercise in space that is segregated and 'sheltered' from official public spaces with other 'normal' women and thus, are already judged as 'abnormal.' Doing exercise moderated feelings of shame and marginalization, but our informants do not experience true empowerment.

Living in a patriarchal world but surrounded by critical voices we propose that women defined as obese should resist the traditional and mainstream ideas about exercise and give more attention to their personal experiences and abilities. Aware that we may be putting yet another requirement onto large women, this position is in line with advocates of size acceptance in the U.S. (Bernell 2000; Shanker 2004). Currently in Norway, there are no programs yet that aim to build on large women's (and men's) embodied experiences. Neither are the culturally shaped ideals about femininity problematized by linking them to the ideals of improvement through hard (individual) work. From a sociological perspective, women are no longer defined, as they traditionally were, by responsibility for and caring toward others, which can be considered oppressive. Instead women receive praise for 'caring about themselves' and taking responsibility for their own health. However, for obese women, taking care of themselves in a medically orientated exercise context is not particularly enjoyable. On the contrary, an oppressive sense of duty overrides ideas of individuality and expressivity that are characteristic of late modernity.

CONCLUSION

In this chapter, we have shown that large women who exercise to lose weight experience repetitive fluctuations of weight, but still hope to find the perfect training program. However, the type of exercise that has been chosen for them provides little opportunity to go beyond a gendered framework. Due to collective cultural norms there seems to be a mutual agreement that slim, well-toned bodies represent the ideal 'normal' woman. In this medical context, to be considered a woman who wants to change and who accepts being instructed toward a changed body size, achieves a more credible feminine identity.

However, the routine of the training program prevents the exploration of personal kinaesthetic experience and reflective subjectivity. The large women seem to be 'forced' to (re)produce the idea that they should work to change their bodily appearance. The chapter illustrates how women, who are defined as obese, express the importance of getting visible results from the training. They had nearly no fun and instead of enjoying the exercise experienced pain, discomfort and dissatisfaction. They, nevertheless, persisted with their exercise program. This chapter demonstrated that public training programs offered to women defined as obese engage them in an attempt to obtain an impossible body ideal. These programs are necessarily not suitable for large women. Rather, these programs can result in the participants' constant dissatisfaction and ill health.

NOTES

1 Here we use 'obese' because we describe how BMI is defined within the exercise context
2 Mensendieck gymnastics, named after its originator Bess Mensendieck, is a form of low-intensity training. By emphasizing slow movements, it aims to build strength; although not in the form of 'pumping up' the muscles to maximum size. Focus is put on developing the core musculature in a thorough and basic manner to enable us to carry our bodies in a correct manner. This can be best achieved with tranquil and gentle exercising, which also enables persons suffering from injuries or problems in the spinal or neck area to engage in it safely. The exercises themselves are unique (termed Mensendieck exercises) both in their manner and the way in which they are performed. All exercises are performed in a prescribed manner, and nothing is left to chance. Bess Mensendieck was preoccupied with the idea that a correctly performed exercise is worth hours of exercising in the wrong manner (Dahl-Mikkelsen 2007). Mensendieck gymnastics is currently being used all over Europe, particularly in the Netherlands and in Norway, which has a physiotherapist education founded on Bess Mensendieck's ideas. Hence, in Norway Mensendieck is used as a physiotherapy method, and only physiotherapists are entitled to call themselves Mensendieck instructors.

REFERENCES

Bernell, B. 2000. *Bountiful women: Large women's secrets for living the life they desire.* Berkeley: Wildcat Canyon Press.
Berry, B. 2008. *The power of looks. Social stratification of physical appearance.* Burlington, Hampshire: Ashgate Publishing Limited.
Dahl-Mikkelsen, T. 2007. From aunt to expert (Fra tante til ekspert). Master's thesis, University of Oslo, Faculty of Medicine.
De Beauvoir, S. 2000. *The second sex* (Det annet kjønn). Oslo: Pax Forlag A/S.
Dworkin, S. L. and F. L. Wachs. 2009. *Body panic: Gender, health and the selling of fitness.* New York: New York University Press.
Engelsrud, G. 2009. Aerobic exercise and health—a tenuous connection? In *Normality/Normativity*, ed. K. L. Folmarson. Uppsala: Center for Gender Research, University of Uppsala.

Featherstone, M. 2000. *Body modification*. London: Sage.

Haravon Collins, C. L. 2002. Working out the contradictions: Feminism and aerobics. *Journal of Sport and Social Issues* 26(1): 85–109.

Johannisson, Karin. 1966. *Det møke kontinent: kvinner, sykelighet og kulturen rundt århunderskiftet* (The dark continent; women, illness and culture around 1900). Oslo: Aventura.

Kenttä, G. 2001. Overtraining, staleness and burnout in sports. PhD dissertation, Stockholm University.

Kvale, S. 1996. *InterViews: An introduction to qualitative research interviewing*. London: Sage.

Kvale, S. and S. Brinkman. 2009. *Interviews: Learning the craft of qualitative research interviewing*. 2nd ed. London: Sage.

Lloyd, M. 1996. Feminism, aerobics and the politics of the body. *Body & Society* 2(2): 79–98.

Maguire, J and L. Mansfield 1998. No-body's perfect: Women, aerobics and the body beautiful. *Sociology of Sport Journal* 15: 109–37.

Markula, P. 1995. Firm but shapely, fit but strong, strong but thin. The postmodern aerobicizing female bodies. *Sociology of Sport Journal* 12(4): 424–53.

Merleau-Ponty, M. 2002. *Phenomenology of perception*. London: Routledge and Kegan Paul.

—— 2004. *The world of perception*. London: Routledge.

Moi, T. 1998. *Hva er en kvinne? (What is a Woman?)* Oslo: Gyldendahl.

Murray, S. 2005. (Un/be)coming out? Rethinking fat politics. *Social Semiotics* 15(2): 153–63.

Sassatelli, R. 1999. Interaction order and beyond: A field analysis of body culture within fitness gyms. *Body & Society* 5(2–3): 227–48.

—— 2007. *Consumer culture, history, theory and politics*. London: Sage.

Shanker, W. 2004. *The fat girl's guide to life*. London: Bloomsbury.

Steen-Johnsen, K. 2004. Individualised communities. Keep-fit exercise organizations and the creation of social bonds. Dissertation from the Norwegian University of Sport and Physical Education.

Svenaeus, F. 2000. *The hermeneutics of medicine and the phenomenology of health*. Dordrect: Kluwer Academic Publishers.

7 Obesity, Body Pedagogies and Young Women's Engagement with Exercise

Emma Rich, John Evans and Laura De Pian

In a time of dramatic social, cultural, and political transition, young women are being constructed as a vanguard of new subjectivity. They are supposed to offer clues about the best way to cope with these changes. Power, opportunities, and success are all modelled by the 'future girl' a kind of young woman celebrated for her 'desire, determination and confidence' to take charge of her life, seize chances, and achieve her goals.

(Harris 2004, 1)

Harris' observation neatly alludes to the individualism that has dominated the political and educational culture of recent years. Its vocabulary and syntax (its 'voice') position young women (and young men) as active abstractions, 'agents' ultimately being in control of and responsible for their own destinies/futures. Such thinking rarely appreciates or acknowledges the socio-economic, material and regional influences that bear upon young women's opportunities to either develop or achieve normatively sanctioned (usually 'westernized') forms of health and well-being. It is now well established, however, that political individualism has dominated (and adversely affected) health policy (Babones 2009) of recent years and influenced profoundly the way in which particular populations (e.g., factions of the working class, single women) and individuals are perceived and held responsible for their own (ill-) health (see Armstrong 1995; Crawford 1980). In this chapter, we examine how recent health discourses associated with obesity, when configured within a culture of individualism, bear upon young women's understanding of, and relationships with, exercise. Within obesity discourse young women are seen to be in control of their own destiny, and are assumed to be able to shape their future lives and health if only they undertake the regulative practices which it prescribes (e.g., pursuing 'good' diets, exercising and losing weight). Such thinking reflects the image of 'future girls' (Harris 2004) in control of their own destiny and able to shape their own life (and health) now celebrated in cultural and political debate in many westernized countries. Like Rail (2009) and Warin et al. (2008, 1), however, we "problematise the universality of health promotion messages" of this kind. We are particularly concerned with how exercise and physical activity practices associated with new health imperatives tend to homogenize young people's diverse interests, needs and opportunities across ethnicity, class, age, culture and ability. Within obesity discourse the possibilities for health are often announced through 'one size fits all' policies advocating practices that are deemed appropriate for everyone. Such policies and practices may thus fail to give due attention to broader social-cultural contexts which may mediate opportunities and prohibit choice, and thus reify a form of political individualism (see Evans et al. 2008).

Policy makers' obsession with 'weight issues' and national obesity standards, especially when reported as international league tables comparing 'their' nation's/populations' collective girth size, has been remarkable. Moral panics associated with obesity have further intensified the pressures on young people to regulate their behaviors (e.g., alter their eating habits, take more exercise and lose weight). 'Facts' around levels of exercise also fuel the obesity debate and are regularly used with impunity to rationalize weightloss programs. Yet, we know relatively little about how young women are reading and experiencing these discourses in relation to their own bodies, identities and experiences across myriad social settings. Therefore, by drawing upon feminist post-structural theory and analytical tools developed in recent studies on obesity and pedagogy, we examine how prevailing discourses of health, gender and the body are interpreted and how young women understand exercise as a bodily practice.

OBESITY, BODY PEDAGOGIES AND THE CONSTITUTION OF 'HEALTHY' SUBJECTIVITIES

In our discussion we draw upon feminist post-structural theory and analytical tools developed in recent studies on obesity and pedagogy. Drawing on Foucault's (1979) concept of bio-power, Wright and Harwood (2009) have developed the notion of biopedagogies as a theoretical concept through which to examine the relationships between bio-power, obesity discourse and pedagogical practices. The discourses connected to this epidemic may shape specific body pedagogies—instructional forms through which an individual learns to understand his/her body—in both formal and popular sites of learning. Through such practices of instruction, new forms of normalizing practices emerge also in schools. Biopedagogies are now recognized as part of the bio-political landscape of contemporary Western cultures oriented toward healthism and more specifically escalating concerns associated with obesity. In this chapter, we have sought to examine how these biopedagogies are shaped from the body pedagogies of both popular culture and more formal contexts of schools.

Increasingly, both individuals and populations are being ascribed responsibility for their health and its reductive constituent 'weight,' and are relentlessly monitored in their capacity to do so. The need for populations to protect themselves from the assumed risks associated with obesity reflects a broader shift toward 'surveillance medicine' (Armstrong 1995). Armstrong argues that in the current society, medical attention is now extended also to those considered 'healthy' through an increasing emphasis on illness prevention. The focus of medicine turns on the healthy population rather than the ill. According to him, this emphasis results in 'healthy' individuals constantly surveying for possible early symptoms for illness. Health problems become, then, constructed by continually problematizing anyone as healthy or 'normal.' The control of populations through medicalization is not an enforced action but one which normalizes particular health practices within everyday contexts. We have been interested in exploring how this process of normalization involves a pedagogical dimension through which young people 'learn' about acceptable health behaviors and body types.

While we observe that prevailing discourses of obesity shape policy and 'produce' individual subjects in particular ways, we also acknowledge the complex interplay between these discourses and active negotiations around the constitution of girls' subjectivities. Following Foucault (1997) we recognize the body as a site on which various discourses are contested and negotiated. However, this is not to suggest that girls are passive recipients of discourses acting upon their bodies (see Youdell 2006). We recognize that girls' identities are not fixed, nor are they acted upon by discourses of gender and health which simply *determine* and shape their identities. Rather, there is a need to account for the pervasive impact of health discourse, but also the *active role* that girls may play in constituting their subjectivities particularly in relation to 'the body' (Davies 1989 Francis and Archer 2005; Skelton and Francis 2009; Susinos et al. 2009; Youdell 2005). Although health discourses may pervade culture, their meanings may be recontextualized, resisted and made meaningful in the lives of girls as they intersect with other categories of experience such as age, family location, social class, sexuality, gender and ethnicity. Understanding girls as active consumers allows us to explore how they may continue to invest in, resist or negotiate particular discourses associated with health and exercise (see Atencio and Wright 2009; Skeggs 1997; Youdell 2006; Hauge 2009; Zannettino 2008). We, thus, explore how girls, through the active negotiation of discourses, take up exercise to constitute themselves in particular ways. Although health messages may be announced through 'universal' (essentially white, middle class, westernized) *ideals*, certain opportunities and subjectivities may only be available to some girls depending on the particular contexts of their lives. We explore how obesity discourse and its associated practices of the body may provide certain 'subject positions' (Davies and Harré 1990) as ways of being and naming oneself or others.

Our interest in this chapter is to examine how exercise as a bodily practice is defined through obesity discourse and featured in "the ways in which subjective gender is constituted and mobilised" (Zannettino 2008, 66). In other words, we seek to examine how young women negotiate the relationships between dominant discourses on health, the body and gender, and how they actively constitute their subjectivities through these discourses in relation to exercise.

Research Design

The chapter is based on data from a study funded by the Economic and Social Research Council (ESRC Reference RES-000-23-2003) entitled 'The Impact of New Health Imperatives on Schools.' The study has investigated how health imperatives and associated curriculum initiatives are operationalized within and across a range of schools located in Middle England with parallel studies pursued in Australia and New Zealand.[1] The methodology was designed to explore the relationships between demographic 'resources' (socio-cultural capital) born of age, gender, class, ethnicity, and (forms of) schooling; sites and sources of influence on 'body knowledge,' and individuals' relationships to their embodied selves. Data sets were collected across eight schools in England selected to reflect a range of social, cultural and policy contexts enabling the in-depth analysis required to capture the interplay between cultural forces, social institutions and their impact on young people's embodied identities. All were policy-saturated environments wherein policy on and commitments to health education sit alongside many other more pressing demands, for example, of literacy and numeracy. The methodology that brings together data sets from teachers, students and the policy context of each school, has enabled us to derive the regulative functions of 'biopedagogies' present in both formal and popular pedagogic sites of learning about the health and body.

This chapter draws specifically on a combination of quantitative and qualitative data derived from some 1,176 questionnaires administered to pupils aged from 9 to 16 years of age, in eight schools in Middle England, U.K. (see table 7.1), and qualitative data drawn from interviews with 90 pupils and 19 staff (see De Pian et al. 2008). Given the diversity of the school contexts selected for the research, the young people occupy a broad range of socio-cultural categories across class, gender, ethnicity and culture. Whilst quantitative data is said to "obliterate individuality and richness" (Greene and Hill 2005, 4), statistics obtained through the pupil questionnaire were used as a backdrop to the qualitative, descriptive data obtained through interviews that registered students' perceptions of health, their bodies, and school health policies and practices. Semi-structured interviews were conducted with a total of 90 pupils, in pairs where possible, although due to time and space constraints some interviews were conducted in groups of three or four. The interviews were based around four themes: health, school, the body and obesity. Each of these was written on a colored card placed face-down in front the participants. The young people took one in turns to reveal the topic to be discussed which was intended not only to redress the power imbalance (Greene and Hill 2005) present in adult-child interviewing but also give the participants a sense of control during the interviews but actively engage them in the process. This was particularly useful for some of the younger participants who reported enjoying the interview process due to the familiar 'game' format.

Talking with young people about sensitive topics such as body-self relationships and issues of weight presented some ethical challenges which we addressed in a number of ways. The study was guided by ethical clearance via the University Ethical Advisory Committee with data collection completed under the remit of the ESRC-funded study. Furthermore, given the sensitivity of issues associated with young people talking about their body, photo-elicitation techniques (Heisley and Levy 1991) were used during interviews, whereby photos of different body types from popular culture were presented to participants as prompts for discussion. All interview quotes are reported using pseudonyms, school year where appropriate, and the school type represented by a letter (e.g., school X) referred to in table 7.1.

Table 7.1 School Contexts

School	Type/Description	Groups included in research sample
B	Large, independent, secondary school for boys (10–18 year olds).	12–13 year olds and 15–16 year olds (years 8 and 11)
F	Large, independent, co-ed., preparatory school (4–11 year olds).	9–11 year olds (Years 5 and 6)
G	Secondary school for girls (11–18 year olds).	12–13 year olds and 15–16 year olds (Years 8 and 11)
H	Large, co-ed., rural state middle school (11–14 year olds).	11–14 year olds (Years 7–9).
L	Large, co-ed., multi-ethnic, state middle school (11–14 year olds).	12–13 year olds (Year 8)
R	Large, co-ed., multi-ethnic, inner city, state primary school (4–11 year olds).	9–11 year olds (Years 5 and 6)
W	Very small, co-ed., middle class, rural/village, state primary school (4–11 year olds).	9–11 year olds (Years 5 and 6)
X	Large, co-ed., deprived, multi-ethnic, inner city college (11–16 year olds).	13–15 year olds (Years 9 and 10)

Source: ESRC, 'The Impact of New Health Imperatives on Schools.'

KNOWLEDGE, EXERCISE AND 'BEING HEALTHY'

The emphasis on diet and exercise as health-enhancing strategies, both in public health promotion and public pedagogy, as well as in more localized contexts of school-based practices and pedagogies has been well documented in recent work (Burrows and Wright 2007; Evans et al. 2008; Wright and Dean 2007; Wright and Harwood 2009). In this first section we outline how these prevailing discourses of health and obesity provided powerful ways of framing exercise as a meaningful practice *upon* the body, as reflected in official discourse on obesity. As Foucault describes: "discourse finds a way of limiting its domain, of defining what it is talking about, of giving it the status of an object—and therefore of making it manifest, nameable, and describable" (1972, 46). Obesity discourse not only names how one is to understand the 'problem' of *obesity* through biopedagogies, but has come to limit and prescribe particular frameworks for *health* more broadly. In the data we report later, we reveal how girls routinely make reference to this framework and rehearse its storyline. Data from both the survey and interviews suggest that girls articulated understandings of health through references to weight, body size and shape and a broader presumption that achieving health was primarily achieved through eating well and exercising. A total of 83.7 percent of girls in the sample (survey data) listed exercise as one of, if not the most important things that someone can do to stay healthy. Similarly, in interviews, participants marked out exercise as a key way to stay healthy, rehearsing dominant western ideals of health: "Get more active and don't just sit around and watch telly and stuff, get more active" (Roopa, Year 5, R).

Data clearly suggested that the students were able to identify exercise as a necessary feature of being and staying healthy. The pervasiveness of this imperative is such that it was an association made by the majority of girls in our survey across all of the schools, regardless of socio-economic context, year group or ethnic make-up, although it is noteworthy that nearly all of 16-year-old girls (97.1 percent of girls aged 16) listed exercise as one if not the most important thing they can do to stay healthy. Eating the 'right' foods, predominantly vegetables and fruit, and exercising regularly were regarded as necessary practices which could make a significant difference to one's health: "Exercise can make a difference" (Ingrid, Year 5, F). When asked what the participants would do to help the children in their school stay healthy if they were the head teacher, many of the participants listed biopedagogical strategies to enhance young peoples physical activity and dietary regimes, often making reference to disciplined practices to achieve this:

Amy (Year 6, F):	I would do a morning exercising
Interviewer:	OK, for everybody?
Amy:	Yeah

Marie (Year 6, F):	Yeah so like in assembly we'd make them do star jumps or something.
Amy:	Yeah or in the morning on the playground, just so you get them going.
Marie:	Or when we're on the apparatus you've got to like jump onto each obstacle. Yeah, don't talk just like star jumps and everything.

This ability to describe health imperatives was unsurprising given that it often aligned with the policies and biopedagogical practices utilized in their schools. Typically, teachers described the health challenges in school as being concerned with instilling knowledge about exercise and ill-health, as evidenced by Jane's comments:

> I think they need to have plenty of fitness, they need lots of exercise, lots of energy and a good basic diet . . . We should be sending the message out that if you eat too much and you don't exercise you'll get fat, if you eat a sensible diet and you exercise enough that's good for you and that's the end of the message.
>
> (Jane, teacher, F)

Knowledge about the role of exercise is thus perceived to be crucial in the campaign for getting children healthy. Many children are exposed to, understand, and reiterate the widely promulgated messages associated with anti-obesity campaigns as they are recontextualized into body pedagogies:

> Yeah, irrespective of size, doesn't matter. If my colleague sitting next to me is twice the size of me and I think oh I'm thin I don't have to do anything that's not going to help me is it? At the end of the day I'm just going to sit in a chair and I might not get fatter because my metabolism might not be like that but I'm not healthy am I? I'm not as healthy as I am if I exercise.
>
> (Jane, teacher, F)

This tendency for young people to conceive of health as eating the right foods and exercising regularly has been observed in other studies of international cohorts of young people (e.g., Beausoleil 2008; Burrows 2008; Rail 2009). It is clear that when asked about health young women were able to rehearse particular storylines about the value of exercise. Although obesity discourse provided a dominant way to understand exercise, the students' experiences were mediated by exposure to other discourses. As Hauge suggests: "girls learn which practices are acknowledged and expected, and do practices on and with their bodies in ways which position them within and according to a multiplicity of discourses which address categories such as gender, sexuality, ethnicity, and age" (2009, 295). Data revealed that while the participants engaged in physical activity for 'health' purposes, they also took up exercise as practice through which to address negative body image. In the remainder of this chapter we examine in greater detail how they subsequently take up exercise as a 'bodily practice' (Hauge 2009) in the process of constituting particular subjectivities.

DIVIDING PRACTICES OF HEALTH: "I DON'T WANT TO BE OBESED"

Interview data revealed how obesity discourse constructs certain ways of being and practices which have profound implications for the way girls conceive of their bodies and the meaning of exercise in their lives. Exercise featured significantly when the girls were constructing themselves as 'healthy.' In what follows, we unpack the relationships between gender, exercise and health to show how different dichotomies manifest in relation to the ideal body and the obese body in girls' and teachers' talk.

Many girls contrasted the concept of 'healthy', which implied being active, with unhealthy which implied a lack of mobility and associated fatness: "You can't like do any like exercise because you're too like big to do it" (Salina, Year 10, R). Discourses associated with obesity across public pedagogy and official health promotion (Evans et al. 2008) have become so pervasive that they effectively construct certain subject positions. For many participants, the changes in body size—becoming 'fat' that was a process over which some felt they had very little control—was to represent not just a physical change, but an obvious change in one's subjectivity:

> I probably wouldn't like it because it would be a complete change 'cause everyone calls me kind of small and petite so it would be a big change and I'd probably get looked at in the streets if I was going into town or something.
>
> (Kaitlyn, Year 5, W)

> 'Cause if you're too fat you could not be really fit and walk around as much as you normally do and it would be more unhealthy to be more fat than thin I think it would be hard to exercise and I think I wouldn't really like it 'cause I would just like to be normal like everyone else
>
> (Phillipa, Year 6, F).

Thus, whilst bodies were constructed in different ways, some were more open to interrogation than others. Following the prevailing discourse of obesity, there was an assumption that those who were 'overweight,' were irresponsibly inactive and lazy: "A lot of people just can't be bothered to do the exercise if they have obesity or whatever" (Kirsty, Year 6, W). Another observed "that it (obesity) has risen in the country and that lots more people are obesed" (Sarah, Year 8, G).

In these spaces, the young women actively refer to the fat child as 'obesed,' a term circulating in popular peer culture. This locates fatness as a disease category, but also creates an abject position in which one becomes a 'beastly' body (through a play on words whereby obesed also sounds like o-*beast*). However, constituting the 'obesed' subjectivity provided no discursive space for the complexities of weight (i.e., that one might be overweight and healthy, or physically active). Girls as young as 10 were reading health in this way and were cognizant of the moral imperative and duty to be healthy and of the body as an indicator of one's health (e.g., Crawford 1980; Markula 1997; Tinning 1985). In particular, it was supposed that one's weight was a result of whether one exercised and ate well (as described and defined in obesity discourse):

> Like on the news when they say someone's died from being obese, and all the schools, they switched didn't they and I think that was really good. If someone tries hard enough to get it to stop then I think we will become like non-obese.
>
> (Milly, Year 7, H)

Girls across all school types, ethnicity and age categories engaged in what Foucault refers to as 'dividing practices' (see Harwood and Rasmussen 2004; Atencio and Wright 2009). This involved 'othering' the 'obesed person' and reiterating the need to exercise so as to avoid "becoming like that":

> I wouldn't like it because I watch Newsround, it's a CBBC channel and it said that people who are obese can't do as much exercise 'cause they have to move more muscles because they're overweight and they've got more weight to move. I like doing sport so I wouldn't really like it. And I'd get stared at.
>
> (Rebecca, Year 5, W)

This process of othering was underpinned by very specific categories of embodiment, projected through future images of what their lives would be like if they were to become obese: "They get pushed around and no-one wants to be friends with them and no-one wants to meet them" (Ingrid, Year 5, F).

> And everyone makes fun of you, you don't usually get any friends. But there's some people that are really skinny and they don't have

any friends. 'Cause people think they're really ugly but sometimes if you're fat you're really pretty but people still don't like you 'cause you're fatter than somebody else.

(Marie, Year 6, F)

Being overweight was, thus, associated with being socially isolated, immobile, unable to move or engage in any form of physical activity or exercise. In this sense, exercise featured as means to not only achieve a physical body, but also a socially acceptable body: a body which protected the participants from the stigma of being overweight. These girls' empowerment or alienation tended to depend on the nature of relationships between their own bodies and the ideal bodies presented through discourses. A 'healthy' looking body, thus, became an important form of social capital when these young women were actively constructing dominant subjectivities through displays of the ideal body. Those without such a body were positioned as 'other':

Hannah (Year 11, G):   I don't feel under pressure personally but I know, you will know who I'm talking about, somebody who gets, two people actually who feel very under pressure.

Interviewer: Why do you think that is?

Hannah: Because they are overweight. Basically they are not the ideal weight but they're doing something productive about it like they go to the gym on a Monday and Thursday I think and they get involved with loads of hockey and loads of sport, but before they did loads of sport I think they just got to this point where they thought 'we have to do something about this now,' because I don't think people from this school were saying it but especially people from School B, the pressure from the boys is a lot bigger than from the girls in this school.

Many of these girls referred to undertaking exercise as a way to differentiate their bodies from others. Particular practices were associated with the category 'healthy.' Thus, body shaping emerges as a particularly important aspect in constituting these subjectivities. Interviews revealed that exercise was constructed as means through which to shape bodies in particular ways to avoid exclusionary practices: "Like show some people who are obese and then you can put them into a gym and then a few weeks later you can show them or however long it takes show them how slim they are" (Ingrid, Year 5, F).

Interviewer: What would you think if you put on a bit of weight?
                        How would that make you feel?
Orla (Year 6, W):   I'd try to do more exercise.

Given that a substantial body of literature points to the escalating pressures concerning body ideals placed on adolescent young women, it is perhaps unsurprising that these pressures were particularly acute for the girls in our study (Evans et al. 2008; Wright et al. 2006). As Hauge notes, the body becomes meaningful through intersections with categories such as child and adolescent, and carries "certain expectations regarding how to perform particular bodily practices" (2009, 293). While some of our younger participants included 'play' in their descriptions of their physical activity patterns, older participants tended to talk about physical activity 'instrumentally' with reference to health and fitness activities, or organized sport, rather than broader conceptions of recreational or educational/enrichment activity. In other words, exercising to achieve 'health' was actually mediated by assumptions about the *outcomes* this would yield, most notably losing weight or shaping one's size or appearance. Obesity discourse becomes so salient in the lives of these young women, because of the observable outcomes of 'weight loss' rather than broader concepts of health and well-being.

AVOIDING 'OTHER' AND BEING A HEALTHY YOUNG WOMAN

While many of our participants talk about the 'health' benefits of exercise, these were often connected to the reshaping of the body and with broader concerns about their appearance. In order to achieve corporeal changes or weight loss, participants made reference to *particular* practices of exercise and physical activity, and focused on individual parts of their bodies, such as thighs or tummies: "I enjoy swimming and I really enjoy bike riding 'cause it works all of your muscles and so does swimming. I'm trying to work on my thighs at the minute" (Marie, Year 6, F).

Marie, who attended an independent school, recognizes the benefits of exercising in terms of 'working her muscles' but then makes reference to 'working on her thighs' to constitute a particular gendered subjectivity; Marie's social class location mediates her understanding of health where she emphasizes responsibility in actively *working* on her body. This positions her within middle-class, neo-liberal discourse in which the individual is deemed responsible for solving health problems (Armstrong 1995; Crawford 1980) through working on oneself:

> Yeah, I try *to work* on it. When I'm sitting down I try and lift my legs up and down so I'm working them [. . .] I go on my mum's foot pedals

as well and she's got a sit-up machine and I've got a Davina exercise DVD that I do with my mum.

(Marie, Year 6, F, our emphasis)

The association of working on oneself as a reflection of the good middle-class citizen affords subject positions through which some young women are able to recognize themselves and others. Marie invokes an unspoken subjectivity as the white middle-class neo-liberal girl: an active healthy young woman who takes the responsibility to actively *work* on their body. She exercises to shape her body toward the ideal *healthy girl*:

Marie (Year 6, F):	Eat good food and exercise everyday 'cause it will burn off your carbs and make you fitter.
Interviewer:	Why do you think you do those activities and try to eat healthily like you do? What are the main reasons?
Marie:	Well I don't want to be fat. I don't want to be thin either, I just want to be average size [. . .] I've lost quite a lot of weight since I've been eating my bananas and everything and doing my dancing.
Interviewer:	How do you feel about that?
Marie:	I feel really happy with myself because I've gone on a bit of a diet. This morning I didn't have any breakfast [. . .] I have, I've got one on my bike. it tells me how many meters I've done in a day and when I clip it onto my belt it will tell me how many steps I've done in a day [. . .] I just want to know if I need to do more. I try to improve it, so say if I've done 50 in a day I'd do like 70, and it also tells me how many carbs you've burnt off and how many stones you've lost.

Through exercise, she is able to constitute an embodied subjectivity. Marie buys into the health benefits of exercise because it helps to reshape her body in specific, gendered ways (i.e., working on her thighs and other feminized practices). In this sense, a thin body complies with both gendered norms and becoming the hetero-feminine subject, but also with the official discourse of obesity. Health knowledge legitimates other readings of the body connected to the hetero-feminine subject. Such findings reflect "the inseparability of sex–gender–sexuality" (Youdell 2005, 268).

The focus on shaping particular parts of the body through exercise in many ways reflects the widely acknowledged pressures on young women to subscribe to body ideals associated with femininity (Bordo 1990; Hesse-Biber 2006; Markula 1998. Indeed, majority of the girls in our survey (60.9 percent) reported that they 'NEVER feel good about their bodies,' and the 54.3 percent were 'NEVER happy about their current weight and size.' Research elsewhere reports similar findings where improved 'appearance' consistently emerges as the reason for young women to exercise (Strelan et al. 2003). When asked "Have you tried to lose weight?" 45 percent of boys responded 'yes' compared to 64.5 percent of girls. Thus, girls expressed a particularly strong desire to get thinner as compared to boys. Of those who had tried to lose weight, 44 percent had done so *through exercise*. Whilst the survey data revealed that girls were clearly able to see the value in exercise as a means to lose weight, very few alluded to potential dangers associated with over-exercising. While 50.4 percent of the participants listed patterns of exercise as one of, if not the main thing that stops people being healthy, 72 percent of those participants claimed 'no exercise or sport' was unhealthy whereas only 1.2 percent referred to over-exercising as unhealthy. Given these findings, a conflation between health and appearance is hardly surprising in Marie's concerns about exercise. She recognized that exercise will make her 'fitter,' but also celebrated the weight loss achieved through dancing. This conflation thus limits her willingness to display alternative physicalities:

> So like me now I'm always worried about what I look like and I always have to be perfect . . . I've done it since I've been 9–10 really I've been wanting to make my hair look nice I'd like make myself look perfect if there was a boy I liked and I wanted to impress him I just want to make myself look perfect and I want to make myself look skinny and I want my hair to be right.
>
> (Marie, Year 6, F)

These narratives reveal the extent to which exercise featured in young people's understandings of what it means to have a 'healthy' body size, not the social and emotional features of health and well-being. Exercise was taken up as a bodily practice through which one works instrumentally on the body to control weight: "I'm not always conscious about it but just like feel better in myself that I'm doing something, I'm not like lounging around. And dancing is proper hard work isn't it, proper sweat" (Jordan, Year 10, X).

Girls described exercise in particular ways, as vigorous activities involving sweating and getting out of breath in order to 'work off weight.' In doing so, they position themselves as morally good and feel better for being responsibly healthy. Exercise became less about the pleasure of movement than the means through which bodies can be shaped and trained toward achieving often 'unachievable ideals' (Markula 1995): "But if you ate a whole pizza you would have to run a whole marathon to burn it off so I'm not having pizza" (Lauren, Year 5, W). Indeed significant proportions of female students at all schools (i.e., 9.1 percent in the independent, co-education, primary school, to 48.8 percent in the independent, girls' secondary school) indicated that they had, at some stage, been 'bullied about their weight.' The emotions associated with fatness prompted us to think about how "discursive processes work in and through desires, feelings, anxieties and defenses" (Zannettino 2008, 477). Schools were instrumental in promoting a classification into fat and thin. This was played out through the health imperatives which stressed the dangers of obesity and those at risk. For example, Marie reported that her teachers were not scared to stress the risks of obesity and invoke fear: My Mum's not scared to say anything so in like PSHE (personal, social, health and economic education) they're not scared to tell me about it or anything (Marie, Year 6, F).

For Marie, the effects of these biopedagogical apparatus were particularly strong, instilling feelings of fear:

> Will I die because I'm overweight and you won't get any sleep because you'll be thinking about will I die or not. Some people don't sleep at all because they think that they're going to die in their sleep because they're so obese.
>
> (Marie, Year 6, F)

Fear of being obese also restricted possible ways these girls felt comfortable about their bodies. Girls across all school settings reported that when they did display alternative bodies, they were often called names like 'fatty': "You get called more names if you're overweight" (Leonne, Year 9, H). Such naming reveals the often emotional consequences of trying to develop alternative ways of being:

> When I was younger I was quite fat (laugh) at primary school, about year 4 or 5 and some people used to call me names and I think children will grow up and other people will start taking the mick out of them and they'll feel shy and they might want to change, they might starve themselves.
>
> (Emma, Year 8, H)

Salina stated, "Yeah my teacher told me to stay healthy because if you are overweight people won't be your friend and they'll like be mean to you" (Year 5, R).

Negotiating the Norm: 'You Could be Overweight and Hate Your Body and You Could be Skinny and Still Hate Your Body' (Katherine, Year 9, H)

The categorization into thin and fat bodies impacted the ways girls mediated their own categories of social class, race and gender. Like Broadfoot, we have registered how pupils' needs, interests, embodied dispositions and abilities interrelate with "the various cultural settings they experience, at home, at school, in their peer group and elsewhere" (2001, 264). The girls in our study made reference to the variety of discourses through which fluid ways of learning about the body occurred in cultural, public and official sites of learning. In particular, they reported drawing on discursive resources made available to them within popular culture to make sense of the body.

Although a thin body was admired, many girls were conscious of walking a very delicate tightrope between constructing an ideal body and a body that was too thin. Being a 'healthy girl' was mediated by their reading of wider popular and consumer culture such as teenage magazines through which they also learnt about acceptable bodies (see Davies 1993; Oliver and Lalik 2000; Walkerdine 1997). Despite an apparent adherence to orthodox notions of health there was evidence within participants' narratives of a critical reading of thinness. Rather ironically, they were critical of those who are too thin, For example, Victoria Beckham (former pop star and wife of the soccer star David Beckham and who is often criticized in popular magazines for being too thin) was frequently constructed as 'overstepping the boundary' and representing all that was bad about being too focused on one's body and losing too much weight:

Interviewer: What about Victoria Beckham, do you like the way she looks?

Marie (Year 6, F):   I think she's really pretty and she's got a really good figure but she's just too skinny for me . . . hmm the right weight . . . well I wouldn't like to be Paula Radcliffe (an international runner).

Abi (Year 6, F):   Personally I wouldn't like to be that skinny.

Marie: Because she's so skinny. I'd more like to be her really (points to picture of Anna Kournikova [a tennis player]).

While slenderness has long been the ideal, a more nuanced reading of 'being too thin' may be equally emphasized. Indeed one might argue that thinness is being refashioned through particular magazines where an individual's body is criticized for one day being too fat, and the next too thin. In earlier extracts where Marie talks about exercise as a means for being healthy and avoiding being fat, she does not want to be too thin. In the active constitution of her healthy thin body, Marie maintains the normative feminine, heterosexual body: she does not want to lose too much weight to achieve a particular body ideal.

Thus health discourse is circumscribed by peer culture, where being the successful popular girl mediates the degree to which one shapes one's body through exercise. We draw on extracts to illustrate how the meaning of sport, exercise and physical activity *within the school context* appeared to have a bearing on the particular discourses these girls chose to invest in. Some girls, for example, made reference to exercise as a way to constitute a different, 'fit, strong and toned' body. Only 16.9 percent said that being healthy is important to them for physical reasons such as being able to participate in sport (36.5 percent). Over half of those girls (51.6 percent) were from the Girls' Independent Secondary School and located in the higher social classes (1–3). Those were the schools where reputation and recognition of sports performance were vital, and part of the broader neo-liberal incentive toward marketization of the school. In such cases, the school's desire appeared to impact young women's understanding of the role of physical activity in their lives. This was unsurprising given the importance of sport in these schools in the process of marketization associated with notions of free choice characteristic of neo-liberal policy within these independent (fee paying) schools. In these contexts, the young women negotiated meanings around the value of exercise in distinctive ways.

Elizabeth (Year 11, G):   Yeah, like I agree with Hannah, toned is good because it makes you look healthy.

Hannah (Year 11, G):   For example in this picture you can see that without doing anything you see she's got like muscles not like a bodybuilder or anything, you just see they're there and she's obviously played sport whereas if you went and had a look at these guys (Posh Spice) you can see their muscles because they've got no fat there. They just have no fat on them at all, it's like "oh my God, it's like skin and bones"—and the only reason you can see the muscles because they've got no fat there.

Elizabeth: Yeah, that's just a bit minging—that just scares me.

For girls like Hannah from the independent (fee paying) school, athletic toned bodies define the 'fit' and 'sporty' body with the emphasis on academic performance in the wider school context:

Hannah: I like her (Anna Kournikova) anyway. She's really nice, when you see her play, I've seen her loads of times, she's really toned but she's not thin. When you're a tennis player, I used to play a lot of tennis but I do hockey and netball now, but she's just so toned; she just looks really good, she's not like a stick thin person, she's just really toned and looks really good.

(Hannah, Year 11, G)

Hannah describes how she engaged in body work in a quest to cultivate a 'healthy' physical body which coalesced with a 'sculpted lean muscled femininity' (Heywood 2007, 113) which represents the 'can do' girls of neo-liberalism.

> Because I do a lot of sport so I would say I'm quite a healthy person: I eat healthily and I would say that I have quite a good body but then there's always an issue, because I cut down on sport so like I have my rest period then I put on weight and then I lose weight so I prefer how I am when I'm being sporty, when I'm doing loads of sport rather than in the summer when I'm doing it perhaps once or twice a week rather than once a day, so that's my preference.
>
> (Hannah, Year 11, G)

The constitution of a successful healthy girl in these school settings carried very clear expectations which influence how girls may shape and perform their bodies. It differed considerably from other schools within our research study where such a powerful culture of sport performance did not prevail. This involves the active negotiation of the display of particular corporeal identities across a variety of social-cultural contexts (see Ali 2003). As Skelton and Francis argue "the achievement of such balances may be particularly challenging for those girls who do not fit the 'norm' of white middle class girlhood" (2009, 43). In this sense "intersections of categories such as gender, age and ethnicity produce different possibilities in terms of which subject positions girls may take up" (Hauge 2009, 302).

CONCLUSION

The prevalence of obesity discourse within contexts of learning is occurring at a time when popular culture is becoming increasingly narrow in its expectations of a normative body. Girls in our study reported that they have to negotiate a complex and delicate series of discourses in constituting gendered bodies in this terrain. Our research data reveal how obesity discourses which shape popular and official pedagogies, exist alongside emerging shifts in popular culture and media toward the critique of 'being too thin' as non-feminine. In this sense, it revealed how young women attempt to constitute healthy subjectivities through obesity discourse, but at the same time have to accommodate tensions which surround the gendered body. Because young women have to resolve tensions between particular subjectivities, the data suggest a nuanced and complex relationship between health, weight and gender. On the one hand, they must meet the ideals and expectations of health imperatives which define health through weight management. Concomitantly, through discourses of sport, and contemporary shifts in femininity and thinness, they must avoid being 'too thin.' Our analysis indicates that although particular bodies were normalized within peer and institutional culture, they are often unachievable 'ideals.' The health discourses benefited those bodies that meet the ideals rather than 'other' alternative body types. Furthermore, these negotiations created particular ways through which exercise became a *particular* body practice. The girls' engagement with exercise was significantly shaped by the cultural pressures toward instrumental relationship with exercise instead of experiencing the joy of movement.

NOTE

1 Involving Professor Jan Wright, Dr Valerie Harwood and Dr Ken Cliff in Australia and Dr Lisette Burrows and Jaleh McCormack in New Zealand

REFERENCES

Ali, S. 2003. To be a girl: Culture and class in schools. *Gender and Education* 15(3): 269–83.

Armstrong, D. 1995. The rise of surveillance medicine. *Sociology of Health and Illness* 17(3): 393–404.

Atencio, M. and J. Wright. 2009. 'Ballet it's too whitey': Discursive hierarchies of high school dance spaces and the constitution of embodied feminine subjectivities. *Gender and Education* 21(1): 31–46.

Babones, J. 2009. *Social inequality and public health*. Bristol: The Policy Press.

Beausoleil, N. 2008. Meanings of health, physical activity and schooling in Newfoundland and New Brunswick youths' narratives. Paper presented at the Australian Association for Research in Education Conference, November 30–December 4 dates in Brisbane, Australia.

Bordo, S. R. 1990. The body and reproduction of femininity: A feminist appropriation of Foucault. In *Gender/body/knowledge* eds. A. Jagger and S. Bordo, 13–33. New Brunswick: Rutgers University Press.

Broadfoot, P. 2001 Editorial: Culture, learning and comparative education, *Comparative Education*. 37(3): 261–66.

Burrows, L. 2008. 'Fit, Fast and Skinny': New Zealand school students 'talk' about health. *New Zealand Physical Educator* November 1st.

Burrows, L. and J. Wright 2007. Prescribing practices: Shaping healthy children in schools. *The International Journal of Children's Rights* 15(1): 83–98.

Crawford, R. 1980. Healthism and the medicalisation of everyday life. *International Journal of Health Services* 10: 365–88.

Davies, B. 1989. *Frogs and snails and feminist tails: Preschool children and gender*. Sydney: Allen and Unwin.

—— 1993. *Shards of glass: Children reading and writing beyond gendered identities*. St. Leonards, NSW: Allen & Unwin.

Davies, B. and R. Harré. 1990. Positioning: The discursive production of selves. *Journal for the Theory of Social Behavior* 20(1): 43–63.

De Pian, L., J. Evans and E. Rich. 2008. Young People's Decision Making about Health as an Embodied Social Process: Reflections from the field. Paper presented at the Annual Australian Educational Research Conference Brisbane, November, 2008

Evans, J., E. Rich, B. Davies and R. Allwood. 2008. *Education, disordered eating and obesity discourse: Fat fabrications.* London: Routledge.

Foucault, M. 1972. *The archeology of knowledge* (A. M. Sheridan-Smith trans). London: Tavistock.

—— 1979. *Discipline and punish.* London: Peregrine.

—— 1997. The ethics of the concern for self as a practice of freedom. In *Michel Foucault: Ethics, subjectivity and truth. The essential works of Foucault, vol. 1*, ed. P. Rabinow, 281–302. New York: The New Press.

Francis, B. and L. Archer. 2005. Negotiating the dichotomy of boffin and triad: British Chinese pupils' constructions of laddism. *The Sociological Review* 53(3): 495–520.

Greene, S. and M. Hill. 2005. Researching children's experience: Methods and methodological issues. In *Researching children's experience: Approaches and methods,* eds. S. Greene and D. Hogan, 1–21. London: Sage.

Harris, A. 2004. *Future girls: Young women in the twenty-first century,* New York: Routledge.

Harwood, V. and M. L. Rasmussen. 2004. Studying schools with an ethic of discomfort. In *Dangerous coagulations? The uses of Foucault in the study of education,* ed. B. Baker and K. Heyning, New York: Peter Lang.

Hauge, M-I. 2009. Bodily practices and discourses of hetero-femininity: Girls' constitution of subjectivities in their social transition between childhood and adolescence. *Gender and Education* 21(3): 293–307.

Heisley, D. D. and S. J. Levy. 1991. Autodriving: A photoelicitation technique. *Journal of Consumer Research* 18: 257–72.

Hesse-Biber, S. 2006. *Am I thin enough yet? The cult of thinness and the commercialisation of identity.* New York: Oxford.

Heywood, L. 2007. Producing girls and the neoliberal body. In *Physical Culture, power, and the body,* eds. J. Hargreaves and P. Vertinsky, 101–20. London: Routledge.

Markula, P. 1995. Firm but shapely, fit but sexy, strong but thin: the postmodern aerobicizing female bodies, *Sociology of Sport Journal* 12(4): 424–53.

—— 1997. Are fit people healthy? Health, exercise, active living and the body in fitness discourse. *Waikato Journal of Education* 3: 21–39.

—— 1998. Women's health, physical fitness and ideal body: A problematic relationship. *Journal of Physical Education New Zealand* 31(1): 9–13.

Oliver, K. and R. Lalik. 2000. *Bodily knowledge: Learning about equity and justice with adolescent girls.* New York: Peter Lang.

Rail, G. 2009. Canadian Youth's discursive construction of health in the context of obesity discourse. In J. Wright and V. Harwood, eds. *Biopolitics and the 'Obesity Epidemic': Governing bodies,* 141–56. London: Routledge.

Skeggs, B. 1997. *Formations of class and gender.* London: Sage.

Skelton, C. and B. Francis. 2009. *Feminism and the schooling scandal.* London: Routledge.

Strelan, P., S. J. Mehaffey and M. Tiggemann. 2003. Self-objectification and esteem in young women: The mediating role of reasons for exercise. *Sex Roles* 48: 89–95.

Susinos, T., A. Calvo and S. Rojas. 2009. Becoming a woman: The construction of female subjectivities and its relationship with school. *Gender and Education* 21(1): 97–110.

Tinning, R. 1985. Physical education and the cult of slenderness: A critique. *The ACHPER National Journal,* 107: 10–13.

Walkerdine, V. 1997. *Daddy's girl: Young girls and popular culture.* London: Macmillan Press.

Warin, M., K. Turner, V. Moore and M. Davies, M. 2008. Bodies, mothers and identities. Rethinking obesity and the BMI. *Sociology of Health and Illness* 30(1): 97–111.

Wright, J. and R. Dean. 2007. A balancing act: Problematising prescriptions about food and weight in school health texts. *Education and Democracy: Journal of Didactics & Educational Policy* 16(2): 75–94.

Wright, J. and V. Harwood, eds. 2009. *Biopolitics and the obesity epidemic: Governing bodies.* New York and Oxon: Routledge.

Wright, J. E., G. O'Flynn, and D. Macdonald. 2006. Being fit and looking healthy: Young women's and men's constructions of health and fitness. *Sex Roles—A Journal of Research* 54(9–10): 1–15.

Youdell, D. 2005. Sex—gender—sexuality: How sex, gender and sexuality con- stellations are constituted in secondary schools. *Gender and Education* 17: 249–70.

—— 2006. Subjectivation and performative politics—Butler thinking Althusser and Foucault: Intelligibility, agency and the raced-nationed-religioned subjects of education. *Gender and Education* 27: 511–28.

Zannettino, L. 2008. Imagining womanhood: Psychodynamic processes in the 'textual' and discursive formation of girls' subjectivities and desires for the future. *Gender and Education* 20(5): 465–79.

Part III

In the Name of Health

Women's Exercise and
Public Health

WESTERN HEALTH PROMOTION DISCOURSE: HOW 'HEALTHY' IS IT?

Health promotion campaigns have been used to encourage people to take responsibility for their health. The term 'healthy lifestyle', for instance, is one of many mobilized by health promoters to persuade people to change the way in which they live their lives to improve their health (Wray 2007). The development of this type of lifestyle often involves avoiding particular types of behaviors and practices that are deemed to be risky to health and promoting others, such as exercise and dieting, that result in improved health. Western public health advice is often presented as based on bio-medical research, the source of 'pure' knowledge. Media reports then repeat these 'facts' to the general public. There have been, however, increasing criticisms of this type of approach to health promotion.

Some researchers point to the increased expectation of the individual to take responsibility for one's health. As state responsibility for health has decreased in modern western societies, the desire to exert autonomy and control over individual bodies has increased (Armstrong 1995; Rose 1999). As a consequence, the individual is more likely to be constructed as the main agent of change (Bunton and Burrows 1995; Furedi 2004; Rose 1999; Sointu 2005; Wray 2007). This means that ill health is now more likely to be attributed to risky lifestyle choices and a lack of health maintenance and self-care (Burgess 2008; Peterson and Bunton 1997). As a result, women's lifestyles and behaviors have also increasingly come under the scrutiny of public health, This is evident in health promotion research and practice that focus on women's 'lifestyle factors' and behaviors. For example, Waters et al. (2001) examined African-American women's risk of developing diabetes, hypertension and stroke. Although the authors argue that it is important "to understand health behaviours in the context of 'that' culture, which profoundly influence beliefs and behaviours," emphasis is still placed on changing individual behavior to fit a particular model of health (Waters et al. 2001, 84). There is an underlying expectation that the participants of the study will conform to scientific models of a healthy lifestyle and adjust their behavior accordingly. This approach is problematic as it fails to question whether it is possible to 'choose health' (Department of Health 2004) regardless of the social and cultural complexities of people's lives (Segal 2003). This leads to the second critique of the current mode of health promotion.

Some researchers point out that the current health promotion strategies ignore social, political and cultural factors that influence people's health behavior (Segal 2003; Wray and Deery 2008). The assumption is that it is appropriate to promote a western healthy lifestyle through often western-centric health promotion interventions (Furedi 2004) to everyone regardless of cultural background. This is evident in current exercise and physical activity campaigns that have relentlessly promoted activity and eating particular foods as essential components of a 'healthy lifestyle.' Because contemporary cultural meanings around healthy lifestyle are often filled with inconsistencies, its applicability across cultures has been questioned (Maynard et al. 2008; Wray and Bartholomew 2006). In addition, uncritical promotion of scientifically based notions of health as 'truth,' marginalize those alternative knowledges that may "expose the very power relations that create . . . and prop up those . . . with a vested interest in the status quo" (Holmes et al. 2006, 185). There is clear research evidence to suggest that ethnic inequalities in health in Britain are influenced by experienced and perceived racism (Karlsen and Nazroo 2002; Krieger 2000; Wray and Bartholomew 2006). For example, Karlsen and Nazroo argue the health consequences of indirect and direct racism include damaged self-esteem and 'poorer physical and mental health' (2002, 17). Other research findings suggest that ethnic and cultural background strongly influences perceptions and experiences of health (for example, Ahmad and Bradby 2008; Gunaratnam 2001; Moriarty and Butt 2004). However, although attempts have been made to provide health services that are 'culturally sensitive,' there is evidence to suggest that minority ethnic groups continue to experience racism and discrimination (Ahmad and Bradby 2008; Blakemore and Boneham 1994; Gunaratnam 2001; Karlsen and Nazroo 2002; Wray and Bartholomew 2006).

Gunaratnam argues that current multi-culturalist approaches to health service policies and services tend to be based on a "celebratory politics of acknowledgement and inclusion" (2001, 293). These often rely on categories of ethnicity and culture, which may inadvertently reproduce processes of "othering" by inclusion (Ang 1996, 37). For example, health promotion policies and strategies that aim to be culturally sensitive or 'inclusive' may reify aspects of cultural and ethnic identities and reproduce stereotypes (Gunaratnam 2001). One example of this is the over reliance on what Gunaratnam (2001, 292) calls 'categorical thinking.' This refers to the construction and use of "highly stylised, stable and homogenous categories of need" to make recommendations about the health and care needs of minority ethnic groups (Gunaratnam 2001, 292). Such categories are often based on stereotyped assumptions about minority ethnic needs and fail to recognize the temporary and fluctuating nature of identity (Brah 1996, 2008). As Brah comments: ". . . multiculturalism should avoid discourses of finality and closure and operate on the basis that identities are contingent, fragmentary and continually in process" (2008, 388).

Conceptualizing ethnic identity as static positions minority ethnic 'needs' as 'special' or problematic and as opposition to the 'normal,' 'unproblematic' needs of the majority of the population (Gunaratnam 2001).

Another difficulty with this type of approach is a lack of acknowledgement of the socio-cultural locatedness of the meanings attached to moral actions. As Gergen points out, the meanings attached to a moral action are communally derived:

> Morality is not something one possesses within, it is an action that possesses its moral meaning only within a particular arena of cultural intelligibility. . . . A moral life then, is not an issue of individual sentiment or rationality but a form of communal participation.
>
> (1994, 103)

Thus, it is likely that cultural and ethnic values and beliefs influence the significance women attach to health. It is surprising then, that these underlying factors are often neglected in health promotion practice that too often emphasizes the individual's responsibility to attend to one's health, and fails to adequately consider the circumstances in which people live their lives.

Feminist research also points to the often unquestioned connection between, health, thinness and beauty. Scholars have explored the links between what is perceived to be a healthy and feminine body and have questioned how exercise and health promotion came to be entangled with the western ideal 'feminine' body (e.g., Brace-Govan 2002; MacNevin 2003; Markula 1995, 2001, 2003; Wolf 1991). These studies have led to new insights into how the rhetoric on health, beauty and well-being, intersect in ways that often make them difficult to differentiate (MacNevin 2003). Exercise participation, in particular, has been identified as a site where feminine-masculine bodies and identities are constructed and/ or subverted (Markula 1995, 2001, 2003, 2004; St Martin and Gavey 1996). In this chapter, I will demonstrate how women may actively resist dominant ideas about health, fitness and beauty and choose to ignore the hegemonic messages emanating from them. In order to explore the idea of 'resistance' I will turn to Foucault's theory of power relations.

Foucault's (1979) conceptualization of power as relational is useful in highlighting the subtle and diverse forms that resistance may take. He notes that individuals are both subjects and objects of power: they both experience and exercise power. Additionally, the forms that resistance takes may be influenced by ethnic and cultural power relations. As I noted earlier the individualizing discourse on health and fitness is commonly rooted in western scientific/medical perspectives. In this formation, health promoters inadvertently take on the role of legislator, as they advise women how to become healthy through participating in various western-specific exercise and dietary interventions. When faced with such advice, women are both objects and subjects of health promotion discourses: they may choose to comply with or resist what are often western-centric perspectives on health and fitness (Wray 2002). As I also demonstrated, there are competing discourses on healthy lifestyle that may be influenced by ethnic and cultural power relations. These competing discourses are often subjugated. For example, Muslim lifestyle and ideas of health may be perceived and defined as a subjugated discourse as it does not fit with the characteristics associated with a healthy life in western society. In my study, I examine the intersections of such competing health discourses through women's experiences in exercise classes.

METHODOLOGICAL BACKGROUND

> Certainly there are very real differences between us of race, age and sex. But it is not those differences between us that are separating us. It is rather our refusal to recognise those differences, and to examine the distortions which result from our misnaming them and their effects.
>
> (Lorde 1984, 115)

In this quote Audre Lorde notes the importance of naming the differences that exist among women and how these create different effects. The methodological approach, of the study on which this chapter is based, aimed to examine ethnic and cultural differences in women's experiences of their bodies and their perceptions of the advice received from white English health and fitness promoters. It also sought to explore how these health and fitness promoters constructed and disseminated health knowledge. A feminist qualitative approach guided the methodology which was underpinned by the following themes: the representation of diversity, reflection on the how the researcher's biography influenced the research process, the belief that women's lives are important, and finally, an aim to uncover the different ways that power operates in women's lives (Gunaratnam 2003; Maynard 1994; Reinharz 1992, 1997).

One aim of the study was to explore how ethnic and cultural background influenced the way midlife women experienced their bodies and health. A second aim was to examine the extent to which women might use exercise to regulate and control their bodies and identities to a particular ideal, as they became older. This included consideration of the opportunities available for the participants to resist dominant western health and beauty rhetoric, and how this might be influenced by ethnic and cultural background (Wray 2001).

In this chapter, ethnicity is defined as "shared identities built on common cultures, histories, languages, religions and regional affiliations" (Ahmad and Bradby 2008, 48). It is important to note that the concepts of ethnicity and culture need to be used carefully. This is highlighted by Ahmad and Bradby who argue that cultural background and lifestyle have often been used to absolve "states from responsibility" (2007, 798) for health which serves to reinforce individual responsibility for health while underplaying structural and material causes of ill health, such as poverty, sexism and racism (Nazroo 1998; Wray 2002).

The research took place at three exercise classes; the first was held at an Asian women's center, the second at a private gym and the third at an African Caribbean community center. The 24 women who participated in the study self-defined their ethnic identities as: British Muslim, Pakistani, white English, British, British Caribbean and African Caribbean/Afro-Caribbean. The three health and fitness instructors shared similar ethnic backgrounds, which they described as white British and English. The methods of participant observation, focus group and semi-structured interviews were used to generate data. The use of a range of research methods made it possible to capture and make visible the fluctuating nature of understandings of health, beauty and well-being. Additionally, it highlighted how women's views on these may be influenced by a desire to maintain the cultural values and beliefs that signify their belonging to a collective ethnic identity (Brah 1996).

Participant observation enabled me to develop a social relationship with the women and gain an insight into the dynamics of the groups. Prior to joining the classes, I provided information about participant observation and gained consent from the class members. Participant observation involved taking part in a weekly exercise class at each of the centers, over a period of 4 to 5 months. Areas for observation included: interactions between the health and fitness instructor and the class members; interactions between the participants, the instructor and myself; interactions between participants; physical and social territory and space; appearance; body movements; type of exercise; health advice; competition; types of relationships between participants; atmosphere of the class; shape and size of the room; values and beliefs of the group; perceptions of the body; non/compliance with non/hegemonic health/beauty discourse; and cultural capital. The main themes generated through participant observation were then used to create themes and questions for the focus group and semi-structured interviews (Mason 2001).

Participant observation also facilitated my entry to and acceptance in the groups. However, aspects of my identity and biography as a white, English-speaking researcher, affected my position. Position in this instance does not signify essential fixed qualities and traits but instead refers to "the disjunctions and contradictions of the different positions we occupy as both materially structured and subjectively experienced" (Burman 1994, 158). Thus, my position as a researcher undertaking participant observation constantly shifted so that I often felt I was both insider and outsider.

Three focus groups took place at the Asian Women's Center exercise class. The remaining groups of women, from the African Caribbean Center and the private gym, did not want to participate in focus groups, due to a lack of time. A total of 19 women agreed to take part in semi-structured interviews, each of which lasted an average of 45 minutes. The interview questions aimed to generate data on the following themes; participant experiences of exercise participation, perceptions of health across the life-course, the embodied experience of aging, health promotion and responsibility for health, and ethnic and cultural background.

Analysis and interpretation of the data was ongoing and not limited to a particular phase. As one of the research aims was to capture ethnic and cultural diversity it was important to identify the relational meanings attached to health and healthy lifestyle, and avoid the imposition of fixed western-centric understandings. This meant examining the particular and common circumstances in which women live their lives, and the power relations that may create different forms of oppression and limit opportunity (Maynard 1994).

This research followed the British Sociological Association ethical guidelines for research. The research was fully explained to potential participants who were then given one week to decide if they would like to participate. The ethical issues arising from the research include those relating to consent, anonymity, confidentiality, privacy and those arising as a consequence of researching across ethnic and cultural diversity, such as the presence of an interpreter. Pseudonyms chosen by the participants were used throughout the research. It was also made clear that intermediaries would not have access to transcripts or any other potentially identifying information without the written permission of the participant.

HEALTH AND FITNESS INSTRUCTORS' PERCEPTIONS OF WOMEN'S HEALTH AND EXERCISE NEEDS

This section explores some of the views expressed by the health and fitness promoters who took part in the study. The health and fitness instructors shared a concern to improve the general fitness of the participants of their classes. However, they differed with regard to what their perceptions of being 'fit' meant:

> The main aim is to encourage them to take exercise and to exercise as a way of looking after yourself. (. . .) Mmm . . . the main aim is for health reasons we could put a lot . . . well you're not allowed to anyway . . . but there could be a lot more exercises in. We have covered health topics and just in all things you keep trying to reinforce these things, 'cause whatever diet things we tell them, whether it's blood pressure the losing weight or joints or anything like they're all the same lifestyle changes they need to . . . [make].
>
> (Norma, English, health and fitness instructor,
> Asian women's center)

Norma's view is that exercise is a means of 'looking after yourself.' This message is evident in current health discourses that promote self-surveillance as a form of self-care (Markula 2003; Rose 1999; Wray

2001, 2007). Given the current commodification of health and the accompanying expectation that individuals should participate in various forms of body maintenance, this view is not uncommon (Featherstone 1996; Wray 2007). Western hegemonic discourses on health, health promotion and individual moral responsibility are often used to cultivate consumerist idealization of the fit and attractive body. One effect of this is that looking and feeling good are often seen as one and the same thing. Moreover, the 'healthy look' promoted and desired in western societies is mostly associated with a body that is "firm but shapely, fit but sexy, and strong but thin" (Markula 1995, 424).

When asked the same question the health and fitness instructor at the African-Caribbean community center commented:

> My aims are just to get them active in whatever way we can, just to get them active. For me, exercise is really to get other women motivated because I've always had exercise as part of my life. I found I got a lot out of it emotionally, physically and mentally . . . if you're all right with two of those it helps with the third. So that's what I'm hoping other women get out of it.
>
> (Nicola, white British, health and fitness instructor,
> African-Caribbean community center)

Thus, Nicola associates exercise with both physical and psychological well-being. In her comment about motivation she links physical activity to empowerment. It is also evident that Nicola conceptualizes health holistically, drawing on her own experience to suggest that exercise participation improves emotional and psychological well-being as well. Her comments show the extent to which exercise participation has come to be associated with psychological well-being (Sointu 2005).

The health and fitness instructor at the private gym exercise class spoke of 'improving' the body through exercise:

> I just like them to increase their fitness. I mean I don't . . . you know say right you came to me this 'big' . . . you are going to . . . you know? I'd like to see improvement in their body obviously in the way they are . . . fitness wise. A lot of them have come right from the beginning, five years ago, and I've seen them come and watch what they eat and really improve.
>
> (Wendy, white English, health and fitness instructor, private gym)

In this quotation, Wendy associates fitness with a reduction in body size. This is a common assumption that is often found in western health promotion discourse and is rooted in bio-medical messages about what constitutes a healthy body weight. Consequently, even though there is evidence to suggest otherwise, a higher body weight becomes negatively linked to a lack of general fitness (Burns and Gavey 2004; Wray and Deery 2008). Women have historically been advised to put on weight or lose it according to the feminine ideals and medical fads of the particular time. The impact of this on women's well-being and how they see their bodies, is well documented (e.g., Bordo 1995; Burns and Gavey 2004; Orbach 1978; Wolf 1991; Wray and Deery 2008).

From the discussion so far it is evident that the three health and fitness instructors view exercise as a way of controlling the health and appearance of the body. Their opinions are, to some extent, rooted in the bio-medical body and they promote exercise as a means of body maintenance and self-care. This highlights the extent to which ethics of self-responsibility for health and well-being have become firmly embedded within health promotion discourse. This is evident in the current western obsession with adherence to "self-monitoring, self-reflection and self-evaluation" (Bauman 1992, 202). One danger associated with these developments is that non-participation in exercise regimes may be constructed as a willful neglect of health and paradoxically lead to a lack of well-being for those who are targeted (Wray 2007).

When asked their views on the current move toward individual responsibility for health, the instructors identified the following as significant: a decrease in State responsibility for the health of the population (Norma), disparities in the targeting of specific groups and communities (Norma and Nicola), and the commercialization of medical health issues (Norma and Wendy). Wendy, for example, gave the following response when asked about the value of health promotion:

> I think there's probably good and bad about it. I mean . . . there's that many diets and things isn't there? And people go to the doctor and the doctor will say 'oh your need lose weight.' I mean what does that person then go and do they'll join Weight Watcher's or something like that. So there's good and bad about health promotion. They should be able to do it theirselves combined with exercise, cut out rather than go to extremes.
>
> (Wendy, white English, health and fitness instructor, private gym)

Here Wendy suggests health promotion advice may be problematic because there is a lack of support for women to enable them to fulfill its expectations, in this case to lose weight. However, in the last sentence she again places the responsibility on the individual who 'should be able to do it theirselves.' This highlights the individualistic premise of health promotion and how it controls women by differentiating and judging them (Foucault 1977, 184). It is unsurprising that the promotion of healthy lifestyles has coincided with a rise in the marketing of body maintenance consumer-based goods such as detoxification diets, food supplements and gym membership (Featherstone 1991; Maguire and Mansfield 1998).

In contradicting her earlier comments on body weight Wendy also felt that the women who attended her class did not attend to lose weight:

> I would say that they (white English, British exercise class participants) definitely come to stay healthy and very rarely I'll get somebody who comes and says 'look I want to lose half a stone.' People do come up to you after class and say 'oh I really want to work on my abs, my thighs or one area.' But I tell people you can't just spot reduce you've got to do the whole thing you can't just work on an area . . .
> (Wendy, white English, health and fitness instructor, private gym)

However, despite Wendy's insistence that different parts of the body could not be 'spot reduced,' during the class she often spoke of exercise as 'good' for particular parts of the body: "We do some floor exercises and Wendy says 'this is good for the tummy' and this will help to tone and slim your thighs" (Research diary notes). Norma felt that the women attending her class had a desire to lose weight:

> The biggest problem the ladies are concerned about is losing weight and it's the only thing we don't seem to be able to achieve very well. And I think the main reason for that, in all seriousness . . . is the . . . it's their diet and the lifestyle.
> (Norma, English, health and fitness instructor, Asian
> women's center)

One way that Norma checked whether the women were losing weight or not was to weigh them weekly. The women often tried to avoid this surveillance by going to the toilets or moving away from the front of the class. In my research diary I note that the women tell Norma they cannot lose weight because their husbands do not want them to change the food they cook. This is discussed in more detail in the next section of this chapter.

For Norma, ethnic difference was regarded as a barrier to the promotion and adherence to a healthy lifestyle:

> They're (exercise class participants) never without something to put in their mouths . . . you know. Western women are as bad they just can't stop . . . and then you think no wonder they've got all these eating problems because they never stop between meals eating. Sounds old fashioned but it's true . . . and . . . all of these things that are supposed to be bad for their teeth . . . all that kind of thing. But I think that when you're . . . when you've come from nothing that's an actual thing. I'm a bit more critical on the western women who do it because they can . . . . Without taking the basic message on the advertising they can read and find out about all the other issues around it,

whereas it's much harder for these ladies. Definitely much harder for them . . . they're illiterate in their own tongue . . .

(Norma, English, health and fitness instructor,
Asian women's center)

Here Norma expresses disapproval of women who do not control their eating habits. She goes on to suggest that there are differences between 'western women' and the participants of her exercise class in relation to their ability to access health promotion information. For example, she comments that the British Muslim Pakistani class participants are "illiterate in their own tongue" and that this makes it harder for them to understand health advice. Thus, for Norma the women's resistance to health promotion rhetoric is a problem of communication that is due to their 'illiteracy.' She suggests, then, the women have 'special' needs and assumes their reluctance to change their diets is due to a lack of language skills (Gunaratnam 2001; Wray 2002). There were obvious differences between Norma and the exercise class participants in the meanings they attached to health and healthy lifestyle. For example, during the classes Norma reiterated the message 'less fat, less ghee, more fruit and vegetables' and the sessions ended with a 'weigh in.' Despite this, the women did not change their diets and rarely lost weight. However, Norma felt that the women's rejection of western discourse on healthy lifestyle was a culturally located 'problem' (Gunaratnam 2001; Karlsen and Nazroo 2002). The next section of this chapter will explore the exercise class participants' views of health and exercise rhetoric.

HEALTH PROMOTION DISCOURSE AND ITS SIGNIFICANCE FOR WOMEN FROM DIVERSE ETHNIC BACKGROUNDS

It is often assumed that people will change their 'health behaviors' if the health promotion interventions they are targeted with are culturally sensitive (e.g., Waters et al. 2001). As I explained earlier, such an approach ignores the wider socio-cultural and economic circumstances that influence the choices available to women, and importantly their right to choose not to conform to health promotion rhetoric. The gendered nature of health promotion advice is often promoted uncritically and, as a consequence, has become entwined with western beauty and body ideals (Brace-Govan 2002; MacNevin 2003; Markula 1995, 2001, 2003; Wolf 1991). For the women in this study the reasons for participating in exercise ranged from perceived health benefits to reducing parts of their body they felt dissatisfied with. However, different themes emerged between the groups of women in relation to their main reasons for participating. For instance, the white British, English participants attending Wendy's class were more likely, than the other two groups of women, to prioritize weight loss or changes to their body shape. For example, one such participant commented: "I came to the gym to lose weight to try and keep control of my weight" (Diane, English/British). Another participant indicated:

> I'd like to have my flabby tummy taken away. Yeah I think it's my flabby tummy that's the main reason why I came [to the gym]. I just don't like the way I can't wear what I want . . . I don't feel happy with myself.
>
> (Mary, British)

However, some of the women attending this class felt that exercise could be used to look after their bodies and resist ageing, as they grew older. This is evident in the following remarks:

> I want to stay fit and healthy into my old age and that's one of the main reasons I exercise. I feel that I'm taking care of my body. There's no need in this day and age to look your age.
>
> (Sue, English)

In contrast, African Caribbean women were more likely to associate participation in exercise with health maintenance and socializing:

> I feel that if I stay at home and sit on the couch it's bad for my heart, it's bad for my health . . . it's bad for everything. Because then . . . you get more aches and pains if you sit around. But if you keep going do your exercises . . . I look forward to coming and feel hundred percent better (Jane, Afro-Caribbean).
>   Well I exercise because I like it. I feel better I can do an awful lot more for myself. I can go distances I can walk I can run (Marie, Afro-Caribbean).
>   (. . .) you meet you meet you know in your class you make friends (Lavinia, British Caribbean).

Women attending the exercise class at the Asian women's centre were, similarly to African Caribbean participants, more likely to comment on health and socializing as important reasons for taking part:

> Exercise is very very good. I think so it's my opinion. It's very good for entertainment and good working (of the body).
>
> (Arshad, Pakistani)

Thus, African Caribbean, Pakistani and British Muslim women prioritized the health benefits of exercise participation, whereas English and British women were more likely to speak of both health and appearance benefits. Despite this prioritization the majority of participants, to varying degrees, expressed concerns about managing the appearance of their bodies regardless of their ethnic background:

> Now there are the changes in my body, and I suppose that's why I carry on [exercising]. (...) It's I suppose it's 50 percent vanity and 50 percent because I enjoy it. I daren't give up now because everything will go (moves hands in downward gesture). It happens quick too!
>
> (Helen, British)

As per Tasneem's interpreter "She (Tasneem) says that she just wants to stay fit and she doesn't like fat . . . she doesn't want to get big" (Tasneem, Pakistani, interpreted). Similarly, Marie and Jane indicated "All in all we want to look good and feel good. You want to look good and feel good" (Afro-Caribbean).

However, English and British women were more likely to speak of their desire to resist body changes associated with ageing, and conform to messages about how to maintain health and beauty.

As previously discussed, there were also differences between the instructors in how they promoted health and their views on why women attended their classes. Norma, the fitness instructor at the Asian women's center class, for example, felt that one of the reasons her participants resisted her health advice was due to a breakdown in language and communication. However, although the participants were able to recount most of the diet and exercise advice they had been given, they did not necessarily choose to follow it. For example, British Muslim and Pakistani women were more likely to associate eating particular food with religious or moral risk taking than with danger to health. Some foods, for example, were regarded as spiritually polluting (Douglas 1970; Wray 2001, 2002). "Some things I don't eat because I am Muslim . . . you know? I know fat is very bad for me but I'm not bothered" (Arshad). In this quote, Arshad notes how her choice of food is influenced by her religious beliefs rather than health promotion discourse. Her main aim is to maintain her Muslim identity and she uses food to achieve this (Douglas 1970). This was important to other Pakistani and British Muslim participants who resisted changes to their diet and stated a preference for 'traditional' food, despite the health advice of Norma. Some of the women openly disagreed with Norma when she asked them to cut fat, particularly ghee (clarified butter), from their diets. During one of the classes one of the participants told me: "I cannot make curries without ghee, it spoils the taste and my family will not eat it" (Shazeem, British Muslim). This suggests family, religious and cultural reasons influenced the participant's decision to resist some of the health promotion advice offered by Norma. Additionally, the act of resisting changes to their diet meant that the women were able to reject western ideas about what constitutes a healthy diet and then maintain their ethnic and religious beliefs and identities.

Here food is a symbol of identity so that eating particular foods signifies cultural tradition, values and collective identity boundaries. As Lupton observes: "Food and culinary practices thus hold an extraordinary power in defining boundaries between 'us' and 'them'" (1996, 26). Moreover, eating foods that are considered taboo symbolically breaches collective cultural identity boundaries. Thus, resisting changes to their diets enabled the women in Norma's class to negotiate western health discourse rather than being dominated or controlled by it.

When the British and English participants spoke about their diets they often reproduced biomedical health advice about 'good' and 'bad' foods.

> Well you've got to be careful about what you eat, you know, cholesterol and everything. I try and eat sensibly I try and eat you know fruit and veg. Well I don't drink coffee, I drink water, to get rid of the toxins in your blood, don't eat chocolate. I try to eat a healthy diet all of the time.
>
> (Janette, English/British)

> A week ago I did this detox thing it was supposed to kick-start my immune system. It wasn't to lose weight . . . although I did lose four pounds, because I didn't have any meat, there was no meat in it. The idea was you had a detox day, your first day, where you flush your system out. You just had orange juice and white yoghurt and loads of water and herbal tea. That was supposed to get rid of everything in your body that was rubbish.
>
> (Helen, British)

Both Janette and Helen are knowledgeable about the types of food that are considered to be healthy and they have gone to some lengths to include these in their diet. In this dietary regime, fat and cholesterol are regarded as pollutants that need to be excluded from everyday consumption. There are similarities between the accounts of Janette and Helen and those of Arshad and Shazeem in that all of them choose to eat particular foods because they symbolize particular forms of cultural knowledge. For Janette and Helen western biomedical knowledge of 'good' (pure) and 'bad' (toxic) foods influences their decision to restrict their diet (Douglas 1970; Lupton 1996). Following a detox diet supposedly flushes 'rubbish' out of the body. Moreover, because western normative discourse on health and feminine ideal body shape interconnect, a detoxification diet also involves calorie counting and produces weight loss (Brace-Govan 2002; Duncan 1994; MacNevin 2003; Wolf 1991). Interestingly, although Helen states she does not want to lose weight the diet she chooses involves counting calories.

Historically and across culture, women have exhibited self-control about the types of foods they eat for reasons such as appearance, income, health, and spiritual and religious beliefs (Bordo 1995; Lupton 1996; Wray 2001, 2002). To an extent, control over the type of food that is eaten becomes a moral imperative that can only be maintained through acts of self-discipline. This moral control over the body may be experienced as empowering because it may equate with increased status within a particular community. Thus, for some of the British Muslim and Pakistani participants, dietary control was used to signify conformity to cultural and religious belief systems. British and English participants also attempted to control their diets but were more likely to attempt to conform to western beliefs about healthy food. It is not surprising then that British Muslim and Pakistani participants rarely changed their diets despite the advice of the health instructor, Norma. In this act of resistance, British Muslim and Pakistani participants were able to indicate the significance of their collective religious and ethnic identities (Gergen 1994). Compliance to western healthy lifestyle advice was more prevalent amongst British and English participants because it was less likely to contest their personal beliefs and values.

CONCLUSIONS

This chapter set out to explore health and fitness instructors' perspectives on healthy lifestyle discourse and how women attending their exercise classes experienced this. One of the main aims was to consider the interrelationships between women's ethnic and cultural backgrounds and their perceptions of exercise and health promotion discourse. The discussion has shown how ethnic and cultural background influences the health perspectives and choices made by exercise class participants and their instructors. It has highlighted how ethnic and cultural beliefs often influence the priority women give to western-centric perspectives on healthy lifestyle.

Although the instructors in this research were aware of cultural differences these tended to be perceived as an obstacle to good health. Arguably, there has been a reluctance to critically question the underlying western-centric knowledge that informs notions of healthy lifestyle and how this may, in turn, reify existing cultural and ethnic stereotypes (Gunaratnam 2001). In this research, for example, the health and fitness promoters often drew on stereotyped assumptions about the health needs of women from different ethnic backgrounds. There were also presumptions made about 'correct' body size, shape and diet, which were influenced by western beliefs about the feminine 'ideal' body and what constitutes a 'healthy' lifestyle (Markula 1995).

Nevertheless, some of the participants of this study did not want to adjust their lives to conform to these messages. For instance, Pakistani and British Muslim women resisted advice from Norma, the instructor, to change their diet. African Caribbean women were also reluctant to conform to messages about correct body weight and did not alter their diets significantly. For these women, there was often a disparity between their health priorities and those promoted by the health and fitness instructors. The act of resisting western discourse on healthy eating momentarily disrupts western-centric discourse on what constitutes a healthy diet. Thus, although Pakistani, British Muslim and African Caribbean women enjoyed and benefited from exercise participation, they did not express a desire to adopt a western-centric healthy lifestyle. This resistance enabled the women to maintain religious and cultural collective identity boundaries (Brah 1996). For example, some of these women chose to continue to eat food that symbolized religious and cultural belonging, even if it was deemed to be unhealthy by western standards. This suggests that they were able to negotiate and resist healthy living advice as opposed to simply being dominated or controlled by it. The women both experienced and exercised power (Foucault 1979).

In contrast, British and English participants were more likely to conform to and pursue the healthy lifestyle promoted by Wendy, the instructor. One reason for this is that the ideas and values underpinning healthy lifestyle messages fit more closely with white, western, cultural values. Thus, the health promoters' views were more likely to map onto those held by the white British and English participants, who were more likely to conform to dietary advice and prioritize weight reduction as an exercise goal. Some spoke of using dietary techniques to 'cleanse' their bodies of toxins and counting calories to control their body size and shape. This knowledge on dietary techniques is part of a range of disciplinary coercions that regulate bodies through the jurisprudence of medical knowledge (Foucault 1979). These are techniques of power that are deployed to discipline and regulate bodies according to the latest scientific findings and healthy living advice (Foucault 1979). Arguably, one effect of this is the legitimization and normalization of particular body shapes and sizes for women. This illustrates how power operates on bodies via the knowledge-producing disciplinary mechanisms of medical science.

There needs to be further exploration of how power influences the choices that are available to women from diverse ethnic and cultural backgrounds. The current western-centric spotlight on individual and psychological influences on health behavior dangerously neglects how ethnicity and culture shape people's beliefs, views and behaviors. Additionally, such an approach is likely to increase the 'categorical thinking' that is evident in much of the health promotion literature and to create further dependency on the standardized 'categories of need' that inform policy documents and practices that are insensitive to cultural identity as contingent and constantly undergoing reconstruction (Brah 2008; Gunaratnam 2001). Arguably, this is one of the reasons for a gap between the health and fitness instructors' understandings of health needs and those of the Pakistani, British Muslim and African Caribbean participants. Clearly, it does not make sense to ignore the ethnic and cultural factors that may constrain the choices and opportunities available to women. On the contrary, it is important the question how 'healthy' western ideas about healthy lifestyle are.

REFERENCES

Ahmad, W. I. U. and H. Bradby. 2007. Locating ethnicity and health: Exploring concepts and contexts. *Sociology of Health & Illness* 29(6): 795–810.

—— 2008. Ethnicity and health: Key themes in a developing field. *Current Sociology* 56: 47–56.

Ang, I. 1996. The curse of the smile: Ambivalence and the "Asian" woman in Australian multiculturalism. *Feminist Review* 52: 36–49.

Armstrong, D. 1995. The rise of surveillance medicine. *Sociology of Health and Illness* 17: 393–404.

Battersby, C. 1998. *The phenomenal woman: Feminist metaphysics and the patterns of identity*. London: Polity Press.

Bauman, Z. 1992. *Intimations of postmodernity*. London: Routledge.

Blakemore, K. and M. Boneham. 1994. *Age, race and ethnicity*. Open University Press: Buckingham.

Bordo, S. 1990. The body and the reproduction of femininity: A feminist appropriation of Foucault. In *Gender/body/knowledge: Feminist reconstruction of being and knowing,* ed. A. Jagger and S. Bordo, 13–33. New Brunswick, NJ: Rutgers University Press.

—— 1993. Feminism Foucault and the politics of the body. In *Up against Foucault*, ed. C. Ramazanoglu, 179–201. London: Routledge.

—— 1995. *Unbearable weight: Feminism, western culture and the body*. London: University of California Press.

Brace-Govan, J. 2002. Looking at bodywork: Women and three physical activities. *Journal of Sport & Social Issues* 26: 403–20.

Brah, A. 1996. *Cartographies of diaspora: Contesting identities*. London and New York: Routledge.

—— 2008. Commentary: Dissolving diasporic identities? *Journal of Community & Applied Social Psychology* 18: 387–89.

Bunton, R. and R. Burrows. 1995. Consumption and health in the 'epidemiological' clinic of late modern medicine. In *The sociology of health promotion: Critical analyses of consumption, lifestyle and risk*, eds. R. Bunton, S. Nettleton and S. Burrows, 206–22. London: Routledge.

Burgess, P. 2008. Health scares and risk awareness. In *A sociology of health*, ed. D. Wainright. London: Sage.

Burman, E. 1994. Experience, identities and alliances: Jewish feminism and feminist psychology. In *Shifting identities, shifting racisms: A feminism and psychology reader*, ed. K. K. Bhavnani and A. Phoenix, 155–78. London: Sage.

Burns, M. and N. Gavey. 2004. 'Healthy weight' at what cost? 'Bulimia' and a discourse of weight control. *Journal of Health Psychology* 9: 549–65.

Department of Health 2004. *Choosing health: Making healthy choices easier*. UK Government Public Health White Paper.

Douglas, M. 1970. *Purity and danger: An analysis of concepts of pollution and taboo*. London: Pelican.

Duncan, M. 1994. The politics of women's body images and practices: Foucault, the panopticon, and shape magazine. *Journal of Sport and Social Issues* 18: 48–65.

Featherstone, M. 1991. *Consumer culture and postmodernism*. London: Sage.

—— 1996. The body in consumer culture. In *The body: Social process and cultural theory*, ed. M. Featherstone, M. Hepworth and B. S. Turner, 170–96. London: Sage.

Foucault, M. 1977. *Discipline and punish: The birth of the prison*. London: Penguin.

—— 1979. *The history of sexuality: An introduction volume one*. London: Penguin.

Furedi, F. 2004. *Therapy culture: Cultivating uncertainty in an uncertain age*. London: Routledge.

Gergen, K. 1994. *Realities and relationships*. Cambridge Mass: Harvard University Press.

Grosz, E. 1994. *Volatile bodies: Towards a corporeal feminism*. Indiana University Press.

Gunaratnam, Y. 2001. Eating into multiculturalism: Hospice staff and service users talk food, 'race', ethnicity, culture and identity. *Critical Social Policy* 21(3): 287–310.

—— 2003. *Researching 'race' and ethnicity*. London: Sage

Holmes, D., S. J. Murray, A. Perron and G. Rail. 2006. Deconstructing the evidence-based discourses in health sciences: Truth, power and fascism. *International Journal of Evidence Based Healthcare* 4: 180–86.

Karlsen, S. and J. Y. Nazroo. 2002. Agency and structure: The impact of ethnic identity and racism on the health of ethnic minority people. *Sociology of Health & Illness* 24(1): 1–20.

Krieger, N. 2000. Discrimination and health. In *Social epidemiology*, ed. L. Berkman and I. Kawachi. Oxford: Oxford University Press.

Lorde, A. 1984. *Sister outsider: Essays and speeches*. The Crossing Press Feminist Series. Berkeley, California: The Crossing Press.

Lupton, D. 1996. *Food, the body and the self*. London: Sage.

MacNevin, A. 2003. Exercising options: Holistic health and technical beauty in gendered accounts of bodywork. *The Sociological Quarterly* 44(2): 271–89.

Maguire, J. and L. Mansfield. 1998. No-body's perfect: Women, aerobics, and the body beautiful. *Sociology of Sport Journal* 15: 109–37.

Markula, P. 1995. Firm but shapely, fit but sexy, strong but thin: The postmodern aerobicizing female bodies. *Sociology of Sport Journal* 12: 424–53.

—— 2001. Beyond the perfect body: Women's body image distortion in fitness magazine discourse. *Journal of Sport and Social Issues* 25: 158–79.

—— 2003. The technologies of the self: Sport, feminism, and Foucault. *Sociology of Sport Journal* 20: 87–107.

—— 2004. "Tuning into one's self": Foucault's technologies of the self and mindful fitness. *Sociology of Sport Journal* 21: 302–21.

Mason, J. 2001. *Qualitative researching*. London: Sage.

Maynard, M. 1994. Methods, practice and epistemology: The debate about feminism and research. In *Researching women's lives from a feminist perspective,* ed. M. Maynard and J. Purvis. London: Taylor and Francis.

Maynard, M., H. Afshar, M. Franks and S. Wray. 2008. *Women in later life: Exploring race and ethnicity.* London: McGraw-Hill, Open University Press.

Moriarty, J. and J. Butt. 2004. Inequalities in quality of life among older people from different ethnic groups. *Ageing and Society* 24: 729–53.

Nazroo, J. Y. 1998. Genetic, cultural or socio-economic vulnerability? Explaining ethnic inequalities in health. *Sociology of Health and Illness* 20(5): 710–30.

Orbach, S. 1978. *Fat is a feminist issue.* London: Arrow Books Limited.

Peterson, A. and R. Bunton, eds. 1997. *Foucault, health and medicine.* London: Routledge.

Reinharz, S. 1992. *Feminist methods in social research.* Oxford: Oxford University Press.

—— 1997. Who am I? The need for a variety of selves in the field. In *Reflexivity and voice,* ed. R. Hertz, 3–20. London: Sage Publications.

Rose, N. 1999. *Powers of freedom: Reframing political thought.* Cambridge: Cambridge University Press.

Segal, L. 2003. Thinking like a man? The cultures of science. *Women: A Cultural Review* 14: 1–19.

Sointu, E. 2005. The rise of an ideal: Tracing changing discourses of wellbeing. *The Sociological Review* 53: 255–74.

St Martin, L. and N. Gavey. 1996. Women's bodybuilding: Feminist resistance and/or femininity's recuperation? *Body & Society* 2: 45–57.

Vom Bruck, G. 1997. Elusive bodies: The politics of aesthetics among Yemeni elite women. *Signs: Journal of Women in Culture and Society* 23(1): 175–214.

Waters, C.M., M. Wey, R. Times, M. Crear and A. R. Morton. 2001. Perceptions of health status and participation in present and future health promotion behaviors among African-American women. *Journal of Prevention and Intervention in the Community* 22(2): 81–96.

Wolf, N. 1991. *The beauty myth: How images of beauty are used against women.* London: Vintage.

Wray, S. 2001. The cultural construction of different identities and bodies at midlife. Unpublished PhD thesis, Leeds Metropolitan University.

—— 2002. Connecting ethnicity, gender and physicality: Muslim Pakistani women, physical activity and health. In *Gender and sport: A reader,* ed. S. Scraton and A. Flintoff, 127–40. London: Routledge.

—— 2007. Health, exercise and well-being: The experiences of midlife women from diverse ethnic backgrounds. *Social Theory & Health* 5: 126–44.

Wray, S. and M. Bartholomew. 2006. Older African Caribbean women: The influence of migration on experiences of health and well being in later life. *Journal of Research, Policy and Planning* 24(2): 104–20.

Wray, S. and R. Deery. 2008. The medicalisation of body size and women's healthcare. *Healthcare for Women International* 29(3): 227–43.

Young-Odoms, A. 2008. Factors that influence body image representations of black Muslim women. *Social Science & Medicine* 66(12): 2573–84.

9   Growing Old (Dis)Gracefully?
The Gender/Aging/Exercise Nexus

Elizabeth C. J. Pike

> All right, I'm just going to come out and say it. Aging sucks. As my gener-
> ation of women hits 40, 50, 60, we are for the first time discovering things
> about our faces and bodies that we never noticed before. Icky things like
> age spots, crow's-feet, gray hair, chin hair, marionette lines, saggy boobs,
> spider veins, bunions—need I go on? I don't think so. You know what
> I'm talking about. The question is: What are you—what are we—going to
> do about it? We're going to fight aging—and we're going to have a blast
> while doing it . . . We're not going to grow old gracefully (or gratefully).
>
> (Krupp 2009, 1)

> You gotta stay in shape. My grandmother started walking five miles a day
> when she was sixty. She's ninety-seven today and we don't know where
> the hell she is.
>
> (Ellen DeGeneres)

The Feminization of Aging

Population statistics indicate that by the middle of the twenty-first
century, it is likely that the world's population aged over 60 will have
reached two billion (or 21 percent of the global population), a situation
which has defined the century as "the age of aging" (Magnus 2008). A
specific feature of this population is that as it ages, it is becoming increasingly female-dominated since the further up the age scale the greater the
proportion of women, with women outliving their male counterparts
in nearly all countries (Central Intelligence Agency 2008). Life expectancy for women now exceeds 80 in at least 35 countries, with rapid
economic development contributing to increased life expectancy in many
other nations (World Health Organization 2005). For example, in Japan,
which has the highest life expectancy of any nation, while men can expect
to live on average to age 78.8, women's life expectancy averages at 85.6
(Central Intelligence Agency 2008).

A paradox of the longevity revolution is that, while it might be expected
that the fact of people living longer would be received with celebration,
longer life expectancy is instead often framed as a problem, and variously

described as a demographic time bomb and even an "apocalypse of age-ing" (Haber 2004). Concerns focus mostly on the impact on the economy, social and health care services, and even the environment, as later life is perceived as one of draining rather than contributing to national economies, increasing demands on welfare services, and using more of the world's natural resources. One editorial in a science journal described the situation of increasing longevity as "even worse than expected!" (in Kirkwood 2001).

For the individuals who live into 'deep' old age, most of whom are women, the consequences of these concerns are very real. Recent research found that discrimination against the aged is reported more than any other form of prejudice (Age Concern 2006). This appears to be largely grounded in a perception of aging as a significant health issue, with the aging body viewed as diseased. Older women suffer more negative stereotypes because they live longer and also because gender is so often the basis of social inequalities (see Arber and Ginn 1991; Gibson 1996; Vertinsky 1995). This interplay of gender and age impacts on recommendations for, and experiences of, exercise for older women as will be discussed in the next section.

THE GENDER/AGING/EXERCISE NEXUS

Patricia Vertinsky (1998) argued that older women's bodies are inca-pacitated as a result of the prevalent belief in western cultures of female bodily incompetence. A specific feature of this is the female menopause, which has traditionally been understood through a bio-medical model of aging as a deficiency disease (Bell 1987). During menopause, women are seen as losing not only their economic productive capacity in their post-employment years, but also their reproductive capacity rendering them useless to society (Vertinsky and O'Brien Cousins 2007). If "for women, menarche is the entrance to womanhood, cessation of menses is depicted as the entrance to old age," Ballard et al. (2009, 270) even though many women experience a life free of menstruation as a positive development and are able to distinguish between reproductive aging (i.e., menopause) and other aspects of aging. Despite this, older women are generally encouraged to treat their 'ovarian failure' with, for example, hormone replacement therapy (HRT). This is due to the alleged association between menopause and osteoporosis, coronary heart disease and Alzheimer's: perceived relationships which are grounded in discourses reinforcing the perception of the fragility of the aging female body (Ballard et al. 2009; Vertinsky and O'Brien Cousins 2007). Significantly, this leads to a discouragement of strenuous physical exercise in later years, as it is seen as exacerbating weakening, burning up vital energy and so speed-ing up aging, which consequently obscures the actual benefits of exercise for menopausal women, including the relief of physical and psychological symptoms (see Vertinsky and O'Brien Cousins 2007). According to Vertinsky (1998), such stereotyped loss of physical competence in later life may not be an intrinsic feature of aging but more a consequence of a cultural process of enfeeblement. Furthermore, when aging female athletes have taken HRT for health reasons, many have been banned in international sporting competitions for the use of a 'performance-enhancing substance' by drug-testing regulations which ignore the needs of older female competitors (Burger et al. 1996).

There is also an interesting paradox in the sociology of aging. While older women are more visible as a result of their greater longevity, gender has been traditionally neglected as a focus for analysis (Arber and Ginn 1991). Certainly early gerontology had a 'masculine bias' (Russell 2007) focusing on the problems men encountered far more than their female counterparts. Notably, the British Heart Foundation recently also identified men as a priority target group on the basis that they have earlier mortality and do not use health services frequently as compared to women (Laventure 2007). This chapter contributes to literature which redresses this balance, exploring the policy process underpinning the gender/age/ exercise nexus through the lived experiences of older British women. I will first examine the policy process itself before turning to the women's stories.

An examination of policy documents and media reports indicates a seemingly unquestioning acceptance of the need for an increasingly aging population to engage in 'active aging,' a key theme in the United Nations, World Health Organization and European Commission as well as national and local policies, despite common perceptions of the frailty of the aging female body (European Commission 1999; World Health Organization 2002, 2005). This has also influenced research agendas. For example, in 2009 the combined Research Council U.K. identified aging, lifelong health and well-being as priority research areas. These policies and agendas encompass a variety of ways of maintaining active citizenship and contributing to society in later life, but invariably promote physical activity and exercise as having health and social benefits. These include perceived benefits for physiological functions most notably improved flexibility, balance and muscle tone. The dominant message is that exercise may help to prevent falls, which are the major cause of disability among older people (World Health Organization 2005). In addition, it is argued that exercise improves psychological well-being, addresses social isolation and enables the maintenance of independence in later life, particularly for older women who live longer and often alone (Cattan 2001; Kluge 2002; Department of Health 2004). However, activity statistics demonstrate that involvement in exercise in most developed nations decreases with age, and that women are less active than men throughout the life course (DCMS/Strategy Unit 2002).

An additional concern is that, while it is generally accepted that an active lifestyle will reduce certain diseases (and, therefore, related medical costs) among some population subgroups, there is not sufficient information about the aging process or age-related diseases to be certain of the benefits to women of exercise in its various manifestations (Clements, 2006). Weinert and Timiras identify 15 different theories of what causes aging, and they conclude that despite advances in knowledge "the ultimate causes of aging remain unknown" (2003, 1713). Since the underlying causes of age-related frailty are not well understood, there is at best inconclusive evidence that exercise prescription will prevent falls or improve functional competence (Fair 2006 in Tulle 2008). Indeed, Coalter (2007) even suggests that evidence of health benefits which are based on one single variable (physical activity) are crude, limited, may contain substantial margins of error, and are often based on theoretically informed judgments rather than empirical evidence.

Regardless a plethora of official policy documents, public health messages and increasingly business enterprises continue to draw from this research to promote the physical, psychological, and social benefits of exercise in specific forms and for specific populations. In a survey of the 'position stands' presented in sports science literature, Tulle (2008) identified an acceptance that exercise is at the forefront of the fight against disease and aging, especially the ability to reduce falls in later life. The resulting anti-aging science agenda claims that symptoms can be alleviated, life expectancy and lifespan extended, and aging delayed and/or reversed. The relationship between exercise and the prevention of aging is stated as a 'truth,' it is given substance by 'scientific discovery,' and supports the use of exercise as 'prevention' against disease and aging. These are then applied to the aging population with claims of 'morbidity compression' which means attempts to increase the health span rather than the life span, lengthening the period of active retirement, commonly termed the Third Age, while reducing the Fourth Age period of decline, dependency and ill-health. The rhetoric surrounding the compression of morbidity makes assumptions that it is possible to decouple age and disease. However, it is known that normal aging and age-related diseases share common causes and are directly connected. Therefore, it is impossible to compress morbidity unless we can control the rate of aging (Kirkwood 2001). Against this backdrop of broad policy recommendations grounded in inadequate understanding of the aging process, I examined the lived experiences of older women who negotiated the terrain of expected and acceptable ways of aging.

METHOD AND THEORETICAL FRAMEWORK

The research presented in this chapter draws on participant observation, interviews and the written stories of British women over the age of 60.

This is the current age of retirement in the U.K., and a life stage which is regarded as significant in its impact on lifestyle, access to regular social networks, physical activity and mental stimulation. These women were recruited from a variety of exercise settings: some regularly took part in exercise classes including Masters swimming clubs and a Scottish dancing group, some had been referred to an exercise program for particular health benefits (specifically cardiac rehabilitation and diabetes), others were engaged through a process of snowball sampling as people known to the researcher or other participants.

The participant observation was undertaken by the author over a period of two years by participating in Masters swimming training sessions. Unstructured conversational interviews (Amis 2005) were initiated by the author indicating a general interest in the changing role of exercise in participants' lives as they aged, and then examined emergent themes via prompt questions during the course of the conversation. The interviews lasted between 30 to 120 minutes, were recorded on a dictaphone, transcribed and coded by systematic thematic analysis. Some women were prepared to write down their experiences in addition to face-to-face contact with the author. Others who were not available for interviews were provided with a questionnaire which, after some initial biographical data, simply encouraged them to write freely about their experiences of the aging process, how they felt about their bodies as they grew older, and the role that exercise had played in their lives through the lifecourse. The level of engagement in the research project was varied from those who were interviewed several times, wrote detailed stories of their lives and were regularly observed, to those with whom there were informal conversations or who sent brief notes to the researcher. However, in total, the stories of approximately 50 women are represented in this chapter. For the purposes of anonymity, no names are provided, but the age of each participant is given in brackets following quotations.

The choice of methods and analysis of these women's experiences is informed by the work of Erving Goffman. In particular, the decision to spend time with, and talk to, the participants in the study was guided by his belief that sociology is something that should be 'done' through observing and interacting with everyday life, an approach which led to Goffman being labeled as "the consummate sociologist" (see Birrell and Donnelly 2004, 49). Furthermore, this follows the critique that social gerontology and studies of exercise and aging have tended to be dominated by positivist and survey-style approaches (Grant and O'Brien Cousins 2001; Markula et al. 2001). Such research attempts to systematically place older people in distinctive categories according to, for example, age and lifestyle but "is not particularly good at explaining what it is like to become and be old" (Blaikie 1999, 169). This is important because the longer a woman lives, the greater the array of life experiences that she has had, making older populations increasingly heterogeneous and less easy to categorize in any meaningful way (Nilsson et al. 2000; Thompson 1992). This chapter, therefore, takes as its *point de depart* a need to avoid generalizing the experience of aging and understand individual differences and the ways that older adults interpret their social worlds through qualitative methods of enquiry (Grant and O'Brien Cousins 2001). Specifically the research responds to concerns that there remains limited examination of the meaning and significance of women's involvement in exercise in later life (Langley and Knight 1999; Roper et al. 2003). Furthermore, it will be identified in what follows that an understanding of corporeality is central to the understanding of aging and exercise, and that this is particularly relevant to older women (Wahidin and Powell 2003).

In drawing on the work of Goffman, I take on board the criticisms of his work including his lack of an explicit macro-perspective and what some regard as his failure to appreciate the gendered basis of people's experiences. Goffman was interested almost exclusively in the subtle nuances and minutiae of human speech and activities that underpin human interaction and which he termed "face work" (Goffman 1967). Throughout his writings, he also demonstrates an awareness of how gender, specifically in the case of women, may be interactionally consequential, and a concern with the consequences of gendered practices for the production of gender as a social institution (see Smith 2006). He published two key texts specifically on gender difference: in 1977 a paper entitled "The arrangement between the sexes" and, in 1979, the book *Gender advertisements*. In these writings, Goffman dismisses biological differences as the justification for the 'othering' of women, and argues that society's desire to magnify gender differences means that "gender not religion is the opiate of the masses" (Goffman 1977, 315). It was Goffman's view that gender and age have greater social significance than class and other social divisions. His main interest, and pertinent to an exploration of women's exercise behavior, was in gendered displays which he regarded as "the shadow and the substance" (Goffman 1979, 6) of gendered social life, and he described people's willingness to adhere to depictions of masculinity and femininity in terms of "the ritualization of subordination" (Goffman 1979, 40). This will be illustrated in the stories told in this chapter of older women's experiences of exercise. It is notable that, despite criticisms of Goffman, his argument that "One might just as well say there is no gender identity. There is only a schedule for the portrayal of gender" (Goffman 1979, 8) was adopted in the seminal work of the feminist Judith Butler who also wrote in terms of there being *no gender identity* (1990, 25). Indeed, while Butler conceptualized power in ways that differ from Goffman, her performative conceptions of gender resonate closely with Goffman's (1959) thesis that human behavior may be understood through the interactions between an 'actor' and their 'audience' on the social stage of everyday life—a process that he termed dramaturgy, and a stance which appears to anticipate much of Butler's celebrated work by approximately three decades. Pertinent to my chapter, Goffman's work investigates and illuminates the personal aspects of life that feminism holds to be political (see Smith 2006). I will turn the attention to such lived experiences in the next section.

THE 'AGENDER'

It has long been argued that age may exacerbate other existing social inequalities, in particular gender, and this may be experienced as a 'double jeopardy' of discriminatory practice (de Beauvoir 1972). Furthermore, older women's exercise promotion, often grounded in medical discourse, rarely seems to take into account what may be meaningful to the women themselves. I use the term the 'AGEnder' to explore the nexus where age and gender are key to the experience of the agenda of the exercise policy makers. Clarke and Warren have argued that the "active healthy aging" agenda is "typically framed by policy makers, researchers and service planners, who tend to define activity from middle-aged or youthful perspectives that may not be congruent with older people's experiences" and "seldom is the focus on what older people themselves desire, and more often on 'what you think we need' (Joseph Rowntree Foundation 2004, 39)" (2007, 467). Sam (2003) and Sam and Jackson (2004) further observe that while policies frame social problems and reflect public values and the demands of interest groups, they also shape public expectations in defining the issue and setting the agenda through best practice guidelines for future plans and actions. This in turn can change, exacerbate and create further problems. The policy makers have adopted a view of aging as a period of frailty and decline which needs addressing through a counter-discourse of positive/active/healthy aging. Governmental anti-aging campaigns, medical and social care experts, thus, aim to keep people healthy and independent of the need for socio-economic support (see Dionigi 2006; Dionigi and O'Flynn 2007). This is illustrative of what Katz (1996) has termed an ensconcement in the gerontological web, and was experienced by women in this study:

> I am definitely more aware now about the benefits of regular exercise. The publicity is all around, and I am inundated with junk mail, charity begging letters, etc. all telling me the benefits. Our local council runs promotions and now government is giving healthy living more exposure.
>
> (64)

Higgs et al. describe this as "the rise to prominence of the 'will to health' in later life," whereby individual 'choices' are largely designated and include a target of being healthy as a fundamental goal (2009, 689). These policies and practices continue to be a trend where physical culture is placed at the heart of population regulation dating back to the nineteenth century when exercise was used as a means of developing soldiers for warfare, underpinning a healthy workforce, and socializing youth into the modern social order (Coakley and Pike 2009). The policies also reinforce the notion that there is a "good" and a "bad" way to age (Cavanagh, 2007, 81), or what Higgs et al. describe as the distinction between normal and natural aging:

> The growth in technologies of the self has fostered a distinction between natural and normal ageing, with the former being associated with a cultural and ethical ideal of old age as a time of physical and mental decline, while the latter is associated with an increasing emphasis on maintaining norms of self-care aimed at delaying or denying such a decline. This distinction is then related to how the older consumer is increasingly tied into contradictory notions of natural and normal ageing through the construction of risk and the marketisation of health technologies.
>
> (2009, 689)

The consequences of this good/bad, normal/natural binary determines people's experiences of aging depending on the choices that they make. Refusal to engage in anti-aging is seen as irresponsible because the person remains a threat to social values. In turn, this contributes to differential power relations—if you do not exercise you are a bad person—which further stigmatizes those who are less able or willing to exercise. It is important to note that older women, and those with less economic capital, are particularly 'othered' by this process. For example, several women in this study indicated that gender-defined domestic responsibilities continue to constrain exercise choices in later life. This demonstrates that gender remains an organizing and potentially limiting element in the experience of aging. For example, one woman explained:

> I thought when I retired that I would increase swimming sessions . . . but so far have been too busy with looking after garden, granddaughter, mother, husband et al. In spite of loving some aspects of 'retirement' I am almost resentful that I do not have the time for myself that I thought I would have. (60)

Goffman describes such techniques as a means by which the 'socially dead' (i.e., the old and usually female) are "sorted but not segregated and continue to walk among the living," enabled to continue to co-exist with those deemed 'successful' (in other words, the young and usually male) who, in this case, are those with relative privilege in being able to make socially valued active lifestyle choices (1952, 463).

Furthermore, these policies and practices have contributed to a commodification of aging by business enterprises targeting a "blossoming consumer market" (Neilson 2006, 151): those who wish to continue to appear young. The older population becomes regulated by a complex network of health and beauty industries, particularly older women for whom aging is more problematic than men. It is often assumed that beauty work is grounded in definitions of femininity which are narrower than those of masculinity within patriarchal, ageist societies. Davis (2003) argues that while this many be true, women often demonstrate agency. They are frequently critical of the dominant definition of femininity as illustrated in the following quotations from women in this study who were also discouraged from exercise:

> I don't think I should be more active. I'm fortunate not to have any creaking joints. I have no guilt feelings about the lack of exercise in my life at all and tend to think the current obsession with going to gym and engaging personal trainers . . . both boring and pointless. (65)

> Yes, I'm heavier than I used to be. But I enjoy life and I'm not cutting down on life's pleasures (wine, for example) or changing my lifestyle to look as someone else thinks I should. I never read women's magazines or take any notice of adverts so I'm pretty immune to the dictates of fashion (when it comes to size and shape). My life is too full to think too much about it. (65)

However, on the whole, most women appeared to continue to engage with such practices, even while critical of them, to increase their acceptability in a society which privileges youth. Women's negotiation of anti-aging discourse and practice appears to be framed by the distinction between what Ballard et al. (2009) term the public and private dimensions of aging. This separates those changes which are visible from those which may be kept hidden by careful management of the information revealed to others. I will further demonstrate this in the following section.

PUBLIC AGING

Goffman (1963) distinguished between a person's *social identity*—how people are identified and categorized by others—and their *personal identity* constituted of those dimensions which make people distinctive from others. The social identity may be initially *virtual* based on the anticipations of a person on first appearance. It then develops into an *actual* identity when the attributes of a person become known. A discrepancy between the virtual and actual social identity which downgrades the initial anticipation creates what Goffman calls a stigma. Stigma may be discredited (visible) or discreditable (invisible) but, according to Goffman, everyone will experience stigma "if for no other reason than oncoming agedness" (1963, 129).

A key dimension of the discredited, or public, stigma is that one's external appearance is seen to say something about one's identity. One woman described her lack of exercise as "a failure of character" and something that needed to be addressed: "I should be more active" (77). As older women negotiate the stigma of aging, they may make comparisons between self and others to assess how 'well' they are aging. This is judged largely on the basis of the public, visible features of the aging process. For example, one woman explained how "I regard swimming as of vital importance, especially as at my age I see so many of my peers who do not exercise becoming old, overweight and mentally lethargic" (63). Here, she is able to reduce her perceived self-stigmatization by distancing herself from those who do not conform to the dominant ideas of the 'good,' 'normal' way to age.

Aging, unlike other discredited stigmas which are visible at birth, is one that has to be adjusted to throughout the life course. This presents a specific challenge for women, who simultaneously have to negotiate ageism and sexism. Hurd Clarke and Griffin explain:

> The loss of a youthful appearance is particularly damaging to women, who are socialized to be more concerned with their appearances than their male counterparts (Bartky 1990; Bordo 1993). Indeed, women are harshly judged on the basis of their ability to achieve and maintain the cultural ideal of female beauty, namely a young, thin, toned, yet shapely body (Bartky 1990; Bordo 1993; Cortese 2004; Gimlin 2002; Wolf 1991).
>
> (2008, 655)

In this study, women repeated a concern with weight gain and changes in their body attributed specifically to the aging process: "I don't like the changes . . . I've gained a huge amount of weight over the last 3 years and it becomes more and more difficult to shift" (60); "Gravity in older age is the problem (fat tummy)" (60). Following Wright (2008), the current vogue for a medical preoccupation with weight and the so-called 'obesity epidemic' shapes people's views that there is a proven relationship between weight, health and exercise. This has become the focus for policies, and also for the ways that people (and particularly women) judge themselves and others. Ironically, in some cases negative perceptions of, and a subsequent desire to hide, the excess weight served as a factor to reduce the amount of physical activity undertaken: "The extra stone that has crept on, is disheartening . . . I can't think what would help me to get motivated (to exercise) once more" (76).

An added dimension of the experience of aging is that people often look at same-sex older people, especially those within their own family, and are worried for their own futures. This may exacerbate negative perceptions of self-aging, and can support ageist attitudes and undermine relationships between younger and older people. Previous research in this area has focused on younger women in their twenties, whose concerns centered on age-related changes to the appearance of their bodies including weight gain following childbearing and giving birth (see Phoenix and Sparkes 2006). In contrast to young men, these women experienced a contradiction between their perceptions of older women and their idealized future selves, with negative views of older age focused on loss of mobility and muscle tone, and the development of wrinkles and graying hair. Within my own research, women in their sixties continued to draw on their perceptions of their older female relatives as a key factor in determining whether to engage in exercise. These decisions were framed as negative choices within an anti-aging discourse—to exercise was to avoid/delay aging:

> I am lucky to be fit and pain-free at the moment—though my hip gets stiff sometimes. I then do a cycling exercise on my back and eventually it goes away. My mother had osteoporosis so I take preventative medication and try to take load bearing exercise daily—but could do more—I set great store by my morning yoga type exercise, about 7 to 10 minutes as I dress, so I am bendy and supple but do not have much stamina. (73)

The experience of the visible discredited stigma may lead to a person engaging in impression management to 'cover' the signs of aging and 'pass' as younger (Goffman, 1963). The role of cosmetics and choice of clothing were identified as particularly significant in this process, as illustrated in the words of one woman:

> I don't feel differently about my body or appearance than when I was younger because I color my hair brown and my weight is only 7lbs more than in my teens so I can wear fashionable sports clothes, combat trousers and t-shirts, etc. (69)

Twigg (2007) identifies the ways in which sport and leisure clothing allow women's body movement and body spread in later life, while simultaneously integrating age-related changes with a youthful appearance via a sporting style. However, some also talked of how their desire to cover their body negatively impacted on the choice of exercise participation:

> I am embarrassed about the veins in my legs and no longer wear short skirts. I feel ashamed of showing bare feet, as I now have bunions,

and try to hide them! This manifests itself in swimming pools, show-ers, and walking barefoot when other people are around. (64)

Such choices are illustrative of what Goffman (1963) called the *ego* or *felt identity*, which relates to the feelings people have about their identity. Many of the women in this study were negotiating in-group/out-group alignments, torn between identifying with their stigmatized peer group and those who Goffman termed the "normals" (in this case, the youthful) in society. Such "politics of identity" (Goffman 1963, 123) was illus-trated in the words of two women who disassociated from their own age group. One referred to her peers as "Old dears, the blue rinse brigade" (70) (referring to the fashion of older women dying their hair blue). The other stated: "I believe it is important to color the hair and avoid exces-sive weight gain. If a person sees a white face with white hair in the mirror that is little incentive to get out and enjoy life" (69). In contrast to the findings of Dumas et al. (2005), none of the women in this study demon-strated an age habitus whereby they were able to re-evaluate standards of beauty and embrace different norms of appearance as they grew older. Instead, the emphasis was very much on "keeping slim and 'defying' old age" (63). Furthermore, while the examples presented in this section are of visible and public signs of aging, many of the women also talked of other non-observable, but highly significant, dimensions of aging which impacted on their exercise choices. These will be discussed in the follow-ing section.

PRIVATE AGING

Many of the women talked of more private aspects of the aging process, akin to what Goffman (1963) termed the discreditable or invisible stigma. Some described changes in their musculo-skeletal structure:

If you let your muscles degenerate you never get them back when you're older because they won't regenerate . . . I'm quite old now you know . . . it all went miserably downhill . . . I've got arthritis in my knee . . . Everyone at my age has osteopenia because it's a degenera-tion of the bones. (70)

Others spoke of a more general sense that "age is slowing me down" (66); or more specifically that "reactions are slower . . . it takes longer for the message to reach the feet! Vision has deteriorated . . . Stamina has less-ened" (64). In each case, the women demonstrated negative comparisons to, and a sense of nostalgia for, their younger selves, to the extent that one woman stated that as she wrote her story for this research: "I am in tears now thinking about the things I can't do anymore" (71). Some of the more private aspects of aging also were explicitly gendered, with women describing the effects of the menopause or having borne children. For example, one specifically explained how she would not exercise because "running makes me wee—we were not taught pelvic floor exercises in the '60s!" (73).

The significance of many of the aspects of private aging is that, unlike public aging, there is little opportunity to cover or alter the changes to the body. The private dimensions of aging were experienced as confirmation of the aging process, and the best that the women could do was to try to control the flow of information which threatened the presentation of a youthful identity, even if this meant not engaging in exercise. As one woman explained, the current (public) exercise provision available to her merely ensured her absence: "Definitely do not do enough exercise . . . Would never go to a gym" (67). Indeed, evidence from these women's stories suggest that the emphasis on youthfulness in policy discourse and promotional materials appears to have the unintended consequence of creating the impression that "You have to be young to do sport" (74), with many women choosing not to engage in activities which appear inappropriate to their presentation and sense of (an aging) self.

However, following Goffman, it is important to understand the experience of aging, as with other stigmatized groups, as context specific: "a language of relationships, not attributes" (1963, 3). How a person feels about growing older is likely to vary depending on where the person is. Consequently in certain situations, it is possible for the aging person to interact with those Goffman termed the 'normals' (i.e., the young). One woman said that she "might consider a small, friendlier women's-only organization" (67). A woman interviewed by Hurd Clarke and Griffin embraced the opportunity to experience her age 'privately,' explaining:

> I don't mind being invisible. I quite enjoy that. Like when I go to the gym with all these gorgeous young things around me, I can just look anyway I want and just be peddling away and do whatever I want. No one is paying any attention to me and it's really nice. I really enjoy that.
>
> (2008, 667)

Unlike previous research, my findings question the idea of the aging body as a 'mask' whereby the outer shell merely disguises the belief in a youthful self beneath (Featherstone and Hepworth 1991). In my research, women found it impossible to disguise aging through strategies of masquerade (Biggs 1993) or a masquerade of youth (Woodward 1991) and continue a lifestyle consistent with an 'inner' youthful self. In the case of most women in this study, it was not only the visible aspects of aging which were problematic but also dimensions of the aging process which were not immediately obvious to others. The challenge and experience of aging extends beyond merely maintaining the public image (Ballard et al. 2009).

CONCLUSION

The findings from this study indicate that exercise has multiple and contradictory meanings for older women: while it offers empowerment in developing strength and mobility for independent living, most of the women continue to be oppressed by the impossible body ideals privileging youth and traditional norms of femininity. Furthermore, Dumas et al. (2005) have argued that older women from affluent backgrounds experience the 'loss' of age-related changes more than working-class women who are more used to hardship and marginalization. It should be acknowledged that majority of the stories in this study were from women who appeared to lead a life of relative privilege with respect to physical and cultural capital. For example, most women enjoyed membership of leisure clubs, overseas travel and home ownership. Upper- and middle-class women are more likely to have the time and resources to work on a 'body project' (Shilling 2005), and often demonstrate greater concern with the presentation of their corporeal self. The stories presented here, therefore, need to be read with the caveat that they are unlikely to be fully representative of the experiences of women from less privileged social groups.

However for most women, growing older is experienced within a framework of age fundamentalism which is reinforced by subsequent policy documents based on incomplete scientific knowledge. Youthfulness becomes a totalizing ideology from which there is little chance of escape. Tulle (2008) has argued that recommendations for older women to exercise are framed in an anti-aging remit—exercise eliminates aging—rather than emphasizing how aging women can find ways to increase physical capital and also restore social and cultural capital.

Aging is particularly problematic for older women who often live on the margins of society isolated, in some cases, by widowhood and perceptions of appropriate gendered norms of behavior and appearance. As women age, choices seem to be taken away through processes of stereotyping, overprotection, and poor and inappropriate policies, planning and provision. There is a clear need for policy makers to be aware that investment in exercise programs for older women is also an investment for the current younger generation, most of whom will also grow old. Perhaps a far greater challenge is to modify the current exercise 'AGEnder' and enhance the celebration of life, experience, and character as it is written on the older woman's body and appreciate the beauty therein.

194   *Elizabeth C. J. Pike*

REFERENCES

Age Concern. 2006. *Ageism: A benchmark of public attitudes in Britain*. London: Age Concern.

Amis, J. 2005. Interviewing for case study research. In *Qualitative methods in sport studies*, eds. D. Andrews, D. Mason and M. Silk, 104–38. Oxford: Berg.

Arber, S. and J. Ginn. 1991. *Gender and later life*. London: Sage.

Ballard, K., M. Easton and J. Gabe. 2009. Private and public ageing in the UK: The transition through the menopause. *Current Sociology* 57: 269–90.

Bell, S. 1987. Changing ideas: The medicalisation of menopause. *Social Sciences and Medicine* 24: 535–42.

Biggs, S. 1993. *Understanding ageing: Images, attitudes and professional practice*. Buckingham: Open University Press.

Birrell, S. and P. Donnelly. 2004. Reclaiming Goffman: Erving Goffman's influence on the sociology of sport. In *Sport and modern social theorists*, ed. R. Giulianotti, 49–64. Basingstoke: Palgrave MacMillan.

Blaikie, A. 1999. *Ageing and popular culture*. Cambridge: Cambridge University Press.

Burger, H., J. Canavan, W. Ey, I. Johnston and B. Drinkwater. 1996. *Drug testing in Master's sport: Implications for women*. Canberra: International Task Force for WomenSport International, Australia.

Butler, J. 1990. *Gender trouble*. London: Routledge.

Cattan, M. 2001. *Supporting older people to overcome social isolation and loneliness*. London: Help the Aged.

Cavanagh, A. 2007. Taxonomies of anxiety: Risk, panics, paedophilia and the Internet. *Electronic Journal of Sociology*. http://www.sociology.org/content/2007/—cavanagh_taxonomies.pdf.

Central Intelligence Agency. 2008. *The world factbook*. Washington, DC: Central Intelligence Agency.

Clarke, A. and L. Warren. 2007. Hopes, fears and expectations about the future: What do older people's stories tell us about active ageing? *Ageing & Society* 27: 465–88.

Clements, R. 2006. The effects of ageing, endurance exercise and heart failure on cardiac power output. Unpublished doctoral thesis, Liverpool John Moore University.

Coakley, J. and E. Pike. 2009. *Sports in society: Issues and controversies*. London: McGraw Hill/Open University Press.

Coalter, F. 2007. *A wider social role for sport: Who's keeping the score?* London: Routledge.

Davis, K. 2003. *Dubious equalities and embodied differences: Cultural studies on cosmetic surgery*. New York: Rowman and Littlefield.

DCMS/Strategy Unit. 2002. *Game plan: A strategy for delivery government's sport and physical activity objectives*. London: DCMS/Strategy Unit.

de Beauvoir, S. 1972. *Old age*. London: Andre Deutsch and Weidenfeld.

DeGeneres, E. Undated quotation. www.thinkexist.com.

Department of Health. 2004. *At least five times a week*. London: Department of Health.

Dionigi, R. 2006. Competitive sport and aging: The need for qualitative sociological research. *Journal of Aging and Physical Activity* 14: 365–79.

Dionigi, R. and G. O'Flynn. 2007. Performance discourses and old age: What does it mean to be an older athlete? *Sociology of Sport Journal* 24: 359–77.

Dumas, A., S. Laberge and S. Straka. 2005. Older women's relations to bodily appearance: The embodiment of social and biological conditions of existence. *Ageing & Society* 25: 883-902.

European Commission. 1999. *Towards a Europe of all ages*. Brussels: European Commission.

Featherstone, M. and M. Hepworth. 1991. The mask of ageing and the post-modern life course. In *The body*, eds. M. Featherstone, M. Hepworth and B. Turner. London: Sage.

Gibson, D. 1996. Broken down by age and gender: The problem of old women redefined. *Gender and Society* 10: 433–38.

Goffman, E. 1952. On cooling the mark out: Some aspects of adaptation to failure. *Psychiatry* 15: 451–63.

—— 1963. *Stigma: Notes on the management of spoiled identity*. Englewood Cliffs, NJ: Prentice Hall.

—— 1967. *Interaction ritual: Essays on face-to-face behavior*. New York: Anchor Books.

—— 1977. The arrangement between the sexes. *Theory and Society* 4: 301–32.

—— 1979. *Gender advertisements*. Cambridge, Mass: Harvard University Press.

Grant, B. and S. O'Brien Cousins. 2001. Aging and physical activity: The promise of qualitative research. *Journal of Aging and Physical Activity* 9: 237–44.

Haber, C. 2004. Anti-aging medicine: The history: Life extension and history: the continual search for the Fountain of Youth. *Journal of Gerontology: Biological Sciences* 59: B515–522.

Higgs, P., M. Leontowitsch, F. Stevenson and I. Rees Jones. 2009. Not just old and sick—the 'will to health' in later life. *Ageing & Society* 29: 687–707.

Hurd Clarke, L. and M. Griffin. 2008. Visible and invisible ageing: Beauty work as a response to ageism. *Ageing & Society* 28: 653–74.

Katz, S. 1996. *Disciplining old age: The formation of gerontological knowledge*. Charlottesville: University of Virginia Press.

Kirkwood, T. 2001. *The end of age*. Reith Lectures, BBC Radio 4.

Kluge, M. 2002. Understanding the essence of a physically active lifestyle: A phenomenological study of women 65 and older. *Journal of Aging and Physical Activity* 10: 4–24.

Krupp, C. 2009. *How not to look old*. New York: Springboard Press.

Langley, D. and S. Knight. 1999. Continuity in sport participation as an adaptive strategy in the ageing process: A lifespan narrative. *Journal of Aging and Physical Activity* 7: 32–54.

Laventure, R. 2007. *It's too bloody late for me! Physical activity and older people*. Loughborough: British Heart Foundation National Centre for Physical Activity and Health.

Magnus, G. 2008. *The age of aging: How demographics are changing the global economy and our world*. Chichester: John Wiley and Sons.

Markula, P., B. Grant and J. Denison. 2001. Qualitative research and aging and physical activity: Multiple ways of knowing. *Journal of Aging and Physical Activity* 9: 245–64.

Neilson, B. 2006. Anti-aging cultures, biopolitics and globalization. *Cultural Studies Review* 12: 149–60.

Nilsson, M., A. Sarvimaki and S-L. Ekman. 2000. Feeling old: Being in a phrase of transition in later life. *Nursing Inquiry* 7: 41–49.

Phoenix, C. and A. Sparkes. 2006. Keeping it in the family: Narrative maps of ageing and young athletes' perceptions of their futures. *Ageing & Society* 26: 631–48.

Roper, E., D. Molnar and C. Wrisberg. 2003. No "old fool": 88 years old and still running. *Journal of Aging and Physical Activity* 11: 370–87.

Russell, C. 2007. What do older women and men want? Gender differences in the 'lived experience' of ageing. *Current Sociology* 55: 173–92.

Sam, M. 2003. What's the big idea? Reading the rhetoric of a national sport policy process. *Sociology of Sport Journal* 20: 189–213.

Sam, M. and S. Jackson. 2004. Sport policy development in New Zealand: Paradoxes of an integrative paradigm. *International Review for the Sociology of Sport* 39: 205–22.

Shilling, C. 2005. *The body in culture, technology and society*. London: Sage.

Smith, G. 2006. *Erving Goffman*. London: Routledge.

Thompson, P. 1992. 'I don't feel old': Subjective ageing and the search for meaning in later life. *Ageing & Society* 12: 23–47.

Tulle, E. 2008. Acting your age? Sports science and the ageing body. *Journal of Aging Studies* 22: 340–47.

Twigg, J. 2007. Clothing, age and the body: A critical review. *Ageing & Society* 27: 285–305.

Vertinsky, P. 1995. Stereotypes of aging women and exercise: A historical perspective. *Journal of Aging and Physical Activity* 3: 223–37.

—— 1998. Run, Jane, run: Tensions in the current debate about enhancing women's health through exercise. *Women and Health* 27: 81–111.

Vertinsky, P. and S. O'Brien Cousins. 2007. Acting Your Age: Gender, Age and Physical Activity. In *Gender and sport in Canada* eds. P. White and K. Young. Oxford: Oxford University Press.

Wahidin, A and J. Powell. 2003. Re-configuring old bodies: From the bio-medical model to a critical epistemology *Journal of Social Sciences and Humanities* 26: 10–22.

Weinert, B. and P. Timiras. 2003. Invited review: Theories of aging. *Journal of Applied Physiology* 95: 1706–16

Woodward, K. 1991. *Aging and its discontents: Freud and other fictions*. Bloomington: Indiana University Press.

World Health Organization. 2002. *Active ageing: A policy framework*. World Health Organization.

—— 2005. *Trends in life expectancy*. World Health Organization.

Wright, J. 2008. Biopolitics, biopower and the obesity epidemic. In *Biopolitics and the obesity epidemic,* eds. J.Wright and V. Harwood. London: Routledge.

10 "Doing Something That's Good For Me"

Exploring Intersections of Physical Activity and Health

Lisa McDermott

> Although our subjectivity might appear our most intimate sphere of experiences, its contemporary intensification as a political and ethical value is intrinsically correlated with the growth of expert languages, which enable us to render our relations with our selves and others into words and into thought, and with expert techniques, which promise to allow us to transform our selves in the direction of happiness and fulfillment.
>
> (Rose 1998, 157)

During the fall and winter of 1994/1995 I completed data collection for a research project the focus of which was to understand qualitatively a group of non-athletic women's perspectives on their lived-body experiences of physical activity and exercise in general, and their involvement in aerobics and wilderness canoing more specifically (McDermott 1998, 2000, 2004). Of particular interest was grasping how these experiences related to their lived comfortableness of *being* their bodies, and the implications of this for questions of empowerment and identity (McDermott 1998, 2000, 2004). Central to this earlier analysis was a process of initiating a conversation that theoretically (i.e., feminist) and methodologically (i.e., phenomenology) sought to conceptualize physicality in a way that both embraced and conveyed the women's bodily experiences in order to broaden dominant representations of physicality as inherently masculine.

In the process of reading through the data a seemingly tangential (and until now unexamined) theme materialized in the women's conversations which articulated their exercise involvement to the active pursuit of health in terms of 'doing something good for me.' Describing it as 'seemingly tangential' signals the historically and discursively constituted nature of me as a researcher, both then and now. Certainly, while the data has not changed between my original analysis and now, the interpretation provided through the former reflects the discursive formations (i.e., feminist and phenomenological) in which I was enmeshed at that time (McDermott 1998, 2000, 2004). Analytically I approached the women's experiences through a feminist commitment to the project of making women's (in this case) physical activity experiences visible; very little feminist analysis at that time had been devoted to examining these in contrast to sporting ones.[1] Epistemologically speaking it sought to provide a corrective understanding to the omission of women's physical activity experiences that characterized the sport sociology literature of that time. Central to the logic of this kind of research is its claim to legitimacy on the authority of the women's direct experiences of (in this case) their physicalities. Underpinning such legitimacy is the sense "what could be truer . . . than a subject's own account of what . . . she has lived through" (Scott 1992, 24). The strength of such a methodology lies in its ability to expose the oppressive means through which the male/female binary of difference operates, the effect of which has been to marginalize women's experiences, including their physically active ones. But as Scott (1992) underscores, what this methodology is unable to do adequately is to render discernible the relational workings and logic of that difference. As she argues, by remaining within such an epistemological frame this research is unable to problematize the assumptions and practices of difference occurring within experiences, the effect of which is to naturalize it.

> When experience is taken as the origin of knowledge . . . the person who had the experience . . . becomes the bedrock of evidence upon which explanation is built. Questions about the constructed nature of experience, about how subjects are constituted as different in the first place . . . —about language (or discourse) and history—are left aside. . . . Making visible the experience of a different group exposes the existence of repressive mechanisms, but not their inner works or logics. . . . For that we need to attend to the historical processes that, through discourse, position subjects and produce their experiences. It is not individuals who have experience, but subjects who are constituted through experience.
>
> (Scott 1992, 25)

This conceptual shift that Scott urges ultimately draws attention to the ways in which individuals give meaning to experience based on the circulating discourses in which they are enmeshed that condition the possibilities of what they can think, do, say, be and feel (Cruikshank 1999). This contrasts with the assumption of a transparent relationship between thought and experience that renders the latter as directly accessible (Scott 1992). Rose (1998) speaks to this understanding of experience as discursively constituted through what he terms "devices of 'meaning production.'" In other words, experience is produced through

> grids of visualization, vocabularies, norms, and systems of judgment. . . . These intellectual techniques do not come ready made, but

have to be invented, refined, and stabilized, to be disseminated and implanted in different ways in different practices—schools, families, streets, workplaces, courtrooms.

(Rose 1998, 25)

Here I would also include health-related exercise practices.

What has thus underpinned not only this subtle recognition regarding the different ways in which to conceive experience conceptually, but also this transformation of the 'seemingly tangential' into something of scholarly significance are the discourses through which I am presently constituted as a researcher. As these discourses have broadened (as is often the case over one's scholarly career) to include both critical health and post-structuralist ones, this has enabled me to revisit, 'read' and 'make sense' of this exercise-health theme for its scholarly import; albeit in a manner that differs from the initial analytics brought to bear on the original data set. This kind of research trajectory, in turn, makes obvious Scott's (1992) point that subjectivity within the research process (regardless of whether the *subject* is the object of inquiry *or* the researcher herself) is neither fixed nor autonomous, but rather is discursively and productively constituted.

The other point I want to draw out about the women's articulation of exercise to health concerns how they conceived this interrelationship in terms of working in the service of the self (i.e., 'good for me'). Arguably it was more than just exercise and health that were being articulated to each other, as the self was also being stitched into this complex fabric of understanding, bringing to the fore the relevance of subjectivity to understanding the exercise-health relationship. With this in mind a host of questions began to surface as I re-engaged the data: how did this group of 20 women, all of whom came to physical activity in their adult years, come to identify exercise and health as important practices to be pursuing, and as intimately tied to their own sense of identity? How did being physically active in the name of health translate into the women thinking about their selves through some notion of 'good;' and how does this relate to what Rose (1999) terms contemporary regimes of ethics specifically regarding how the women chose to act upon their selves? What are the relationships amongst the women's seemingly '*private*' decisions to engage in these exercise practices, the emergence of expert health and neo-liberal discourses, and questions of power?

My intent for this discussion is thus to utilize it as an occasion to revisit this data and to use the aforementioned questions as guiding posts for unpacking the associations the women conceived amongst exercise, health and the self in an effort to problematize the relations between the self and power within their exercise practices. Arguably, weaving the question of subjectivity into how the women conceived the exercise-health relationship serves to recognize its centrality as both an essential target and resource for strategies of surveillance within advanced liberal democracies (Rose 1998). To this end, I initially begin by outlining the theoretical perspective taken up, notably a Foucaultian understanding of the self, government and bio-power. I then set out the discursive terrain in which the women's exercise experiences were enmeshed. The final section of the chapter thus presents the findings of my re-visitation of the data.

FOUCAULT, THE SELF, GOVERNMENT AND BIO-POWER: THEORETICAL CONSIDERATIONS

Within advanced liberal societies, where the modernist narrative continues to hold sway, the self is widely conceived through autonomy, rationality and individual responsibility; it is thought of as a fixed, coherent entity that strives for personal fulfillment, that seeks meaning through acts of choice, that can be apprehended and understood (in an unmediated fashion) through introspection (Rose 1998; Atkins 2005). In contrast to these 'givens,' Foucault (1983) works from the premise of the self as socially, historically and discursively constituted; it is constituted through both the effects of power-knowledge relations, as well as processes of active self-formation. Rose (1998, 1999) elaborates on this power-knowledge relation when he argues that intimately tied to the production of the self is the intersection of liberal government (power) and intellectual technologies that "play a fundamental part in 'making up' the kinds of persons that we take ourselves to be" (1998, 10) and "how we can become what we want to be" (1998, 11). This speaks to Foucault's point that human beings are not born subjects but rather are transformed into them through three specific processes of objectification: 'dividing practices,' scientific classification and subjectification. Of greatest import for this discussion, and what Rabinow (1984) describes as Foucault's most original contribution to discussions of the subject, is subjectification.

Essentially, subjectification encompasses the process by which an individual turns herself into a subject; it concerns the processes and practices through which she constitutes, recognizes and comes to relate to herself as a subject of a certain type (Rose 1998); and it is in this way that Foucault's notion of active self-formation becomes clear (Rabinow 1984). Conceiving a person's active involvement in processes of self-formation is also intimately tied to Foucault's understanding of the nature of power: it only exists when put into *action*; that is, power is "actions brought to bear upon possible actions" (1983, 220); moreover, it is productive "as the creation, shaping, and utilization of human beings *as* subjects" (Rose 1998, 151). In this way, one *becomes* a subject "through a variety of 'operations on [people's] own bodies, on their own souls, on their own thoughts, on their own conduct'" (Foucault 1980, as cited in Rabinow

1984, 11). The self is thus both an effect *and* an instrument of power. Here Foucault's understanding of power hinges on two meanings of the term subject: "subject to someone else by control and dependence, and tied to his [sic] own identity by a conscience or self-knowledge. Both meanings suggest a form of power which subjugates and makes subject to" (1983, 212). Power thus ties an individual's subjectivity (i.e., conscience, self-knowledge, identity [e.g., the healthy subject]) to her subjection (i.e., control by another). Within such logic "the subject is one who is both under the authority of another and the author of her or his own actions" (Cruikshank 1999, 21), illustrating Foucault's (1983) point that power necessarily operates through its interplay with freedom.

Rose (1998) proposes that relations between self and power can be examined along three interconnected dimensions: the political (i.e., governmentality), the institutional and the ethical. Most germane to this discussion are the political (addressed later) and ethical dimensions. For Foucault, ethics involve the meticulous types of practical advice that one uses for evaluating and acting on the self, which he explored through what he termed technologies of the self (Foucault 1988; Rose 1998); that is, techniques "which permit individuals to effect by their own means or with the help of others a certain number of operations on their own bodies and souls, thoughts, conduct, and way of being, so as to transform themselves in order to attain a certain state of happiness, purity, wisdom, perfection or immortality" (Foucault 1988, 18).[2] Central to the workings of these technologies "is the belief that one can . . . tell the truth about oneself," notably through scrupulous self-examination, itself a fundamental component of power (Dreyfus and Rabinow 1983a, 175). At the interface of technologies of power and technologies of the self is what Foucault calls government.

Government

Foucault's (1991) conceptualization of government references both an older, more comprehensive understanding of this term, as well as political rationalities that emerged in the sixteenth century with the modern Western state's development.[3] These rationalities, in turn, were contoured by an issue that had become central to matters of rule: the problem of population. Questions of government, which proliferated during this period, were thus "concerned with . . . how to introduce economy, that is the correct manner of managing individuals, goods and wealth" (Foucault 1978, cited in Rabinow 1984, 15). As government's primary target and concern, population became something to be administered "in its depth and details" (Foucault 1991, 102), which necessitated a "more detailed consideration of how to introduce economy and order (i.e., government) from the top of the state down through all aspects of social life" (Rabinow 1984, 15). Central to the workings of this "new political form of power" embodied in government is "this kind of political 'double bind,' which is the simultaneous individualization and totalization of modern power structures" (Foucault 1983, 213, 216), in terms of 'each and all.'

Drawing on this older understanding of government, Foucault (1983) broadly defines its purview as encompassing techniques and procedures concerned with the 'conduct of conduct'; here it is important to understand what he describes as conduct's equivocal nature: "to 'conduct' is at the same time to 'lead' others . . . [as well as] a way of behaving within a more or less open field of possibilities." In this way government is "modes of action, more or less considered and calculated" that "act upon the possibilities of action of other people. To govern, in this sense, is to structure the possible field of action of others" (Foucault 1983, 220–21). [4] Government is thus a deliberate activity whose tactics and strategies seek to enable certain conditions to shape and guide people's conduct (Gordon 1991; Dean 2006). This ranges from 'governing others' to 'governing the self,' illustrating, in the latter instance, how individuals become both subject *to* and a subject *of* power. Government is consequently defined and accomplished through the calculated management of a population's life forces (Nadesan 2008) and welfare (i.e., its wealth, health, needs, happiness, etc.) in terms of 'each and all' towards particular sought-after ends (Foucault 1991; Rose 1998) thereby securing social order and its reproduction.

But this shaping of conduct is not simply directed at controlling, disciplining and/or normalizing the ways of individuals; rather it works on the subject's capacities to act on her own interests to make her "more intelligent, wise, happy, virtuous, healthy, productive, docile, enterprising, fulfilled, self-esteeming, empowered, or whatever" (Rose 1998, 12). Central to the logic of governance is its simultaneously voluntary and coercive nature. Its interests are not established through force but rather it "operates to invest [individuals] with a set of goals and self-understandings, and gives [them] an investment in participating voluntarily in programs, projects, and institutions set up to 'help' them" (Cruikshank 1999, 41). In this way social order, as achieved through government, rests upon self-managing individuals making the choice to act in ways that ultimately serve to reproduce it (Dean 2006).

A governmental analysis thus seeks to connect questions of government, politics and administration to bodies, lives, selves and persons (Dean 2006) by focusing on "the forms of power that subject us, the systems of rule that administer us, [and] the types of authority that master us" (Rose 1993, 286). In doing so, it affords three things. First, it provides a framework for assessing relations of power, authority, self and identity relative to "the organized practices through which we are governed and govern ourselves" (Dean 2006, 18). Second, it engages issues of subjection in a way that allows one to understand how individuals are both subject *to* and a subject *of* power without getting trapped in the structure-agency binary (Yeung 2007). And third, it makes intelligible the multiplicity of authorities (utilizing diverse techniques, strategies and knowledges,) shaping our conduct "by working through our desires, aspirations, interests and beliefs, for definite but shifting ends [e.g., national prosperity, therefore productivity, social order, self-realization, etc. (Rose 1998)]" (Dean 2006, 11). At the heart of governing thus is a process of facilitating the public's identification of these definite ends (i.e., what is considered 'good'), which individuals are urged to act upon for the sake of their own interests (Lupton 1995). Importantly, as Rose (1998) points out, these strategies for conduct frequently operate through technologies of the self, revealing how the latter can be integrated into structures of coercion (Burchell 1996).

Bio-Power

Foucault's work on government introduced the term 'bio-power,' conceived as a technology of power focused on the body's life forces, and as a fundamental dimension through which government is accomplished (Dean 2006). Foucault explains this technology of power positing that the classical period marks a transition from sovereign power to bio-power, signalling "the entry of life into history . . . into the order of knowledge and power, into the sphere of political techniques" (1984, 264). Whereas the right to *take* life or *let* live characterized sovereign power as negative, "the right to intervene to make live" (i.e., to secure, extend and improve life [Foucault 1997, 248]) typifies bio-power as a positive influence on life "that endeavours to administer, optimize, and multiply it, subjecting it to precise controls and comprehensive regulations" (Foucault 1984, 259). With this entry of human life into history,[5] and as an object of power-knowledge, the question of how humans live becomes the focus of concern; it becomes something to be understood, regulated and controlled.

Foucault (1984, 1997) uses a bi-polar model to represent bio-power's technologies, which, despite being established at different times, ultimately dovetail and are articulated. The first pole, taking shape in the seventeenth and early eighteenth centuries, is an *anatomo-politics of the human body* involving disciplinary technologies centered on the individual body, maximizing its capacities and forces, rendering it both economically useful and docile. The second pole, emerging in the latter half of the eighteenth century, is a *bio-politics of the population* that necessitates regulatory technologies directed at the social body to ensure the regularized homeostasis of life's biological processes (e.g., propagation, births, mortality, health, longevity, etc.). Bio-politics is thus concerned with the administration of life as it exists at a population level (Dean 2006), where population is conceived as both a political and scientific problem, whose biological mechanisms require careful calculation, administration and management. Accordingly, bio-politics endeavors "to rationalize problems presented to governmental practice" by "a population: health, sanitation, birth rate, longevity, race" (Foucault 1997, cited in Dean 2006, 99); from the eighteenth century onwards bio-politics became a fundamental arc through which life processes are governed.

While bio-power's first pole entails bodily subjugation through discipline, the second one involves population control by regulation. The link between the two, and lying at bio-power's heart, as Gordon explains, is its concern with "subjects as members of a *population*, in which issues of individual . . . conduct interconnect with issues of national policy and power" (1991, 5). Importantly, as Foucault explains, the second pole does not supersede the first one; rather the former seeks to "integrate it, modify it to some extent, and above all, use it by sort of infiltrating it, embedding itself in existing disciplinary techniques" (1997, 242). Hook (2003) suggests bio-power valuably allows Foucault to connect "'bottom-up' and 'top-down' 'flows' of power, whilst maintaining an emphasis on technical and tactical imperatives" (cited in Harwood 2009, 18). The example through which Foucault examined the tandem operation of these two poles was sexuality; health practices and outcomes, arguably, is another area where such an articulation functions. Moreover, these two poles of bio-power clearly map onto the individualizing and totalizing effects of government.

In a discussion seeking to provide both conceptual clarity to bio-power, and to assess its relevance for contemporary analyses, Rabinow and Rose (2006) note not only Foucault's limited elaboration of bio-power due to his death, but also the lack of scholarly attention directed at expanding Foucault's "sketchy suggestions" regarding it. In an effort to initiate such a process, they posit that operationalizing bio-power involves an assessment of three interrelated dimensions: the existence of 'truth' discourse(s) about human life and authorities considered proficient to speak that 'truth'; strategies and technologies for intervening on the social body in the name of life and health; and modes of subjectification, whereby "individuals are brought to work on themselves, under certain forms of authority . . . by means of practices of the self, in the name of their own life or health" (Rabinow and Rose 2006, 197). Rabinow and Rose's proposition usefully contours the ensuing discussion in which I illuminate the interplay of these three dimensions in terms of the emergence of the discourses of neo-liberalism and the New Public Health (NPH) approach, with its health promotion strategies and interventions, which operated as fundamental discursive resources that the women in the research subjected their selves to through their identifications with the healthy subject position.

THE DISCURSIVE CONTEXT OF THE WOMEN'S EXERCISE INVOLVEMENT

One may legitimately query, what scholarly significance is to be gained by re-visiting data nearly 15 years on? Beyond elucidating the self-power relationship inherent in women's exercise practices, I argue the merit lies in being able to make sense of how they conceived the exercise-health relationship in light of two significant and interrelated contextual discourses of that day, whose effects and complexities can be better grasped historically than could necessarily have been discerned at the time of the data collection and my earlier analysis. What were these interrelated discourses?

NEW PUBLIC HEALTH

The first was the emergence of the NPH discourse in the late 1980s. While the 'old' public health movement of the late nineteenth/early twentieth centuries directed its efforts at controlling the spread of contagions and infectious diseases, the 'new' movement takes as its primary concern the categories of population and the environment (broadly conceived as encompassing the psychological, physical and social),[6] specifically in relation to chronic diseases and their prevention through lifestyle prescriptions (Petersen and Lupton 1996). Significantly, exercise and diet are represented as two of the primary prescriptive mechanisms for preventing the onset of ill-health.

New Public Health's focus on bodily surveillance and regulation, at both individual and population levels, operates by seeking to transform individuals' knowledge and understanding of 'good' health and 'risky' behaviours (via the dissemination of expert knowledges, norms, documentation, etc.), with a view to encouraging people to assume greater personal responsibility for them. In this way, NPH seeks to work through the "'responsibilized' and 'educated' anxieties and aspirations of individuals" (Rose 2005, 88). Its attention to population, health and prevention signal NPH's quintessential operation as a technology of bio-power, where power is "situated and exercised at the level of life" (Foucault 1984, 260), focused on maximizing its vitality; here its inherently moralistic and normative nature, operating in the service of governance, is revealed (Petersen and Lupton 1996). An essential NPH strategy is health promotion, through which its education and disease prevention efforts are disseminated. Significantly, Canada played a principal role in the emergence and development of this practice at a political level (e.g., Lalonde 1974;[7] Epp 1986). It staged the first international conference on health promotion in Ottawa in 1986.[8] Arguably, in the late 1980s/early 1990s (when data collection occurred) Canada was a critical context for incubating health promotion knowledges and practices, particularly through a focus on health education and social marketing (Bunton and MacDonald 2002), that was, and continues to be, deployed through various sites (e.g., educational, media,[9] medical, etc.).

Critical to NPH's operation is[10] not only its vocabulary of empowerment and self-care,[11] but also a self-reflexive and entrepreneurial (i.e., through exercising rational choices) subject who is not passively dependent but rather is actively (Petersen and Lupton 1996) pursuing a normative self constitution. Thus, the healthy subject is not just the bearer of rights, but is also necessarily obliged

> *to be free*, to understand and enact [her] li[fe] in terms of choice . . . where competent personhood is thought to depend upon the continual exercise of freedom, and where [she] is encouraged to understand [her] life . . . in terms of [her] success or failure acquiring the skills and making the choices to actualize [her]self.
>
> (Rose 2005, 87, emphasis in original)

To paraphrase Foucault (1981), NPH is arguably animated though 'the will to' health (cited in Mills 2003).

Neo-liberalism

New Public Health's establishment and entrenchment as a dominant discourse shaping the public's understanding of health as pro-actively achieved through self-discipline, responsibility and choice coincided with the second significant contextual factor at play: the nascent turn to and implementation of neo-liberalism in Canada.[12] Macroeconomic policy, organizational culture, social welfare, as well as conceptualizations of citizenship came to be restructured (Rose 1998) at both the provincial and federal levels. As Cameron (2001) notes, beginning in the mid-1980s and gathering momentum in the 1990s, the conventional Canadian take on the role of politics, and the nature of government and the market began to be undermined by numerous powerful forces, including neo-liberalism and globalization. This, in turn, propelled a change in political rationality in Canada, which aspired to create what Rose (1998, 1999) terms an "enterprise culture." Within this rationality, the self is made thinkable, judged and acted upon in a particular kind of way, specifically in terms of the "enterprising self."

> Enterprise here designates an array of rules for the conduct of one's everyday existence: energy, initiative, ambition, calculation, and personal responsibility. The enterprising self will make an enterprise of its life, seek to maximize its own human capital, project itself a future, and seek to shape itself in order to become that which it wishes to be.

The enterprising self is thus both an active self and a calculating self, a self that calculates *about* itself and that acts *upon* itself in order to better itself.

(Rose 1999, 154)

The synergies between neo-liberalism and NPH discourse become obvious, as its practices are dependent upon this enterprising self.[13] Initiative, self-discipline, risk calculation, personal responsibility coupled with a commitment to better oneself fundamentally underpins the healthy subject as conceived through NPH discourse. This signals how the effects of these discourses are not discrete. Rather the interests of one is served and supported through the other. Arguably, neo-liberal and NPH discourses operate as

> an ensemble of arts and skills entailing the linking of thoughts, affects, forces, artefacts and techniques that do not simply manufacture and manipulate, but which, more fundamentally, order being, frame it, produce it, make it thinkable as a certain mode of existence that must be addressed in a particular way.
>
> (Rose 1998, 54)

Accounting for the constellation of these mutually supportive discourses in which the women's lives were enmeshed is fundamental to understanding both how they conceived of exercise as articulated to health, and the implications of this for grasping questions of self and power within advanced liberal society.

THE RESEARCH AND FINDINGS

Ten women participated in the data collection (participant observation and interviews), all of whom were white, self-identified as heterosexual, ranged in age from 28 to 52, and lived in either an urban or a rural location in Ontario, Canada. They also identified a variety of physical activity and exercise regimes in which they were involved including running, cycling, aerobics, weight training, swimming, cross-country skiing, walking, horseback riding and hiking. Their level of involvement, in turn, ranged from daily participation to two times per week. In addition to these exercise practices they also identified dietary ones (the other normative component of healthy lifestyle prescription) as something they actively focused on and worked at.

The women foremost conceived their engagement with these practices as 'doing something that's good for me.' Describing their involvement in this way (i.e., 'good' for them) is interesting on a couple of fronts. On the one hand, the term 'good' implies a moral framework (i.e., 'good' is the binary of 'bad') for understanding one's actions. The consistency with which the women drew on this frame for making sense of their exercise and dietary practices signals the particular grid of meaning-making made possible through NPH discourse. Undoubtedly, such a frame holds consequences for the subject of that 'good' (i.e., 'me') in terms of evaluating one's self to be either satisfactory or wanting. On the other hand, determinations of 'good,' particularly at a public level, are central to the workings of government. At the heart of governing *is* "facilitating the [population's] development of certain characteristics considered 'good' and 'desirable' and of eliminating or minimising others" (Evans and Davies 2004, 44) in the name of its own welfare. Understanding the women's use of such language thus required grasping it in relation to these forces in order to account for their discursive effects. As one scratches below the surface of the women's use of 'good,' three themes emerge as fundamental to their conceptualization of it in relation to the exercise-health-self articulation. First, was the women's identification with the healthy subject position as constituted through NPH and neo-liberal discourses. Second, was the centrality of expertise, and what Rose (2005) terms the generosity of expertise to the workings of government and the formation of enterprising subjects. And finally, was the sense of accomplishment the women derived from their exercising and dietary practices, which held implications for how they evaluated their selves.

Exercise-Health-Self Articulations: Identifications with the Healthy Subject

Common to the women's sense-making of their exercise involvement was their articulating it to health. While this was not the only reason[14] underlying their exercise engagement, it was a salient one coming through the data. This articulation reflects an ethical decision to act on their selves in pursuit of both normative notions of 'good' health and a healthy subjectivity. This articulation, in turn, was conceived in a variety of (knowledge-informed) ways as: "doing something to keep my heart and lungs in better shape"; "mak[ing] my heart stronger"; "[a] cardiovascular challenge working a lot of muscles"; "a way of dealing with "high cholesterol" and "high blood pressure"; "[a means] to los[ing] some weight"; helping "to have good muscle tone so I don't hurt my back"; and most explicitly it was conveyed as being "tied up with the whole concept of health and wellness." But, as Anne's and Rachel's comments demonstrate, it was more than just exercise and health that were being articulated: "physically I know it's good for me just to get a good cardiovascular workout. Get my blood pumping and get energized" (Anne); "[aerobics] give me a good sense I've done something for my heart and I'm healthier" (Rachel).

　　While the former examples signal the specific identifications the women made regarding what they conceived exercise afforded them health-wise, the latter ones (Anne and Rachel) point to the rationales underlying their decisions to act on their selves in the name of health. This decision to act on their selves in this way was, in turn, dependent upon the women's identification with the appropriately valorized subject position contained within health promotion discourse, a point that requires further elaboration.

Central to the working of any discourse are the various subject positions (including 'the other') they bear, and from which its knowledge and meanings makes the most sense. It is through the process of locating oneself in said position(s) that one becomes its subject, subjecting oneself to its meanings, power and regulation (Hall 1997). All of the women readily identified themselves with, and therefore assumed, the primary subject position offered within normalizing health promotion discourse: the healthy subject. One of the ways in which this positive identification materialized was through their self-description as being "health conscious." Grace illustrated this sensibility when she explained:

> I feel good about myself and the way that I exercise and that I'm not a couch-potato[15] and I hope I never will be. I have to say I feel pretty good about myself and my health. I think it's good to be health conscious of what you're eating and what you're doing physically to keep yourself going. I think it's important to take care of myself. Keep yourself as healthy as you can for as long as you can.

Grace's comment made obvious the discursive effects of neo-liberalism and NPH (e.g., Epp 1986) to naturalize self-care and self-responsibility for one's health as commonsense, the net effect being to shore up their representation of 'good' health as achieved through individualized actions, themselves normative and regulative, on one's bodies and thoughts. At the same time, her comment was interesting in light of her (and more generally some of the other women's) age(s).[16] Their active self-formation into the healthy subject was evidenced through them talking about their 'former' selves who, for the better part of their lives, had not engaged in such health practices, illustrating not only their purposeful intent to act on their selves toward particular ends, but also the power of NPH discourse's 'will to' health.

> I think we've become a fairly health conscious family. I've changed our eating habits a lot. We eat very little beef anymore and pork very, very rarely. We eat mostly chicken and fish. . . . Two years ago I had my husband buy me a bicycle for our anniversary. And he said "a bicycle for our anniversary?!?" And I said, "yes I really want a bike!" I'm not into sports which keeps everyone physically active, but I think that's why I enjoy aerobics, and why I wanted a bike!
>
> (Grace)

Linda, who was 48 and started doing aerobics when she was 45, provided an even more forceful illustration of her subjectification and transformation into the healthy subject:

> Before I used to think well, the body, it's just a body; it carried you from here to there, you fed it. It didn't matter what you put in it. But now, I want my body to be healthy through diet and exercise. I'm into healthy foods, healthy eating. I really want to go that way. And in terms of exercise, I don't know how people cannot do something aerobic and feel good about themselves. I can't comprehend it because I like to stay active.

Illustrated through these examples of the women subjecting their selves to normalizing health promotion discourse is Foucault's understanding of power (as both productive and tied to knowledge, a point to which I return), and the self (as an effect and instrument of power). Through the women's exercise and dietary practices the self became both subject *to* and a subject *of* power through their self-responsible acts of monitoring and regulating their behaviors in a way that aligned with the expectations of the healthy subject, with the net effect of functioning in the service of health governance. In other words, while the women's sense of selves *as* healthy selves was enacted through *their* decision to employ exercise and dieting techniques, it was also under the authority of *others*, both those holding political power (e.g., implementing the NPH agenda and neo-liberal rationalities) and experts (e.g., health-related ones) who create 'truths' on which the women's conceptions of self were hung, demonstrating this double meaning of subject that Foucault (1983) argues power hinges upon.

At the same time, having 'former' selves afforded the 'older' women (40+) the opportunity to recognize the historical trajectory of constituting one's self *as* healthy. As Kathy astutely observed:

> With health promotion, which we didn't even know what that was 10 years ago [1980s], exercise is more in vogue now I think than it used to be for people. It was like if people were 40 and they were out riding a bicycle people would have laughed at them. To be physically active, I don't think it was in vogue then. Healthy lifestyle hadn't been invented. But that has changed.

Anne similarly discerned:

> Definitely the trend of the '90s is eating better, shaping up, that kind of thing. I feel it doesn't matter what magazine you open or program you're watching there's a little bit of something there *encouraging* it. . . . It's more like—doing things that are healthy for you and changing

your lifestyle. And I don't feel that's been—a negative influence. I think that it's been more of information for me, changing, being aware of fat intake or why exercise is good for my lungs and those kinds of things. So I've been influenced but in a positive way. I just *know* it's a good thing to do.

A few points require drawing out here regarding the "invented" and relative newness of this "trend" towards healthy "lifestyles." The first one concerns time. The women's observations readily map to the turn to the NPH agenda in Canada, and its use of the media as an apparatus of governance. Strategies such as Body*Breaks* (noted earlier) and other forms of media, to which Anne gestured, operated as key sites in the relay of expert exercise and nutritional knowledges to the population with a view to shaping Canadians' health habits, which the women viewed as positive "encourage[ment]" rather than as an intrusive strengthening of the grip of power over their lives.

The second point connects to issues raised in Markula's (2004) discussion of the potential resistive elements contained within Foucault's technologies of the self. As she asserts, fundamental to accomplishing this is a process of critical self-reflection that involves the constant questioning of the seemingly 'natural' and inescapable nature of one's identity; by interrogating its limits the potential for transgression emerges. Suggestively, the 'older' women's recognition of the historical trajectory of the healthy subject afforded them an occasion for such critical self-interrogation, to query for what purpose they engaged in their exercise and dietary practices. However, like Markula's (2004) fitness instructors, this opportunity was not seized upon, demonstrating both the inherent challenges for subjectivities to practice ethical self-care, and, as Rose (1998, 2005) and others (e.g., Coveney 1998; Cruikshank 1999; Dreyfus and Rabinow 1983a; Lemke 2000; Yeung 2007) have noted, how strategies of governance, in this case health, can operate through technologies of the self, making one's ability to discern their power effects even more difficult.

Finally, even though these health "trends" and "inventions" were relatively new when I interviewed the women, the deep identifications (e.g., Anne's conviction: "I just *know* it's a good thing") they made with normalizing health promotion discourse spoke both to its success at becoming an important constitutive discourse, even in its infancy; as well as revealing its nature as a technology of power whereby it worked, to paraphrase Rose (1998), simultaneously to maximize certain capacities (e.g., to exercise regularly, to eat 'properly,' etc.) and aspirations ("to be healthy through diet and exercise"), and constrain others (e.g., to be "a couch-potato") in agreement with particular expert knowledges (e.g., medical, epidemiological, physiological, psychological, etc.) towards particular ends (e.g., population health objectives). Its effect was thus to more or less structure the women's field of possible actions, illustrating how government operates "*through* the freedom and aspirations of subjects rather than in spite of them" (Rose 1998, 155). Here one can see the import of Foucault's understanding of the relational nature of the self (i.e., one's relation to oneself as the subject of thoughts and actions) that "provides a point of entry into [the women's] own thought processes (and subjectivity) through the mediation of normalizing [e.g., health promotion] discourse" (Atkins 2005, 208). It was their own actions (i.e., power) brought to bear on their bodies and thoughts, via dietary and exercise techniques, that transformed their selves into healthy subjects. In so doing, they assumed "responsibility for the ideas and actions to which the discourse gave rise" (Atkins 2005, 208) and became the bearers of its power/knowledge, with the net effect being the normative force of health promotion discourse being sustained. Central to the women's constitution as healthy subjects was knowledge, to which I now turn my attention.

Expert Knowledges

While the women clearly identified with the healthy subject position produced through health promotion discourse, their decisions to act on their selves in the name of health was equally dependent upon expert knowledges, which assume a dual role from a governmental perspective. On the one hand, they document the capacities and forces of individuals, transforming that into expert regimes of 'truth', which serve to constitute and define governmental activities and monitor their advancement. On the other hand, expert knowledges play a central role in the production of subjectivities notably through what Rose terms the *generosity of expertise*, which operate to shape individuals' conduct.

> The key to the transformations in our present wrought by expertise of human conduct lies in the way in which certain knowledgeable persons . . . have lent their vocabularies of explanation, procedures of judgments and techniques of remediation 'freely' to others. . . . And this includes their subjects. . . .
>
> (2005, 92)

The relation between subjects and expertise, Rose argues, is one of 'making up' individuals whose ethics (i.e., relations to themselves) are configured through expert-based "devices of 'meaning production'" (i.e., norms, knowledges, vocabularies, evaluative methods, etc.). The relation between the two is thus one of subjectification. Dreyfus and Rabinow further add that through such generosity

> the individual . . . become[s] an object of knowledge . . . to himself [sic] . . . an object who tells the truth about himself in order to know

himself and be known, an object who learns to effect changes in himself. These are the techniques which are tied to scientific discourse in the technologies of the self.

(1983a, 175).

Clearly, the women were indebted to such generosity, evidenced by the way in which they conceived their exercise involvement in terms of the prevention and/or management of chronic health conditions. Here they specifically referenced their exercise practices to existing conditions including arthritis, asthma, back problems, high blood pressure or cholesterol, and osteoporosis. Fundamental to their exercise involvement was their belief in its efficaciousness to manage these conditions. Suggestively, while we culturally tend to view chronic disease prevention and management as two separate spheres of activity, arguably managing them can be seen as another form of prevention, that is, preventing these health conditions from worsening. Yet, prevention, principal to the NPH discourse, is by its very nature a bio-political technology of governance that "work[s] as a kind of recruitment . . . [whose] method is to govern people by getting people to govern themselves" (Cruikshank 1999, 39) through the freedom of their 'choice' to do "things that are healthy for you and chang[e] your lifestyle" (Anne). This ability of expert knowledges to illicit such acts of self-governance were evidenced in the ways in which the women conceived exercise in relation to chronic disease prevention and/or management.

> Exercise just makes me feel better about my body. I *know* that I'm doing something that's good for it. I *know* that I'm doing something to keep my heart and lungs in better shape. That's important because I have asthma. So it's [exercise] a good thing.
>
> (Anne, emphasis added)

> I started out with the aerobics because of the high cholesterol. . . . When I finish aerobics, I *know* I'm one step ahead. That's one session that's made my heart stronger. When I found out my cholesterol was high I really panicked and I thought: "oh my god, I could have a heart attack." And I said to my husband "what I do now is keep moving. I keep doing my exercise and keep with my diet because if I stop—*then* I will do damage."
>
> (Linda)

Characteristic of all chronic health diseases is their complexity, evidenced by the limits of bio-medical knowledge to 'cure' them. Yet despite expert knowledges detailing the multiplicity of factors at play in their determinations, exercise was/is represented at a public level as an unequivocal ticket to 'good' health. But for someone like Anne, who was coping with asthma, arguably the exercise equals good health equation was not so straightforward given the broader context of her life in Ontario where the implementation of neo-liberal government policies resulted in the dilution of environmental regulations, including pollution controls; arguably structural determinations such as this hold much greater health consequences for individuals dealing with respiratory problems, and yet, it is at the level of individual action that Anne makes sense of her respiratory health. The women's decision to assume self-responsibility for their health rather than critically interrogate its structural determinations speaks to the early success of NPH and neo-liberal discourses in establishing themselves as dominant "devices of 'meaning production.'" Moreover, it also demonstrates the subtle and effective mechanisms through which health governance operates, whereby "one is largely self-policed" with no force being necessary as the women voluntarily complied "in the interests of their health" (Lupton 1995, 11).

As the women's discussions revealed, in making meaningful their techniques of the self, one found this weaving of expert health knowledges regarding prevention practices into their own conceptualizations of what was in "their best interests."

> Initially I started with aerobics to build up my muscle tone because I wanted to make sure that I had muscles so I wouldn't pull anything [due to her physically demanding job as a nurse]. And then I realized after I got there the benefit you have of the aerobic part for your heart and then you read the various things about the benefits for osteoporosis and your cholesterol. And so once you realize "okay this is why were doing this," considering that I'm better to be exercising.
>
> (Kathy)

> I'm approaching menopause and so I'm caught up on osteoporosis. I'm reading everything that I possibly can to see how I can't get osteoporosis because I know my aunt has it and she's in a wheelchair now. So I walk and do what I can physically so that I can avoid it. Because according to some of the new books they say walking, weight-bearing exercises are extremely important. The more you use your muscles against a resistance the more your bones get stronger.
>
> (Laura)

Two significant points require highlighting in relation to these excerpts. First, is the striking nature of the women's appropriation and use of expert health knowledges, whether this be in terms knowing about and using Body Mass Index (BMI) measurements for managing their weight, identifying 'good'/'bad' fat content in foods, accepting the dominant representation of overweight/obesity as an energy intake and expenditure imbalance, or knowing the risk factors for heart disease, osteoporosis, diabetes, etc. Through constituting themselves as the healthy subject, the women used the knowledge provided by NPH to act on their bodies *and* their thoughts (Atkins 2005), demonstrating the nature of exercise and dietary practices as both technologies of governance and techniques of the self that provided the women the means by which to transform their selves into healthy selves.

This leads to the second point. The women's transformations into the healthy subject did not occur in a vacuum, but rather in a context where the neo-liberal self was/is conceived as an autonomous subject making rational choices, who is self-responsible, and 'naturally' pursuing self-realization. In other words, their subjectification to NPH discourse occurred in a context where the enterprising self was/is highly valorized, and where the interests of government are seen to be the interests of each and all (Rose 1999). Characteristic to such a context, Rose (2005) suggests, has been a re-thinking of the social-economic relation, which came to the fore in the post Thatcher-Reagan era; in other words, the period of my data collection.

> All aspects of *social* behaviour are now reconceptualized along economic lines—as calculative actions undertaken through the universal human faculty of choice. Choice is dependent upon a relative assessment of costs and benefits of 'investment' in light of environmental contingencies. . . . And the paths chosen by rational and enterprising individuals can be shaped by acting upon the external contingencies that are factored into calculations. The notion of enterprise thus entails a distinct conception of the human actor . . . [as] an entrepreneur of his or her self. The human beings who [are] to be governed . . . [are] now conceived as individuals who [are] *active* in making choices in order to further their own interests. . . . [T]hey [are] thus potentially active in their own government. The powers of the state thus [are] directed to empowering the entrepreneurial subjects of choice in their quest for self-realization.
>
> (2005, 141–42)

Essential to this economization of the social is a logic of productivity and a belief in the importance of people productively living their lives on all fronts, including their health. How the women conceived their exercise involvement points to this calculating entrepreneurial subject that Rose describes. Their active deliberation on the benefits of such an investment to their health was fundamental to their decision to self-realize as a healthy subject.

> When you are exercising—well you know you're doing something that's good for you health-wise [because] you're going to lower your bad cholesterol, you're going to burn off calories and I think you feel

a sense of accomplishment in that instead of knowing you're deteriorating or not very fit. . . . So the best way to cope with that is to help myself as much as possible to avoid that by exercising.

(Kathy)

Moreover, this type of self is ultimately represented as productively contributing to the nation rather than being a drag on it, especially at an economic level. As Kathy noted in a conversation about the emergence of health promotion:

they [governments] realized that a lot of money can be saved if people eat properly and are physically fit. There's going to be a lot of money saved by their healthy lifestyles when they get older . . . which has made people more aware that they should be trying to be fit.

This idea of the women as entrepreneurs of their selves, actively making healthy (rational) choices in their own best interest was also commonly referenced to siblings and parents who had not made the 'correct' choice, and who implicitly became the specter of the *un*healthy subject—a subject position to be avoided. Rebecca was emblematic of this type of logic.

Initially it [doing aerobics] was about liking the way I look with exercising but now it's more the health. I'm concerned because my dad died of a stroke. He was diabetic and smoked. I have a sister that's insulin dependent. She's heavy and smokes. I'm worried she's next in line [to die]. My brothers and sisters all seem to have allergy problems. I don't and I sometimes think it's because I take care [of myself]—I won't smoke because I don't want to smoke. I don't *want* to be like my sister or my dad. I don't *want* to be like that. I don't *want* to be unhealthy. I'm a firm believer when your time's up, your time's up. But if you can prolong it in any way—that's why I'm doing it [exercise].

Factoring into the women's active rejection of an *un*healthy subjectivity was the fact that many of them had lost a parent and/or sibling to these chronic diseases at relatively young ages (n = 38–62), illustrating this idea of cost/benefit analysis relative to external contingencies. Their decisions to act on their selves in the name of health also resided, therefore, at the discursive-material juncture. On the one hand, their health-enhancing actions were incited by expert health knowledges regarding both exercise/diet as strategies for preventing chronic disease onset, as well as understanding their hereditary implications. The effects produced through dominant mortality discourses, in turn, undoubtedly compounded this. On the other hand, was/is the material reality that bodies, including one's own, are finite.

I was 12 when my father died of a heart attack. He was a big man. He smoked. I think they said it was a heart attack. He sort of dropped dead. Now he'd be an example of an unhealthy lifestyle. I think you certainly realize that you're not infallible when your father died at 44 and you're 43. And my mother died of melanoma. . . . at 55 . . . You realize that life can be short.

(Kathy)

As part of the repertoire of techniques the women drew upon to mediate their subjectivities in light of the injunction to health (e.g., "I'm doing my part by exercising" [Beth]), exercising and eating 'properly' also mediated their selves in relation to this material-discursive interface, which facilitated their ability to constitute a self not psychically paralyzed by the material frailties of life. Here Foucault's understanding of the productive nature of power illustrates how the effects of bio-power can be positively re-couped by the women to negotiate such psychic realities. Yet, the women's *knowing*[17] deployment of these techniques illustrated the effectiveness of NPH discourse, even its formative days through its normative and regulatory effects, in enhancing the grip of bio-power to *each* (of the women's lives) and *all* (of our lives). One of the obvious effects of this, as manifested through the women's discussions of their parents and siblings, was the naturalizing of methods of dividing and classifying (both of which are fundamental to the operation of government) people as a function of health practices and outcomes, rendering some subjectivities as morally desirable while positioning other ones as wanting.

'Doing Something Good for Me': Accomplishment and the Construction of the Self

One of the distinct contributions a Foucaultian perspective offers is its analytic objective of not adjudicating discourses to determine if they are 'good' or 'bad.' Rather, its intent is to shift one's analytic focus to understanding the effects produced (in this case, through the operation of NPH and neo-liberal discourses) for the ethical subjectivities the women constituted. In attempting to answer this question I draw on an observation Foucault made in a conversation with Dreyfus and Rabinow (1983b): "'[p]eople know what they do; they frequently know why they do what they do; but what they don't know is what what they do does' (personal communication)" (Foucault cited in Dreyfus and Rabinow 1983b, 187). What did the women's subjecting their selves to NPH and neo-liberal discourses *do*? As the discussion thus far demonstrates, the women were able to articulate meaningfully (albeit within the discursive limits of NPH discourse) what they conceived they did, in terms of acting on their bodies and thoughts via specific techniques of the self (i.e., exercise, diet, etc.), and why they did it (i.e., to be healthy subjects). And I would argue that, to a certain degree (and only at a micro level), they were also able to articulate "what what they do does." As the women explained, engaging in these particular techniques of the self afforded them a sense of accomplishment for having met the normative expectations of the healthy subject. That, in turn, was conceived as making them better selves.

> Getting a good workout gives me a greater sense of accomplishment because I know it's bettering me physically, health-wise. When you exercise, you feel like you've done something, you've accomplished something. The interesting thing about aerobics is that it's up to you to put as much into it as you want. There are days that I feel like "ugh I don't want to go tonight" but when I get there I think "alright, come on, push yourself a little." And when I do the extra 10 push ups that feels good. Getting a good workout gives me a greater sense of accomplishment because I know it's bettering me.
>
> (Anne)

> I have a membership at the "Y" and I find that it [working out] elevates my spirits. And there's the research[18] talking about the links between being physically active and mental well-being and I feel that pretty clearly; that's part of the appeal for exercising then. There's also being able to conform to some sort of discipline, which also made me feel good. I can say at the end of the week I went to the gym three times; I did this activity. I set my goal and achieved it. That's self-imposed discipline.
>
> (Julie)

Implicit to the logic of both Anne and Julie's explanations of the sense of accomplishment they derived from meeting normative expectations the NPH's was the neo-liberal enterprising self who demonstrates initiative, a commitment to her betterment, energy, ambition and makes the 'right,' rationally-determined choices to not only be physically active and 'healthy,' but to do so even when tempted otherwise, and to challenge oneself ultimately to do *more*. Lemke (2001) explains that fundamental to the workings of neo-liberal rationality is the congruence it endeavors to produce between a responsible-moral individual and an economic-rational individual. Here the responsible subject's moral quality is conceived through the belief that she rationally assesses the cost-benefits of an act (e.g., exercising, eating properly) versus other alternative ones (e.g., not exercising, eating anything). As understood through neo-liberal grids of meaning-making, the choice of options for action is represented as the expression of self-determined free will (shoring up the modernist narrative of the autonomous self in the process) resulting in the consequence(s) of that action(s) being shouldered alone by the subject. Put this way it begins to make sense why the women conceived their exercise involvement as such a significant accomplishment given the discursive terrain made available to them for assessing it in relation to their selves. In a context where one's sense of moral worth is determined by calculating the right 'choice,' at stake was not just the risk of failing to self-realize as a healthy subject, but having an ethical relation to one's self mediated through the binary to this good (healthy subject): the bad (unhealthy subject).

Fundamental to the women successfully acting on their selves, via techniques of exercise and diet, was another crucial component of the enterprising self; specifically discipline, which Julie astutely discerned as pivotal to both her sense of accomplishment and feeling good about herself. But techniques of discipline, as Julie and others illustrated, are not just a fundamental characteristic of the neo-liberal subject; importantly they also interact with techniques of the self (i.e., exercise and dietary practices). As Foucault explains:

> The contact point, where the individuals are driven by others is tied to the way they conduct themselves, [which] is what we can call . . . government. . . . Power consists in complex relations: these relations involve a set of rational techniques, and the efficiency of those techniques is due to a subtle integration of coercion technologies and self technologies.
>
> (1993, 203–204)

The sense of accomplishment the women derived from their faithful commitment to exercising and eating 'properly' was not just a critical aspect of their constitution as a healthy subject, but equally crucial to their constitution as a '*good*' subject.

> In the back of your mind you're going "okay, I'm going to aerobics twice a week. I'm making an attempt to be healthier, to be physically fit." And I think you think, "well, that's good. I'm glad I did it. I feel better about myself than if I never got away from the television." I've been able to discipline myself to get me there, and able to discipline myself to keep going, which makes me feel better about myself. I think you feel better about yourself because you know you're doing something positive, that's more healthy for yourself. It's that knowing that I'm doing something that's good for me; it's just knowing that you should.
>
> (Kathy)

Similarly, when asked to describe how she felt after doing aerobics Rebecca responded:

I feel I've done myself some good. I just feel good about myself when I am active. Like I know if I stop doing all activity for a couple of weeks, I know I'm going to feel frumpy. When I'm working out I'm feeling better about me and I'm feeling healthier. And it makes me feel good to know I'm healthier for it.

Two points need drawing out here regarding the women's active stitching of their selves to the exercise-health articulation they conceived. First was the double meaning the word 'good' assumed in the women's deployment of it. On the one hand, expert knowledges, which hold considerable cultural sway, sanctify exercising and eating properly as good for one's health, and therefore something responsible individuals do. On the other hand, exercise was "good for" the women because it facilitated their enactment of a type of subjectivity that demanded and demonstrated the qualities through which competent personhood is conceived within neo-liberal rationality.

The second point is that inherent to the workings of this logic of feeling good about themselves for having acted on their bodies was a binary framework of meaning: to exercise (as required of a healthy subjectivity) was to feel *good* about their selves; to not exercise was to feel *bad* about their selves as evidenced by the negatively imbued terms they used to describe themselves when they did not exercise: "frumpy," "slovenly," "less energetic," "deteriorating" and "sloppy." Juxtaposed to this were terms through which they conceived exercise: "positive," "right," and "good." Foucault (1993) suggests that fundamental to understanding the ethical field an individual negotiates with one's self are the twinned dimensions of evaluation and action, both of which are discursively produced. The parameters upon which evaluation occurs are discursively determined as a function of what is considered true, permitted and desirable, which in turn inform the actions brought to bear on one's body and thoughts. No doubt the women actively chose to subject their selves to health promotion discourse, but once subjected to it the idea of choice becomes a more complicated affair given the moral implications for evaluating one's self if one *did not* exercise. This was the reality the women faced in making sense of their selves in relation to their healthy subjectivities, whereby exercise and dietary techniques became the moral barometers demarcating a 'good' from a 'bad' self, explaining the sense of currency they attached to accomplishing these techniques on their bodies.

CONCLUSION

Two significant discourses that fundamentally shape contemporary exercise practices are NPH and neo-liberalism. Within the Canadian context their historical trajectory dates back to the late 1980s/early 1990s. Coinciding with their nascent appearance was my collection of qualitative data relating to a group of women's lived-body experiences of physical activity and exercise. At that time, my feminist interests lay in exploring, from the women's perspectives, how these experiences contributed to their understandings of their physicalities, with a view to grasping the empowering effects of them. What also emerged in that data, but left unexamined due to its seemingly peripheral nature to my then interests, was the women's articulation of their exercise involvement to the active pursuit of health in terms of 'doing something good for me.' Fast-forward to the present and the peripheral has been transformed into the meaningful, imbued with scholarly import that is recognized as warranting analysis. This, in turn, is due to the changed nature of my discursive constitution as a researcher, which has broadened from my earlier feminist-phenomenological one to a Foucaultian governmental one, with my primary intellectual interests now lying at the exercise-health interface.

With this in mind, I have used this discussion as an opportunity to examine the exercise-health articulation that emerged in the 1990s data; but to do so in a manner that both reconceives experience as something discursively produced, which foregrounds the two contextual discourses (i.e., NPH and neo-liberalism) in which the women's exercise experiences were enmeshed, and necessarily conditioned the possibilities of what they could think, say and feel about those experiences. Arguably, NPH and neo-liberalism's discursive effects could only be discerned retrospectively. Thus my focus has not only been to examine how the women conceived this exercise-health articulation, but to problematize the weaving of their selves into it in order to bring to the fore the relevance of subjectivity to it, and to scrutinize critically the relations between the self and power within those exercise practices.

What this retrospective governmental analysis ultimately revealed was the ability of these discourses to take hold of the public imagination and convincingly establish themselves as constitutive over a relatively short period. The women's subjectification to them provided the knowledge and rationale through which they conceived exercise, health and the self as deeply articulated. Here the sense of satisfaction they derived with exercise, with doing something 'good' for themselves, demonstrates how exercise has become an important technique of the self through which the 'good' subject and the healthy subject interface and are secured; and where the ethical relations and interest of the self intermingle with state interests. Underpinning this edited collection is an understanding that exercise is felt to be an important (but conflicting) thing to women. What this analysis reveals are some of the meanings and multiple registers through which feeling 'good' about exercise is produced, and which are inescapably tied to the generosity of experts. As the women's experiences revealed, this facilitated their ethical negotiation of their selves allowing for their transformation "in the direction of happiness and fulfillment" (Rose 1998, 157).

NOTES

1 Notable exceptions include Gilroy (1989, 1997), Markula (1993, 1995), Wright and Dewar (1997), Castelnuovo and Guthrie (1998).

2 Foucault's conceptualization of technologies of the self has primarily been advanced in two ways in the literature, which are not mutually exclusive within a given analysis (e.g., Dumm 1996). First, are those analyses taking it up as practices that free the individual from technologies of domination, which, Markula (2003) suggests, involves processes of ethical self-care, aesthetic self-stylization and critical self-awareness (see also Besley 2005; Lloyd 1996; Markula 2004). Second, are those analyses positing that technologies of the self are also tied up in power relations, whose net effect is to extend the grip of surveillance and control in people's lives through self-governance. This discussion primarily draws upon the latter literature.

3 Foucault demonstrates that up until the eighteenth century the term government was used within philosophical, religious, medical and pedagogic texts, rather than simply being limited to the political meaning it assumes today. This older interpretation of government also signified problems of self-control, and guidance for the family, children, the household, soul, etc., thereby transcending its contemporary understanding as simply state administration (Lemke 2000).

4 My earlier notation of Foucault's understanding of power as action assumes a greater depth of relevance regarding his perspective of power through government.

5 Foucault clarifies, this is not to suggest that this was "the first contact between life and history;" rather he argues through economic advancement, demographic changes and the development of expert knowledges of life, "control over life averted some of the imminent risks of death" resulting in "biological existence . . . [being] reflected in political existence" (1984, 264).

6 Petersen and Lupton (1996) argue that NPH's wide-ranging conceptualization of environment serves to redefine many areas of personal life as health-related, thereby extending its grip to multiple facets of people's lives.

7 The influence of this report by the then Canadian Minister of Health, Marc Lalonde (1974), was felt worldwide. Its introduction of the health field concept argued improved population health status required a multifactorial approach beyond simply focusing on access to institutionalized health care. Also factoring into the equation were "self-imposed risks due to lifestyle choices," the environment (both social and physical) and biology. This document is also recognized as laying the groundwork for both NPH and health promotion (Leeder 2005).

8 At this conference health promotion's definition was set out in the *Ottawa Charter of Health Promotion*.

9 Media dissemination of expert health knowledges in Canada has occurred through not only the usual venues (i.e., newspapers and magazines), but also televised public service announcements, with one of the most widely recognized ones being Body*Breaks*. These 90-second commercials, which first aired in 1989, sought to provide expert-based knowledge on exercise/physical

activity and nutrition, in an effort to urge Canadians to adopt healthier lifestyles (Body*Break* 2009). The other significant player on this educative front has been the Canadian Fitness Lifestyle Research Institute (CFLRI), a national research agency whose mandate is to educate Canadians "about the importance of leading healthy, active lifestyles" (CFLRI 2005a). In 1991 it launched both the *Research File* (monthly one-page summaries of synthesized and interpreted scientific research findings about active lifestyles for professionals) and *Lifestyle Tips* (articles published in community newspapers for the general public) (CFLRI 2005b, n.d.).

10 While I am writing about the past, the effects of the NPH discourse continue to operate. For the sake of simplicity I use the present tense.

11 Indeed, in *Achieving health for all,* which set out the federal government's blueprint for addressing how Canada would meet the objectives of the *Ottawa Charter,* one of the triumvirate mechanisms of health promotion is "self-care," understood as the actions "individuals take in the interest of their own health" (Epp 1986, 7). But, as Cruikshank (1999) astutely observes in her seminal work *The Will to Empower,* projects organized to engender empowerment, self-esteem and self-care are far from politically neutral; rather she draws attention to how these discourses operate as technologies of power.

12 Ronald Reagan and Margaret Thatcher are perhaps the most identifiable faces of this logic. Within the Canadian context, the seeds of neo-liberalism were first planted by former Prime Minister Pierre Trudeau in the 1970s (Brownlee 2005), but it was the conservative government of former Prime Minister Brian Mulroney (1984–92; a Thatcher and Reagan contemporary) that actively sought to implement, against considerable public resistance, a neo-liberal political rationality in Canada, which was subsequently entrenched by Jean Chrétien's liberal government (1993–2003) (Cameron 2001).

13 Petersen and Lupton (1996) use the phrase "entrepreneurial self" in a similar way.

14 Rose (1998) talks about the subject as constituted through a constellation of discourses, and this was certainly evident with the interviewed women whose exercise practices were conceived not just through health discourses, but also, for example, gender and beauty ones as well. However, due to space constraints, my focus is limited to examining the women's constitution through the former.

15 Illustrated here is 'the other' subject position of health promotion discourse.

16 Half of the women interviewed were 40 and older, including Grace who was 50.

17 *Knowing* is italicized to signal not only the women's belief that they 'freely' chose to engage in particular exercise and dietary practices (and necessarily the monitoring and disciplining of the self that goes with that) in order to produce a healthy self, but also their conviction of NPH discourse as a regime of 'truth' (i.e., "I just know it's a good thing to do").

18 The knowledge-power effects become clear here as exercise discourse is clearly drawn upon for making sense of her mental well-being.

REFERENCES

Atkins, K. 2005. Commentary on Foucault. In *Self and subjectivity*, ed. Kim Atkins, 206–10. Malden, MA: Blackwell Publishing.

Besley, T. 2005. Foucault, truth telling and technologies of the self in schools. *Journal of Educational Enquiry* 6: 76–89.

Brownlee, J. 2005. *Ruling Canada: Corporate cohesion and democracy*. Toronto: Fernwood Publishing.

Bunton, R. and G. MacDonald. 2002. *Disciplines and diversity*. New York: Routledge.

Burchell, G. 1996. Liberal government and techniques of the self. In *Foucault and political reason*, eds. A. Barry, T. Osborne and N. Rose, 19–36. Chicago: University of Chicago Press.

Cameron, D. 2001. Putting the 'public' back in government and the economy back in its place. Paper presented at the conference 'Beyond the Washington consensus: Governance and the public domain in contrasting economies: The cases of India and Canada', February 12–14, in Toronto, Canada. http://www.yorku.ca/robarts/archives/chandigarth/index.html.

Castelnuovo, S. and S. Guthrie. 1998. *Feminism and the female body. Liberating the amazon within*. Boulder, Colorado: Lynne Rienner Publishers.

CFLRI (Canadian Fitness and Lifestyle Research Institute). (n.d.) Milestones of CFLRI. http://www.cflri.ca/eng/about/milestones.php

—— 2005a. Who are we. http://www.cflri.ca/eng/about/whoweare.php

—— 2005b. The research file. http://www.cflri.ca/eng/research_file/index.php

Coveney, J. 1998. The government and ethics of health promotion: The importance of Michel Foucault. *Health Education Research* 13: 459–68.

Cruikshank, B. 1999. *The will to empower*. Ithaca, NY: Cornell University Press.

Dean, M. 2006. *Governmentality. Power and rule in modern society*. Thousand Oaks: SAGE Publications (2nd reprint).

Dreyfus, H. and P. Rabinow. 1983a. The genealogy of the modern individual as subject. In *Michel Foucault. Beyond structuralism and hermeneutics*, eds. H. Dreyfus and P. Rabinow, 168–83. Chicago: University of Chicago Press.

—— 1983b. Power and truth. In *Michel Foucault. Beyond structuralism and hermeneutics*, eds. H. Dreyfus and P. Rabinow, 184–204. Chicago: University of Chicago Press.

Dumm, T. 1996. *Michel Foucault and the politics of freedom*. Thousand Oaks: SAGE Publications.

Epp, J. 1986. *Achieving health for all: A framework for health promotion*. Ottawa: Ministry of Supply and Services.

Evans, J. and B. Davies. 2004. Sociology, the body and health in a risk society. In *Body knowledge and control. Studies in the sociology of physical education and health*, eds. J. Evans, B. Davies and J. Wright, 35–51. New York: Routledge.

Foucault, M. 1983. The subject and power. In *Michel Foucault. Beyond structuralism and hermeneutics*, eds. H. Dreyfus and P. Rabinow, 208–26. Chicago: University of Chicago Press.

—— 1984. Right of death and power over life. In *The Foucault reader*, ed. P. Rabinow, 258–72. New York: Pantheon Books.

—— 1988. Technologies of the self. In *Technologies of the self: A seminar with Michel Foucault*, eds. M. Luther, H. Gutman, and P. Hutton, 16–49. Amherst: University of Massachusetts.

—— 1991. Governmentality. In *The Foucault effect. Studies in governmentality*, eds. G. Burchell, C. Gordon and P. Miller, 87–104. London: Harvester Wheatsheaf.

—— 1993. 'About the Beginning of the Hermeneutics of the Self'. Two Dartmouth Lectures. *Political Theory* 21: 198–227.

——1997. 17 March 1976. In *Society must be defended*, 239–63. New York: Picador.

Gilroy, S. 1989. The em-Body-ment of power: Gender and physical activity. *Leisure Studies* 8: 163–71.

—— 1997. Working on the body: Links between physical activity and social power. In *Researching women and sport*, eds. G. Clarke and B. Humberstone, 96–112. London: MacMillan Press.

Gordon, C. 1991. Government rationality: An introduction. In *The Foucault effect. Studies in governmentality*, eds. G. Burchell, C. Gordon and P. Miller, 1–52. London: Harvester Wheatsheaf.

Hall, S. 1997. The work of representation. In *Representation: Cultural representations and signifying practices*, ed. S. Hall, 13–74. Milton Keynes: Open University Press.

Harwood, V. 2009. Theorizing biopedagogies. In *Bio-politics and the 'obesity epidemic,'* eds. J. Wright and V. Harwood, 15–30. New York: Routledge.

Lalonde, M. 1974. A new perspective on the health of Canadians. Ottawa: Minister of Supply and Services. http://www.phac-aspc.gc.ca/ph-sp/phdd/pdf/perspective.pdf.

Leeder, S. 2005. The new public health. http://www.ahpi.health.usyd.edu.au/pdfs/srlpresentations2005/nphtnvl070305.pdf.

Lemke, T. 2000. Foucault, governmentality, and critique. Paper presented at the Rethinking Marxism Conference, University of Amherst (MA), September 21–24, http://www.andosciasociology.net/resources/Foucault$2C+Governmentality$2C+and+Critique+IV-2.pdf.

—— 2001. "The birth of bio-politics"—Michel Foucault's lecture at the Collège de France on neo-liberal governmentality. *Economy and Society* 30: 190–207.

Lloyd, M. 1996. A feminist mapping of Foucauldian politics. In *Feminist interpretations of Michel Foucault*, ed. Susan Hekman, 241–64. University Park, PA: Pennsylvania State University Press.

Lupton, D. 1995. *The imperative of health. Public health and the regulated body*. Thousand Oaks: SAGE Publications.

McDermott, L. 1998. Physically active bodily practices: Towards an understanding of women's physicalities. PhD diss., Leeds Metropolitan University.

—— 2000. A qualitative assessment of the significance of body perception to women's physical activity experiences: Revisiting discussions of physicality. *Sociology of Sport Journal* 17: 331–63.

—— 2004. Exploring intersections of physicality and female-only canoeing experiences. *Leisure Studies* 23: 283–301.

Markula, P. 1993. Looking good, feeling good: Strengthening mind and body in aerobics. In *On the fringes of sport*, ed. L. Laine, 93–99. Augustin, Germany: Academia Verlag.

—— 1995. Firm but shapely, fit but sexy, strong but thin: The postmodern aerobicizing female bodies. *Sociology of Sport Journal* 12: 424–53.

—— 2003. The technologies of the self: Sport, feminism, and Foucault. *Sociology of Sport Journal* 20: 87–107.

—— 2004. "Turning into one's self": Foucault's technologies of the self and mindful fitness. *Sociology of Sport Journal* 21: 302–21.

Mills, S. 2003. *Michel Foucault*. New York: Routledge.

Nadesan, M. 2008. *Governmentality, bio-power, and everyday life*. New York: Routledge.

Petersen, A. and D. Lupton. 1996. *The new public health. Health and self in the age of risk*. Thousand Oaks: SAGE Publications.

Rabinow, P. 1984. Introduction. In *The Foucault reader*, ed. P. Rabinow, 3–29. New York: Pantheon Books.

Rabinow, P. and N. Rose. 2006. Bio-power today. *BioSocieties* 1: 195–217.

Rose, N. 1993. Government, authority and exepertise in advanced liberalism. *Economy and Society* 22(3): 283–99.

—— 1998. *Inventing our selves. Psychology, power and personhood*. Cambridge: Cambridge University Press.

—— 1999. *Governing the soul. Of the private self*. New York: Free Association Books, 2nd Edition.

—— 2005. *Powers of freedom. Reframing political thought*. Cambridge: Cambridge University Press.

Scott, J. 1992. "Experience." In *Feminists theorize the political*, eds. J. Butler and J. Scott, 22–40. New York: Routledge.

Body*Break* 2009. The Body*Break* story. http://www.bodybreak.com/News_TheBodyBreakStory.php.

Wright, J. and A. Dewar 1997. On pleasure and pain: Women speak out about physical activity. In *Researching women and sport*, eds. G. Clarke and B. Humberstone, 80–95. London: MacMillan Press.

Yeung, S. 2007. Working the program: Technologies of self and citizenship in alcoholics anonymous. *Nexus* 20: 48–75.

Part IV
Lived Body Experiences
Exercise, Embodiment and Performance

11 The New 'Superwoman'

Intersections of Fitness, Physical Culture and the Female Body in Romania

Jessica W. Chin

Under communism media images of 'superwomen' were commonly printed in Eastern Europe (Gal and Kligman 2000). Such women master-fully handled the triple burden of running a household, working full-time and rearing children. During this period women in Romania were valued for their productive—and indeed their reproductive—capacities, admired and praised for their strength and resilience in the face of severe economic and social hardship (Gal and Kligman 2000). In postcommunist Romania, however, the superwoman image no longer holds the same importance it once did. Women, however, continue to work full-time while maintaining their primary role in childcare and housework, all the while seeking ways to improve their life that "continues to be seen primarily in terms of 'survival,' in terms of social fragmentation, and stress-based existences" (Michelson 2001, 57). Persistence of the survival mentality is due in part to the diminishing number of industrial jobs for women and an enduring legacy of male management in the transitional economy (Shelley 2002); the feminization of poverty (Roman 2001; Shelley 2002); privatization of firms resulting in the loss of full-time jobs; and disappearance of the second economy in which women played a significant role (Chelcea 2002; Verdery 1996). Whatever status women had achieved during socialism was, thus, quickly forgotten as socialist policies were given over to efforts toward building a functional democracy and market-based economy. In this instance, women were freed from the explicit control socialist state regulations had placed over their bodies, but were subsequently faced with new forms of body control and regulation in the postcommunist context.

To date scholars have given limited attention to analyses of the female body and its relationship to the state and physical culture in Romania after communism.[1] Most of the literature in this regard has focused on the ways in which the state, under the leadership of communist dicta-tor Nicolae Ceauşescu, exerted its control over women's bodies in the name of socialism. This was made possible, for example, by mandating participation in the workforce, strictly enforcing pro-natalist policies and creating a culture of shortage that directly affected the role of women in both the public and private spheres (see in particular, Gal and Kligman 2000; Kligman 1998; Verdery 1996). In the present study I draw from this select body of literature that provides insight into the persisting legacies of communism and politics of gender under Ceauşescu, but rely on Foucauldian analyses of the body more prevalent in Western studies of physical culture to theorize the modes of power which are evermore distinct in the postcommunist era.

Because I attempt an examination of shifting gender norms and expectations which are reproduced through the body, my research requires serious consideration of the forms of power by which these norms are socially inscribed and reinforced. Michel Foucault (1977) argues that self-surveillance and self-discipline have become the regulatory mechanisms by which modern forms of power are sustained. It could be argued that during communism women self-corrected deviations from social expectations for fear of persecution by government authorities; and yet in the postcommunist era, free from the threats of government persecution which once dominated the socio-political landscape of Romania, women continue to self-regulate and correct what may be perceived as deviance from social codes in the postcommunist era. In postcommunist Romania socially acceptable behavior, attitudes and styles have been subsumed under an established code of conduct, which is reinforced in social circles, for example through the media and publications of 'scientific' health and fitness guidelines. In Foucauldian terms, the body has remained a vehicle of control that continues to be disciplined through regulatory technologies of power. The following sections address the ways in which women's bodies were disciplined in the socialist society of Ceauşescu and draw a comparison to the regulatory mechanisms which have surfaced in the developing democratic context.

THE POSITION OF WOMEN AND THE TRIPLE BURDEN UNDER SOCIALISM

While this study is an analysis of the position of women in the postcommunist context, such an analysis requires an understanding of the roles and responsibilities of women during communism. Communist legacies, including the position and status of women, continue to persist in the current period of political and social transformation in Romania. Under the reign of Nicolae Ceauşescu, Romania's leader from 1965 until his execution in 1989, both women and men were subjected to strict laws that dictated how their time and energy were best spent in service to the nation—to the socialist system in general and national production in particular (Verdery 1996). The private sphere was commandeered in the sense that daily life was highly regulated by the State which determined how one could spend leisure time, which goods and services were available for consumption, and the ways in which one could modify outward appearances (Verdery 1996). The freedom to express difference, whether through the consumption of exported goods and services or fashion and leisure activities, was severely curtailed by strictly enforced work, dress, food and media restrictions.

The political and ideological control Ceaușescu exerted over the basic needs of the people involved enacting normalizing technologies of the body (Foucault 1977) that promoted 'needs' as defined by the State over personally empowering needs. These practices were consistent with Marxist-Leninist interpretations of socialist doctrine of which Ceaușescu claimed to be a staunch follower. Breda Luthar explains the nature of socialism and its powerful mechanism of ideological control in this way:

> Socialism . . . represents a political and social project and a form of economic organization characterized not only by cultural, legal, and economic constraints and control of demand, but also direct political forms of disciplining and limiting demand (i.e. the political and ideological 'dictatorship over needs'). . . . However, political control over needs under socialism is not just the consequence of the power interests of a 'unified apparatus of power,' but is based on the ideology of socialist egalitarianism and through it on the essentialist view of human needs and the division of needs into 'real' ones and 'false' ones.
>
> (2006, 233)

The socialist government defined the real needs of the people as only those which promoted socialist doctrine and its version of egalitarianism. The Ceaușescu regime took such extreme measures in creating a classless and genderless society, however, that the ideological battle of real and false needs was soon overshadowed by the reality that the basic needs of the people to survive were not being met.

By the 1980s, far from reaching a socialist utopia, Ceaușescu had succeeded only in isolating Romania from the rest of the world. Further, while amassing his own fortune, he created a dearth of food, consumer goods and freedom for Romanians then struggling to survive in a 'culture of shortage' (Verdery 1996). One of Ceaușescu's stated goals was to populate the nation and thus grow the workforce, and to this end he enacted laws against birth control and abortion (Kligman 1998). Furthermore, every citizen was subject to the close eye of the *Securitate*, Ceaușescu's secret police force, for which even one's close friends and family were recruited, thus creating an atmosphere of fear and distrust (Boldur-Lătescu 2005). Living in an atmosphere of fear, women for the most part succumbed to the restrictions placed on their bodies: participating in the workforce, caring for their household, rearing children and seeking ways to overcome the shortage of food and consumer goods. Women were thus affected by the many restrictions which dictated how, where and when they spent their time, forcing them to daily negotiate state-imposed limitations with the necessities of survival (Gal and Kligman 2000).

Acts of resistance did exist in the form of 'black markets,' border crossing and industrial stealing and bartering, which led to the formation of a 'second economy' (Verdery 1996). But for the most part, living in a culture of shortage and a society of limited consumption opportunities, food and otherwise, heavily contributed to the depravity of the nation. Thus, it was not just that women had to bear a triple burden, but they had to do so under very difficult circumstances. The superwoman succeeded in surviving within a social system that forced her to assume full-time responsibilities at home and in state-run factories, and a failing economic system that limited the resources needed to comfortably provide for herself and her family.

The promotion of socialist egalitarian ideology is somewhat controversial. Although scholars recognize that the State never fully supported the realization of gender equality, many of the policies which were enacted did, in fact, provide some benefits to women and helped to integrate them into society and the economy. For example, the establishment of subsidized childcare, summer programs, and cultural and athletic programs for children, allowed women to take part in the workforce, while still maintaining familial responsibilities, thus becoming "an integral part of Soviet economy" (Shelley 2002, 207). Women also played a significant role in the underground 'second economy,' many times becoming the primary source of purchasing or trading over their male counterparts (Chelcea 2002). In this environment, while bearing the triple burden of raising children, managing the household and holding an industrial job, many women actively negotiated their position and identity within the socialized system into which they were wholly integrated. With the collapse of communism in 1989, however, the system that once contributed to the growing role of women in society and the economy would also fall, and in its place would be a system requiring different modes of survival than what Romanians had grown accustomed to under the previous regime.

Although women have suffered after the official fall of communism in 1989, with the promotion of the individual has come new opportunities of expression and identity construction through leisure consumption, physical activity and aesthetic modifications. For example, how are women affected by global fitness trends and shifting standards of beauty and health while still addressing the issues of family and finances? The next section is an analysis of the ways in which fitness is promoted by the media and a spreading rhetoric of lifestyle change. Changes in body management and lifestyle practices among women are explored to reveal parallels with the U.S. fitness boom, particularly in regard to the added burden placed on women with the conflation of such notions as health, beauty and individual responsibility. With the influx of global media images and messages that flaunt extravagant lifestyles of (oftentimes American, if not Western European) icons, as well as promote popular health and exercise regimes, gender norms and expectations are shifting.

TECHNOLOGIES OF THE POSTCOMMUNIST FEMALE BODY

Foucault (1977) argues that the fragmented and inconsistent nature of the body leaves it vulnerable to a variety of disciplining technologies. The process of identity formation for women in postcommunist Romania is complicated by aesthetic and body modification practices. These practices have already been instilled with socially and culturally constructed meanings. In this context, opportunities for women to construct their identity through physical activity and lifestyle changes, and consequently through body modification and consumerism, are being shaped by, in and through the newly constructed spaces and gendered discourses of society in general.

In the meantime, women must also negotiate consumptive limits imposed by social and material realities with imported images of fashion and beauty. Just as the unmet promise to meet basic needs through a distinctive socialist consumer culture contributed to a growing enchantment with the West behind the iron curtain (Stitziel 2005), legacies of communism continue still to encourage an enchantment with Western fashion, beauty and the body. Even though bourgeois prosperity, symbols of modernity and Western ideals of beauty were scorned and ridiculed by socialist governments, they "remained virtually identical on both sides of the iron curtain" (Stitziel 2005, 167). Now free to consume these images, encouraged through popular media and empowered by neo-liberal discourse to do so, women are challenged to come to terms with notions of 'modernity,' 'femininity' and 'individual responsibility.'

On my third trip to Romania in 2007, I flew into Timişoara, a major urban center located on the west side of the country. When I arrived, I spent a little time at the airport browsing through a small rack of advertisements and picked up a business card that had caught my eye. The card advertised "Alana's perfect body," a company that specializes in "Ladies Fitness and Personal Training." The pitch read, "Alana, a beautiful woman, a perfect body, a healthy lifestyle." Only one of the approximately 160 beauty centers in Timişoara (www.Timisoreni.ro), Alana's conveniently complements the rising number of 'sporting clubs' in this city, demonstrating a growing emphasis on promoting women's beauty, health and lifestyle change in the new economy.

With only a cursory glance at the publications offered at the many newsstands in the city, the growing attention to women's health and beauty is evident. Magazines and newspapers now have special sections (if not the entire publication) devoted to women's health and nutrition, diet tips and exercise recommendations. Media outlets are capitalizing on and perpetuating the spread of global (body) consumerism through their own dissemination of gendered images and expectations, promoting especially Western constructions of the ideal female body. As health, beauty and fitness discourse fill the pages and air time of Romanian media, Romanian women are now more than ever exposed to Western images of idealized femininity and female beauty. These messages convey that to be healthy is to be beautiful, and meeting the standards of both requires significant lifestyle changes. It is becoming increasingly evident that at the core of a Romanian female subjectivity is a new body aesthetic and mentality (Roman 2003).

Within the contemporary historical context, bodies are shaped and disciplined by popular discourses of health, fitness and lifestyle improvement. These discourses are then fueled by a number of sources including media, scientific reports, surveys and commercials (Howell and Ingham 2001). Current shifts in fitness trends in Romania demonstrate a strong resemblance to those witnessed during the rise of the fitness culture in the US context during the 1980s. In both instances, a dramatic shift from a more socialized, government-supported health care system to a market-driven system that preached individual accountability was met with the timely emergence of a changing lifestyle rhetoric. In their study of US fitness culture, Howell and Ingham argue that:

> despite the fact that there can never be any guarantee as to how these 'knowledges' and 'effects' will be articulated together, as we moved into the 1980s the venerable theme of improving your life via the fitness marketplace, the belief that the individual was solely responsible for acquiring the skills needed for personal well-being, became increasingly discursively evident.
>
> (2001, 335)

In the context of postcommunist Romania, mobilization of an individualization that reinforces notions of survivorship in an uncertain economy of bodies, health and capital, articulates these 'knowledges' and 'effects' with perhaps even more consequence than that discussed by Howell and Ingham in the US context of the 1980s and 1990s. In other words, locating the female body within traditional ideals of motherhood and childcare alongside new images of improving and meeting health and beauty standards, we see how constructed 'knowledges' and subsequent expectations and established norms continue to discipline and regulate the female body through neo-liberal self-betterment. David Harvey explains the impact neo-liberalization has had on women in this way:

> The social consequences of neoliberalization are in fact extreme. Accumulation by dispossession typically undermines whatever power

women may have had within household production/marketing systems and within traditional social structures and relocates everything in male-dominated commodity and credit markets.

(2005, 170)

Neo-liberal rhetoric merely masks the inability of the state to sustain the legacies of full employment and investment in women's education (Shelley 2002). In the meantime, the reality of limited reform possibilities and outcomes inevitably shine through this mask as institutional deficits continue to impede successful reform (Cook 2002). Women therefore, continue to be burdened with household, childcare and work responsibilities.

In response to the growing influence of lifestyle and body consumerism and global capitalism, I argue that women are now challenged by the 'postsocialist triple burden' of family, fitness and finances. Further, as the ideological emphasis shifts from socialist equality to democratic freedoms, I argue that the disciplining of female bodies is only thinly veiled by the rhetoric of new opportunity, freedom and individual responsibility. In this chapter, the main research question I address is how postcommunist physical culture, including shifting body management practices related to health, fitness and exercise, is shaping and defining the female body. I argue that though Romania is undergoing significant social, economic and political changes, which are directly (and differently) affecting the status and place of women post-1989, the socialist superwoman image which once symbolized the strength of women remains relevant in the expectations of women in the current context. The new superwoman, however, embodies the struggles and pressures of living in a democratic, consumer society which is no less demanding on her time and energy than was surviving under the constraints of socialism.

METHODS

The present study is based on extensive research completed in 2008. In total I spent 24 weeks in Romania collecting data through ethnographic participation and semi-structured interviews. Data used for this chapter comes specifically from interviews I conducted with university students whom I met during the spring semester of 2007.

Participants

Interview participants were recruited through a sport and physical education department at a major university in the west of Romania. All of the students were in their early twenties and in their final semester at the school. Volunteers to participate in the interviews were sought from two classes at the university. A total of 20 students volunteered, thirteen males and seven females. Many of the students were former elite-level athletes, having had competed at the junior national and/or national level in their respective sport. Most of them had 'retired' by this point, but their sport experiences provided a unique standpoint from which they answered the interview questions.

Data Collection and Analysis

A consent form approved by the university's Institutional Review Board (IRB) and description of the study was provided to each student prior to the interviews at which time the student was given the option of whether to be audio recorded or not. The consent form was provided in English with a Romanian translation. I did the original Romanian translation, but had it checked for grammatical errors by two native Romanian speakers who were fluent in English. In addition, I had a Romanian university professor help translate the interview guide. All interviews were conducted in Romanian—except in the rare instance a student wished to speak English—and recorded with a digital recording device. All interviews were conducted at the university which made it convenient for both me and the participants. A native Romanian speaker transcribed the recordings, and with the help of multiple native Romanian speakers who were fluent in English, I completed the translations of the transcribed interviews.

For this project I took an interpretivist epistemological stance with a view that researchers and subjects are co-participants in the research process as they interact and shape one another (Denzin and Lincoln 2003, 33). I would be remiss if I made it seem as though the cultural and language barriers were not major hurdles, especially in terms of data collection and analysis. In order to tackle this obstacle, I was fortunate to have been awarded a grant to enroll in an intensive language and culture program in Romania; the program included both group and one-on-one language lessons as well as excursions to various cultural sites around the country.[2] Upon completion of the course, I had reached a basic level of fluency which became a key step in making entry into the field more feasible. Fortunately, I have also made connections with Romanians who speak fluent English and have helped me tremendously throughout my research. During my time in Romania, one of my goals was to immerse myself in the culture and become fluent in the language not so much to attain an insider status, but to achieve a "privileged outsider status" (Shaffir 1999, 683). The "privileged outsider status" I earned provided a level of mutual trust and intimacy that I protected and valued, not only for moral and ethical reasons, but also for reasons related directly to collecting more and richer data (Harrison et al. 2001). As with translation in general, recognizing the "reductive and generative nature of methodological translation" (Sykes et al. 2005, 200) helps the qualitative researcher come to terms with the many shortcomings of representing others' stories. Naturally, I had to acknowledge that "[a]s is true for all systematic studies, we are limited by the tools that we use to gather data, in this case ourselves" (Fine 1999, 535). Though there is much that I could offer in terms of self-critique and shortcomings—for example, a certain level of dependence on Romanian translators, an incomplete understanding of cultural innuendos and language nuances—I am convinced that this work offers a unique contribution to the existing body of knowledge. Markula and Denison explain, "It's important, then, that qualitative researchers celebrate the unique access they have to people's lived experiences and try to evoke those experiences with as much drama and detail as possible" (2005, 165).

The next section is an analysis of interview data which offers a look into gendered social expectations and the efforts of women to achieve the normalized female body, not only through their work in and outside of the home, but also in the fitness realm. Recognizing that the specific population of university students is not fully representative of the entire population, their perspective nonetheless provides insight into some of the general social norms and gender roles in contemporary Romanian society. I would argue also that their perspective as young university students, males and females in their early twenties, provides a unique angle from which to engage the transforming society and physical culture more specifically in postcommunist Romania.

NEGOTIATING THE POSTSOCIALIST TRIPLE BURDEN

From the interviews conducted at the Romanian university, three major themes related to gender roles and expectations emerged: 1) gender roles, particularly in relation to the family and household, are ambiguous, an indefinite mix between shared and separate responsibilities between men and women; 2) women and men are subject to gender-based aesthetic standards, such that while women can participate in sports and physical activity, more value is placed on achieving an ideal body aesthetic than sporting success; and 3) even though women are expected to be fit and beautiful, they are not viewed as (naturally) active, a contradiction that presents yet another obstacle for women to overcome in order to challenge male dominance in society and sport.

Ambiguous Roles

Traditional gender roles as understood in the West do not correspond exactly to the Romanian context because of the differences in women's roles during and after socialism (Gal and Kligman 2000; Kligman 1998; Roman 2001, 2003). The essential function of women in the workforce

during socialism and the integral role they assume in a struggling economy after socialism do not have an exact parallel in democratic societies.
Furthermore, the structure of the family and the private sphere prior to
socialism was disrupted by the effects of communism, and in the current
moment both the legacies of communism and of pre-communist traditions and values meet at a challenging intersection in the postcommunist
context. Consequently, in general there is much ambiguity in how the
family is viewed, especially with regard to the specific responsibilities of
the mother and father within the family unit. It could be argued that this
ambiguity is indicative of the tenuous gender boundaries informed by a
tension between communist and pre-communist legacies and postcommunist social developments. In the interviews with university students,
conflicting viewpoints concerning the roles of women and men in the
family were apparent. While some students related the women's role to
caring for children and the household and the father's role to working
outside the home, earning money and protecting his family, others saw
shared roles and less of a gendered division.

However, there were differences in the perspectives of male and female
participants. Some of the participants felt that even if separate roles and
social inequality existed in the past, this was no longer the case. Darius
and Ovidu,[3] young men in their early twenties, saw it this way:

> Society doesn't make a difference anymore. There's no difference like
> there was in the past when women were put to only cook, take care of
> the children. Now we are sharing the load . . . it is getting better and
> better . . . meaning men can go shopping too and can take the kids
> home. It's not only the women who cook anymore and the men only
> bring home the money. . . . Now they both bring home the money
> and there's equality.
>
> (Darius)

> Not now, but there were [different roles] in the past when the woman
> had to stay at home with the kids, prepare the meals and the man
> worked. Nowadays they both work and take care of the kids. Now
> they have equal roles, half and half, they share the roles.
>
> (Ovidu)

While some students believed that equality exists between men and
women, others were not as easily convinced. A number of students shared
their skepticism about claims of equality and shared roles:

> Yes [there are different roles]. They all say that they [women and
> men] are equal, but they aren't. There are rules between men and
> women and I think that way [too]. The men have to do men things.
> The men have to earn money, have to support the family and the

women have to take care of the child, do homework business, domestic business. They all say that they are equal, but they really aren't. In high society they are trying to do that [practice equality], but here in Romania, 90 percent have 'old culture' I think.

(David)

Yes [there are different roles for women and men]. For example, how there's the old saying that the women have to stay and prepare the meals, take care of the children, and the man's role is to bring home the money and to keep the family.

(Silvana)

In our country, yes. I don't say this, but I heard from [my] parents that the woman's role is to stay at home with the children, to cook, to take care of the children, the housework. And the men have to work and bring home the money. I think that a woman can make as much money as a man and I think that home obligations should be shared.

(Diana)

Different roles still exist [for men and women]. I'm referring to how it's still considered that men run the world, although many more women are coming to power in sport and in other domains. So, there still exists this mentality but I believe that little by little women want to be at the same level as men. And I hope so!

(Maria)

Whatever their stance on the current situation, students recognized that socially prescribed gender roles in the home did exist at some time in the past. When they referred to "old culture" (David) and the "old saying" (Silvana) and what was "heard from my parents" (Diana), they indicated that these practices and modes of thought are viewed as dated. Though there was a fair mix of opinions, with few exceptions, the males had a stronger tendency to opine that gender equality in Romania had already been realized. David, for instance, was one of those exceptions, estimating that only 10 percent of the population had broken social gender divisions. In contrast, the female participants more frequently implied that a clear distinction between male and female roles continues to exist. But they generally did not hesitate to add that they were not content with the prevailing trends that consistently placed men higher on the gender hierarchy, contending that women not only should, but could achieve the same social status as men. For example, Silvana, after sharing her thoughts on traditional gender roles (quoted earlier), added with a hint of optimism:

. . . I believe that a woman can be independent, too, and be more authoritative—even more than a man, even if they say otherwise.

Now, of course, people's mentality has changed and women will be equal to men. . . .

(Silvana)

Not unlike many of her female colleagues, Silvana noted a significant shift in "people's mentality," an imperative for any degree of social change.

Interestingly, there were also small hints of a backlash similar to that found against Title IX in the U.S. One young male spoke about his feelings of being discriminated against *as a man* in the current climate of equal rights awareness.

From my point of view as a man, women are fighting for equal rights but this doesn't exist vice versa, meaning men can't do a lot of things women can. There's also discrimination [against men]; especially here in Romania there are some posts where it clearly specifies, "Waitresses wanted." They don't say that they are looking for waiters, so they specifically say that you have to be female (*de sex feminin*). This is a form of discrimination in my opinion. Obviously, I can do what a woman does and a woman can do what a man does but very few men are given the chance to do what women do.

(Bogdan)

A practitioner of Romanian popular dance, Bogdan may have been more reactionary than the majority of his male colleagues because of his experience with competing and practicing in a physically challenging environment where women's participation is already commonly accepted. This is a topic to be further explored elsewhere, but it is important to note the various opinions regarding shifting gender roles in contemporary Romania, including the opinion of Bogdan who clearly felt his prospects (and those of men in general) were being negatively affected at the expense of increasing opportunities for women. Indeed, the challenge for women does not simply consist of balancing family obligations with work and leisure, but also involves convincing others that theirs actually is a position of inferior status in need of elevation and social support.

Reconciling Standards of Aesthetic Beauty and a Fit Body

Obviously, there is no *one* standard of beauty, of a perfect body, of the ideal contemporary Romanian woman despite the many advertisements for beauty products and fitness centers, imported images of Western standards of beauty, and articles related to health, nutrition and the body, which filter into Romanian society through available media outlets. Or is there? Are women expected to consume the newly available products and services to achieve a certain feminine aesthetic? In Foucauldian terms, how is the female body disciplined by normalizing (postcommunist) technologies and with what consequences? The postmodern superwoman has been placed in a precarious position in terms of constructing her identity; for amongst the swell of images portraying the fit, beautiful female body are the barriers that preclude her from working toward that image. Resources, in the form of time and money, remain limited as she continues to work and provide for her family in a struggling economy.

The majority of the interviewees had experience on elite level sports teams, many competing at the national level. Though there were various responses to the question asking about different expectations between women and men, there was a general consensus that women were expected to adhere to 'feminine' qualities and men to 'masculine' ones. The distinct elements associated with these gendered categories resonated with essentialized categories of gender that U.S. and Western scholars have been diligently working to deconstruct. Raluca, a competitive handball player, believed that "Women are expected to be more feminine, to have other [physical] forms; not like men who are muscular." Carmen, a former competitive volleyball player, provided more specific details about the ideal body: "90-60-90 for women; and for men, well-built muscles. . . ." The measurements 90-60-90 (breast, waist, hips) were commonly given when I asked about expectations of the female body or perceptions of the ideal female body. Even if women are not actively working toward those proportions, it was evident that respondents had been conditioned to believe—to whatever degree—these were ideal female body measurements. Diana who had competed as an elite athlete in track and field added, "Yes, from women [society is] looking for them to be beautiful, intelligent, hardworking," indicating that beauty is only one of the characteristics expected of women. Otilia went into greater detail, explaining the social consequences of dominant gender norms in Romanian society:

> Men have more open doors in sports and in society. Women have to struggle more and men have more safety in society. Here, for example, a man looks for a woman who is more submissive, who knows her place and so the woman has to know her place, not try to surpass the man. Yes, there are women who are strong, [but there's] always a stronger man next to her . . . Here, women have to be skinny, frail, to be beautiful . . . women don't eat very much to keep their silhouette and men have to be muscular.

Otilia felt that women are pressured by society to conform to normalized images of femininity. Her comments also imply that opportunities for women are not only fewer, but also less secure, especially for those who reject conventional standards of femininity.

In the postcommunist moment, an increasing number of women who have the resources are taking advantage of new opportunities to change their body, social status and indeed their lifestyles. Although both men and women are affected by the changing physical culture of postcommunist Romania—a consequence of opening markets, globalization of body consumerism and health and fitness rhetoric, a growing middle-class, widespread dissemination of Western and local images of beauty, and an expanding fitness industry, among other major processes of transformations since 1989—in some instances there is a fine line of separation in terms of how males and females are changing body image and consumption patterns. In other words, the male body cannot claim exemption from the disciplining technologies that shape and govern its production. As one student observed: "Now, there's not really a difference because as an example, if a man wants to have an operation to look better, he can. Men have taken things from women to enhance their looks . . . they shave, pluck their eyebrows . . ." (Silvana).

Silvana was quick to observe changing aesthetic practices among men, even implying that at some level it is acceptable for men to have "taken" body modification practices from women to look better. Women's perceived attention to their appearance, despite the many aesthetically-oriented activities men take part in, may be due in part to the amount of physical activity that women and men are perceived to do (or not) on a regular basis. In other words, as men play sports, train at the gym, run on the track, or perform other physical activities of choice for leisure, they create an image of being fit, healthy and physically active: the focus of the activity is not on building muscle or burning fat per se, but rather on simply engaging in physical activity. Because there are not as many sporting opportunities for women—opportunities in terms of number of clubs, leisure time and disposable income—they are commonly on the sidelines or away from sporting spaces altogether. Consequently, apart from competitive female athletes, women are not readily associated with sports and physical activity. The perceived function of physical activity thus appears to be different for women and men, and as a consequence, the image of the strong superwoman of socialist times is giving way to a more delicate, beauty-oriented character. Yet, just as the superwoman under socialism embodied the ability of women to survive in a system that did not adequately provide substantive provisions, so the modern superwoman embodies the struggle to meet mounting expectations of fitness and beauty (while still maintaining her role at home and work) in an environment lacking an adequate support system.

Contradicting Expectations of the Female Body

If in the past, through their active participation in the industrial workforce, second economy, and elite sporting competitions, women were seen as strong and indefatigable, after socialism women are more commonly seen as physically inactive, disinterested in physical activity except for body modification purposes. The assumption that the female body is not (naturally) active, reinforces women's inferior status to men in both sport and society. Positioning the female body on the margins of an expanding physical culture, while expecting a fit and healthy (commonly read as skinny and feminine) body, presents major hurdles for women in challenging dominant gender norms.

Bogdan expresses his views on the current expectations for women and the changing roles that require them to consciously raise their level of physical activity:

> Probably that a woman has to have suppleness, without a lot of muscle mass (*să nu aibe o masă musculară mare*), whereas men are the opposite and are to be well developed. That's how it should be . . . From the communist concept that still exists here, women shouldn't really participate in recreational activities, but modern women are coming who are spending their time doing sports activities, training for health as well as for looks. And it's worth it. I'm OK with them doing sports—I don't want to see fat; it's better [for them] to go to the gym. When you have an old-fashioned woman who is a housewife, there are whole different sorts of activities that you can consider as exercise—lifting . . . mixing, they exercise doing what they do for the household, preparing meals, holding a child in her arms. Holding a child who weighs five kilograms is like me going to the gym to lift weights. Only now, she doesn't do anything—she stays at home and watches TV and so she has to go do some exercise, too.

Bogdan explained that he did not mind women playing sports and exercising, and in fact he favors the idea, since, "now, she doesn't do anything," and "it's better [for them] to go to the gym," *particularly since he doesn't like to see fat.*

Radu, who used to play competitive soccer, identified "running, fitness, gymnastics, aerobics and Tai-bo" as physical activity opportunities available to women in their free time. He added, however, that women "all" watch *Telenovele*, popular Spanish soap operas: "That's what the majority of women do. Instead of doing a sport, taking a walk, they get in bed and watch *Telenovele*." Like Radu, other interview participants easily listed off opportunities available for women to participate in physical activity, but there was a general sense that on a whole, women are less interested than men in physical leisure activities. Two key contradictions regarding the female body are presently exposed: First, while the modern woman is more involved in a variety of fitness- and leisure-based physical activities, she is viewed as being *less* physically active than in the past. Second, the female body must be fit and strong, but without muscle mass. Challenging prevailing notions of femininity that discipline the female body is made all the more difficult by this disconnect in social expectations.

I want to stress that the conditions which make balancing the postsocialist triple burden so challenging are also those that provide opportunity for empowerment and change. Living in a society with ambiguous gender roles and shifting expectations for women and men, within a growing consumer market, and a developing democracy, women are confronted but not necessarily threatened by the conditions of the transforming society. As many of the interviews showed, the young generation is optimistic for what the future holds, readily observing that they are living in a period of great change. Perhaps it is only a matter of time before women and men are put on equal footing. Certainly the upcoming generation, which just began grade school when the change of administration occurred, shows evidence of shifting mentalities in the postcommunist moment. When asked about his thoughts on whether different aesthetic expectations for men and women existed, for example, one student replied:

> No, I don't think so. I don't know, maybe there are but I don't think so, and I wouldn't agree. It doesn't matter how a woman looks; it matters how she thinks, how she expresses herself, what her goals are.
>
> (Manu)

A former elite competitor in soccer, what many consider the country's most masculine sport, Manu presents a glimpse into the counter discourse that will be critical in supporting the new superwoman as she negotiates the conflicting expectations of the postcommunist female body.

CONCLUDING THOUGHTS

Today, over 20 years removed from the official fall of communism in 1989, Romanians have become familiar with the daily responsibilities critical to their survival in an increasingly globalized, market-driven and consumer-based society. Where once social equality and indeed gender neutral, if not gender homogenizing, policies promoted the 'erasure' of sexual difference, two decades of increased exposure and access to Western trends has complicated the gendered terrain of postcommunist Romania. The generation coming of age has very little if any memory of the communist dictatorship under Nicolae Ceauşescu, and socialist rhetoric of equality between the sexes has all but been completely supplanted with democratic, neo-liberal ideals of individualism and personal responsibility. Further, centrally-planned state systems have given way to enterprising capitalists and consumer markets, both local and global. In turn, the transforming socio-cultural, economic and political landscape of this region continues to become ever more complex in the postcommunist context, and the place of women within it even more so. The politics of the body in Romania will be of notable concern in the context of the growing democratic marketplace that promotes the power of certain marked bodies over others. It, thus, remains vital to expose the obstacles that prevent women from constructing and using their bodies in socially empowering ways, revealing opportunities to achieve social equality and opening new spaces for physical cultural resistance by the new 'superwoman.'

NOTES

1 After an exhaustive search I found only two peer-reviewed articles (Svendsen 1996; Mîndruţ 2006) related to women, female bodies and physical culture in postcommunist Romania. Both studies focus on dominant discourses and images which shape women's participation experiences in aerobics. The only other related article is a short theoretical exploration piece I wrote as a graduate student for a Romanian journal (Chin 2007).
2 I must acknowledge the American Council of Learned Societies (ACLS) for providing me with this competitive language training grant which afforded me a great many opportunities, not the least of which was learning the language and providing the means for me to spend time in Romania to pursue my dissertation research.
3 All interview data is reported using pseudonyms to protect the confidentiality of the participants.

REFERENCES

Boldur-Lătescu, G. 2005. *The Communist genocide in Romania*. Trans. D.Teodorescu. New York: Nova Science Publishers.

Chelcea, L. 2002. The culture of shortage during state-socialism: Consumption practices in a Romanian village in the late 1980s. *Cultural Studies* 16(1): 16–43.

Chin, J. W. 2007. Post-communist body construction and global consumer culture. *Annals of the West University of Timişoara: Philosophy and Communication Sciences Series* II(XIX): 108–13.

Cook, L. J. 2002. Institutional and political legacies of the socialist welfare state. In *The legacy of state socialism*, ed. D. Lane, 107–25. Lanham/Oxford: Rowman & Littlefield Publishers.

Denzin, N. K. and Y. S. Lincoln. 2003. Introduction: The discipline and practice of qualitative research. In *The landscape of qualitative research: Theories and issues*, ed. N. K. Denzin and Y. S. Lincoln, 1–45. Thousand Oaks, CA: Sage.

Fine, G. 1999. Field labor and ethnographic reality. *Journal of Contemporary Ethnography* 28(5): 532–39.

Foucault, M. 1977. *Discipline and punish: The birth of the prison*. Trans. A. Sheridan. NY: Vintage Books.

Gal, S. and G. Kligman. 2000. *The politics of gender after socialism*. Princeton, N.J.: Princeton University Press.

Harrison, J., L. MacGibbon and M. Morton. 2001. Regimes of trustworthiness in qualitative research: The rigors of reciprocity. *Qualitative Inquiry* 7(3): 323–45.

Harvey, D. 2005. *A brief history of neoliberalism.* Oxford: Oxford University Press.

Howell, J. and A. Ingham. 2001. From social problem to personal issue: The language of lifestyle. *Cultural Studies* 15(2): 326–51.

Kligman, G. 1998. *The politics of duplicity: Controlling reproduction in Ceauşescu's Romania.* Berkeley: University of California Press.

Luthar, B. 2006. Remembering socialism: On desire, consumption and surveillance. *Journal of Consumer Culture* 6(2): 229–59.

Markula, P. and J. Denison. 2005. Sport and the personal narrative. In *Qualitative research in sports studies,* ed. D. L. Andrews, D. S. Mason and M. Silk, 165–84. Oxford: Berg.

Michelson, P. E. 2001. Romanian Unity, 1859, 1918, 1989: Beginnings, opportunities . . ., and illusions. In *Tradition and modernity in Romanian culture and civilization, 1600–2000,* ed. K. W. Treptow, 47–64. Iaşi, Romania: The Center for Romanian Studies.

Mîndruţ, P. 2006. Aerobics and self-asserting discourses: Mapping the gendered body in post-socialist Romania. *Anthropology of East Europe Review* 24(2): 13–24.

Roman, D. 2001. Gendering Eastern Europe: Pre-feminism, prejudice, and east-west dialogues in post-communist Romania. *Women's Studies International Forum* 24(1): 53–66.

—— 2003. *Fragmented identities: Popular culture, sex, and everyday life in post-communist Romania.* Lanham, MD: Lexington Books.

Shaffir, W. 1999. Doing ethnography: Reflections on finding your way. *Journal of Contemporary Ethnography* 28(6): 676–86.

Shelley, L. I. 2002. The changing position of women: Trafficking, crime, and corruption. In *The legacy of state socialism and the future of transformation,* ed. D. Lane, 207–22. Lanham/Oxford: Rowman & Littlefield.

Stitziel, J. 2005. *Fashioning socialism: Clothing, politics, and consumer culture in East Germany.* Oxford/NY: Berg Svendsen, M. N. 1996. The post-communist body: Beauty and aerobics in Romania. http://www.antrhobase.com/xt/S/Svendsen_M_N_01.htm.

Sykes, H., J. Chapman and A. Swedberg. 2005. Performed ethnography. In *Qualitative methods in sports studies,* ed. D. L. Andrews, D. S. Mason and M. Silk, 185–202. Oxford: Berg.

Verdery, K. 1996. *What was socialism and what comes next?* Princeton: Princeton University Press.

12 Keep Your Clothes On!

Fit and Sexy Through Striptease Aerobics

Magdalena Petersson McIntyre

Stockholm, January 23, 2010. I have gone to see *Battle of the Pole*, an event advertised as "the first time ever cross Northern European championships in Pole dancing." It is a contest in one of several different exercise forms under the name 'striptease aerobics.' The event is located in a traditional theater/hotel in the city center. As I check in, the receptionist apologizes for not answering the phone while we're talking. "I already know what they want," she says. "What time does *Battle of the Pole* start? Are there any tickets left?" She explains "it's been going on like this all day." *Battle of the Pole* is held in an elegant hall with gilded walls, large mirrors, sculptures and balconies. At the front is a large stage and on the floor approximately 200 padded chairs, behind the chairs there is space for standing. To the left is a bar and to the right a table with a white tablecloth for the five members of the jury. In the middle of the stage is a platform with a four to five meters tall pole that is held in place by four steel wires. Disco balls are hung on the stage and loud music is pumping out of the speakers. The event is sold out.

The audience appears to be in their twenties or early thirties, comprising men and women in equal numbers. They look dressed for a night out, sophisticated and elegant and fit well into the stylish setting. Many are sipping white wine out of tall glasses. They seem to be couples and groups of friends. The atmosphere is friendly, relaxed and well-behaved. Displayed on the stage are the prizes: one trophy for each category, a high-heeled shoe with straps made of sparkling stones. Functionaries, men and women dressed in white cotton t-shirts, walk around. Three women in hotpants and training tops come out onto the stage. The audience cheers when they take turns in swinging around the pole. One of them climbs up the pole, turns upside down and back again and then slides down the pole to land on the floor in a split. They leave and the hostess of the evening appears. She does a 'shimmy' and the audience cheers again. A male functionary climbs up to polish the pole. The hostess explains that it is important to get good grip and that's why the pole is going to be cleaned between every performance. While he is polishing she introduces herself. It all began when she was in New York: "A friend took me to pole dance and two guys had to push my butt up the pole." The audience laughs. "But I still thought, Wow! It was so hard and I had bruises all over." The audience laughs again. 'But it gave me a new respect for pole dancing. It's going to look easy tonight, but there will be lots of sweat.' The hostess is dressed in a tight dress sponsored by Karen Millen, we are told, and she wears high heels. She then introduces the jury. Tania from Finland is going to judge technique, execution and choreography. Mariana from France is going to judge fluidity. Kiera from New York will focus on the creative part and Lara from Iceland on technique. The only man in the jury is a well-known Swedish photographer and publisher of sexual images of women for men's magazines and he will offer a photo session to the winner. He is introduced as the "pride of Sweden and chair of the jury." When the microphone is passed to him, he says that there is another battle going on at his house, with his girlfriend: "I told her it's a sport," he says and brings a narrative to the fore that is repeated many times during my study. This is exercise—not striptease! The hostess joins in to explain that her Dad freaked out when he first found a strip pole in her house but quickly understood that pole dancing was good exercise. We get the point.

The first of the 14 contestants enters the stage. First out are 'the Kittens' presented as beginners and later 'the Lionesses' who are more experienced. The hostess explains the rules: 'Kittens must at least include 1 inversion, 2 spins, floor walk, 1 inner thigh hold and one split in their program. The Lionesses must at least include 2 inversions, 4 spins, 1 being a back spin, floor work, 2 inner thigh hold and two splits.' Other than that they are free to create their own choreography. The contestants come from Sweden, Norway, Finland, Denmark and Russia. They look to be in their twenties or perhaps early thirties. All are women. They swing around the pole, lift themselves up and spin around while holding on with one arm. They walk around the pole, climb up and down the pole, turn upside down on the pole, hold on with their arms while separating their legs and flaunting their groins to the audience. They slide down the pole, some alternately clutching with their legs. The hostess finds the performances 'lovely' and regarding one competitor comments that "she was like Spiderman." There is a combination of references to strength and beauty. The chair of the jury is asked between performances whether he prefers the Kittens or the Lionesses. He prefers his pregnant girlfriend, he answers rather unexpectedly, and thereby presents himself as a family man while giving the show a respectable and heterosexual framing. The audience are encouraged to shout 'No,' but don't seem too bothered.

Most of the contestants are dressed in black hotpants and black training tops. Two have bikini-like suits with sequins. Some have strong eye-makeup, in strong colors and with false lashes. A few have shoes with high heels, but most are bare-footed. Two or three have garments that they throw off, one a sequined hood jacket, another a corset like training top and mini-skirt. All have black hotpants and training tops underneath. The dress code is clear. High boots are not permitted. Nude or partially nude performances will lead to disqualification. They are allowed to remove clothing but shorts or hotpants that cover most of the buttocks must be left on. Thongs or tassels are not allowed and "Upper coverage must be of style as sports bra with cross back or halter neck" (www.battleofthepole.se/rules).

The audience cheers when the clothes are thrown off, though the cheering seems rather dutiful. It is the display of physical strength that really seems to wake their enthusiasm. Two women sitting beside me sigh in awe when one of the contestants uses her arm strength to turn upside down on the pole. The show leaves me with a strange feeling. The spectacle, location and the audience's expectations seem to contrast with the lack of stage experience of many of the performers. The display of groins, high heels, eye makeup and exposure of the dancers seems in turn to collide with the exercise apparel that covers their torsos, the display of arm and leg strength, and the absence of any sexualized facial mimicry. Back home I find a blog written by the chair of the jury's also well known girlfriend. She comments that the show hadn't been as "porny/strippy/sexual" as what she had expected. The most talented and serious girls hadn't at all "shown off," but exercised acrobatic moves. This is what seemed so contradictory: while on the one hand the erotic and suggestive content was dismissed by onlookers in favor of the display of physical strength, on the other, an aerobics show would not have attracted any crowds, sponsors or acquired this attractive venue. So what was really going on?

STRIPTEASE AEROBICS AND POLE DANCING AS CULTURAL FORMS

Striptease Aerobics took off as a new 'trendy' form of exercise in Swedish health clubs in 2007. The inspiration came from New York fitness trends and exercise videos sold on the Internet by Hollywood celebrity Carmen Electra (www.aerobicstriptease.com). It received plenty of media coverage from the start, partly due to the fact that the first health club owner to take in the new trend was a member of the Royal family,[1] a point often made and an expression of the 'respectability' for this new form of exercise. Most articles had headlines such as "do it like the Hollywood stars," "pursue the latest fitness trend," or "it's already big in the U.S., now it has finally come to Sweden."[2] The homepage of Sweden's leading striptease aerobics center describes it as "the most entertaining way to keep in shape while you soften up your body and get the opportunity to fully express yourself." It tells the story of how the owner walked into 'Crunch Fitness' in Downtown Manhattan in New York to obtain private lessons to develop her own skills as instructor. She continues:

> We even visited strip clubs for 'study' purposes and it was far from the gritty hangouts I have seen on television documentaries on poverty in Sweden . . . Here the women were well-trained and all had their own routines, a bit like Flash dance.

The story then takes yet another turn: "Then I believe that one should not glorify the whole industry, but they could really dance!" (www.stripaerobics.se). This story reflects some of the points that I will develop in this chapter. First, striptease aerobics is described as something fun that makes one feel sexy. Second, while it should not be seen as sexual exploitation, some precautions need to be taken to avoid such risks.

Pole dancing is culturally associated with striptease, a form of sex work where (usually) women undress before (usually) men to tease and create sexual arousal (Attwood and Holland 2009, Liepe-Levinson 2002). It builds on the tensions between teasing, showing, hiding and the built-up expectations of what is seen and what is not. The spread and acceptance of this new form of exercise needs to be seen in the light of a normalization of striptease and pornography that has taken place since the 1990s. During this period of time striptease and cultural goods and products inspired by striptease spread throughout the world of fashion, music and entertainment. The music video industry in particular has systematically adopted choreography inspired by striptease. Striptease has become a noticeable part of the entertainment, art and media industries and sexiness has become a part of the desired body ideal (Attwood 2009; McNair 1996, 2002). In this context it became possible to promote striptease as an inspiring exercise form. It took off as the exercisers increasingly want to be recognized as desirable subjects in contemporary popular culture, but also as the fitness industry continually searches for new ways to sell physical exercise. Attwood (2009) calls this development "the sexualisation of culture": porn has turned chic and pole dancing has been repackaged as fitness. In this culture, the sex industry has become more mainstream allowing porn stars to enter mainstream society and ordinary people to circulate their own sexual images through the Internet (see also McNair 1996, 2009; Hubbard 2009).

Despite this normalization of striptease in popular culture, Swedish public discourse is generally critical of striptease and, on the rare occasions that striptease is discussed in the press, media coverage focuses on the exploitation of women. In 1999 a new law made the buying of sex illegal in Sweden while the selling of sex remained legal. While many saw the new law as a victory for feminism, critics argued that it victimized sex workers, reflecting moralistic value judgments rather than concern for the lives and experiences of sex workers (Lorentzi 1999; Dodillet 2009). Sex work was understood as one-way exploitation and no clear difference was made between porn, prostitution and striptease (Östergren 2006). The law against the buying of sex hence builds on a cultural understanding of sex work that many Swedish fitness consumers are well familiar with; strippers are victims of patriarchy. This also explains why, the cited homepage description of striptease aerobics earlier, emphasized that striptease aerobics should not be confused with the ways that striptease is portrayed in social realist TV documentaries. It is an association readers are expected to make. It cannot be taken for granted, therefore, that the spread of striptease builds on a more liberal view of sexual politics. Rather, it needs to be understood as part of the fitness culture where new, fun, challenging activities are eagerly sought. On one hand sex work is condemned as oppressive exploitation and on the other, it is sold as inspiration for exercise.

Dworkin and Wachs (2009) refer to "commodity feminism" whereby the culture industry has appropriated the concepts of femininity and feminism to capture market shares. In this process the commodities tied to feminist imagery and a feminine appearance have simultaneously come to represent feminism (Goldman, Heath and Smith 1991, in Dworkin and Wachs 2009). Dworkin and Wachs critique commodity feminism as it reflects an "aesthetically depoliticised feminism" (2009, 130). For example, in this process striptease aerobics can be interpreted by exercisers as feminist empowerment, but the connection between feminism and femininity is unproblematized. This undermines the feminist political struggle by associating it with consumer culture (see also McRobbie 2009). Striptease aerobics can, nevertheless, be argued to actually empower the exercisers.

In postfeminist consumer culture consumers are offered ways of understanding beautification of the body and engagement with consumer practices as empowering. The practices and cultures of lap and pole dancing can also be taken to symbolize sexual liberation, economic freedom and feminism (Attwood and Holland 2009, see also Hubbard 2009). In her research, Merl Storr (2003) examines home parties where women buy sexy lingerie, erotic fashion and sex toys. While Storr finds that the parties have a postfeminist character, they do not only celebrate traditional "womanly abilities" but new kinds of "womanly values" which emphasize the primacy of pleasure and the centrality of active (hetero)sexuality in women's selves and lives (2003: 32). In this chapter, I will discuss how three instructors of striptease aerobics make sense of exercise, gender and bodies within commodity feminism and how embodiment is constructed through this particular form of fitness culture.[3]

METHOD

My research is based primarily on participant observations and ethnographic interviews (for more on this type of interview, see Clifford and Marcus 1986). I align my research with a cultural studies approach that builds on an interest in lived experiences, discourses, texts and social context (Marcus 1998; Saukko 2003). Qualitative participant observations and interviews offer ways of reaching people's negotiations between the ways different cultural definitions of gender, bodies and dress are expressed contextually (see also Sassatelli 1999). Media texts do not necessarily convey exercisers' thoughts about gender and fitness. During qualitative interviews meanings are changed and alternated. When the women negotiated with cultural representations of gender and fitness, they often ended up contradicting themselves.

The three instructors I interviewed for this study have middle-class backgrounds and an 'urban' lifestyle. In other words they are typical of Scandinavian fitness consumers (Engelsrud 2009). I detail each instructor's background hereafter.

Anette is 32 and works in marketing for an international sports brand. She has a background as a semi-professional in a team sport and has a lifestyle in which fitness and sports culture play a major role. She also runs her own center where she teaches different classes. In addition to providing instruction in striptease aerobics, Anette jogs and strength trains. According to her, striptease aerobics only complements, but cannot replace other training.

Camilla is in her late 20s and works in her family's business during the day. She has practiced fitness since she was 16 and prefers classes such as aerobics. She too teaches classes in striptease aerobics in the evenings. She became interested in striptease aerobics when she came across the exercise videos by Carmen Electra. Camilla thought it was a form of exercise that really suited her and then qualified as an instructor.

Maria is around 30 years old and trained as a professional dancer. She teaches many different classes and her professional career is completely focused on dance, health and exercise. For a couple of years she has been teaching classes in striptease aerobics. Maria has also trained as a school teacher and has, what she calls, lots of experience in how to talk to young girls. Maria asserts that knowing dance makes it easy to pick up striptease. From her point of view, it is based on jazz dance with exaggerated curving and straightening of the back.

CONSTRUCTING GENDER THROUGH STRIPTEASE AEROBICS

Fitness can be seen to reflect the cultural gender order: it appears to make the gender differences between men and women natural as it is often constructed around gendered ideals of beauty, sexuality and health. Fitness practices illustrate the pervasiveness of gendered beauty ideals when men build big, muscular upper bodies and women build thin and toned bodies. At the same time exercise has served to empower women, because through fitness practices women can build strong and muscular bodies

(Dworkin and Wachs 2009; Heywood 1998). The striptease aerobics instructors also refer to such gender differences when they talk about their fitness form.

The informants speak of striptease aerobics as something that combines exercise, sexiness and fun. Camilla likes striptease aerobics because of the combination of high intensity, aerobic training, and dance. She repeatedly describes this form of exercise as 'sexy' without explaining what 'sexy' might mean. Sexiness, or this particular form of sexiness, is understood as something feminine and the sexiness is contrasted with men and men's training. Both the movements of the body and the way of exercising are referred to as feminine. As pointed out by Smith Maguire (2008) fitness has to fight against boredom, the inherent idea that exercise is considered something like a necessary evil, plainly boring. Anette explains: "Men are much simpler and easier satisfied when it comes to training," but women are in need of more varied forms of exercise to motivate them. Men are understood as simple and straightforward, women as more complex beings, but also more sensible. This sentiment might constitute striptease aerobics as empowering in a postfeminist sense (Storr 2003). Women collectively need special training because many exercise forms are modeled on men and better suited to their minds and bodies. It also reflects the cultural association of men with large, muscular bodies and women with agile, slim bodies. In my previous study with aerobicizers, many liked yoga because of the long and flexible muscles it helped develop and avoided exercises that were perceived to result in small, rounded muscles associated with men (Petersson McIntyre 2009).

> A guy can go in and lift iron and enjoy watching his muscle do a biceps curl and feel it grow. But a girl, we don't have the will or lust to look at ourselves in that way, it just feels ridiculous. We need this kind (striptease aerobics) of training to gather energy to go and lift junk because we know it's good for our bodies. Because this is exercising just for fun.
>
> Anette

Camilla too thinks that men exercise to get bigger muscles, and that women want slimmer muscles and desire to burn fat.

Camilla: It's more rewarding. You have fun, learn to know your body more and it's . . . I think that it's important that you . . . You get to know your body better.

Magdalena: In what way?

Camilla: To dare to dance and to be sexier . . . it's hard to explain.

Striptease aerobics is clearly more suitable for women than for men. It is the performance of femininity, an inner femininity that is enacted and performed through flexible bodies and sexy moves. This doesn't necessarily mean that it is only objectifying women's bodies. Camilla thinks that striptease aerobics helps the participants dare to be sexier and learn to know their bodies better. This means that striptease aerobics can be interpreted as a way of taking control over the performance of sexiness and of being an active sexual subject, a part that women rarely play in culture. The femininity in striptease aerobics is, however, rather narrow and consistent with norms and conventions of popular shows such as MTV. Striptease aerobics provides an opportunity for women to perform as active sexual subjects as long as they do it within the limits of the dominant heterosexual culture (see also Attwood and Holland 2009).

Even though the women thought of striptease aerobics as a feminine form of exercise that did not really suit men's bodies and movements, they all wished for more men to take part in classes, in line with the ideal of gender equality in Sweden (Martinsson 2000). At the same time there was some ambivalence concerning the participation of men. Striptease aerobics allowed women to move in sexy ways and when the informants on rare occasions had men participating in classes (which only two of them actually had experienced) they modified the moves to suit the men. Maria explained that she changed the choreography to be more about 'bump and grind.' Men were neither considered to be able to do the regular moves, nor were they thought to want to try. These understandings were taken for granted. The movements had to correspond with the supposed inner gender identity of the person performing them to make cultural sense.

Pleasure for Oneself

MTV is a continual point of reference for both Anette and Camilla. They situated fitness in a larger sphere of popular culture where exercise is not just understood as a way of improving one's body, but it is placed in a larger context of music, film and fashion. They also thought that many Swedish fitness consumers had seen strip dance on MTV and that the desire to look and feel like one of those dancers has direct impact on the popularity of striptease aerobics. When I asked Anette what she likes so much about striptease aerobics, she mentions MTV right away:

> [I liked] to be able to let loose, the feeling of being in the middle of an MTV music video, to move to the music from the coolest clubs, to feel gorgeous, and on top of it all your body is getting good exercise. It triggered me into challenging expectations, but I admit that I wasn't really feeling comfortable with all the movements.

To "feel like you're in an MTV music video" can be interpreted as a desire to be at the center of the latest trends in contemporary popular culture. The fact that fitness and fit bodies are given meaning in relation to the popular culture illustrates that improving one's physical condition alone is no longer an adequate reason to exercise. When striptease makes Anette feel "gorgeous" she uses it as a means to obtain the contemporary beauty ideal. Her statement illustrates the transformation of fitness culture into pleasure-seeking.

During the late 1970s and1980s fitness emerged as a field on its own right and health clubs became places not just for exercise, but for an investment into one's self. From then onwards fitness turned into an individualistic and sometimes narcissistic project of improving one's own body (Bauman 1993; Featherstone 1991, 2001; Giddens 1991; Smith Maguire 2008). Fitness and training have since then been construed as pleasurable experiences, as ways of getting time for oneself, to relax and simultaneously improve one's body capital in an ever more competitive society (Featherstone 1991, 2001; Smith Maguire 2008). Exercise has become a means of improving one's strength and energy, appearance, and professional and private life. Exercise is also advertised as a way to improve oneself (Dworkin and Wachs 2009; Featherstone 1991, 2001; Smith Maguire 2008).

Striptease aerobics could also bring out a woman's inner sexiness as one might learn to look like someone famous by experimenting with the limits of acceptable feminine sexuality. Anette liked the way striptease aerobics felt "challenging." In the context of postfeminism "challenging" can be interpreted to convey new ways for women to act as sexual subjects. At the same time Anette felt confused as to whether some of the choreography really was challenging in the right way. She did not feel "comfortable with all the moves." Her ambivalence reflects the complex interplay of empowerment and exploitation that make this new form of exercise both alluring and challenging in this particular context of Swedish fitness culture.

ADAPTING TO THE SWEDISH MARKET

This ambivalence is articulated even more clearly when Anette explained how she first decided to offer classes in striptease aerobics to Swedish fitness consumers. She felt convinced that the classes that she had participated in while in New York would need some adjusting. She replaced certain movements, particularly those that explicitly expressed the essence of striptease: getting undressed. She created a version of the moves that she called "different—with a higher tempo, faster and less sexy, and more about exercise." She also made 18 years the age limit to participate in the classes.[4] According to Anette, the age limit signals that she keeps a serious business that is not in any way connected with 'real' striptease:

It might give the wrong associations (to allow all ages) and attract many young girls for the wrong reasons. The average age during our classes is between 30 and 35. They (the participants) are strong, independent women in the middle of their careers and in the middle of life. They do it for fun, with a sense of humor, and that's exactly what I was looking for when I started it all up.

Anette also stressed the importance of locating her classes in a health club, not in a night club or bar, which she found more common in other countries, like in the U.K.[5] She explained: "We said from the very beginning that we had to signal that very clearly; this is more serious." To make it more serious she employed "the right people:"

All the instructors are really high educated, are managers in high positions and have gone to college. It can't be the 'bimbo-silicon-girls,' you have to have a sense of humour, be a little sexy, and have a big smile and a lot of 'come on' spirit.

Anette

Anette did not think the New York style striptease aerobics would suit the Swedish market without modifications. Therefore, when new cultural influences, often through transnational corporations, spread all over the globe, they also need to be adapted to local markets in order to become successful (Brembeck 2007). To avoid an association with sexual exploitation she excluded some sexual overtones, enforced an age limit, targeted her business toward women with careers, and employed instructors that wouldn't be mistaken for "oppressed victims." These strategies were all part of walking the tightrope between empowerment and exploitation.

EMPOWERMENT OR EXPLOITATION: AMBIVALENT READINGS

On one hand striptease aerobics celebrates an active female sexuality, and on the other it builds on repeating a body language developed to entertain an audience and arouse sexual excitement in onlookers. These contradictions are not limited to striptease aerobics. Katherine Frank (2007), however, criticizes research on striptease for an inability to move beyond the divide of exploitation versus empowerment. Theorists of striptease have long been caught up in either pointing out the sex industry as the most obvious example of male oppression or assigning the dancers as the winners in the struggle for power. More recent research has moved toward problematizing ideas of power, control, agency and subjectivity. Frank (2007) for example, states that the most frequent analysis demonstrates that stripping is neither entirely liberating nor oppressive as power and resistance come in different forms. Striptease, therefore, has to be understood as both exploitation and empowerment (Frank 2007, see also Egan 2003, 2005).

The fitness context sheds light on the contradictions embedded in striptease in a particular way. This is evident when the three women instructors navigate exploitation and empowerment in their practice. Even if the sexual content can be understood as empowering, the instructors consider it crucial to hold 'striptease' at a distance. For example, they present striptease aerobics as an activity suited for middle-class and middle-aged women preferably with careers. Consequently, in addition to gender, intersections of social class and age contribute to the construction of striptease aerobics as 'acceptable'. Skeggs (1997) has pointed to the difficulties involved in identity processes of class and gender and how definitions of respectable women conflate with middle-class ideals. In their interviews, Camilla and Anette brought up the fact that striptease aerobics is not something that only younger women do. The fact that many 'older' women participate in these classes became, for Camilla and Anette, a way of asserting respectability. Striptease aerobics was often described through what it is not, and through who is not the right type of consumer. These are strategies applied to turn striptease aerobics into a culturally acceptable form of exercise and as such they reflect the current understandings of class and gender in Swedish culture.

The instructors constantly negotiated the question of whether striptease in general, and striptease aerobics in particular, should be understood as exploitation, empowerment, or both. Although ambivalent themselves, they constantly dealt with questions and comments from other exercisers, strangers or family and friends regarding striptease aerobics. Camilla indicated that she has had to convince strangers about the 'respectability' of striptease aerobics many times. All the instructors used a combination of different strategies—in varying measures—to deal with this ambivalence. The first strategy was to understate the sexual content and emphasize the type of person that would practice striptease aerobics. This strategy further accentuated the dressed body during the class. The second strategy was to describe how striptease aerobics builds on ironic presentations of femininity. The third strategy was to characterize striptease aerobics as an opportunity to recharge the meanings of women's sexual subjectivity. I will discuss each of these strategies in more detail.

Understating the Sexual Content

Camilla found that the difference between the chair dance[6] that she teaches and more conventional aerobics was the chair. "Other aerobic classes can be just as sexy," she continued and contradicted her earlier statement of 'sexiness' being the most important distinguishing factor. For Camilla, it was of utmost importance that the participants do not actually get undressed during classes, because "in Sweden, you don't take your clothes off in class." It was her only rule. When I asked a similar question about striptease aerobics movements she explained that the movements can never be wrong as long as they are fun. Clothes and dress are hence given a more important role in constructing an acceptable form of striptease than the actual exercises. Camilla defined the movements as somehow 'neutral,' indicating that it is the clothes that infuse them with meaning. Anette recommended loose fitting clothes for striptease aerobics: "Loose fit gives a more dance-like feeling." She explained, however, that pole dance is an exception, because there one needs hot pants to be able to climb the pole with one's thighs. Camilla told that she uses her face and head to signal sexiness but keeps her body, through un-erotic dress, in the realm of 'safe' aerobics:

> I wear a lot of make-up during classes. And my hair hangs freely. I have large ear-rings, a tank top or sweater. Better looking training clothes that are comfortable and made of good fabric. I wear baggy pants . . . I tell the participants to put on earrings, let their hair down and [wear] whatever looks good on them.

Camilla's choice to restrict the sexiness to the head and face illustrates the rather small space of cultural acceptance within this form of exercise. Camilla explained regarding training in comfortable clothes that it is "more fun that way." The exercisers should dress for a workout and not look too much like a stripper in order to enjoy the class. The make-up and hairdo are very important, she continued, "because you get in the right atmosphere when you have the right gear, you let loose." She also dims the lights to create the right feeling and to make the participants more "daring." Maria too, kept a strict 'clothes on' policy:

> In my classes, you keep your clothes on. If you want to get undressed, put on an extra sweatshirt and wear a tank top underneath. My classes are not about getting undressed, they are about a language of movements.

Sometimes the participants' expectations clashed with this strategy of understating the sexual content. Maria recounted a time when the participants got undressed despite her instructions. It was an unpleasant experience for her:

Maria: I didn't know where to look, what to do and what they were expecting of me.
Magdalena: Was it a misunderstanding, you mean?
Maria: Yeah! During warm up someone took her top off, stood there in her bra and the others said "let's strip." I had forgotten that very few people in Sweden actually think that they are going to strip for real.

Striptease aerobics has a complex and complicated relationship with dressing and undressing, with revealing to and concealing the body from the gazes of others. The interviewees emphasized the dressed body to keep within the boundaries of what they thought was culturally acceptable exercise. However, in striptease aerobics the participants must look, and above all, feel sexy. The clothes that can be pulled up or down, spun around and thrown around the head must conceal and reveal the body in the right way. The dress becomes an integral part of the ways this particular form of exercise is represented. As opposed to conventional striptease the dress code during these classes is more loose-fitting, comfortable and un-erotic. Compared even with regular aerobics where dress is mostly very tight fitting, striptease aerobics apparel was comfortably loose (Petersson McIntyre 2009).

'Keeping the clothes on' can also been seen as a way of displaying 'sexiness' within the realm of heterosexuality. Anette, for example, instructed her participants: "you will not have time to look at each other, and no one will look at you." The participants are expected to interact with their own reflections in the mirror and not with the female dancers beside them. In this sexually charged situation where a group of women perform eroticized movements together, focusing on yourself becomes a way of maintaining heterosexual order.

Emphasizing the Ironic Representations of Femininity

The fact that striptease can be interpreted as 'challenging' representations of femininity was important for all three instructors. Maria, similar to Camilla and Anette, explained striptease as a choreography that helps the participant to know and use her feminine side in a somewhat ironic matter, as a way of experimenting with femininity. Striptease aerobics is a type of stage performance. Camilla understood the 'performativity' and being on stage as "good." For Maria, the performance aspects, the playing with representations of femininity, is what makes striptease possible:

> If I would say in class that today we are going to learn how to be sexy so that you will be able to go and be sexy at home, I think that people would get uncomfortable. But since I exaggerate everything and share my own weaknesses they feel, 'Oh God, we are just having fun!' I can curve my back and pout my mouth and do 'ridiculous' moves. You allow yourself to do what's a little . . .; you might have seen it on TV and wondered what it would be like? And now you can try it, it's completely legit! It's in a gym. We do the moves. I'm fully dressed! There's nothing . . .

As a performance, striptease aerobics can be seen as a cultural site where gender is created, but also challenged. As a concept, performance is often associated with transgression (Carlson 1996). Katherine Liepe-Levinson (2002) points to the theatrical and performative aspects of striptease and sees exotic dance clubs as sites where hegemonic gender roles are both upheld and contested. Exotic dance is not simply a site of exploitation of women and men, but a site of agency and resistance. Theatrical performances can be used to make a mockery of social norms, because the safety of the stage makes it possible to break the otherwise strictly held rules. Stripping has been also been interpreted as transgressive and carnivalesque, a form of inversion, or mockery of social norms and gender roles (Liepe-Levinson 2002). For Maria, exaggerated performance became an ironic representation of femininity that revealed the performative aspects of being a woman.

Magdalena: Are there any moves that the participants don't like to do?
Maria: No, but some can hesitate. I have included a move where we stick our finger into our mouths and look cute, or a bit dim, if I may say so. Some don't like it. But I tell them already in advance that I only have three rules; to have fun, to be as vulgar as possible and to put on an obscene facial expression. But we don't grab our groins. We might put our hands on our bottoms and shake a little. My classes are all about dance and play and you could of course make it more like porn if you wanted to. But I don't think that people are very in to that. Sometimes I make a joke. I pull my hand along my legs but always stop at my thighs shout 'oh' and give my hand a slap with the other one and I say that "we are not slutty strippers, we have class." It's really funny to say the words class and stripper together; everyone thinks it's really funny, that we have class, when really we are being very slutty.

Maria not only plays with conventional representations of femininity, she also creates a performance of class and gender: you are 'classy' when you so clearly are not. The participants appreciate it too: it is okay to be 'slutty' as long as one maintains a middle-class respectability by pretending not being 'slutty.' The 'sluttyness' also illustrates the borders that cannot be crossed in this context. To 'grab your groin' would be taking it too far and, according to Maria, "people would not like it."

The instructors carefully maintain the difference between striptease and striptease aerobics. This enables the ironic display of femininity in striptease aerobics and aligns this practice with the ideals of gender equality characterizing Swedish society. However, the performance of femininity originates from popular culture where women usually are exposed to the sexualizing male gaze. The ironic performance does still illustrate that striptease aerobics is far more complex than women learning to look attractive for men as it illustrates how gender is constantly negotiated and renegotiated in an interplay of consumption and popular culture.

When the instructors characterized striptease aerobics as a perform-ance, they signalled that they would not engage with it 'off stage,' it is not 'real life.' At the same time it would be a simplification to say that striptease aerobics only becomes culturally possible when it is construed as something other than getting undressed. The fact that striptease has become a form of exercise illustrates the current borders for culturally acceptable gender performances that are constantly challenged and rene-gotiated by consumers within fitness culture.

Recharging the Meanings of Women's Sexuality

Maria promotes a healthy lifestyle by lecturing to young girls and women about topics such as anorexia nervosa, which, in her experience, is very common in the dance world. She has also studied sexology at the university and is, according to herself, interested and open-minded about issues relat-ing to human sexual interaction. Striptease aerobics made sense for her against this context. Maria made the sexual content of striptease into a site for empowerment where women can oppose the beauty ideals by gaining sexual confidence and by taking control over sexualized representations.

> Some clients approach me and say: "well I can't support this" and I say "yes come on, try it" and I try to have a discussion. They don't always want to, but I say that just because I'm doing this doesn't mean that I support exploitation of women. I don't support strip clubs where women take their clothes off for men to watch them. It's more that I am tired of beauty ideals with photoshopped images in men's magazines. I don't think that shouldn't be the definition of a sexy woman. I want mothers of three leaving my classes thinking "I'm so god damned hot right now." And they do. They leave the classes snapping their fingers, and it's a powerful feeling.

Maria engaged in further interventions to help young girls build up their confidence. She saw a risk in striptease aerobics but believed that it can be balanced by teaching classes about beauty ideals. Maria shared an episode with me where a group of high school girls asked her to come to their school and teach striptease aerobics for a health and physical activity class. Maria then demanded to include a discussion about beauty ideals in the program because she was afraid that young girls will use her classes as a way to learn striptease. She did not promote such a body ideal:

> Sometimes I get asked if I can teach striptease, like for working at a club. Well I'm not interested in teaching that, but at the same time, if I don't someone else will and at least I get the opportunity to include my ideas. I can't control the world.

Storr (2003) examines home parties where women buy sexy lingerie, erotic fashion and sex toys. She argues that such parties enable women to transgress social taboos in the comfort of their homes. They are, nevertheless, also means of constructing and enforcing heterosexual femininity. The classes in striptease aerobics offer similar space for heterosexual women to have fun together and behave as sexual subjects and objects in ways they otherwise would not do. Storr envisions the parties as a space where women can take pleasure in the simple fact of being heterosexual women and where they can have fun on the condition that they are willing to follow the rules of heterosexuality (see also Holland and Attwood 2009). All three instructors were very careful to point out that they would like men to participate in classes and that participants could pretend to perform for a boy- or a girlfriend, regardless of whether they were a man or a woman. At the same time, it is necessary to strictly conform to the acceptable behaviors of heterosexual respectability.

As a result, Maria created a form of striptease aerobics that allowed women to act both as sexual subjects and objects, play with accepted representations and transgress borders for accepted behavior. In their discussion of pole dancing in the U.K., Holland and Attwood (2009) conclude that in a climate where women are encouraged to be actively sexual, yet have inherited a tradition which provides them with little idea of how to manifest this, the pole may stand in for women's sexuality and give them a means of articulating it (Holland and Attwood 2009). Striptease aerobics, thus, becomes a mixture of objectification, power and negotiation of femininity, exercise and pleasure.

CONCLUSION

For a pole dancing contest to take place in one of Stockholm's most attractive venues, it had to undergo a process of re-signification. While still associated with women's objectification and the sex industry, pole dancing can also represent a challenge and transgression for female sexuality. A cultural frame of reference where it could be understood as an exciting, trendy and challenging form of exercise aligned with gender equality in Sweden made pole dancing an acceptable practice.

The narratives of the three striptease aerobics instructors were also structured around finding an acceptable, new femininity. They clearly distinguished between striptease as exercise that women perform for their own benefit and striptease as entertainment where women get undressed for a male audience. At the same time, the appeal of striptease aerobics is its potential to 'challenge' acceptable femininity. Thinking of striptease aerobics as performative separated it from real life and in this context, 'stripping' could be understood as something other than being 'a stripper.' The instructors navigated the contradictions of empowerment and objectification through strategies that understated the sexual content, emphasized the ironic presentations of femininity and recharged the meaning of women's sexuality. Striptease aerobics emerged as a space for the construction of feminine identity where women experienced empowerment though the performance of active sexual subjectivity and staged a desired femininity defined through culture. The commodity feminism in Sweden might have created a space where women want to deal with these contradictions even through there are many other exercise forms where participation requires less negotiation.

Notes

1 Daniel Westling who is married to Crown Princess Victoria since Jume 2010 owns the health club Balance which first offered striptease aerobics in Sweden. The couple met while he was her Personal Trainer.
2 See for instance: 'USA:s nyaste trend' *Västerbottens-Kuriren* October 27, 2006. 'Daniel Westling lär folket att strippa' www.tv4.se/Artikel_519470. 'Träna som en strippa – Ny trend på Daniel Westlings gym. *Aftonbladet* January 17, 2007. 'Strippa på gymmet' *Pressens mediaservice* April 7, 2008. 'Strippa dig i form' *Vi iVasastan* June 14, 2008. 'Carmen Electra, Kate Hudson och Lindsey Lohan gör det' *Aftonbladet* September 15, 2008. 'Träna fram din sensuella sida'. *Metro* September 14, 2009. 'Vårens hetaste träningstrender'. *Aftonbladet* January 16, 2010.
3 It is part of a large Norwegian/Swedish research project titled "Beauty comes from within" that studies the intersections of health and beauty at some different Scandinavian contexts (Engelsrud 2009).
4 The minimum age limit is 16 years for chair dance and 18 years for pole and floor dance.
5 See Holland and Attwood (2009) for a study of pole dancing in a pub in the U.K.
6 Chair dance is similar to pole dance, except the dancer uses a chair instead of a pole.

REFERENCES

Attwood, F., ed. 2009. *Mainstreaming sex: The sexualization of western culture.* London and New York: I.B. Tauris & Co.
Bauman, Z. 1993. *Postmodern ethics.* Cambridge: Polity Press.
Brembeck, H. 2007: *Hem till McDonald's.* Stockholm: Carlssons.
Butler, J. 1990. *Gender trouble.* New York and London: Routledge.
—— 1993. *Bodies that matter.* New York and London: Routledge.
Carlson, M. 1996. *Performance: A critical introduction.* London: Routledge.
Clifford, J. and G. E. Marcus. 1986. *Writing culture: The poetics and politics of ethnography.* Berkeley: University of California Press.
Dodillet, S. 2009. *Är sex arbete? Svensk och tysk prostitutionspolitik sedan 1970-talet.* Stockholm: Vertigo.
Dworkin, S. and F. Wachs 2009. *Body panic: Gender, health, and the selling of fitness.* New York and London: New York University Press.

Egan, D. 2003. Eroticism, commodification and gender: Exploring exotic dance in the United States. *Sexualities* 6(1): 105–14.

—— 2005. Emotional consumption: Mapping love and masochism in an exotic dance club. *Body and Society* 11(4): 87–108.

Engelsrud, G. 2009. Aerobic exercise and health—a tenuous connection? In *Normality/Normativity*, ed. L. F. Käll, 155–86. Uppsala universitet, Centrum för genusvetenskap: Crossroads of Knowledge.

Featherstone, M. 1991. *Consumer culture and postmodernism*. London: Sage.

—— (2001 [1982]). The body in consumer culture. In *The body: Social process and cultural theory*, ed. M. Featherstone, M. Hepworth and B. Turner. London: Sage.

Frank, K. 2007. Thinking critically about strip club research. *Sexualities* 10(4): 501–17.

Giddens, A. 1991. *Modernity and self-identity*. Stanford: Stanford University Press.

Heywood, L. 1998. *Bodymakers: A cultural anatomy of women's bodybuilding*. New Brunswick N.J.: Rutgers University Press.

Holland, S. and F. Attwood. 2009. Keeping fit in six inch heels: The mainstreaming of pole dancing. In *Mainstreaming sex: The sexualization of western culture*, ed. F. Attwood, 165–83. London and New York: I.B. Tauris & Co.

Hubbard, P. 2009. Opposing striptopia: The embattled spaces of adult entertainment. *Sexualities* 12(6): 721–45.

Liepe-Levinson, K. 2002. *Strip show: Performances of gender and desire*. London and New York: Routledge.

Lorentzi, U. 1999. Samtal om prostitution, lagstiftning, queerteori och feminism mellan Don Kulick och Pia Laskar. *Bang: feministisk kulturtidskrift* 3: 18–21, 60.

McNair, B. 1996. *Mediated sex: pornography and postmodern culture*. London: Arnold.

—— 2002. *Striptease culture: Sex, media and the democratization of desire*. London and New York: Routledge.

—— 2009. From porn chic to porn fear: The return of the repressed. In *Mainstreaming sex: The sexualization of western culture*, ed. F. Attwood, 55–76. London and New York: I.B. Tauris & Co.

McRobbie, A. 2009. *The aftermath of feminism: Gender, culture and social change*. London: Sage.

Marcus, G. E. 1998. *Ethnography through thick and thin*. Princeton NJ: Princeton University Press.

Martinsson, L. 2000. Olikhet som fetisch. In *Porträtt utan ram*, ed. Y. Hagström, L. Martinsson, M. Mörck and M. Petersson. Lund: Studentlitteratur.

Östergren, P. 2006. *Porr, horor och feminister*. Stockholm: Pocketförlaget och Natur och kultur.

Petersson McIntyre, M. 2009. Genus, sportmode och flexibla fibrer. In *Modets metamorfoser*, ed. L. Gradén and M. P. McIntyre. Stockholm: Carlssons.

Sassatelli, R. 1999. Interaction order and beyond: A field analysis of body culture within fitness gyms. *Body and Society* 5(2–3): 227–48.

Saukko, P. 2003 *Doing research in cultural studies*. London: Sage.

Skeggs, B. 1997. *Formations of class and gender: Becoming respectable.* London: Sage.

Smith Maguire, J. 2008. *Fit for consumption: Sociology and the business of fitness.* London and New York: Routledge.

Storr, M. 2003. *Latex and lingerie: Shopping for pleasure at Ann Summers parties.* Oxford: Berg.

13 Becoming Aware of Gendered Embodiment
Female Beginners Learning Aikido

Paula Lökman

This chapter examines how engaging in exercise has the potential to increase awareness and initiate questioning of gendered embodiment. Based on an ethnographical study of female beginners' experiences of learning a Japanese self-defense sport, Aikido, I will discuss the changes in gendered bodily dispositions and relation to movement that occurred as a result of doing this exercise. Employing a phenomenological framework, I will illuminate how the female Aikido beginners developed an understanding of 'the body' as the means through which one relates to and experiences 'the world around her' (Davis 1995; Merleau-Ponty 1962).

In Maurice Merleau-Ponty's (1962) phenomenology, embodiment is the very basis of experience: we always perceive the world from our embodied position. It is a subject's relation to her own body that provides the basic spatial concepts used to reflect on her position. Space becomes comprehensible to the subject through movement, thus movement is a variation of that subject's hold on their world. The way in which a body moves and the techniques it draws on, tells how its environment is made functional to it, and therefore, practical action should be understood as "a way of taking up a meaningful position in the world" (Crossley 1995, 61). Indeed, through learning new ways of moving and occupying space, the female beginners of this study awoke to bodily realizations. They became aware of their physical capabilities, re-learned bodily dispositions and started questioning gendered patterns of movement.

In the following I will first briefly introduce the phenomenological framework that was used to explore gendered embodiment in an Aikido practice hall, 'the dojo.' This is followed by a discussion of oriental physical arts in Western consumer domain. Then the theoretical ideas will be presented in action through an ethnographical study on female beginners learning Aikido.

PHENOMENOLOGICAL FRAMEWORK AND
GENDERED EMBODIMENT

Merleau-Ponty (1962) claims that a person's movement is a variation of that subject's hold on their world. Thus, the experience of embodiment consists of implicit borders set by culture and context and is constructed for and by an individual. There is an "interpenetration between the concept of the body as a surface of inscription and as a (lived) way of being-in-the-world": we exist by "means of embodied action" and therefore, it matters "how our bodies are treated and how they perform" (Crossley 1996b, 114). Embodiment is above all an active process, not a static condition. It is about interaction, movement; about the ways we relate to the world with and through our bodies (Crossley 1996a; Davis 1995; Merleau-Ponty 1962). Embodiment, and therefore by extension, movement, is gendered (Budgeon 2003; Crossley 1996b; Young 1989). According to Grosz (1995), the sex that is assigned to the body makes a great difference to the mode of embodiment that is assigned to the social subject, which means that the bodies of each sex occupy a different spatial framework. Arguably, the biological division of bodies into female and male is an insufficient account for an analysis of embodiment and therefore, we need to acknowledge the notion of 'gender.'

A much cited study on gendered embodiment in sport is Iris Young's (1977/1989) "Throwing Like a Girl." Young (1989) uses a phenomenological approach to look at habitual body schemas stating that physical negotiation of our environment reflects socially mediated gender difference. She claims that gendered styles of movement and the predisposition to movement is not a result of biology, but there are specific aspects of "feminine body comportment" (Young 1989, 52): a woman's relation to her body is hesitant and the body is experienced as a thing at the same time as a capacity. As a result of this, women perceive themselves as the object of motion rather than the originator, performing physical tasks through testing and reorientation.

The key argument in Young's theorization is that these differences between men and women in physical activities cannot be explained by muscular strength, but by gender—the way each sex uses the body in approaching tasks is different due to social expectations. Women's bodies reflect their subordinate position in a patriarchal society and their "expected gender behaviour" even within the realm of sport (Cronan and Scott 2008, 19). Similarly, MacKinnon claims that

> . . . we [women] have learned actual disability, enforced weakness, lack of spirit/body connection in being in motion. Men are trained to be strong and women are trained to be weak. It is not *not* learned; it is very specifically learned.
>
> (1987, 120, emphasis in original)

Young's (1989) elaborations on gendered embodiment can partly explain women's experience of sport and exercise. However, as embodiment is a continuous process, new physical skills have the potential to initiate change. Chisholm (2008), for example, notes how Young's idea of typical experience of embodiment

> presumes a situation wherein girls are restrained by systemic sexism from acquiring and exercising forceful, full-bodied movement. Given that the situation has changed since 1977, when Young first presented her paper . . . this description of girls' 'typical' motility is radically outmoded.
>
> (Chisholm 2008, 33)

Furthermore, based on a female free-climber's autobiography, Chisholm emphasizes the phenomenological category of lived body over that of gender, showing "how women can, by cultivating the body's full and free movement, surmount the gender limits of their situation" (2008, 28).

Women are not without agency, and the belief regarding insufficient "body ability" can be confronted by using the body to perform meaningful and challenging physical tasks (Cronan and Scott 2008, 19). McDermott (2004) emphasizes the importance of physical experience in the processes of gender construction pointing out how women's empowerment within Westernized societies is inextricably tied to their bodily experiences. In her study, a canoeing trip provided the opportunity to experience embodiment in a new way. Enabling women to be "conscious" about their body beyond scrutinizing its appearance, the event offered a positive, gender resistive experience of physicality (McDermott 2004, 293). Glimpses of this process were also apparent in the Aikido dojo when female beginners began to question their gendered patterns of movement through the learning of this oriental physical art.

ORIENTAL PHYSICAL ARTS AND WOMEN IN WESTERN CONSUMER CULTURE

Eichberg (1998) notes that since the 1960s there has been a rise of exercise forms from East Asia, such as Yoga, Tai Chi, Aikido, Kung-Fu and Tae Kwon Do, in Westernized countries. These meditational exercise forms have been attracting broad interest in Europe and America and the opportunities to practice a form of these oriental physical arts have multiplied. Their social appeal ranges from middle-aged women to the alternative youth scene. Furthermore, as the interest in bodily strength has diminished, it has been replaced by the fascination with speed and velocity, and therefore what is required now, is the streamlined body whose energy gets transformed into "modern dynamic" (Eichberg 1998,

143). Martial arts emphasize skills and fast movements, and stress the spiritual side in using and mastering one's body (Goldman 1997). Therefore, a powerful or muscular body is not a requirement for self-defense. These qualities can create an image of a 'low threshold sport' for many different kinds of groups of women (Thing 2001). In my research I focus on one form of Oriental physical art, Aikido, in the context of British culture.

The British Aikido Association (BAA), founded in 1966, has Sports Council recognition and brings international high-grade instructors to Britain at regular intervals to further promote and develop Aikido (British Aikido Association web site). There are several branches of Aikido that have developed from the mother system, the Ueshiba Aikido. My research focuses on 'Tomiki-style Aikido', or so-called 'sports Aikido,' which is characterized by the attacking and defending competitions in which a rubber knife (tanto) is used (Draeger and Smith 1987). For example, one club's web site described Aikido to be: " [A] relatively modern, non-competitive martial art for the development of mind, body and spirit . . . It is practiced by men and women of all ages not just the young and fit!" (Tetsuhinkan oriental physical arts web site)

Although my ethnographic study focused on women's lived experiences of Aikido, it is clear that the cultural notions of Oriental physical arts partly informed these experiences.

Chan (2000) observes that mythology plays a large role in the internationalization of Japanese martial arts such Aikido. Apart from electronics, cars and cuisine, these arts are Japan's greatest export (see also Miles 1998). Oriental physical arts or, as they are often termed, martial arts have become a commodity in big budget Hollywood productions and subsequently are familiar to consumers of these cultural products. Action-packed films use these physical arts in their narratives in multiple ways and the popularization of martial arts is also apparent in newspapers and magazines. Massey notes:

> [T]he postmodern condition in which the link between culture and place is currently being ruptured can be seen for example in the commodification processes of oriental physical arts that have produced several hybrids to appeal to western consumers.
>
> (1994, 161)

It is worth noticing that many contemporary oriental physical arts movies offer women a subject position of an active agent and the hero. The literature of these arts also often displays women as active subjects (see for example Draeger and Smith 1987, Goldman 1997, Stepan 2002). Media images have become interwoven in everyday-life practices and the different forms of oriental physical arts become more familiar and easily accessible for women as self-defense practices.

Whitson remarks that "for some women martial arts have provided a context in which they have learned to express force and to overcome the sort of partial, tentative movement habits described by Young (1989) [Whitson refers to Iris Young's theorizations on 'feminine body comportment']" (1994, 361). Hargreaves (1994) argues that women's interest in oriental physical arts, such as Aikido, Judo, Karate and Tae Kwon Do, is as forms of self-defense. Furthermore, Hargreaves (1994, 1997) notes that the number of women participating in self-defense courses has grown as a reaction to the power of sexist ideology and the fear of sexual harassment and abuse. Self-defense draws on the martial arts skills, but it is not perceived as competitive. It is, rather, linked to women's desire to live safely in this society and to the feeling of vulnerability that often comes with being a woman. For example, when the U.S. media during the 1980s began to cover more cases of sexual violence, the number of women taking self-defense classes increased in New York (McCaughey 1997, 4).

The discipline of these arts has also challenged the conventional taboo against women fighting (see also Mennesson 2000). The traditional separation of male and female categories is broken down in the martial arts, and often men and women train together. Despite the complex meanings that these activities have within the countries of their origin, these sport forms do not occupy the same place in British culture as the heavily class- and gender-coded sports like football and rugby do. For women interested in exercise, the oriental physical arts allow for more fluid ideas about gender and physicality. However, while women are not the only victims of violence, an attacker is often considered a masculine position and the victim a feminine position (Gill 2007). For example, in the women's Aikido class, the alleged attacker was always referred to as being male: "if a man grabs you from your wrist," "if a guy tries to steal your necklace," "the male genitalia are one of the most vulnerable places in a body . . ." (Diary, women's group, 13 January 2004).

Thus, the key to understanding how oriental physical arts as an exercise form have an impact on women's perception of 'the world' and their selves in it, lies in the uneasy nexus between body-power/self-defense/ aggression. This kind of physical training has the capacity to signify leisure and freedom, as well as to increase the possibility of defense from attack. As it appeared, the encouraging experiences in the dojo revolved around the moments when a technique was executed successfully, and the female learners realized the power their bodies wielded. This, however, was accompanied by the realization that in an unfortunate situation, these techniques might need to be used to the full and this would mean hurting another person.

The next section introduces the research project, based on which I will discuss in more detail two aspects of the lived experience: body-power and assertiveness. These highlight how new ways of moving enabled the female beginners to realize that gender is but one factor in embodied experience—not a source of bodily incapacity but more of a social and cultural background to a bodily disposition (Chisholm 2008).

RESEARCHING GENDERED EMBODIMENT IN AN AIKIDO DOJO

Former studies of women and oriental physical arts have emphasized an increase or a change in aggression through the practice of these arts (see for example Björkqvist and Varhama 2001; McCaughey 1997). Instead of measuring these attitudes, my study of Aikido concentrated on bodily experiences—gendered embodiment—as experienced by a group of female Aikido beginners, including the author (see also Kohn 2003).

The theoretical framework of phenomenology (Crossley 1996a, 1996b; Merleau-Ponty 1962; Young 1989) that was employed underpins interpretive approaches as a style of thinking, not explaining or analyzing. Uniquely, phenomenology has had "the tradition of allowing the subjective experience in to the scholarly discourse" (Eichberg 1994, 102) and emphasizing knowledge as an intersubjective, situational and interactive meaning-making activity (Crossley 1996a). Elaborating on research methodology on female sporting bodies, Hall stresses that "we need concrete, material analyses of diverse women's 'body' experience in sport" (1996, 64). She strongly argues for the unification of theory and practice, "the personal and the political" and suggests that research process should concern actual "living, breathing, thinking, theorizing people" (Hall 1996, 73–74). I employed reflexive methodology in order to conduct research on lived experiences and question gendered embodiment. I kept a rigorous diary detailing my experiences of joining and practicing with an Aikido club, writing down the process of developing new skills of movement through this physical training. The diary allowed me to reflect on my relationship to gender, embodiment and space, and provided a means of documenting my changing experiences. Doing reflexive ethnography (Ellis and Bochner 2000) meant that I as the researcher was very much part of the lived reality in the Aikido dojo. I used all my senses, my body, movement and feelings to learn about embodied space in the Aikido classroom. Thus my personal experience is "an important and integral part of illuminating the culture under study" (Ellis and Bochner 2000, 740–41). In addition, parts of the diary were used as "stimulus texts" (Törrönen 2002) when interviewing the other female participants.

Most of my study took place in a south-London BAA dojo that teaches 'sports Aikido.' The data included observations, participant observations and interviews with stimulus texts, over a period of one year in a women's group for beginners (n = 11) and a mixed group (n = 15, 3 women) for both men and women of all skill levels.

In the women's group the beginners were more eager to try out new movements than the female beginners in the mixed group setting where the majority of the participants were men, who figuratively and literally occupied more space (McDermott 2004). As McDermott (2004) suggests, the experiences through which women are presented with alternative understandings of their physicality did not occur to their fullest in the company of men. The valorization of technical skill and physical competence as masculine created an atmosphere in a mixed-gender space in which women were assumed to lack bodily capability.

> There is a lot of things that you become aware of, like . . . how women sometimes naturally react to things girly around men . . . sometimes there is sexism in men in the way they approach you, the way they treat you as well . . .
>
> (Sarah, interview, mixed group)

For example, a banal routine in the beginning and the end of each Aikido class was the act of carrying exercise mats that covered the dojo floor, from and back to a storage room. This seemingly insignificant exercise did, however clearly display the attitude toward carrying as an unsuitable task for female bodies and the hierarchy of embodiment in the mixed class setting. I often felt that I was more in the way than of help when dragging a mat into the storage and some of the men felt obliged to give way and nodded their heads to communicate 'ladies first,' thereby slowing the pace and disrupting the flow of work. In the women's group the carrying of the mats 'naturally' became part of the routine for the women, and there was no lack of confidence in being able to carry a mat nor self-consciousness about appearing "awkward" or "too strong" (Young 1989, 56 and 59). McDermott (2004) notes that, similar to the women learning Aikido, the women in her study were clearly embodying dominant notions of femininity, which led to the underestimation of their skills. This physical hesitancy was then challenged and changed during the canoeing trip where women participated in activities such as carrying heavy equipment packs. Their hesitant attitudes toward their bodies changed when they had the opportunity to experience something else. These women said that they would not have participated in the carrying activities as much as they did had there been men on the canoeing trip (see also Cronan and Scott 2008).

The content for the mixed group differed from the female beginners' group. In the latter group, the teaching covered more streetwise techniques said to match 'the reality' of the city. The movements and techniques were often demonstrated in a 'mugging' context, and most of the female beginners were happy to rehearse these staged situations, often performing self-defense shortcuts better than the official Aikido techniques. As one of the interviewees put it: "It's not like we're doing competitions, you want it (the Aikido skills) for practical reasons" (Catherine's interview, women's group).

In the following vignettes, I use my diary entries from the mixed group and the women's group, and the interview transcripts to explicate some key dimensions of how the experience of practicing Aikido initiated a process of becoming aware of gendered patterns of movement and resulted in subtle changes in how the group lived their bodies.

BECOMING AWARE OF GENDERED EMBODIMENT

In the dojo the body was seen as the means through which one relates to the world, something to defend. The assimilation of the Aikido techniques that connotate masculine physicality—"being in control and having power over others and the environment" (Alsop et al. 2002, 160)—into one's way of being in the world, challenged the female beginners' subjectivities.

What was learned in the dojo extended beyond Aikido techniques and the developing awareness of embodiment shed light on how certain dispositions are the result of lifelong learning and gendered socialization into movement:

> I realize that Caroline and I stick to the procedures while the male beginners are able to improvise their movements more freely. I could not see Caroline or myself 'wrestling' with the opponent if the defending technique would not be successful and the opponent would not go down in the first instance. Instead, if we do not remember how to proceed we stop and wait for instructions. The aim for us is to complete a pure technique, not to win the opponent. The men, on the other hand, are playing around, laughing, and Caroline says that this is just like being in the playground.
>
> (Diary, mixed group, 10 November 2003)

> A black belt commands me after my gentle attack: "Stop being a lady! You can go back to being a lady after the movement."
>
> (Diary, mixed group, 15 December 2003)

> It is so alien, isn't it, you know, women don't do that (punching). Boys do, men do, they grow up, and you can see when a man punches it looks totally different than how you punch, its just not how you do it, you have to learn that.
>
> (Tina, Interview, women's group)

These reflections on the difference of bodily movement styles illustrate the process of becoming aware and questioning gendered patterns of movement. Femininity with its 'throwing like a girl' (Young 1989) connotation was strongly present when the female participants compared their efforts to those of the male participants. These differences were not confined to the strength of the body or men's 'natural' skills but were specifically discussed as something that had to be learned. This reflection of the situations combined with the accumulation of physical experiences enabled questioning of this femininity. I, for example, started to wonder, "Am I learning new ways to position myself in space or actually returning to my bodily hexus that got lost or become more restricted over the years?" (Diary, women's group, 28 October 2003).

A breakthrough realization was that body-power does not necessarily equal strong muscles. The incompatibility of a commonsensical reality and the lived reality led to paradoxes that were most apparent in the negotiations regarding powerful bodies. It was not clear who was powerful, what type of body was dominant, or even what bodily skills would count. Physical strength was constantly challenged by other elements, such as flexibility, light movement, quick response, smaller bodies and the ability to follow a movement smoothly.

> A high-rank male Aikidoka explains to me that based on his experience, women are often good in Aikido because we tend to follow "what comes naturally," not like "the men who are trying to show power because they can."
>
> (Diary, mixed group, 3 November 2003)

Qualities, like being supple and having rhythm, granted a person a powerful body position regardless of the muscle strength or gender. This led to a complex situation of shifting hierarchy between the muscular bodies and the more supple bodies. Both of these types of power were at work in the dojo, manifesting the convoluted nature of gendered hierarchy embedded in bodies. The women's class assistant teacher actually told me that he felt sick when watching Sarah twisting my arm because compared to most male participants, I am so agile that to him it looked 'unnatural.' Through the learning of new physical skills and adopting alternative dispositions, the exercise disrupted the commonsensical understanding of who has a powerful body, that is, a dominant subject position and agency in the world.

Learning to Use the Body in New Ways

Learning Aikido allowed the women to understand their bodies in relation to the world around them: the streets of London were present in the classroom and the city seemed to act as a framework for the learning of self-defense techniques. The learning of Aikido did lead to an increased feeling of security outside the dojo, and many of the female participants became more vigilant about their surroundings and more aware of their relation to urban space. Avoidance and using 'a look' were examples of the acquired bodily dispositions.

[A]voidance is, I think, a very good technique and I have used it as well if somebody's gone, like if you are in a pub and someone's falling towards me or running towards me, I have actually avoided them. I have reacted and stepped away.

(Sarah, interview, women's group)

I think the avoidance moves register more and you tend to move away from people keeping the distance . . . Yes, I do feel it's made me more aware of how to keep my distance.

(Catherine, interview, women's group)

Immediate reaction and the ability to sustain as wide a personal space as possible were thought to be practical safety measures. Learning to use 'the look,' instead of being the object of 'the gaze' (for further discussions on 'the male gaze' see Mulvey 1989) or passively adopting an unseeing stare made an interviewee feel 'more comfortable' in the public space:

. . . a man walking behind me [in the street] and when I feel comfortable I turn around and look at them . . . if you get a funny feeling about them—if you actually look at them, that makes them a little bit nervous.

(Sarah, interview, women's group)

Realizing that the body is capable of moving differently than before led to micro-level changes in the way the women carried themselves. The developing dispositions and the changing embodiment communicated a new way to occupy space, 'the world' (Merleau-Ponty 1962).

I always presume that someone's gonna grab your bag or something . . . Maybe your action would be different than it would be before you started this class, maybe you'd be able to do a bit more . . . probably you would act differently.

(Tina, Interview, women's group)

Because you have the option with Aikido, so far I've seen that you have the option of really hurting somebody. If they don't get the message—lay off—you can tighten the screw, can't you? But you don't have to tighten the screw if they get the message that you are in the position to defend yourself. So that's the beauty of it.

(Anna, Interview, women's group)

Avoidance was seen to be a useful technique, but learning to be assertive with one's body triggered mixed emotions in the female beginners. The thought of hurting another person often stood in the way of efficiently executing a technique. Even in the context of Aikido class, playing the role of the attacker resulted in feelings of "guilt" and "feeling bad"

(Tina's interview, women's group). Some of the female beginners apologized even before they had tried a technique, and often afterwards. Many of us did not put any effort on the shoves and said that it was "difficult to push another person" (Diary, mixed group, 3 February 2004).

> I think you have to learn how to be assertive with your body in martial arts . . . it's like when I first started attacking I was a bit wimpy (laughs) . . . I think I've got a bit stronger in my movements to actually say, yeah, I've got the intention of attacking them . . . it's learning to be more assertive in a movement and that helps with your confidence.
>
> (Sarah, Interview, women's group)

The teacher encouraged me to make my moves stronger: "Just think of someone you really dislike, a man or a woman, doesn't matter. Think Freddy Krueger, if it helps—just push me down towards that corner!" I try three times, but I can feel it that I am not doing well. "You like everyone" murmurs the teacher. (Diary, mixed group, 24 February 2004)

Some of the women experienced a conflict with embodying movements that have the potential to hurt another body, and they felt that they had to 'give permission to themselves' to be assertive:

> I just wonder whether there is some conflict within my role as a nurse . . . Is that why I'm not able to [push another person]? I'm not the gentlest person by any means, I'm sure there is aggression within myself as well. I'm sure . . . but why is it so suppressed?
>
> (Anna, Interview, women's group)

> There is aggression in me, obviously, but I haven't used it in that way so it is like . . . trying to use some of that, you know, trying to be forceful, obviously if you got someone attacking you, you need to be.
>
> (Sarah, Interview, women's group)

Wearing (1998) remarks that "anger, hostility, physical aggression, and violence remain illegitimate emotions for women" adding, "it was surprising to hear how two dozen women talk about the deep feelings of anger which rose to the surface in a self-defense class where they were encouraged to express physical aggression" (121). Thus, "men who use their bodies as weapons by engaging in sport define masculinity through their embodiment. Women, who likewise embody violence, redefine what it means to be feminine" (Gill 2007, 417). McCaughey (1997) argues, that women's aversion to seeing their defensive violence as legitimate, changes when their own bodily boundaries might be intruded upon, and is also possible in relation to the protection of others. She suggests that women must either imagine that they are defending someone else or redefine themselves as worth defending. While women are glad they learn self-defense they still wish they did not have to. For some women it seems like a 'male-mode' of interaction and it should be men's responsibility to stop assaulting women (McCaughey 1997, 132):

> The option of being able to hurt another person is acknowledged by the men in the group. Even though Aikido is considered to be a non-violent martial art, in which injuring your opponent tells about a lack of skills, the teacher sometimes finishes a technique by saying "from here we could break his jaw or nose" and threatening the opponent's face with his elbow or fist. Tonight a black belt man threw down a brown belt man and then lifted his foot above the brown belt's elbow to demonstrate how easily he could crack his bones. The black belt was smiling with satisfaction, looking arrogant. In these situations I feel like an outsider, observer, since such performances are not done on me, nor am I expected to act in such way.
>
> (Diary, mixed group, 1 December 2003)

In my study, developing or awakening aggression was not appreciated or named as the female beginners' aim. It was more important to have control over your embodied space and, through that, the other bodies violating your personal space. The complexity of the situation was apparent; there were extraordinary spectacles of self-defense but sometimes, when expected to perform a defense technique, female beginners replaced the physical actions with quiet words, "Go away."

CONCLUSIONS

The learning of Aikido techniques changed the ways the women of the study related to their bodies and, as a result, to everyday realities. It became clear that the accrued gender restrictions to movement could be challenged. This process initiated subtle changes in the way the female Aikido beginners saw themselves and acted in 'the world.' The lived body (Merleau-Ponty 1962; Chisholm 2008) surpassed gender expectations (Young 1989): by reflecting on the experience and questioning the limits of femininity, a new kind of body consciousness emerged. This awareness of physicality—the wonderment of, at first how some movements felt off limits, and then through the accumulation of confidence gradually became part of the repertoire of inhabiting the body—was above all a positive experience. In the mixed group moments that supported this development appeared occasionally, but were less often witnessed than in the women's group, where in most of the classes peers were supporting and cheering (see also McDermott 2004).

Accompanied by body awareness, learning Aikido resulted in micro-level alterations in bodily dispositions. What was developed was an embodied consciousness that mediated the politics of everyday life: relating to the metropolis with vigilance and, if needed, being assertive with the body. Reflexive understanding of the newly acquired skills changed the women's relation to the institutional understanding of gender (e.g., having weaker bodies, a hesitant disposition). Thus exercise was not a separate entity from other areas of everyday life but had far-reaching consequences for the female Aikido learner's understanding of herself.

REFERENCES

Alsop, R., A. Fitzsimons and K. Lennon. 2002. *Theorizing gender*. Cambridge: Polity.

Björkqvist, K. and L. Varhama. 2001. Attitudes toward violent conflict resolution among male and female karateka in comparison with practitioners of other sports. *Perceptual and Motor Skills* 92: 586–88.

British Aikido Association web site. http://www.aikido-baa.org.uk/baawhats.htm (accessed August 23, 2003).

Budgeon, S. 2003. Identity as an embodied event. *Body & Society* 9(1): 35–55.

Chan, S. 2000. The construction and export of culture as artefact: The case of Japanese martial arts. *Body & Society* 6(1): 69–74.

Chisholm, D. 2008. Climbing like a girl: An exemplary adventure in feminist phenomenology. *Hypatia: A Journal of Feminist Philosophy* 23(1): 9–40.

Cronan, M. K. and D. Scott. 2008. Triathlon and women's narratives of bodies and sport. *Leisure Sciences* 30: 17–34.

Crossley, N. 1995. Merleau-Ponty: The elusive body and carnal sociology. *Body & Society* 1(1): 43–64.

——— 1996a. *Intersubjectivity: The fabric of social becoming*. Sage: London.

——— 1996b. Body-subject/Body-power: Agency, inscription and control in Foucault and Merleau-Ponty. *Body & Society* 2(2): 99–116.

Davis, K. 1995. *Reshaping the female body*. New York: Routledge.

Draeger, D. F. and R. W. Smith. 1987. *Comprehensive Asian fighting arts*. Tokyo: Kodansha International Ltd.

Eichberg, H. 1994. Biographical. Scandinavian sociology of body culture traying a third way. *International Review for Sociology of Sport* 29(1): 99–116.

——— 1998. *Body cultures: Essays on sport, space and identity*, ed. J. Bale and C. Philo. London and New York: Routledge.

Ellis, C. and A. Bochner. 2000. Autoethnography, personal narrative, reflexivity: Researcher as subject. In *Handbook of Qualitative Research*, ed. N. K. Denzin and Y. S. Lincoln, 2nd ed., 733–68. Thousand Oaks, London and New Delhi: Sage.

Gill, F. 2007. 'Violent' femininity: Women rugby players and gender negotiation. *Women's Studies International Forum* 30: 416–26.

Goldman, J. 1997. *A step-by-step introduction to Tae-Kwon-Do, Judo, Ju-Jitsu, Karate and Kung-Fu*. London: Tiger Books International.

Grosz, E. 1995. *Space, time and perversion: Essays on the politics of bodies*. New York and London: Routledge.

Hall, A. M. 1996. *Feminism and sporting bodies: Essays on theory and practice.* Champaign, IL: Human Kinetics.

Hargreaves, J. 1994. *Sporting females: Critical issues in the history and sociology of women's sports*, London: Routledge.

—— 1997. Women's boxing and related activities: Introducing images and meanings. *Body & Society* 3(4): 33–49.

Kohn, T. 2003. The Aikido body: expressions of group identities and self-discovery in martial arts training, in *Sport, dance and embodied identities*, eds. N. Dyck and E. P. Archetti, 139–55. New York and Oxford: Berg.

McCaughey, M. 1997. *Real knockouts: The physical feminism of women's self-defense.* New York: New York University Press.

McDermott, L. 2004. Exploring intersections of physicality and female only canoeing experiences. *Leisure Studies* 23(3): 283–301.

MacKinnon, C. A. 1987. Women, self-possession, and sport. In *Feminism unmodified: Discourses on life and law*, ed. C. A. MacKinnon, 117–24. Cambridge, MASS and London: Harvard University Press.

Massey, D. 1994. *Space, place and gender.* Cambridge: Polity Press.

Mennesson, C. 2000. 'Hard' women and 'soft' women: The social construction of identities among female boxers. *International Review for the Sociology of Sport* 35(1): 21–34.

Merleau-Ponty, M. 1962. *Phenomenology of perception.* London: Routledge and Kegan Paul.

Miles, S. 1998. McDonaldization and the global sports store: Constructing consumer meanings in a rationalized society. In *McDonaldization revisited: Critical essays on consumer culture*, eds. M. Alfino, J. Caputo and R. Wynyard. London: Praegar.

Mulvey, L. 1989. *Visual and other pleasures.* Basingstoke: MacMillan.

Stepan, C. A. 2002. *Tae-Kwon-Do: The essential guide to mastering the art.* London: New Holland Publishers Ltd.

Tetsuhinkan oriental physical arts web site. http://www.movingeast.co.uk/tetsu-shinkan/aikido.html (accessed August 12, 2003).

Thing, L. F. 2001. The female warrior: Meanings of play-aggressive emotions in sport. *International Review for the Sociology of Sport*, 36(3): 275–88.

Törrönen, J. 2002. Semiotic theory on qualitative interviewing using stimulus texts. *Qualitative Research* 2(3): 343–62.

Wearing, B. 1998. *Leisure and feminist theory.* London, Thousand Oaks and New Delhi: Sage.

Whitson, D. 1994. The embodiment of gender: Discipline, domination, and empowerment. In *Women, sport and culture*, eds. S. Birrell and C. Cole. Champaign, IL: Human Kinetics, 353–71.

Young, I. M. 1989. Throwing like a girl: A phenomenology of feminine body comportment, motility, and spatiality. In *The thinking muse: Feminism and modern French philosophy,* eds. J. Allen and I. M. Young, 51–70. Bloomington and Indianapolis: Indiana University Press.

14 Running Embodiment, Power and Vulnerability

Notes Toward a Feminist Phenomenology of Female Running

Jacquelyn Allen-Collinson

Over the past 25 years the sporting body has been studied in a myriad of ways including via a range of feminist analyses (George 2005; Hall 1996; Hargreaves 2007; Lowe 1998; Markula 2003) and gender-sensitive lenses (e.g., Aoki 1996; McKay 1994; Woodward 2008). Despite this developing corpus, studies of sport only rarely engage in depth with the 'flesh' of the lived sporting and exercising body (Allen-Collinson 2009; Wainwright and Turner 2003) at least from a phenomenological angle, and in relation to female embodiment. It seems that a more corporeally-grounded, phenomenological perspective on women's sporting embodiment would be a welcome addition to extant studies. In this chapter I suggest that employing a feminist phenomenological framework can provide a powerful lens through which to explore the subjective, richly-textured, lived-body experiences of sport and exercise. Phenomenology of course offers only one of a multiplicity of avenues to investigate the body in sport, and this chapter provides just a small glimpse of its possibilities. To-date studies of sporting experience employing a phenomenological theoretical framework remain surprisingly under-developed (Kerry and Armour 2000), as do those using its ethnomethodological offspring (Burke et al. 2008; Coates 1999). Further, as Fisher (2000) notes, the significance of the interaction between phenomenology and feminism has only relatively recently begun to be explored. It seems timely, therefore, to address this intriguing, potentially productive, but sometimes uneasy nexus, focusing upon female running embodiment in this case.

With some notable exceptions (e.g., Rail 1992; Young 1980, 1998), there is a relative lack of research on women's experiences of sporting/ exercising embodiment utilizing an explicitly phenomenological theoretical framework. Methodologically-speaking too, a phenomenological approach can offer insightful avenues into female sporting experience. In this chapter, I link feminist phenomenological theoretical perspectives with phenomenology as method, employing what has been termed 'auto-phenomenography' (Allen-Collinson 2009; Gruppetta 2004), described later, to examine my own situated experience of female running in 'public' space. While this experience is certainly lived and felt at the subjective, individual level, it is also structurally shaped by "women's inability to secure an undisputed right to occupy that space" (Hanmer and Saunders 1984, 39). To consider some of these complexities, the chapter is structured as follows. I begin with a brief portrayal of phenomenology as both a theoretical and methodological perspective. Two research projects are then described, and key themes emergent from the data are portrayed in relation to my lived-body experiences of the paradoxes and tensions of the vulnerable but also powerful female running body. I then turn to the ways in which feminist existential phenomenology in particular can offer us distinctive insights into women's sporting embodiment.

PHENOMENOLOGY, FEMINISM, EXISTENTIALISM

Described as perhaps the major philosophical movement of the twentieth century (Embree and Mohanty 1997), modern phenomenology, founded by the philosopher Edmund Husserl (1859–1938), now constitutes a wide-ranging, multi-stranded theoretical and methodological approach. In general, phenomenology focuses upon subjectivity, and accords primacy to lived experience. Seeking to transcend mind/body dualism, it focuses upon embodied experiences and aspires to reveal the 'essences' of phenomena, the essential—but always situated—structures of experience. Very different ontological and epistemological positions underlie the many, complex strands of phenomenology; in Ehrich's (1999) evocative metaphor, its 'tangled web.' Transcendental, existentialist and hermeneutic phenomenologies, for example, all have distinctive but interrelating perspectives (see Allen-Collinson 2009 for a general overview in relation to sports studies). Existentialist phenomenology, and the oeuvre of Maurice Merleau-Ponty in particular, have engaged extensive feminist theoretical attention (e.g., Coy 2009; de Beauvoir 1972; Fisher and Embree 2000; Olkowski and Weiss 2006). Indeed, Fisher (2000) posits that of the earlier 'founding phenomenologists', Merleau-Ponty is the most discussed and drawn upon by feminist writers.

My focus in this chapter is on the ways in which phenomenologically inspired insights, in combination with feminist theory, might be brought to bear on the study of specific, situated, gendered sporting experiences. In common with existential phenomenologists, feminist theorists (see for example, Grosz 1995) have subjected to trenchant critique the dominance of 'reason' and the systematic denial of the importance of the body in human experience. Criticisms have, though, been leveled at some forms of phenomenology for insufficient analytic attention to 'difference,' including gender, and the social-structural influences and constraints upon individuals. Forms of more sociologized or 'cultural' phenomenology (Csordas 1994), including feminist phenomenology, explicitly recognize the structurally influenced, historically-specific, and culturally situated

nature of human experience, along with the importance of intersubjectivity and 'intercorporeality' (Merleau-Ponty 2001). For, as Weiss (1999)
notes, our experience of embodiment is never a private affair, but always
already mediated by our continual interactions with other human and
non-human bodies. Csordas' concept of 'somatic modes of attention' is
particularly apposite to my analysis here, because it focuses on the "culturally elaborated ways of attending to and with one's body in surroundings that include the embodied presence of others" (2002, 244). In the
current analysis, this includes my corporeal dealings with the presence of
other, sometimes threatening and harassing, bodies.

Although departing in some ways from original Husserlian transcendental phenomenology, more 'sociologized' forms of phenomenology
interweave insights from other theoretical traditions such as feminism
(Bartky 1990; Butler 2006; Young 1980, 1998), queer studies (Ahmed
2007) and critical sociology (Hughson and Inglis 2002). Here I focus
upon the ways in which feminist phenomenology offers powerful analytic
insights into female sporting embodiment. Although 'traditional' existential phenomenology has sometimes been accused of taking as tacit norm
the masculine (white) body, Merleau-Ponty's work nevertheless has been
adapted and utilized inventively and productively by feminist scholars
when addressing female lived experience (e.g., Butler 2006; Olkowski
2006; Weiss 1999). Indeed, de Beauvoir signaled the importance of his
writings to feminist thought, and her work provides a classic intersection
of feminism and phenomenology in addressing gendered being-in-the-
world. Kruks argues that, in spite of his sexism, Merleau-Ponty's account
of the pre-personal body can in fact help us grasp significant aspects of
human existence that span distinctions such as class, race and gender
(2006, 35). Conversely, with regard to those very differences, Merleau-
Ponty's existential phenomenology, aligned with feminist theory, allows
for conceptions of bodies and action as highly situated, socially related
and interacting from particular structural standpoints.

Furthermore, existentialist phenomenology offers a 'third way' ontologi-
cally- and epistemologically-speaking, for it starts not from the assumption
of an objective world 'out there', nor from a pure, constituting consciousness, but rather from their dialogical relationship. The world, body and
consciousness are fundamentally intertwined and inter-related. One's own
body (le corps propre) is the subject of perception, the instrument of human
grasp on the world (de Beauvoir 1972). As Mensch notes, our awareness
has a "first-person character" and is always from a particular point of
view, a "hereness" specific to 'me' (2006, 73). Perception, a key concern for
Merleau-Ponty, is portrayed as an active, creative receptivity. Phenomena
are not merely abstract things 'out there,' separate from our experience,
but form part of our human incarnate subjectivity. We have existential
unity with the flesh (chair) of the world, and can experience phenomena at
a deeply corporeal, pre-(perhaps ultra-) linguistic level. This is powerfully

illustrated by Pace's account of her father's death: "Bodies respond, often before thoughts enter the mind. Narratives materialize, fear pours over flesh, stealing breath and flattening the world. I felt as though I had no language" (2009, 411–12). Similarly, as Alcoff notes in considering feminist phenomenology, experience is sometimes "inarticulate," exceeding language (2000, 47).

For the in-depth portrayal of our corporeally-grounded experiences of sport and physical activity, Merleau-Ponty's form of existentialist phenomenology is particularly well-suited, given his interest in embodied consciousness, perception, intentionality (described later) and the ways in which we experience lived spatio-temporality. In relation to the time-space nexus, for example, Masciotra et al. (2001) provide a detailed phenomenologically grounded account of spatiotemporal 'distancing' and coordination in Karate. The dialectical relationship between 'player-body-subject' and the lived-space of the playing field has been evocatively portrayed in relation to 'the beautiful game' of (male) soccer, and the 'silky touch' aesthetics of star players (Hemphill 2005). Merleau-Ponty's work has been taken up by various scholars examining mind-body practices and physical cultures. Samudra (2008), for example, portrays kinaesthetic experiences in Silat Bangau Putih, a Chinese Indonesian self-defense and health system, whilst Morley (2001) examines yoga practice and breath-control, utilizing some of Merleau-Ponty's constructs relating to the lived body, whilst also drawing comparisons between the practice of yoga and phenomenology itself, including in relation to 'bracketing' (see description later). Drawing upon Merleau-Ponty's framework of embodied consciousness and being-in-the-world, McDonald (2007) considers Kalarippayattu, a martial art of southern India, and the politico-philosophical significance of corporeal activity. Addressing sports and physical activity more generally, Hockey and Allen-Collinson (2007) explore the sensory dimension of the sporting body and the centrality of sense perceptions, employing Merleau-Ponty's (2001) work on the body as subject of perception. Before proceeding to describe the sports-related research on which this chapter is based, for those unfamiliar with phenomenological tenets, I give a basic portrayal of some key qualities within the phenomenological method.

THE PHENOMENOLOGICAL METHOD

The phenomenological method, for many, is the phenomenological approach itself (Kerry and Armour 2000). This 'method' is for many of us, however, perhaps more accurately described as a phenomenological attitude, an orientation to the world, an attitude of attentiveness, rather than any particular set of prescribed techniques or procedures. Indeed lively debates flourish amongst phenomenologists as to how best to undertake this form of research (see Finlay 2009). In general, our aim is to provide rich, textured, complex descriptions of phenomena as they are lived and experienced in actual situations. Four key themes or qualities, derived originally from Husserlian phenomenology, provide a useful starting point in my brief consideration of the phenomenological method: 1) description 2) epochē and reduction 3) essences and 4) intentionality. I then proceed to describe the actual methods utilized in my own phenomenologically inspired research project.

For phenomenologists, description is a core concern, but may have very different meanings according to the particular phenomenological framework adopted. It is perhaps more useful to think of this in terms of a descriptive/interpretive continuum. At one end of the continuum, Husserlian forms of descriptive phenomenology have as their aim to 'go back to the things themselves' (zu den Sachen selbst) to describe structures of experience in everyday terms without resorting to more abstract theorizing. Those working within the hermeneutic tradition, on the other hand, focus more centrally upon the role of interpretation, noting that interpretative activity is an inevitable part of our being-in-the-world (Heidegger 1927/1962). But as Langdridge (2008) and Finlay (2009) remind us, there are no hard and fast boundaries between description and interpretation, indeed any such boundaries would be antithetical to the very spirit of phenomenology. For those of a more descriptive orientation, in order to arrive at the phenomenon/phenomena with a fresh and open perspective, efforts are made to suspend as far as possible the researcher's prior knowledge, presuppositions, attitudes and interpretations of the phenomenon, via a process of *epochē* and *reduction*. 'Epochē' (from the Greek 'to abstain, stop, or keep a distance from') is a term used to denote the bracketing of prior assumptions (including 'scientific' ones) about a phenomenon, or at least our best attempts to do so, in order to be able to reduce it to its essential structures of experience, an essence or 'eidos' of an object of consciousness. These terms should, however, be treated with caution, for as Merleau-Ponty (2001) warns, the central lesson of the reduction is the impossibility of a complete reduction! Although standing outside of one's socio-cultural frame to achieve complete bracketing of assumptions and beliefs is impossible, nevertheless in practical research terms, I find the concept of epochē useful in encouraging a more self-critical, reflexive approach. *Intentionality* is the key feature of consciousness within Husserlian phenomenology. Further developed by Merleau-Ponty in relation to the bodily dimension, intentionality centers on the notion that consciousness is always consciousness of something. It is thus intentional, directed or orientated toward something or someone. As Willig neatly encapsulates: "Intentionality allows objects to appear as phenomena," and explains why different people perceive and experience the 'same' environment in radically different ways (2008, 52). This concept is thus highly applicable to my interests in the gendered perceptions of environments.

For me, as for many phenomenologists, any method capable of producing rich, detailed, in-depth and textured descriptions of participants' actual concrete lived experiences of a phenomenon, has the potential to generate data for the application of phenomenological analysis. To illustrate phenomenology's distinctiveness in portraying sporting experience, Kerry and Armour provide the example of glycogen depletion or "hitting the wall" in distance running, contrasting a phenomenologist's approach to this with a physiologist's approach (2000, 3–4). The latter would most likely focus upon holding constant certain variables whilst manipulating others in order to ascertain whether some distinctive, 'objective' process is occurring in the body. Phenomenologists, however, would endeavor to capture as far as possible the lived meaning of hitting the wall for the participant: how it actually feels to experience this phenomenon, irrespective of whether 'the wall' exists in any physiological, cellular sense. There is a burgeoning literature, particularly within psychology (Moustakas 1994) and sports psychology (Dale 1996) centered on operationalizing phenomenology as a distinctive empirical approach. Within psychology and health-related studies, for example, Interpretative Phenomenological Analysis (IPA) has been used extensively, although some IPA-based studies do present methodological challenges for those taking a more descriptive phenomenologically-oriented approach (see Allen-Collinson 2009; Parker 2005). In IPA, semi-structured interviews and forms of thematic content analysis are the primary means used to examine and understand participants' meanings, as well as perceptions of, and beliefs about a phenomenon or phenomena.

Phenomenology (including IPA) has at times been criticized (see, for example, Gruppetta 2004) because many phenomenological researchers, unlike ethnographers, do not themselves participate in the processes under study but rely, instead, upon secondhand accounts (2004, 4). Although this need not necessarily be construed as a weakness of phenomenology per se, or indeed any methodological approach, autoethnographic phenomenology or autophenomenography[1] provides one means of addressing such criticism, and generating the rich, textured descriptions of first-person experience, including sporting embodiment that is central to the phenomenological quest to bring to life and share the felt, lived experience. This approach was used in two research projects that I describe later. One project was a collaborative project with a male co-runner and co-researcher (see Allen-Collinson and Hockey 2001, 2008) and one an autophenomenographic study of female running embodiment.

THE RESEARCH PROJECTS

Congruent with the spirit of feminist phenomenology and the autophenomenographic genre, it is appropriate here to incorporate some personal information regarding my own running biography in order to situate myself as researcher-participant and to contextualize the analysis. A female middle/long-distance runner in my (very!) late forties, I have a running biography stretching over 23 years, which has in the past required sustained commitment to training 6–7 days a week, at times twice daily. Struggling with chronic knee problems since my mid-30s, nowadays I try to restrict myself to running just 5 days per week. Although falling firmly within the non-elite category, I do remain highly committed, a serious runner in Smith's (1998) categorization.

Some years ago, my male running partner and I both incurred relatively severe knee injuries, and decided systematically to document our injury and rehabilitation processes each of two years' duration (for further details of the collaborative autoethnographic study, see Allen-Collinson and Hockey 2001, 2008). We each constructed individual 'injury logs,' while a third 'reflective log' was used to examine the research process itself, to interrogate and synthesize emergent analytic themes and also to exchange at times highly divergent views and experiences. Our logs were read and re-read as part of a lengthy process of data-immersion, employing processes of re-memory (Sanders-Bustle and Oliver 2001) in an attempt to capture and record as vividly as possible our subjective, emotionally-charged and very corporeal lived experiences. The reflective log helped generate new understandings, and to 'attune any dissonances' within what Spiegelberg terms "cooperative phenomenology" (1975, 33). Long-standing careers in running gave us some confidence of fulfilling Garfinkel's phenomenologically-derived "unique adequacy requirement":

> . . . for the analyst to recognize, or identify, or follow the development of, or describe phenomena of order in local production of coherent detail, the analyst must be vulgarly competent to the local production and reflexively natural accountability of the phenomenon or order he [sic] is 'studying'.
>
> (2002, 175, emphasis in original)

In the second study an autophenomenographic approach was used from the outset to examine my experiences as a middle/long-distance runner, training in public spaces. The autophenomenographic method adhered quite closely to Giorgi's (1985, 1997) and Giorgi and Giorgi's (2003) guidelines for undertaking phenomenological research in general, but using myself as both researcher and participant (the 'auto' element). I documented in detail my engagement with training for middle/long-distance running via a research log maintained for a period of 2.5 years (and still ongoing). This involves drafting notes of training sessions, not only in terms of timings, terrain, forms of training undertaken, weather conditions (as is familiar practice to many a 'serious' runner), but also recording in detail specific, concrete, subjective, and corporeal experiences and feeling states (the 'phenomena' element). The length of entries varies between a few sentences and two A-4 pages of notes. Given the temporal pressures of incorporating training sessions into long workdays, however, it is not usually possible for me to write more extended field notes.

Adhering to some of Giorgi's (1985) guidelines, this study includes the following elements: 1) the collection of concrete descriptions of phenomena from an 'insider' (my) perspective; 2) the adoption of the phenomenological attitude, my efforts to be open to the richness and complexity of the phenomena; 3) initial impressionistic readings of the descriptions in order to gain a feel for the whole; 4) in-depth re-reading of these descriptions as part of a lengthy process of data-immersion, to identify themes and sub-themes; 5) free imaginative variation: I search for the most fundamental meanings of a phenomenon, its 'essential' characteristics. This involves imaginatively varying elements of the phenomenon initially identified to ascertain whether it remains identifiable after such imagined changes and so to identify and draw out the 'essences': those elements which are, for me, necessary for the phenomenon to be the phenomenon. Given the ideographic nature of the research, exploring my own lifeworld, I depart from Giorgi's method with regard to constructing general descriptions applicable to a range of participants. Instead, the focus is upon individual experiences of a phenomenon, an in-depth approach which has been used to great effect by other existential phenomenological researchers (e.g., Finlay 2003) including the researcher's powerful account of her own lived experience of the condition (Toombs 2001).

In order to identify and acknowledge—as far as possible—my own pre-conceptions and presuppositions about female running in public space, I engaged in two 'bracketing' practices throughout the study, not only at the research design phase: 1) discussions with insiders and non-insiders of the distance-running subculture, both female and male; and 2) reading ethnographic accounts of a range of other sporting and physical activities in order to compare and contrast the key elements of these with the running experience, including the gendered dimensions. Although I would certainly never claim to have achieved 'full' bracketing (nor consider this possible), these practices greatly helped in increasing critical self-reflection and identifying certain of my assumptions surrounding the experience of being a running woman in public space.

A RUNNING WOMAN IN PUBLIC SPACE: CONTRADICTIONS AND CONTRAINDICATIONS

The following discussion addresses some of the key structures of experience emergent from both sets of data, relating in this case to my use of public space for training purposes, often as a solo runner. Public space has been defined by Chua and Edwards (1992) as space where in principle: 1) everyone has rights of access; 2) encounters between individual users are unplanned and unexceptional; 3) people's behavior toward each other is subject to rules of common norms of social civility. But the 'public' is of course not a homogenous body with equal rights of access and participation. Nor is 'space' homogenous, but subject to differentiation, for example, in relation to urban/rural and indoor/outdoor. The social structuring of such space has been subject to extensive analysis. Lefebvre (1991), for example, signals the political and strategic nature of public space. Indeed far from being universally open to all, feminist researchers have highlighted the ways in which participation in, and use of, public space is structured and constrained by gender. The gendering of public space, and in particular the contestation of women's 'right' of access, has been explored in a range of studies using a variety of theoretical and methodological approaches. Examples include Brooks Gardner's (1980) discussion of men's use of 'street remarks' to underscore women's lack of right to enjoy public space free from harassment; Valentine's (1989) portrayal of the 'geography of women's fear'; Wesely and Gaarder's (2004) account of women's negotiation of vulnerability in an urban wilderness park; and Kilgour's (2007) analysis of young women's experiences of outdoor physical activity in public space.

The social agency of women should not be underestimated. Budgeon (2003) reminds us that it is possible to make new, transformative connections with the body, to live the body in different ways, and to move from experiencing the body as object to living the body in terms of what it can do. Taking a feminist phenomenological stance, de Beauvoir (1972) signaled the empowering force of outdoor recreation for women, whom she exhorted to battle against the elements, take risks and go out for adventure. Battling the elements, active social and corporeal agency, resistance and transformative action certainly constitute core elements in my own lived experience of training for distance running, and are also reflected in accounts of women's physical activity as resistance, which draw upon different theoretical frameworks (e.g., Cronan and Scott 2008; Granskog 2003; Wesely and Gaarder 2004).

In the phenomenological analysis of my data, the paradoxical, contradictory nature of exercising in public space clearly emerged. On the one hand, the negative structures of experience loom large: the dangers of and bodily vulnerability to harassment (verbal and physical), threat and attack. On the other hand, the positive elements include the experience of empowerment, social agency, resistance, bodily power, strength and sensory pleasure. All these elements emerged from data analysis as essential to my experience of training for distance running, although on any single training outing one element might be in greater evidence or predominate entirely. In aggregate, the elements comprise my general structure of embodied vulnerability and power, held in a state of flux. I now attempt to unravel some of the intricacies of these lived-body experiences, drawing upon data from both the projects described earlier.

The Paradox of the Vulnerable/Powerful Woman in the Running Body

Running in public space undoubtedly renders women (and also in some contexts, men) vulnerable to harassment—verbal and on occasions physical, even assault. Indeed, on many occasions men and teenage boys have lunged at me, some grabbing at various parts of my body, including breasts and buttocks; the following field note is unfortunately representative of all too many analogous occurrences of general, low-level (comparatively-speaking) harassment and reveals my embodied response to a sexist street remark:

> Early afternoon, we were running down the high street . . . J diverted off to nip into the gents' toilet, so I jogged around whilst waiting for him. Suddenly felt someone brush against me and comment, quite loudly: "Fantastic arse, Love!". Before I have chance to utter a withering rejoinder, he is vanishing off down the pavement, turning around to smile and nod, presumably in what he considers an appreciative fashion. I feel the heat and colour rise to my skin, seeing red is indeed the metaphor, angry red suffuses my body at that instant. The adrenalin surge lightens my aching legs and I resume the run at a bursting sprint—at least for the first few minutes.
>
> (Log 2, joint study)

Feagin (1991) argues that the relative anonymity of public places emboldens prejudiced individuals to engage in racist behavior inconsistent (one would hope) with prevailing social norms, and this similarly applies to sexist attitudes and behavior exhibited toward women in public. At times, as indicated earlier, such flagrant sexism engenders deeply embodied feelings of outrage and anger, but in other contexts, the vulnerability of my woman's body in public space is brought home to me as I run warily, eyes and ears on full alert, through narrow alleys, dark streets or even just past pub entrances where lascivious comments erupt from boozy male mouths. But running outdoors also makes me feel strong, powerful, honed, dynamic, capable. Granskog (2003) found that triathlon provided a social space where women could attain a greater sense of personal empowerment in a society usually discounting of female capacities and strengths. Analogously, I love the feeling of lived-body empowerment, strength, 'butchness' (c.f. Crawley 2002), of putting my body to the test, stretching its muscles, sinews and capabilities (increasingly so as age takes its toll!), especially after a hard day of university work. The mind/body linkage so fundamental to phenomenology is brought to the fore, as I struggle to gain some bodily balance between long hours of 'mind work,' cramped up in a predominantly sedentary job and the all-too-brief escape, the 'rush' and challenge of physical activity after the working day:

Nearly 3 weeks solid of marking. Legs and arms heavy from it, neck and shoulders rigid, strained, taut to breaking. Eyes red and gritty. It's going to be a hard run tonight, I guess. But, just a few minutes into my stride and the navy-dusk wind is cutting away the work smog, sloughing off the grey skin of the working day. I am being cleansed. I am back. I am back in-body after yet another day of attempted body denial, and enforced focus on the headwork. Quads surge forwards, muscles strong and bulking, pushing against tracksters, abs tighten and flatten against the chill wind as I begin to up the pace . . . Power surges through me, I feel butch, lean, mean and honed, and very much woman.

(Autophenomenography, February 2008)

The Elemental Body-World

Exercising outdoors—whether rural or urban—as opposed to indoors, does engender lived-body vulnerabilities. At times rural isolation seems to hold more danger: distance from people, safety and sources of help, challenging terrain, encounters with animals. But then the urban harbors a set of specific dangers, especially at night: dark alleys and underpasses, doorways where men can lurk and lunge out, drunks, stalkers, gangs of men and youths. But being outdoors is an intrinsic part of running for me (indoor treadmill running is a dire last resort): facing all the elements in the fresh air, battling against vicious wind, stinging hail and pelting rain, sinking in fresh snow, glistening in high summer sun, melting into dark night, coursing over fields eerie in silvery moonlight, running alongside the heavy beat of flying swans. Following de Beauvoir's (1972) exhortation to women to battle the elements, and commensurate with Merleau-Ponty's (2001) portrayal of the intertwining of body and world, my body as part of the elemental world is a fundamental component of my running experience:

> As I set off in the last rays of April sunshine, down the hill towards the playing fields and river, dark, lowering cloud obscures the hills on the other side of the valley. It looks as though it's going to pour down or snow heavily. Sure enough the temperature is dropping rapidly and an icy wind's edge chills my skin, which chafes against thin cotton tee shirt. Shall I head home for warmer gear now, is there time? . . . No, but best divert away from the open fields and head towards the scant cover of early spring trees. As I continue, the thin wind is bitter against my slight body, but as my core begins to warm to the labour, a strange sensation comes over me. Like Baked Alaska in reverse: my wind-chilled outer skin is bitterly cold, grey-blue, but it seems as though just a few layers beneath the epidermis, my inner body is glow-warm orange. The strangeness of the feeling preoccupies me

so that the discomfort of the cold is forgotten for a while and I can concentrate on a steady even pace.

(Autophenomenography, April 2008)

Running Abreast

Contradictions and paradoxes also emerge in relation to which running gear to select—for running-purpose but also for self-presentation in public space: snug-fitting, skin tight, streamlined clothing provides greater functionality for my running body, being neat and aerodynamic, but also attracts unwanted male attention and comments. My clothing compromise is usually to opt for the streamlined, functional kit but to seek anonymity and protection via dark sunglasses and a cap pulled down low; MP3 player and headphones provide a supplementary auditory barrier against lewd street remarks and looks, and can be switched off once I reach the different lived space of the fields and meadows that fringe the city or when running through darkened streets, which require aural attentiveness to potential danger. Looser, baggy clothing is too cumbersome and restrictive, flapping in the breeze, catching against and chafing the body, whilst 'proper' running kit renders me empowered, dynamic, streamlined. Relatedly, it has taken years and years to hone down and 'discipline' the fleshy expansiveness of breasts to create a more 'sleek' running form. From a phenomenological perspective, Young (1992) evocatively portrays how a woman's breasts can form the center of her being-in-the-world, more like fluid than a solid, and in movement being liable to sway, jiggle, bounce and ripple, even when the movement is small. For many women runners, even those who are not particularly full-breasted, such swaying and bouncing can be intensely uncomfortable, even painful when exacerbated by the action of running. Even now, after decades of (non-surgical) breast reduction via exercise, I have to wear two sports bras in order to avoid being the target of unwanted attention, but also to avoid the embodied discomfort, the 'dys-appearance' of my breasted body (c.f. Gimlin 2006):

> Oh no, I find I've forgotten to pack the usual two bras in my training bag. Ach well, I'll just have to try running in the 'day' bra. But minutes into the training run and it's nigh on impossible! Not only is it incredibly uncomfortable, verging on painful, but my whole body feels huge, ungainly, uncoordinated, and very unbalanced. Surprisingly, it's not just my upper body but strangely my quads also feel big and billowy, uncoordinated. The two sports bras combination that I normally wear may be unflattering' to 'feminine curves' but their flattening and constricting presence makes me feel 'contained', streamlined and aerodynamic. How bizarre that their lack makes me feel as though I'm not a real runner at all. The house is

only 10 minutes into the run, so I decide to make a quick pit stop and effect a speedy change.

(Autophenomenography, February 2008)

Sensory Pleasures and Dangers

The centrality of the sensory dimension of sporting embodiment has been signaled in recent years (Hockey and Allen-Collinson 2007; Sparkes 2009), but only rarely provides the focal point within sports studies. Hockey and Allen-Collinson (2007) for example emphasize the importance of 'listening for hazards' when undertaking running training in public, where roads, parks and pathways are replete with hazards—some more deliberate than others—generated by traffic, pavement cyclists, pedestrians and dogs. For me, this awareness of danger can manifest itself not only via the visual and aural, but also at a deeply visceral level, and in quickened, sometimes ragged breathing, elevated pulse rate, a tightening of my abdomen and a hypersensitivity of skin, especially on arms and thighs:

> Decided to take the bracken route down the moor to the track, but as I enter the head-height, dense bracken, I feel hemmed in, trapped—I can't see what's around the corner, who might be lurking at the path sides. My breath catches, holds, ears straining for any sound, goose pimples catch the moor breeze, trying to quieten my heart beat so that I can hear . . . probably just sheep . . . I have to walk some of the way, the path is too steep, too friable for running, but I'm light and primed for flight as any moorland creature . . . Hit the open space with relief.
>
> (Autophenomenography, July 2008)

In contrast, the sensuous pleasures of running form a key structure of my running experience. The olfactory dimension, whilst largely neglected in studies of sport generally (Sparkes 2009), features strongly in more sensorily-focused sporting analyses where smells can confirm the self's involvement in the sporting present moment, and also substantiate sporting identity via memory (Hockey and Allen-Collinson 2007). The smell of fresh-cut grass, for example, evokes in me strong childhood memories of watching cricket or listening to the radio commentary in my old family back garden:

> As I head down suburban streets to the river meadows, the warmed sweet scent of cut grass suddenly meets me, taking me back to those long, summer-haze holiday afternoons as a child, with all the family sitting out in the back garden in deckchairs, cricket on the radio, a tractor busy somewhere in a distant field and the drone of a light aircraft overhead. My memory mind travels, and a long section of the pathway goes missing in my running mind.
>
> (Autophenomenography, May 2008)

Other sensory pleasures of the running body in harmony with landscape and (MP3 player-generated in this case) soundscape also emerge as salient structures of experience:

> One of those 'in the moment' runs tonight. Glorious sunset down by the river, great rhythm, my strides just eat up the ground. Whole sections of the route have gone missing (recalls an earlier fieldnote from a different place, a different time) as John Bonham's[2] great tree trunk sticks beat out the rhythm. Machine-gun the pace. Perfect rhythm, perfect timing. Flow. Breathing and beat in synchronicity. As aquamarine finale of sunset darkens to indigo, as the dying Pagey[3] riffs fade away, I walk the last few steps down the path to my front door. Fade out. Synchronicity.
>
> (Autophenomenography, January 2008)

These then are illustrative of some of the key structures of my lived experience as a running woman who habitually undertakes her training in the contested and gendered zone of 'public' outdoor space.

CONCLUSION

This chapter has sought to contribute, in a small way, to the feminist phenomenological research literature, by examining the nexus of structure and agency in sporting embodiment as played out in my particular lifeworld, that of a female distance runner. This is an under-researched area within the feminist phenomenological tradition, but which provides, I would argue, an excellent domain for the application of its theoretical insights. For me, the constraints of social structure and the potentials of female agency coalesce powerfully in my lived experiences of outdoor running. Their relationship is lived out at a deep, individual embodied level in terms of the endlessly negotiated, fluctuating ways of balancing both corporeal and psychological power and vulnerability. Feminist phenomenology offers one way of 'capturing' these tensions and paradoxes, partial though that capture must always inevitably be within the phenomenological spirit. An analysis of the linkages between our subjective, lived-body experiences and our situatedness within social structures offers a powerful means of investigating female subjectivity and embodiment. In particular, it would seem there is a strong rationale for incorporating feminist-phenomenological perspectives into the pantheon of theoretical and methodological approaches to investigating women's sporting embodiment. These can generate fresh research insights, grounded in the carnal, 'fleshy,' lived, richly textured realities of the moving, sweating, sensuous female sporting body, which of course also holds cultural meanings, significances, purposes and interests.

This is by no means to advocate feminist phenomenology as the only or even necessarily the best way of undertaking qualitative investigation into female sporting embodiment, but to propose it as a potent complementary approach, to widen and deepen the focus of the feminist lens. Linked to the power of feminist theorization, including those of 'difference,' phenomenology encourages a re/consideration of the structures of women's sporting and physical activity experiences, always taking into account the full force of social-structural (including ideological) location and constraint. It can help promote deep reflection upon, and empathic understanding of how it actually feels to be the woman in the sporting body.

NOTES

1 Gruppetta (2004) contends that if a researcher studies her/his own experiences of a phenomenon/phenomena rather than a 'cultural place,' then the appropriate term would be 'autophenomenography.'
2 John Bonham was the legendary drummer with Led Zeppelin until his untimely death; Jimmy Page was their virtuoso lead guitarist.
3 Ibid.

REFERENCES

Ahmed, S. 2007. *Queer phenomenology: Orientations, objects, others*. Durham, NC: Duke University Press.
Alcoff, L. M. 2000. Phenomenology, post-structuralism, and feminist theory on the concept of experience. In *Feminist phenomenology*, eds. L. Fisher and L. Embree, 39–56. Dordrecht, Netherlands: Kluwer Academic.
Allen-Collinson, J. 2009. Sporting embodiment: Sports studies and the (continuing) promise of phenomenology. *Qualitative Research in Sport and Exercise* 1(3): 279–96.
Allen-Collinson, J. and J. Hockey, 2001. Runners' tales: Autoethnography, injury and narrative. *Auto/Biography* IX(1 and 2): 95–106.
—— 2008. Autoethnography as 'valid' methodology? A study of disrupted identity narratives. *The International Journal of Interdisciplinary Social Sciences* 3(6): 209–17.
Aoki, D. 1996. Sex and muscle: The female bodybuilder meets Lacan. *Body & Society* 2(4): 59–74.
Bartky, S. 1990. *Femininity and domination: Studies in the phenomenology of oppression*. New York: Routledge.
Brooks Gardner, C. 1980. Passing by: Street remarks, address rights, and the urban female. *Sociological Inquiry* 50: 328–56.
Budgeon, S. 2003. Identity as an embodied event. *Body & Society* 9(1): 37–57.
Burke, S. M., A. C. Sparkes and J. Allen-Collinson. 2008. High altitude climbers as ethnomethodologists making sense of cognitive dissonance: Ethnographic insights from an attempt to scale Mt Everest. *The Sport Psychologist* 22(3): 336–55.
Butler, J. 2006. Sexual difference as a question of ethics: Alterities of the flesh in Irigaray and Merleau-Ponty. In *Feminist interpretations of Maurice Merleau-*

Ponty, eds. D. Olkowski and G. Weiss, 107–25. University Park, PA: Penn State University Press.

Chua, B. H. and N. Edwards. 1992. Public space: Design, use and management. In *Public space: Design use and management,* eds. B. H. Chua and N. Edwards, 1–10. Singapore: Singapore University Press.

Coates, S. 1999. Analysing the physical: An ethnomethodological study of boxing. *Ethnographic Studies* 4: pp. 14–26.

Coy, M. 2009. This body which is not mine: The notion of the habit body, prostitution and (dis)embodiment. *Feminist Theory* 10(1): 61–75.

Crawley, S. 2002. 'They still don't understand why I hate wearing dresses!' An autoethnographic rant on dresses, boats and butchness. *Cultural Studies and Critical Methodologies* 2(1): 69–92.

Cronan, M. K. and D. Scott. 2008. Triathlon and women's narratives of bodies and sport. *Leisure Sciences* 30: 17–34.

Csordas, T. 1994. *The sacred self: A cultural phenomenology of charismatic healing.* Berkeley: University of California Press.

—— 2002. *Body/Meaning/Healing.* New York: Palgrave Macmillan.

Dale, G. A. 1996. Existential phenomenology: Emphasizing the experience of the athlete in sport psychology research. *The Sport Psychologist* 10: 307–21.

de Beauvoir, S. 1972. *The second sex* (trans. H. Parshley). Harmondsworth: Penguin Books.

Ehrich, L. C. 1999. Untangling the threads and coils of the web of phenomenology. *Education Research and Perspectives* 26(2): 19–44.

Embree, L. and J. N. Mohanty. 1997. Introduction. In *Encyclopedia of phenomenology,* eds. L. Embree et al., pp. 1–10. Dordrecht, Netherlands: Kluwer Academic.

Feagin, J. R. 1991. The continuing significance of race: Anti-Black discrimination in public places. *American Sociological Review* 56: 101–16.

Finlay, L. 2003. The intertwining of body, self and world: A phenomenological study of living with recently diagnosed multiple sclerosis. *Journal of Phenomenological Psychology* 34(6): 157–78.

—— 2009. Debating phenomenological research methods. *Phenomenology & Practice* 3(1): 6–25.

Fisher, L. 2000. Phenomenology and feminism: Perspectives on their relation. In *Feminist phenomenology,* eds. L. Fisher and L. Embree, 17–37. Dordrecht, Netherlands: Kluwer Academic.

Fisher, L. and L. Embree, eds. *Feminist phenomenology,* 39–56. Dordrecht, Netherlands: Kluwer Academic.

Garfinkel, H. 2002. *Ethnomethodology's program: Working out Durkheim's aphorism.* Boulder. CO: Rowman & Littlefield.

George, M. 2005. Making sense of muscle: The body experiences of collegiate women athletes. *Sociological Inquiry* 75(3): 317–45.

Gimlin, D. 2006. The absent body project: Cosmetic surgery as a response to bodily dys-appearance. *Sociology* 40(4): 699–716.

Giorgi, A. P., ed. 1985. *Phenomenology and psychological research.* Pittsburgh: Duquesne University Press.

—— 1997. The theory, practice and evaluation of the phenomenological method as a qualitative research procedure. *Journal of Phenomenological Psychology* 28(2): 235–60.

Giorgi, A. P and B. M. Giorgi. 2003. The descriptive phenomenological psychological method. In *Qualitative research in psychology*, eds. P. Camic, J. E. Rhodes
and L.Yardley, 242–73. Washington: American Psychological Association.

Granskog, J. 2003. Just 'Tri' and 'Du' it: The variable impact of female involvement in the triathlon/duathlon sport culture. In *Athletic intruders: Ethnographic
research on women, culture, and exercise*, eds. A. Bolin and J. Granskog, 27–
52. New York: State University of New York Press.

Grosz, E. 1995. *Space time and perversion: The politics of bodies*. New York,
Routledge.

Gruppetta, M. 2004. Autophenomenography? Alternative uses of autobio-
graphically based research. In Association for Active Researchers in Education
(AARE) Conference Paper Abstracts—2004, ed. P. L. Jeffery. Sydney: AARE,
http://www.aare.edu.au/04pap/gru04228.pdf (accessed June 9, 2009).

Hall, M. A. 1996. *Feminism and sporting bodies: Essays on theory and practice*.
Champaign, Il: Human Kinetics.

Hanmer, J. and S. Saunders. 1984. *Well-founded fear: A community study of
violence to women*. London: Hutchinson.

Hargreaves, J. 2007. Sport, exercise, and the female Muslim body: Negotiating
Islam, politics, and male power. In *Physical culture, power, and the body*, eds.
J. Hargreaves and P. A. Vertinsky, 74–100. London: Routledge.

Heidegger, M. 1927/1962. *Being and time*. Translated from German by permission of Max Niemeyer Verlag, Tübingen. Oxford: Blackwell.

Hemphill, D. 2005. Deeper inside the beautiful game. *Journal of the Philosophy
of Sport* XXXII: 105–15.

Hockey, J. and J. Allen-Collinson. 2007. Grasping the phenomenology of sporting bodies. *International Review for the Sociology of Sport* 42(2): 115–31.

Hughson, J. and D. Inglis. 2002. Inside the beautiful game: Towards a Merleau-
Pontian phenomenology of soccer play. *Journal of the Philosophy of Sport*
XXIX: 1–15.

Kerry, D. S. and K. M. Armour. 2000. Sport sciences and the promise of phenomenology: Philosophy, method, and insight. *Quest* 52(1): 1–17.

Kilgour, L. 2007. Gender, spatiality and fear: Young women's experiences of
outdoor physical activity. *Annals of Leisure Research* 10(2): 215–34.

Kruks, S. 2006. Merleau-Ponty and the problem of difference in feminism. In
Feminist interpretations of Maurice Merleau-Ponty, eds. D. Olkowski and G.
Weiss, G. University Park: Penn State University Press.

Langdridge, D. 2008. Phenomenology and critical social psychology: Directions
and debates in theory and research. *Social and Personality Psychology Compass*
2: 1126–42.

Lefebvre, H. 1991. *The production of space*, translated by D. Nicholson-Smith,
2nd ed. Malden, MA: Blackwell.

Lowe, M. R. 1998. *Women of steel: Female body builders and the struggle for
self-definition*. New York: New York University Press.

McDonald, I. 2007. Bodily practice, performance art, competitive sport: A critique
of Kalarippayattu, martial art of Kerala. *Contributions to Indian Sociology*
41(2): 143–68.

McKay, J. 1994. Embodying the 'new' sporting woman. *Hecate* 20(1): 68–83.

Markula, P. 2003. The technologies of the self: Feminism, Foucault and sport.
Sociology of Sport Journal 20: 87–107.

Masciotra, D., E. Ackermann and W.-M. Roth. 2001. 'Maai': The art of distancing in Karate-Do: Mutual attunement in close encounters. *Journal of Adult Development* 8(2): 119–32.

Mensch, J. 2006. Artificial intelligence and the phenomenology of flesh. *PhaenEx* 1(1): 73–85.

Merleau-Ponty, M. 2001. *Phenomenology of perception,* trans. C. Smith. London: Routledge & Kegan Paul.

Morley, J. 2001. Inspiration and expiration: Yoga practice through Merleau-Ponty's phenomenology of the body. *Philosophy East and West* 51(1): 73–82.

Moustakas, C. 1994. *Phenomenological research methods.* London: Sage.

Olkowski, D. 2006. Only nature is mother to the child. In *Feminist interpretations of Maurice Merleau-Ponty,* eds. D. Olkowski and G. Weiss, 49–70. University Park: Penn State University Press.

Olkowski, D. and G. Weiss, eds. 2006. *Feminist interpretations of Maurice Merleau-Ponty.* University Park, PA: Penn State University.

Pace, L. K. 2009. Ontological explorations: A narrative approach. *Qualitative Inquiry* 15(2): 409–20.

Parker, I. 2005. *Qualitative psychology: Introducing radical research.* Maidenhead: OU Press.

Rail, G. 1992. Physical contact and women's basketball: A phenomenological construction and contextualisation. *International Review for the Sociology of Sport* 27(1): 1–25.

Samudra, J. K. 2008. Memory in our body: Thick participation and the translation of kinaesthetic experience. *American Ethnologist* 35(4): 665–81.

Sanders-Bustle, L. and K. L. Oliver. 2001. The role of physical activity in the lives of researchers: A body-narrative. *Studies in Philosophy and Education* 20: 507–20.

Smith, S. L. 1998. Athletes, runners and joggers: Participant-group dynamics in a sport of 'individuals.' *Sociology of Sport Journal* 15: 174–92.

Sparkes, A. 2009. Ethnography and the senses: Challenges and possibilities. *Qualitative Research in Sport & Exercise* 1(1): 21–35.

Spiegelberg, H. 1975. *Doing phenomenology.* The Hague: Martinus Nijhoff.

Toombs, S. K. 2001. Reflections on bodily change: The lived experience of disability. In *Phenomenology and medicine,* ed. S. K. Toombs, 247–61. Dordrecht, Netherlands: Kluwer Academic.

Valentine, G. 1989. The geography of women's fear. *Area* 21: 385–90.

Wainwright, S. P. and B. S. Turner. 2003. Aging and the dancing body. In *Aging bodies: Images and everyday experience,* ed. C.A. Faircloth, 259–92. Oxford: Altamira Press.

Weiss, G. 1999. *Body images: Embodiment as intercorporeality.* London: Routledge.

Wesely, J. K. and E. Gaarder. 2004. The gendered 'nature' of the urban outdoors: Women negotiating fear of violence. *Gender & Society* 18(5): 645–63.

Willig, C. 2008. *Introducing qualitative research in psychology* (2nd ed.). Milton Keynes: Open University Press/McGraw Hill.

Woodward, K. 2008. Hanging out and hanging about: Insider/outsider research in the sport of boxing. *Ethnography* 9(4): 536–61.

Young, I. M. 1980. Throwing like a girl: A phenomenology of feminine body comportment, motility and spatiality. *Human Studies* 3: 137–56.

—— 1992. Breasted experience: The look and the feeling. In *The body in medical thought and practice*, ed. D. Leder, 215–30. Boston: Kluwer Academic.

—— 1998. 'Throwing like a girl': Twenty years later. In *Body and flesh: A philosophical reader*, ed. D. Welton, 286–90. Oxford: Blackwell.

Contributors

Jacquelyn Allen-Collinson is a sociologist based in the Qualitative Research Unit, School of Sport and Health Sciences at Exeter University, UK, where she teaches sociological perspectives on sport, and qualitative research methods. Her current research and supervisory interests cohere around sociological and phenomenological analyses of the lived sporting body and sporting activity, particularly distance running; 'identity work' and the management of disrupted identity; chronic illness within sports and physical cultures; narratives of intimate partner violence and abuse; and autoethnographic and autophenomeno-graphic approaches to the sociological study of sporting experiences. Jacquelyn is the Project Director of a multi-disciplinary, multi-institutional research team currently evaluating the Sports Council for Wales' Mentro Allan (Venture Out) national programme, designed to increase and sustain physical activity levels amongst specific target groups across Wales. She publishes in a wide range of sociology and sports sociology journals, including *Sociology*, *The Sociological Review*, *Symbolic Interaction*, *Journal of Contemporary Ethnography*, *International Review for the Sociology of Sport*, and *Sociology of Sport Journal*. Jacquelyn has been involved in middle/distance running for over 20 years.

Jessica W. Chin is an assistant professor in the Kinesiology Department at San José State University, USA. Her teaching and research interests include cultural studies of sport and physical activity. A recent graduate of the Physical Cultural Studies Program at the University of Maryland, she takes a special interest in the role of the active body and its use in the negotiation of power and identity in various sporting contexts. Currently, her research projects focus on elements of an emergent postcommunist female subjectivity articulated with changing patterns of lifestyle and leisure consumption in Romania, looking particularly at corporeal manifestations of the increasing socio-cultural, political and economic tensions within the transforming postcommunist landscape.

Laura De Pian is a doctoral research student in the School of Sport, Exercise and Health Sciences, Loughborough University, UK, currently researching young people's decision making about health as an embodied social process. She is a former Research Associate on an ESRC project "The impact of new health imperatives on schools" and has published in *Policy futures in education*.

Gunn Engelsrud is a part-time professor at the Institute for Health and Society, Faculty of Medicine, University of Oslo and Head of Department of Physical Education Norwegian School of Sport Science. Among her latest publications are: Engelsrud, G., 2008, Teaching styles in contact improvisation: An explicit discourse with implicit meaning, *Dance Research Journal* 39(2): 58–73; Schriver, N. and G. Engelsrud, in press, When life is sport: Examples of patients' understanding of being injured, *Journal of Sport and Social Issues*; and Engelsrud G., 2010, "To allow oneself to dance . . .": Understanding the individual training of a selection of young dancers, *Nordic Journal of Dance* 1: 31–44. Her main research interest is to investigate how meaning is shaped and experienced in performances of movement (yoga, fitness, dance improvisation and martial arts). Her expertise is in qualitative methods and phenomenology.

John Evans is professor of sociology of education and physical education at Loughborough University, England. He teaches and writes on issues of equity, education policy, identity and processes of schooling. With Emma Rich and Laura de Pian, he is currently researching the relationships between formal education, health and identity. He has authored and edited many papers and books in the sociology of education and physical education and is founding editor of the international journal, *Sport, Education and Society*.

Karen Synne Groven has been working as associate professor at Oslo University College, Department of Health, Physiotherapy Education since 2000. She is currently a PhD student at the Institute for Health and Society, Faculty of Medicine, University of Oslo. In her PhD project she explores the experiences of men and women who have undergone bariatric surgery. Among her latest publications are 1) Groven, K. S, 2008, *Exercise—in the Name of Change*. Master's Thesis, Institute for Health and Society, University of Oslo and 2) Groven K. S. and G. Engelsrud, in press, Dilemmas in the process of weight reduction. *International Journal of Qualitative Studies on Health and Well-Being* (in press). Her research interests include empirical projects in the areas of overweight and obesity as well as exploring Norwegians' experiences of health and well-being in different settings (including spas, massage institutes and fitness centers). She is currently working on her PhD project.

Christina R. Johnson is a visiting assistant professor of sport psychology in the department of Health and Sport Studies at the University of Iowa. Her research uses feminist and critical perspectives to examine identity development within the context of sport and physical activity participation.

Eileen Kennedy has a background in philosophy and women's studies. Currently she is an associate researcher in the School of Sport and Education at Brunel University. Her research explores the address of mediated sport and exercise to its various audiences, focusing on intersections of gender, class, race and nation. She has examined various sports including football, tennis, rugby, snooker, athletics, gymnastics and motor racing, and considered a range of media including television, magazines, newspapers and the Internet. She is interested in the relationship between media images and embodied subjectivities. Eileen enjoys working across disciplinary boundaries, and has collaborated with scholars within the arts and sciences. She is co-author of *Sport, media and society* (Berg).

Paula Lökman received her PhD in sport sociology from University of Surrey Roehampton, and her MA in adult education from University of Helsinki. In her doctoral thesis, she drew on research within the areas of sociology of the body, gender studies, cultural geography and the social and cultural study of sport and leisure, to investigate women's experience of their bodies in space, and how physical training in a Japanese self-defense sport, Aikido, changed the way they experienced both their physicality and the world around them. Recently, she has been involved in conducting research in a qualitative study at University of London, Royal Holloway, which explores leadership approaches and patient care within the UK National Health Services. Her research interests center on the exploration of gender and embodiment, construction of social knowledge, and implementation of qualitative research methodologies, in particular ethnographic approaches and narrative research.

Louise Mansfield is senior lecturer in the sociology of sport at Canterbury Christ Church University. She works within the Centre for Research in Sport, Physical Education and Activity Research (SPEAR). Her work on fitness cultures and female bodies embraces the Health at Every Size (HAES) approach to sport and fitness practices (see www.healthateverysize.org.uk). She has published on women, corporeality and fitness, feminist theories for understanding gender, sport and leisure, media representation of female athletes, and fitness and the politics of the environment.

Pirkko Markula is a professor of socio-cultural studies of sport and physical activity at the University of Alberta, Canada. Her research interests include social analyses of dance, exercise and sport in which she has employed several theoretical lenses ranging from critical, cultural studies research to Foucault, Derrida and Deleuze. While her work is based on qualitative research methods (textual analysis, participant observation, interviewing, ethnography), she is also interested in methodological experimentation including autoethnography and performance ethnography. She is the current editor of the *Sociology of Sport Journal*. Her work appears in *Qualitative Inquiry*, *Sociology of Sport Journal*, *Journal of Sport & Social Issues*, *Journal of Sport Management* and *Journal of Contemporary Ethnography*. She is the co-author, with Richard Pringle, of *Foucault, sport and exercise: Power, knowledge and transforming the self* (Routledge, 2006), editor of *Feminist sport studies: Sharing joy, sharing pain* (SUNY Press, 2005) and *Olympic women and the media: International perspectives* (Palgrave, 2009), co-editor, with Sarah Riley, Maree Burns, Hannah Frith and Sally Wiggins, of *Critical bodies: Representations, identities and practices of weight and body management* (Palgrave, 2007) and co-editor, with Jim Denison, of *Moving writing: Crafting movement in sport research* (Peter Lang, 2003).

Lisa McDermott is an associate professor in the Faculty of Physical Education and Recreation at the University of Alberta, in Edmonton, Canada, where she teaches courses in sociology of sport, leisure and health education. Her research interests focus on socio-cultural analyses of physical activity, obesity and health, as well as sport and popular culture. Her work is informed by post-structuralist and feminist perspectives. Her research has been published in journals such as *Sociology of Sport Journal*, *Leisure Studies*, *International Review for the Sociology of Sport* and the *Journal of Canadian Studies*.

Kerry R. McGannon received her PhD (health and exercise psychology) from the University of Alberta after receiving a BA (psychology) and an MA (sport and exercise psychology) from the University of Victoria. She is an assistant professor in the Department of Health and Sport Studies at the University of Iowa. Her research provides a 'bridge' between traditional epidemiological approaches and cultural studies approaches, to understand physical activity participation. Her specific interest is in the social construction of the self and critical interpretations of physical activity and fitness using 'critical constructionist' approaches (e.g., post-structuralism, social constructionism) and qualitative methodologies (e.g., narrative, discourse analysis). The goals of this research are to produce knowledge that (1) contributes toward helping people adhere to lifestyle behavior guidelines to prevent disease occurrence (i.e., primary prevention) and recurrence (i.e., secondary prevention), and (2) improve individuals' overall quality of life through physical activity participation. Her studies focus on marginalized populations, especially women. The journals where her work is published, such as *Quest*, *Sociology of Sport Journal*, *Qualitative Research in Sport and Exercise* and *Journal of Sport and Exercise Psychology*, underscore the interdisciplinary nature of her research.

Magdalena Petersson McIntyre is an associate professor in ethnology at the Centre for Consumer Science (CFK) at the University of Gothenburg, Sweden. Her research concerns gender, embodiment, consumption, design and fashion. Her chapter in this book is part of a large Norwegian and Swedish research project called "Beauty comes from within" where a group of scholars problematize the intersections of health and beauty in different Scandinavian contexts of exercise, spas and magazines. Magdalena Petersson McIntyre has, together with Lizette Gradén, edited a Nordic book on fashion, *Modets Metamorfoser* (2009). She has also published academic texts about gender and technology, shopping, design, fashion and taste. In the book *Bara den Inte Blir Rosa* (2010) she discusses different contemporary design objects where the designers have tried to challenge gender conventions, for instance a concept car built by Volvo in 2004. Currently she is working with a research project that deals with gender, packaging and luxury, and another that deals with aesthetic labor in retail.

Evdokia Pappa is a PhD candidate at Brunel University, London. Her PhD topic is a sociological examination of the media's depiction of doping scandals. Her educational background includes an MA in criminology from Middlesex University, where, in order to provide an in-depth understanding of the use of drugs in competitive sport, she completed a series of interviews with competitive athletes who had used performance-enhancing drugs.

Jaana Parviainen holds a PhD in philosophy from the University of Tampere, Finland. Her research interests include phenomenology, embodiment, philosophy of movement, fitness culture, post-industrial economy and digital technology. Her doctoral dissertation *Bodies moving and moved* (1998) was concerned with the phenomenology of contemporary dance, focusing on the professional development of the dancer and bodily knowledge. One of her recent books *Meduusan Liike* (The Motion of Medusa) (2006) addresses the cognitive, emotional and social meanings of movement and kinesthesia in the ubiquitous society. In 2009, working as a visiting researcher in Austria, she investigated the virtual sonic environment that combines motion capture and sound processing software with movement improvisation. Her research has been published in *The Nordic Journal of Aesthetics*, *Consumption, Markets and Culture*, and *Scandinavian Journal of Management*.

Elizabeth C. J. Pike is a senior lecturer at the University of Chichester where she is Deputy Head of Sport Development and Management. She was awarded a PhD in the sociology of sport by Loughborough University and has since researched and published on risk, injury, ageing and corporeality in sports. She has delivered presentations critically evaluating these phenomena in universities and conferences throughout Africa, the Americas, Asia, Australasia and Europe. Her recent publications include a co-authored book (with Jay Coakley) entitled *Sports in society: Issues and controversies*. Elizabeth is currently a member of the Executive Board of the International Sociology of Sport Association. She serves as the General Secretary of this association and the Sociology of Sport Research Committee of the International Sociological Association. She is also the discipline leader for the sociology of sport on the Scientific Committee for the International Convention on Science, Education and Medicine in Sport for the London 2012 Olympics. She works as a reviewer for several journals and publishers, and is on the Editorial Board of the *International Review for the Sociology of Sport*. She lives in the City of Brighton and Hove, East Sussex.

Emma Rich is senior lecturer in pedagogy, the body and physical culture, School of Sport Exercise and Health Sciences, Loughborough University. She has published work related to the body, education and health in journals such as *Sociology of Health and Illness*, *Discourse*, *Health*, and *Gender and Education*. She is co-author of the books *The medicalization of cyberspace* (with Andy Miah, Routledge 2008) and *Education, disordered eating and obesity discourse: Fat fabrications* (with John Evans, Brian Davies and Rachel Allwood, Routledge 2008) and editor (along with Lee F. Monaghan and Lucy Aphramor) of the forthcoming book *Debating obesity: Critical perspectives* (Palgrave, Macmillan).

Kari Nyheim Solbrække is associate professor at the Institute for Health and Society, Faculty of Medicine, University of Oslo. She holds a PhD (dr. polit) in sociology and her expertise is in gender research related to different aspects of modern working life. She is also a part-time researcher at the Institute for Social Research in Oslo where she is involved in studies related to social integration, gender, and ethnicity. Her methodological expertise is in qualitative methods. Among other things this interest involves both narrative inquiries of patient stories as well as participant observation to interpret how different kinds of health-care technology 'in action' play a crucial role for identity and power distribution in professional health care work.

John C. Spence spends most of his time relaxing in the Sedentary Living Laboratory in the Faculty of Physical Education and Recreation at the University of Alberta. He has expertise in the area of behavioral medicine and research methods. His research focuses on both the benefits and determinants of physical activity and how physical inactivity is related to obesity. He has studied the broad social determinants (e.g., SES) and population physical activity patterns. More recently, he has focused on 1) the physical environment and how it may influence physical activity choices and risk of obesity among both children and adults (e.g., urban form, location of food establishments), and 2) the effect of media (e.g., popular films) on physical activity and diet. John Spence has a strong background in physical activity measurement, meta-analysis and ecological models of behavior and health.

Sharon Wray is a reader in sociology in the Department of Behavioural and Social Sciences at the University of Huddersfield. Her research interests include embodiment and health, aging and ethnic and cultural diversity. Her publications have focused on these issues and developing the concepts of agency and resistance in relation to them. She recently completed a qualitative research study on the quality of life, health and well-being of older (60+) migrant women from India and Pakistan.

Index